POWER RISC
System/6000

AF342488

J. Ranade Workstation Series

DEROEST · *AIX for RS/6000: System and Administration Guide,*
0-07-036439-7

HENRY · *Solaris 2.0: System Administrator Guide,* 0-07-029368-6

JOHNSTON · *OS/2 Connectivity and Networking: A Guide to
Communication Manager/2,* 0-07-032696-7

LAMB · *MicroFocus Workbench and Toolset Developer's Guide,*
0-07-036123-3

LEININGER · *UNIX Power Toolkit,* 0-07-911690-6

LOCKHART · *OSF DCE: Guide to Developing Distributed
Applications,* 0-07-911481-4

SANCHEZ, CANTON · *Graphics Programming Solutions,* 0-07-911464-4

SANCHEZ, CANTON · *High Resolution Video Graphics,* 0-07-911646-9

SANCHEZ, CANTON · *PC Programmer's Handbook, 2/e,* 0-07-054948-6

WALKER, SCHWALLER · *CPI-C Programming in C: An Application
Developer's Guide to APPC,* 0-07-911733-3

WIGGINS · *The Internet for Everyone: A Guide for Users and
Providers,* 0-07-067019-8

*To order or receive additional information on these or any other
McGraw-Hill titles, in the United States please call 1-800-822-8158.
In other countries, contact your local McGraw-Hill representative.*   MH93

POWER RISC System/6000

Concepts, Facilities, and Architecture

Dipto Chakravarty

McGraw-Hill, Inc.

New York   San Francisco   Washington, D.C.   Auckland   Bogotá
Caracas   Lisbon   London   Madrid   Mexico City   Milan
Montreal   New Delhi   San Juan   Singapore
Sydney   Tokyo   Toronto

Library of Congress Cataloging-in-Publication Data

Chakravarty, Dipto.
    POWER RISC System/6000 : concepts, facilities, and architecture /
    Dipto Chakravarty.
        p.   cm.—(Jay Ranade workstation series)
    Includes index.
    ISBN 0-07-011047-6
    1. IBM RISC System/6000 computers.   I. Title.   II. Series.
QA76.8.I25975C48   1994
004.165—dc20   93-34964
                                                                   CIP

Copyright © 1994 by McGraw-Hill, Inc. All rights reserved. Printed in
the United States of America. Except as permitted under the United
States Copyright Act of 1976, no part of this publication may be repro-
duced or distributed in any form or by any means, or stored in a data
base or retrieval system, without the prior written permission of the
publisher.

1 2 3 4 5 6 7 8 9 0   DOH/DOH   9 9 8 7 6 5 4 3

ISBN 0-07-011047-6

*The sponsoring editor for this book was Jerry Papke and the editing
supervisor was Suzanne W. Babeuf. It was set in Century Schoolbook
by North Market Street Graphics.*

Printed and bound by R. R. Donnelley & Sons Company.

Postscript is a trademark of Adobe Systems Incorporated.
Laserjet and PCL are trademarks of Hewlett-Packard Corporation.
Intel is a trademark of Intel Corporation.
AIX, POWER RISC System/6000, PowerPC, RT, PS/2, Micro Channel,
    VM/CMS, and MVS/TSO are trademarks of International Business
    Machines Corporation.
UNIX is a trademark of UNIX System Laboratories.

Information contained in this work has been obtained by McGraw-
Hill, Inc., from sources believed to be reliable. However, neither
McGraw-Hill nor its authors guarantee the accuracy or completeness of any information published herein and neither McGraw-
Hill nor its authors shall be responsible for any errors, omissions, or
damages arising out of use of this information. This work is published with the understanding that McGraw-Hill and its authors
are supplying information but are not attempting to render engineering or other professional services. If such services are required,
the assistance of an appropriate professional should be sought.

To my parents

Contents

Part 2   System/6000 Software Subsystem—User's Perspective

Preface

This book is intended for computer professionals who are interested in gaining an insight into the POWER RISC System/6000. The information included is geared to serve as a single source of reference about the machine hardware and its operating environment. The subtitle, *Concepts, Facilities, and Architecture,* is quite appropriate, as it contains a comprehensive overview of the hardware and the software *concepts* from both user as well as system perspectives. The text introduces the multifarious *facilities* available in the operating system and in the underlying hardware subsystems. Its advanced sections explain the *architecture* of AIX and the design layout of the RISC processor.

The seeds for writing this book were sown in the days when I used to develop developers, prior to the machine's introduction in the market. What started out as training a few hardware engineers on the RISC hardware design and teaching system programmers about how the internals of AIX worked differently than traditional UNIX turned into something a lot bigger. For five years I continued to teach RISC System/6000 architecture and AIX architecture to developers across the United States as well as Japan, Australia, Germany, the United Kingdom, and Canada. This book is a consolidation of my experiences that I wanted to share with the RISC System/6000 community.

The book's contents are organized into four parts. The first two sections introduce the user's perspective of (1) the software subsystem and (2) the hardware subsystem, followed by the latter two sections that present the system's viewpoint of (3) the software subsystem and (4) the hardware subsystem. If viewed as four quadrants of a knowledge domain, the contents of each section are geared to serve professionals with different backgrounds. When viewed along the horizontal axis, one sees a software subsystem and a hardware subsystem. When viewed along the vertical axis, one finds a user's perspective of the machine and a system perspective of the machine. (See Fig. P.1.) Each of the four areas comprises four chapters. The contents of each of the areas are stand-alone and can be studied individually.

	HARDWARE	SOFTWARE
USER	User Perspective of Hardware	User Perspective of Software
SYSTEM	System Perspective of Hardware	System Perspective of Software

Figure P.1   Reader's perspective of different aspects of the RISC System/6000.

The target audience for this book consists of two types of computer professionals: (1) new users, who will benefit from the first part of the book in which a user's perspective of the hardware and software is presented, and (2) experienced users, who will benefit from the second part in which a system's perspective of the hardware and software is explained.

This book is organized as follows:

Chapter 1 introduces the RISC technology in light of its evolution, design goals, and characteristics. It discusses the basic hardware nomenclature that is typical for RISC-based architectures. Some of the fundamental concepts of computer architecture that form the basic blocks of RISC-based computing have been reviewed in detail so that the reader can relate to the heuristic notions of this machine's design philosophy. Chapter 2 introduces the IBM RISC System/6000 family which is based on the POWER (*Performance Optimized With Enhanced RISC*) architecture, developed to meet the needs of the next decade and beyond. All the members of the family are introduced in light of their positioning, orientation, architectural description, and performance. Chapter 3 expands on the introduction of the RISC System/6000 by describing the myriad options available with this machine to meet the diversified needs of the diversified work environments. Different options for memory expansion, storage media selections, choice of graphics as well as communications adapters, displays, and battery backups are described in this chapter. Chapter 4 describes the maintenance and diagnostic components of the machine that users should know about. The product's maintenance package components are explained, along with its reliability, availability, and serviceability features implemented in the hardware. The diagnostics topics explain how to interpret the operator panel and describe the facilities that are available to diagnose the machine hardware.

Chapter 5 introduces the operating environment to the reader. It describes the layout of the user environment so that one knows how to navigate under the AIX (Advanced Interactive Executive) operating system to use the commands, utilities, and facilities effectively. Chapter 6 describes the assorted development tools. The most commonly used tools, such as compilers, debuggers, etc., are described in light of their functions and features. Chapter 7 addresses the networking, interoperability, and standards-related issues. The networking and interoperability options are described to address connectivity of the RISC System/6000 with multivendor UNIX platforms, host mainframes, as well as PCs. The second component of the chapter focuses on standards. It explains the semantics of the industry standards and presents what the numerous POSIX specifications, X/Open conformance, and FIPS compliance are about, in nonspecialist terms. Chapter 8 covers the essential AIX system administration concepts and tuning methods. Emphasis is given to the aspects that are unique for AIX, such as *smit* and ODM. The second part of the chapter deals with fine-tuning AIX. Since both system administration and performance tuning can constitute an entire volume of text by themselves, the discussion here has been focused on the bare essentials.

Chapter 9 explains the layout of the central electronic complex of the System/6000. The machine organization is presented from both a logical as well as a physical perspective. The different implementations of the POWER architecture are described, followed by the details of the planars and the pipelined layout of the execution units. Chapter 10 investigates the cache memory organization of the RISC System/6000. After presenting an overview of cache memory, the functions, features, and layout of the instruction cache and data cache are discussed individually. Chapter 11 demystifies the hardware design and organization of the three execution units. Each of the execution units (branch processing unit, fixed point unit and floating point unit) are examined in detail to illustrate the information flow inside the central electronic complex and explain how the independent execution of instructions is made possible in the three execution units. Chapter 12 delves into the details of the processor's I/O architecture. The first topic is the memory interface, its operational functions, timing diagrams, and transfer methods when transferring *quadwords* from the same and different physical cards. The next topic includes an in-depth discussion of the Micro Channel bus, its different modes of transfer, and its data representation scheme. The third topic covers the storage subsystem, with an emphais on the SCSI protocol, bus interface, controller logic, mailbox implementation, and evolving standards such as SCSI-2 and SCSI-3.

Chapter 13 outlines the design of the AIX operating system, with specific discussions on components of the kernel, structural layout of the kernel, and the characteristic features of the kernel. Further topics include kernel extensions, kernel's view of processes, and notifications means. Unveiling the architecture of AIX concludes with a discussion on internal representation of files, related kernel tables, and allied data structures and buffer pools. Chapter 14 explains AIX processes and their life cycle. It describes the structure of a process, state of a process, process-affiliated kernel structures, and their positioning in the kernel address space. Additional topics include a discussion on how to monitor running processes by learning to traverse through the *kmem*. Ensuing topics covered are process states, context of processes, timer services, and process scheduling under AIX. A thorough discussion of processes is concluded by explaining how asynchronous and synchronous events, like interrupts and exceptions, are handled by the AIX kernel and what interprocess communication mechanisms are available under AIX on RISC System/6000. Chapter 15 presents the available system call interfaces, AIX kernel services, and the kernel extensions. The concept of dynamic binding under AIX is also explained to show how symbols are relocated and external references are resolved. Chapter 16 discusses the software I/O subsystem of the RISC System/6000 in a similar manner as Chapter 12 did for the hardware subsystem. Topics include system perspective of the file management, memory management, device management, and storage management. The first part describes the physical filesystem, pacing and memory mapped files, followed by the journaled filesystem and the logical volume manager. The subsequent discussion focuses on the segmented memory layout and the virtual memory manager. The ensuing topic covers the I/O management strategies.

The material in the first four chapters will be of maximum benefit to system engineers who are dealing with machine configurations. The information in the second four chapters, i.e., Chapters 5 to 8 will serve to introduce users to the machine's operating environment and system administrative functions. The latter half of the book is meant for those wishing to gain an insight into the machine's internals. Chapters 9 through 12 deal with the software architecture of AIX to demystify the design of the operating system components. Chapters 13 through 16 explain the hardware design of the POWER architecture that controls and delivers the precision-crafted performance. In conclusion, this book can be thought about as a single source of information about every aspect of the IBM RISC System/6000. Professionals requiring an immersion training in System/6000, as well as those keen on gaining an insight into the internals of this complex machine, will benefit from this book.

A few caveats need to be mentioned. No attempts have been made to cover details of release-specific software and/or hardware components. Such attributes are likely to change over a period of time. For a release-specific dependency, one is encouraged to refer to the corresponding product reference manuals. Although I have avoided predicting future development of the hardware and software, trends in many of the characteristics are obvious. In that case, this book will serve as the baseline technical reference for the future products such as Power2 and PowerPC that are based on the POWER architecture.

RISC is an evolving hardware technology. AIX is one of the leading variants of UNIX. Together, they have succeeded in the industry as the RISC System/6000 product. This book integrates the RISC-based hardware concepts and AIX-based software concepts, and presents to the readers a single comprehensive reference for the concepts, facilities, and architecture of the POWER RISC System/6000.

Dipto Chakravarty

Acknowledgments

POWER RISC System/6000 and AIX together are notable for having inspired an enthusiastic community worldwide. Innovators, both within and outside IBM, extended these products to a zenith never imagined by their hardware and software designers.

The wealth of information that I assimilated, both as a developer and teacher on the POWER architecture and AIX operating system, is a conglomeration of the valuable contributions made by my colleagues too numerous to mention. Of the many individuals who helped me author this book I would like to express my gratitude to my colleagues at IBM Austin, especially to Fred Strietelmeier for reviewing the section on Micro Channel and managing the review effort of the hardware I/O subsystem, to Ed Silha for reviewing the material on BPU and FXU, to Giles Fraizer for reviewing the material on SCSI, to Steve Thurber for review of the IOCC-related material, to Warren Maule for review of the memory subsystem, to Shawn Seaman for review of RAS aspects, and to Tom McConathy for review of the hardware diagnostic aids. I would also like to thank Jennifer Goff for promptly processing the intellectual property law paperwork to use some of the IBM-published diagrams; Rick Qualters for reviewing the material on the POWER instruction set and cache; Stephan Chan for reviewing the material on POSIX and standards; Alan Thompson for reviewing the material on AIX process structure; and Elizabeth Lewis of IBM U.K. for reviewing the material on process management, VMM, and I/O management. Thanks to Sasmith Reddi, Ashok Thareja, Sudha Velamati, and Shlomo Weiss for their help with various aspects of the book.

A special mention should be made of editors Jay Ranade and Jerry Papke for providing me with ongoing advice and guidance. My warmest thanks to Christine Furry and the production staff who adhered to a tight schedule to get this book out on time.

The person to whom I owe the most for this book is my wife, Aloka Chakravarty. She put the publication of her own Ph.D. thesis on hold so that she could help me complete this work. Not only did she draw all the diagrams, but she also proofread every page of this book and managed the life cycle of each chapter from its outline, to draft, to production. When the going got tough during the final few weeks, she never let me miss a beat.

System/6000 Hardware Subsystem—User's Perspective

RISC Technology

1.1 PHILOSOPHY OF RISC ARCHITECTURE

The System/6000 is based on RISC architecture. The term *RISC* (Reduced Instruction Set Computer) is somewhat misleading in the context of the present era. Today's so-called RISC machines display more hybrid traits than pure RISC characteristics. The traditional notion of RISC was to create a machine with a very fast clock cycle that can process instructions at the rate of one per cycle. Pipelining became a default trait of this so-called RISC machine, as it is a natural technique to achieve the goal of executing one instruction per machine cycle.

The first seeds for RISC were sown as a result of development of a telephone switching network in the mid-seventies. Nobody may remember the telephone switching network anymore, but the progress made on the design of a prototype machine at that time was taken up as a research project at the T. J. Watson Institute. The low cost-performance ratio of this prototype machine was exceedingly encouraging. Led by John Cocke, this prototype machine emerged as an internal machine called the IBM 801. Named after the building number in which the machine was developed, its features continued to be improved upon. The 801 was the predecessor to the IBM RT. Although the 801 could handle one instruction per cycle for specialized code, the rate fell short when used with general purpose code. In the continuing effort to smooth out the delays caused by storage access and conditional branching with additional pipelines, a new design was formulated. Referred to as the AMERICA, this new design made use of three semi-autonomous processors. The design of AMERICA later evolved into RIOS, which came to be known as the POWER architecture in the commercial world.

1.2 RISC CHARACTERISTICS

Traditionally, RISC machines had a set of typical characteristics. They all had fixed-size instructions. They also supported a reduced instruction set. Instructions were typically implemented in the hardware for performance reasons as opposed to being microcoded. A desired side effect of doing so was that it freed up a lot of the chip area which would have been used to store the microcode. Also, a generous supply of general purpose registers was inherent to the design of RISC machines since their architectural design called for instructions to be brought in to registers before being able to process them. These traits are further elaborated in the ensuing sections.

RISC machines of the present day often incorporate hybrid features from other types of architectures to marry the best of available technologies into one microprocessor. There is nothing wrong with doing so, but the phrase *RISC* does get weakened as far as references to the type of architecture are concerned.

1.3 LOAD-STORE ARCHITECTURE

The load-store type of computer architecture is also referred to as a register-register architecture or RR architecture. In this class of machines, operands and results are retrieved indirectly from the main memory through the use of a large number of scalar or vector registers. Compared to an RR architecture there is a class of architectures called the memory-memory architectures in which source operands' intermediate and final results are retrieved directly from the main memory. As a result is retrieved from storage, the shorter notation for this class of machines is SS architecture. RISC machines are of the RR-type architecture.

1.4 HARDWARE CONTROL

RISC machines support hardware control instructions, as opposed to microcode. Implementing instructions in hardware may be expensive but it offers unparalleled performance in terms of execution. Hardware control also facilitates a higher degree of accuracy. This facilitated the implementation of *fused instructions* in the design of the

POWER architecture. By making certain frequently occurring instructions execute atomically as fused instructions, the gain on clock cycle savings was doubled. In terms of accuracy, the reduction from six connections to four in the fused multiply-add instruction (called *fma*) of the floating point unit is consistent with the RISC philosophy of producing heavily optimized units to tackle the most frequently required functions.

1.5 PIPELINED IMPLEMENTATION

Instruction execution in the System/6000 takes place in a way which is quite different from the classical machines that executed one instruction at a time with a program counter pointing to the current instruction being executed. A pipelined architecture of the three execution units of System/6000 has added a new set of complexities to its instruction execution mechanism while yielding a high degree of performance. In order to best explain the functions, features, and benefits of pipelining, we first explain its basic design philosophy, followed by the implementation. The basic principle of pipelining is quite natural; it is not specific to computer technology. The notion of a pipeline can be conceptualized with quite a few real-world examples. The first analogy can be made with petroleum pipelines where a sequence of hydrocarbons is pumped through a pipeline of treatment phases. The last product may be entering the pipeline before the first product has been removed from the terminus. Our second analogy is made with an assembly line in an industrial plant. Consider automobile manufacturing plants that build cars using an assembly line of phases. The initial phase could be molding of the chassis itself, with the final phase being assembly of the engine. The last automobile may very well enter the pipeline before the first vehicle has been removed from the terminus. In both the analogies notice the fact that the net yield will be directly proportional to the number of phases of the pipeline or the assembly line. Later, we will be using this simile to relate to the yield of a pipeline in the System/6000 computer.

Once basic ideas about pipelines have been discussed, it is time to understand their key benefits. The most significant contribution of pipelining is that it provides a way to start a new task before an existing one has been completed. Hence the completion rate (or throughput) is not dependent on the total processing time, but rather on how soon a new process can be introduced in the pipeline.

To further illustrate this important concept, we analyze the aspects of general purpose processing. Consider Fig. 1.1, which depicts a (simplified) sequential process being done step-by-step over a period of time. Assume three distinct stages in the automobile assembly are molding of the chassis, painting of the frame, and, last, the installation of the engine. If each stage takes one time unit, then the total time for the processing will be three units. So, to build three automobiles it will take nine time units. To perform the same process using pipelining technique, consider a continuous stream of the jobs going through the three stages. In this case each horizontal row represents the time history for one job. Each vertical column represents the activity at a specific time. Note that up to three independent jobs may be active at any time in our example. Hence, to build three automobiles using this three-stage pipelining technique, it will definitely take less time than the nine time units that were required in the earlier case using sequential processing.

Relating the general ideas presented in Fig. 1.1 to computer design is quite straightforward. Executing a single computer instruction is analogous to the automobile assembly line process. Instruction processing is done in a number of pipeline stages. Each phase of computer instruction processing is conceptualized to be a stage in the pipeline. Typically, an instruction is first fetched, then decoded, and subsequently executed. So, the three pipeline stages, (1) instruction fetch, (2) instruction decode, and (3) instruction execute, can be correlated to the three stages in the assembly pipeline. Figure 1.2 illustrates the analogy by substituting the names of the stages. In the specific sense, each of the three instruction processing stages is significant. The instruction fetch stage consists of obtaining a copy of the instruction from memory when the program begins. The instruction decode stage comprises examining the instructions and initializing the control signals that would be required to execute the instruction in the subsequent step. The instruction execution essentially executes the specific instruction in the processor.

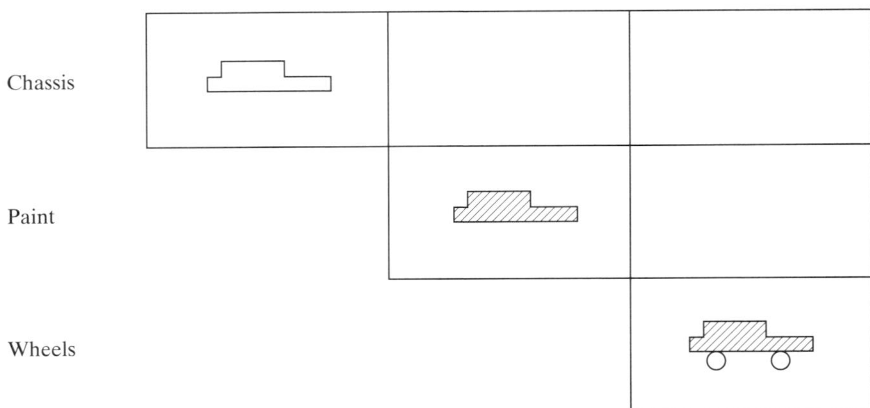

Figure 1.1 Pipelined execution for a three-stage automobile assembly line.

	1	2	3	4
Fetch	i_1	i_2	i_3	i_4
Decode		i_1	i_2	i_3
Execute			i_1	i_2

Figure 1.2 Pipelined execution of computer instructions.

In this generic example, we assume that each of the stages takes one time unit to complete. This time unit is referred to as a *clock cycle* throughout the remaining discussion. In the normal mode of operation, the first stage of the pipeline will continuously fetch instructions, the second stage will decode instructions, and the third stage will continue to execute the decoded instructions. If you were to have a sequential stream of instructions, this pipelining scheme would be adequate to handle a program execution efficiently. But in the real world almost all programs have branches that lead to nonsequential execution of the code. When a conditional branch instruction is detected, its address cannot be determined until it is executed. If the branch falls through, the sequence of instructions will remain unaffected. However, if the branch is taken and it happens to be a forward branch, its address will remain unresolved. As a result, we will end up with a "hole" in the pipeline. The "holes" are also known as "bubbles."

Figure 1.3 illustrates a simplified instruction stream that contains a forward branch instruction. Its pictorial representation is portrayed in Fig. 1.4, illustrating the temporal positioning of bubbles in a two-stage pipeline. If too many of these bubbles were to develop in our pipeline, the performance penalties (encountered by the idle clock cycles) will increase significantly. Although we can guarantee the proper execution of the instruction stream in the pipeline by interlocking the execution of the conditional branch fetched by the first stage such that no further fetches take place until the execution of the branch instruction in the next stage, we are penalized by acute performance costs. The method guarantees proper instruction execution, but it wastes too many clock cycles. So, one has to be able to deal with these bubbles in the pipeline in a reasonable way.

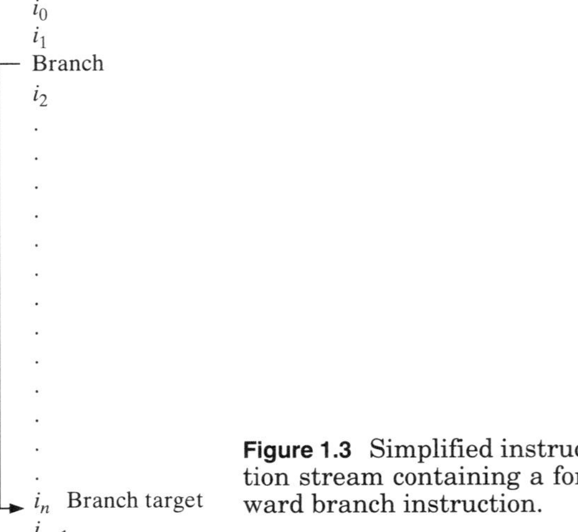

Figure 1.3 Simplified instruction stream containing a forward branch instruction.

Dealing with bubbles in a pipeline requires us to understand the fact that when a processing stage lies idle on a particular cycle and the idleness is due to the lack of available input rather than to a potential future collision, the idleness eventually propagates through the entire pipeline and deteriorates the overall pipeline efficiency.

We now explore several techniques that best suit the design of RISC architectures. A *delayed branching* technique that is suitable to sustain high performance is discussed first. It is based on our attempt to manipulate the sequence of instructions in the instruction stream at compilation time. An optimizing compiler is used to perform this feat. Figure 1.5 shows how a normal instruction stream is altered by realigning an independent instruction to execute immediately follow-

	1	2	3	4	5
Fetch	i_1	Branch		i_n	i_{n+1}
Execute		i_1	Branch		i_n

Figure 1.4 A two-stage pipeline showing bubbles generated by an instruction stream.

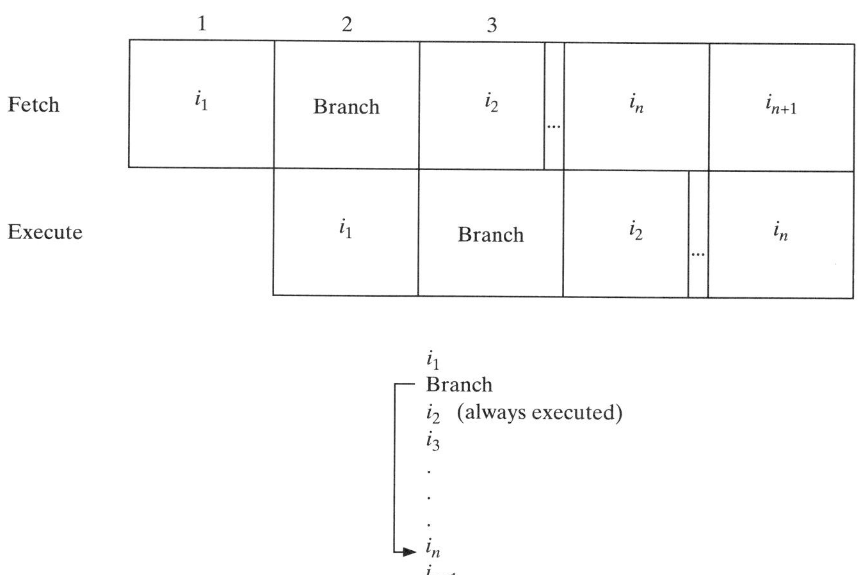

Figure 1.5 Delayed branching technique that allows a potential bubble to be replaced with an independent instruction that can be made to execute.

ing the branch instruction fetch. The branch instruction is now followed by an independent instruction i_2, so that the execution phase following the decode phase always remains full, as shown in Fig. 1.6. Owing to the fact that RISC machines attempt to execute one instruction per cycle and the delay in the execution pipeline is two or more stages, this technique of delayed branching has become quite attractive. However, when the depth of the pipeline gets longer (like four or six stages) it becomes exceedingly difficult to find independent instruc-

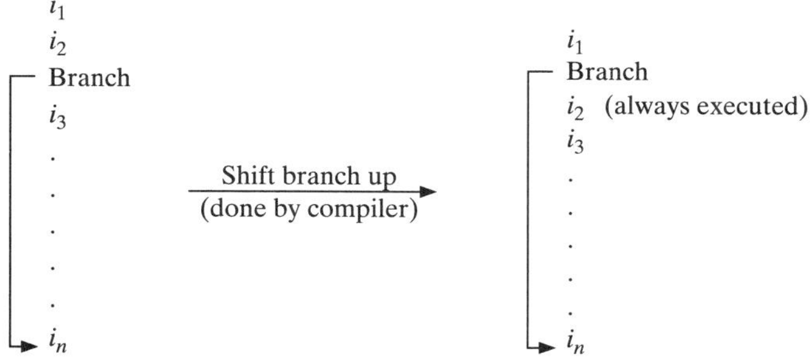

Figure 1.6 Outcome of realigned instruction processing (1) with and (2) without delayed branching technique.

tions that can fill up all the bubbles. As a general rule of thumb, this technique becomes difficult to design for pipelines with depth of three or greater.

A *branch prediction* technique is another way to sustain high performance, in which the branch target is guessed in advance and the instructions in the pipeline are marked provisionally. After the outcome has been resolved, the temporarily tagged results are made permanent if the guessed outcome was true; these tentative results are purged if the guessed outcome was false and the operations in progress are all canceled. The algorithm looks like this:

```
guess branch outcome
proceed on that path
  .

  .

  .
if prediction correct
      < no bubble in the pipeline >
if prediction incorrect
      partially executed instruction cancelled
      < bubble left in the pipeline >
```

It is intuitively obvious that this technique is very effective when the guesses are correct most of the time.

In the FOR or DO/WHILE statements in FORTRAN or C programming languages, backward branches are usually loops. All loop closing branches are taken except for the last one. So, for these types of branches, if one were to predict that the default case is the branch not taken, then the prediction will be true for all except the last case. In the last iteration of the loop the value of the loop control variable will render the comparison logic false. Due to the availability of a branch-and-count instruction in some of the RISC machines' instruction set, counting the number of loops becomes easy. The issue becomes challenging when branch instructions are used differently by different software, particularly when generated by different compilers. The IF/THEN statements that generate forward branches allow a guess to be correct only 50 percent of the time. Moreover, the branch address of a jump instruction might be the normal-case branch produced by one compiler and might be the exceptional-case branch in the code produced by another compiler. Which case should the hardware guess to be the normal case and decide whether the branch is to be taken or not? With a random choice of guessing the outcome one will have the probability of being right half of the time.

In order to do better than mere random prediction of branch outcome, a *branch history table* is used in some machines. The idea of a cache is applied here to optimize the accuracy of prediction by maintaining a table of frequently taken branches. The branch history table is essentially a cache memory accessed concurrently with each instruction fetch to a cache. If a match is found, an instruction address is generated that will be used in the next cycle of the pipeline. The execution from here on is similar to the branch prediction scheme, with all results marked as tentative until the true outcome of the branch is known. (Note the fact that the very first execution is the same as that of a branch prediction method, where it is pure guessing without a history.) Figure 1.7 illustrates the layout of the branch history table, with its branch and target address fields, and the fetch-decode-execute logic. The table is updated each time the execution of a branch is completed, with each update entering (1) the instruction address of the branch just executed and (2) the target address to which it branched.

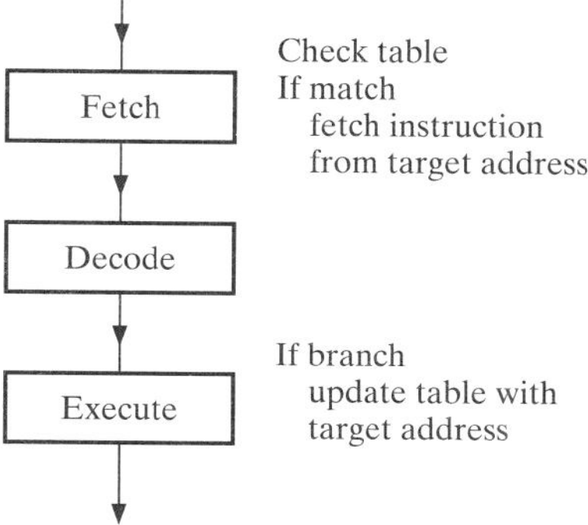

Figure 1.7 Structural layout of a branch history table.

An extension to the concept of a branch history table is a *decode history table,* in which the table update is minimized by accessing it only after the decoding stage, i.e., when the instruction has been identified as a conditional branch instruction.

Out of the four methods of dealing with bubbles in the pipeline, the System/6000 makes use of the branch prediction method. For FOR and DO/WHILE loop constructs it assumes that a branch is not taken. Due to the availability of its branch-and-count instruction, counting the number of loops is easy. So, for a loop of 100 iterations, all but the last iteration will succeed, thereby yielding a 99:1 success ratio. For IF/THEN constructs, the outcome has a 50:50 chance of succeeding. In real life, an instruction mix usually consists of three different types of branches: (1) unconditional, (2) loop closing, and (3) forward branches. With all of the three branches occurring in equivalent proportions, it is imperative that the unconditional branches occur a third of the time, the loop closing branches occur a third of the time, and the forward branches occur for the remaining third of the time. As the probability of the untaken forward branches is 0.5, the total likelihood of predicting the branches correctly is $\frac{1}{3} + \frac{1}{3} + (\frac{1}{2} * \frac{1}{3}) = \frac{5}{6}$. So, only $\frac{1}{6}$ of the branches (taken conditionals) may waste cycles and cause bubbles in the pipeline.

1.6   DEDICATED CACHE

RISC System/6000 uses two separate cache memory units for instructions and data.* Recognize that cache is functionally just a memory. What separates cache from system memory is that cache is implemented in hardware using faster memory chips. Being fast, cache is expensive. And being expensive, it is used frugally. Traditionally, a single cache memory would handle both instructions and data. But by separating out the instruction stream, contention is reduced. Since there are lesser constraints and conflicts with the cache line, it is no surprise that it results in a net increase in performance.

1.7   INSTRUCTION SET CHARACTERISTICS

The POWER instruction set architecture defines a total of 184 instructions which may be executed by the execution units of the System/6000. This large instruction set is contrary to the classical definition of the RISC systems (such as Berkeley RISC I, Berkeley RISC II, and IBM 801 that had a total of 39, 55, and 120 instructions, respectively).

---

* There are a few exceptions, as some of the entry-level models in the product line feature a combined instruction and data cache.

The availability of independent execution units in the System/6000 that are capable of concurrent execution of instructions justified a large instruction set so rich that the machine could execute multiple instructions in a single clock cycle. This implementation, i.e., the ability to process multiple instructions in a single clock cycle, is referred to as *superscalar* architecture. Available VLSI and CMOS technology was exploited to provide this feature, i.e., parallel execution of up to five operations per clock cycle, with the ideal instruction mix.

1.8 RISC/CISC TRADEOFFS

One of the typical characteristics of RISC machines is their simplified instruction set. This notion of a simplified instruction set can be best explained with the help of a practical everyday-life scenario. Consider an option to build a five-foot-high wall using either (1) fewer large concrete blocks or (2) a large number of small bricks. The amount of work done in both cases is quite different. Although the larger blocks would be slower to carry (performance deterioration), there would be fewer to fetch (performance amelioration). Likewise, the small bricks would be much faster to haul (performance amelioration), but there would be more to fetch (performance deterioration). Now if the rate at which the fetches are performed can be increased, then the latter method will end up being faster.

This is exactly how the performance metrics for RISC and CISC machines compare. The pros for CISC machines may be that there are fewer instructions to fetch and the size of the object code is smaller. But the cons are the time to decode variable-length complex instructions and the slower rate of execution for their microcoded instructions.

1.9 EFFECT OF PIPELINING

A pipelined architecture of the three independent execution units of System/6000 has added a significant yield to the instruction processing rate. In the earlier sections, the concept of a pipeline was explained, demonstrating that yield was directly proportional to the number of phases of the pipeline. If the pipeline can be kept full for any of the execution units, then every clock cycle will result in multiple instruction processing. The pipeline gains are not only within an execution unit but there is also the cumulative effect of multiple execution units processing as many instructions as their pipeline's depth, per clock cycle.

1.10 REDUCED INSTRUCTION SET CYCLES

Most of the performance leverage is in making optimal trade-offs between instruction set functionality (the power of each instruction) and the clock cycles per instruction. Hence, the design of the POWER instruction set was made with the focus on optimal functions per instruction. First, the cycles per instruction were minimized (using simplified instructions). Second, the path length was reduced as much as possible. Having optimized these two attributes, we now see how the net program execution time is affected.

As the overall *program execution time* is really the number of instructions executed (*path length*), each using the given number of clock cycles that the architecture supports, with the *cycle time* being fixed for the given architecture, the performance metric can be expressed as

$$\text{program execution time} = \text{path length} \times \text{CPI} \times \text{cycle time}$$

All three variables contribute equally to the overall performance of the system. Note that variables one and two, i.e., the path length and cycles per instruction (CPI), can be controlled, while the third one will remain constant for a given architecture. Minimizing the first two variables augments the overall performance metric. Having understood that this performance leverage is in making optimal trade-offs between instruction set functionality and cycles per instruction, it is easier to appreciate how the POWER architecture was defined with as much function per instruction as possible. This resulted in exhibiting to the compilers the parallelism that exists among the three independent execution units of this machine in order to harness the capabilities of the machine's ability to handle multiple operations per clock cycle.

1.11 SUPERSCALAR IMPLEMENTATION

Unlike the previous generation RISC processors, the System/6000 does not have a single microprocessor which can be called the CPU per se. The machine harnesses its power from three separate execution engines, each of which performs dedicated duties. The first of the three execution units is called the *branch processing unit,* which deals with branch instructions. The second processor, which is the *fixed point unit,* essentially executes fixed-point instructions within the machine. The third processor is the *floating point unit,* and it processes the floating-point instruction stream. Collectively, these three processors are referred to as the *execution units.*

The availability of independent execution units in the System/6000 that are capable of concurrent execution of instructions justified a large instruction set so rich that the machine could execute multiple instructions in a single clock cycle. This implementation, i.e., the ability to process multiple instructions in a single clock cycle, is referred to as *superscalar* architecture. Available VLSI and CMOS technology was exploited to provide this feature, i.e., parallel execution of up to five operations per clock cycle, with the ideal instruction mix.

1.12 SUMMARY

The advent of RISC architecture creates a new milestone in the field of hardware technology for computer systems. The architectural traits of a RISC design has its obvious benefits—so much so that RISC-based architecture will be the next generation of personal computers. With the best cost-versus-performance ratio, the RISC architecture is seen as mingling with industry standard CISC designs.

The biggest advantage of RISC-based architecture is that we now have the speed-matching peripheral components to take advantage of the raw performance that the processor is capable of delivering. That the RISC architecture of the System/6000 is scalable makes it likely to emerge as an industry leader not only in the entry-level market, but also in the high-end computing arena. It has already been demonstrated that megahertz are no more the criteria for speed, since System/6000's 20 MHz is completely different than an 80386's 20 MHz. The parallelism achieved through the presence of multiple independent execution units propels the effective performance of the machine above and beyond what was previously characterized as CPU throughput.

This chapter discussed the fundamentals of RISC technology and the evolutionary path for this machine. Each of the remaining chapters refers to a particular facet of the RISC System/6000.

Product Family

All the models in the System/6000 product line are based on a scalable architecture which is based on RISC technology. The product line was introduced in early 1990. Since then, the scalable architecture has been made available in three different implementations. The first two are multichip implementations and are characterized by the presence of two or four semicustom data cache chips. The third one is a single-chip implementation that can be distinguished by a combined data and instruction cache. A shorter notation used to represent these three processor chip sets is RS 1.0 (with four data cache chips), RS .9 (with two data cache chips), and RSC (single-chip module).

All the models offer one of these three variants of the chip technology in over a dozen different configurations ranging from high-end multiprocessors to entry-level workstations. A processor roadmap is illustrated in Fig. 2.1. The speed of the oscillator on assorted models ranges from 20 to 62.5 MHz (as of current availability) and is denoted by a numbering code of the form *xxyy*, where *xx* represents the oscillator speed and *yy* describes the data cache size. The hardware used in the System/6000 was developed by IBM to meet the computing needs of the next generation of computers. Its design is referred to as the Second Generation RISC-based architecture, or SGR architecture. The IBM RT System (formerly known as IBM RT Personal Computer) was the first generation of RISC-based machines when it became commercially available in 1986.

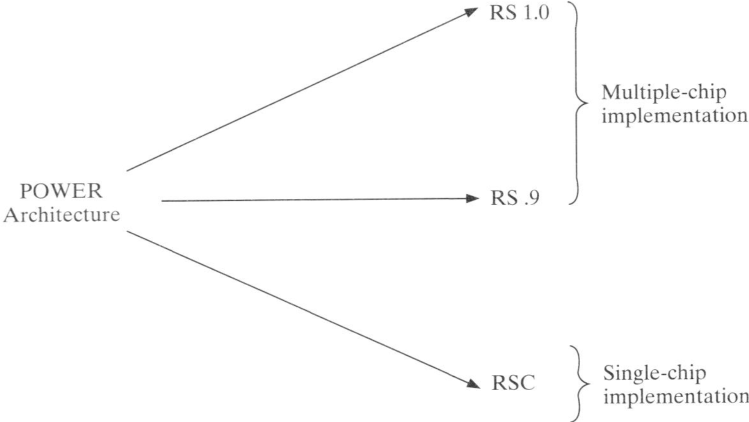

Figure 2.1 POWER processor roadmap.

The architecture that is implemented in the RISC System/6000 product line is commonly referred to as the POWER architecture, POWER being an acronym for *Performance Optimized With Enhanced RISC*. The POWER architecture that has evolved out of classic RISC architecture also blends in selected features of the traditional CISC architecture for optimizing performance. Currently there are three implementations of the POWER architecture available. Over a period of time more implementations are going to be built based on the POWER architecture.

2.1 SERVER/WORKSTATION ORIENTATIONS

The System/6000 has been targeted for two major market segments. These are the engineering/scientific and high-function graphics market, and the commercial data processing market. Diverse types of system configurations are made by combining various components and peripherals. Based on the configuration of the machine, the system is viewed as a workstation (for individual users' use) or a server (multiuser environment).

For engineering use, the System/6000 may be configured as a personal graphics workstation to perform tasks like stress-strain analyses in Computer Aided Design (CAD) or program generation for industrial parts fabrication with numerical control machine tools in Computer Aided Manufacturing (CAM). For the scientific workplace, the system may be configured as a server to handle numerically intensive computations like projection pursuit analysis in statistics, quadrature integrations in mathematics, or weather data analyses in geology. Scalable parallel systems can be utilized to further augment the capabilities of a single node to a higher degree. For the commercial data processing market involving transaction processing needs, the machine can be configured as a multiuser system. A newer market has evolved which consists of deploying dedicated high-performance processors in communication systems, network gateways, routers, and multimedia servers. The near future is likely to see the advent of symmetric multiprocessors that harness the power of multiple nodes to deliver a level of compute power never achieved before.

The following four denominations are assigned to the System/6000 currently available. This label is based on packaging, configuration, and the intended use of the system.

1. POWERstation
2. POWERserver
3. POWERparallel System
4. POWER Network Dataserver

2.2 PACKAGING AND CONFIGURATION

Since the introduction of the System/6000 product line in 1990 there have been several models announced across all the families. Over a period of time, the evolution of the product line along with the evolving needs of the market have introduced as well as discontinued manufacturing of specific models. Although a specific model may be unavailable after a period of time, its equivalent (and superior) configurations are always there to fill the gap. This section documents all the individual members of the System/6000 offered to date. Individual models that have been discontinued (as of the preparation of this book) are noted. Since the announcement and retirement of models is a sliding window, it must be recognized by the readers of this book that these annotations will change over time.

Individual models are packaged in a variety of configurations that include diskless, desktop, deskside and rack-mounted orientations. As per the present convention, the 300 series machines have desktop orientations, the 200 series machines have what is called a compact-desktop setup, the 500 series machines have deskside orientations, and the 900 series machines have a rack-mounted orientation. The 700 series machines are regarded as special offerings. An 800 series has been introduced with its first member being a network server.

More than one model may use the same mechanical frame that houses the system unit. Each of the mechanical frames is represented by a four-digit number *nnnn,* prefixing the model name. For example, the 7011 system unit frame denotes the compact frame used by the Model 220, whereas the 7012 system unit frame refers to the desktop enclosure used by the 300 series models. The 7013 denomination is used for all the deskside systems in the 500 series, and 7015 is used to represent the rack-mounted frame for the 900 series. Individual system unit frame numbers for each of the models appear in the following sections.

2.3   200 SERIES

The 200 series class of machines emphasizes compact packaging. The compactness in the physical size of this desktop model is achieved by smaller components—3.5-in disks and surface-mounted chips. An optional tower configuration is also available. The front of the housing contains a row of vents for cooling the internal components, as well as a key-lock mode switch, LED operator displays, and an optional diskette drive. Currently, there is only one member in the entry-level product line, which is Model 220. The 200 series family is also the newest of the families in the POWER product line.

2.3.1   Model 220 specifics

The 7011 System/6000 Model 220 features a 33-MHz RSC (RISC single chip) as the main processor which implements the single-chip version of the POWER architecture. In terms of cache memory, the system offers a combined 8-KB instruction and data cache. The path between the data cache and memory is 64 bits wide, thus giving the system a memory bandwidth of 264 MB/s for information transfer to and from the memory. The model comes standard with 16 MB of main memory installed on two 8-MB SIMMs (single in-line memory modules), leaving the remaining six available for future upgrade by pairs of 1-, 2-, 4-, or 8-MB SIMMs. The model comes standard with a POWER Gt1 graphics adapter and an option for the more powerful Gt3 to be installed in a Micro Channel slot. No diskette bays come standard with this model. However, if desired, a 200-MB, 400-MB, or 1-GB disk drive and a 2.88-MB diskette drive can be attached. An integrated Ethernet and SCSI connector is available on this model so that two Micro Channel slots can be freed up for use by other I/O devices like disk, CD-ROM, and tape drives.

2.3.2   Model M20 specifics

The 7008 System/6000 Model M20 features a 33-MHz RSC as the main processor. In terms of cache memory, the system offers a combined

8-KB instruction and data cache. The path between the data cache and memory is 64 bits wide and gives the system a memory bandwidth of 264 MB/s for information retrieval. The model comes standard with 16 MB of main memory installed on two 8-MB SIMMs that can be upgraded to 64 MB. This model offers graphics function and performance comparable to that of the POWER Gt1 adapter on Model 220 machines—the only exception is that it supports a single, integrated display included with each system. No diskette bays come standard with this model, thereby emphasizing the notion of the diskless workstation. An integrated Ethernet and SCSI adapter port leaves both the Micro Channels free for use with one or more external I/O devices like disk, CD-ROM, and tape drives.

2.4   300 SERIES

The 300 series class of machines has a desktop orientation, since the mechanical chassis was designed to reside on the user's desktop. The front of the housing contains a row of vents for cooling the internal components. The front panel also contains the key-operated mode switch, the reset button, an LED display, a 3.5-inch diskette drive, and the power switch. Unless stated explicitly, all drive interfaces are SCSI-based. The number of Micro Channel slots varies between one and four, depending on the individual model. The model-specific features are described below.

2.4.1   Model 320* specifics

The 7012 System/6000 Model POWERstation 320 features a 20-MHz processor chip. 8 MB of memory installed on a single memory card is standard with this model. There is provision for the memory on the card to be upgraded to a maximum of 128 MB with two 32- or 64-MB memory cards. The system uses an 8-KB instruction cache and a 32-KB data cache. The path between the data cache and memory is 64 bits wide, thus giving the system a permissible memory bandwidth of 160 MB/s for information transfer to and from the memory bank. The system comes standard with a 160-MB hard disk drive. (Note: Some older Model 320s may have a 120-MB drive in them.) An option for additional disk storage allows up to 800 MB, using SCSI drives. Note that this model uses an ESDI hard disk drive for its base configuration which has its own built-in adapter on the planar; hence, all of the four Micro Channel slots in this system remain open instead of one being taken up by the SCSI adapter.

---

* This model is no longer in regular production.

2.4.2 Model 320H specifics

The 7012 System/6000 Model 320H uses a 25-MHz processor as its engine. The model comes standard with 16 MB of memory, which is installed on a single memory card. The memory on the card can be upgraded with a 32- or 64-MB memory card. A second memory expansion card may also be added for a maximum of 128 MB. In terms of cache memory, the system offers an 8-KB instruction cache and a 32-KB data cache. The path between the data cache and memory is 64 bits wide, thus giving the system a memory bandwidth of 200 MB/s for information transfer to and from the memory bank. The system offers 400 MB of disk storage with an option to support up to 800 MB of data storage. There are four Micro Channel slots in this system, with one of them remaining occupied with a SCSI disk controller card.

2.4.3 Model 340 specifics

The 7012 System/6000 Model 340 uses a 33.3-MHz processor. 16 MB of memory, residing on a single memory card, are offered standard with this model. It can be upgraded with a 32-, 64-, or 128-MB memory card. A second memory expansion card can be added in the memory adapter slot to provide a maximum of 256 MB of real memory. The cache offered is an 8-KB instruction cache and a 32-KB data cache. A 64-bit-wide memory bus interface allows the system to have a memory bandwidth of about 266 MB/s for information transfer to and from the memory bank. The size of the standard disk drive offered is 160 MB which can be upgraded to a 400-MB or 1-GB drive. On this model, a SCSI interface is integrated into the system board, thereby leaving all four Micro Channel slots in this desktop model to house other optional cards. An integrated Ethernet port is also found on the planar board.

2.4.4 Model 350 specifics

The 7012 System/6000 Model 350 utilizes a 41.6-MHz processor as its engine. The model comes standard with 32 MB of memory installed on a single memory card and 400 MB of disk storage. The memory on the card can be upgraded with a 64- or 128-MB memory card. A second memory expansion card can be added in the memory adapter slot provided for a maximum of 256 MB of memory on the system. The instruction cache size is 8 KB, and the data cache is 32 KB. The path between the data cache and memory is 64 bits wide and gives the system a memory bandwidth of up to 332.8 MB/s for information transfer to and from memory. A 160-MB drive in one of the two disk bays is standard, with an optional upgrade to a 400-MB or 1-GB disk drive. Using a second drive, a maximum of 2 GB of storage can be handled. An Ethernet port and a SCSI interface built on an integrated system board leaves the four Micro Channel slots open for other components.

2.4.5   Model 355 specifics

The 7012 System/6000 Model 355 uses a 41.6-MHz processor as its engine. This model comes standard with 16 MB of memory and the option to upgrade to 128 MB. This model features a 32-KB instruction cache as well as a 32-KB data cache. With a 64-bit path between the cache and memory, the system is able to provide a memory bandwidth up to 200 MB/s. The system comes configured with a 400-MB disk drive and can be upgraded to support up to 2 GB of storage. The Micro Channel on this machine has been extended to provide a throughput of 80 MB/s. The single Micro Channel slot that comes with this model is available for use since the SCSI adapter circuitry is integrated onto the system board. Its interface is a 64-bit extended I/O (called XIO) channel, which provides notable improvement in overall system performance. An integrated Ethernet port is also found integrated onto the planar board for network connectivity.

2.4.6   Model 360 specifics

The 7012 System/6000 Model 360 employs a 50-MHz chip as its engine. On this model, standard memory offered is 16 MB, with an option to upgrade to 256 MB. In terms of cache memory, it offers a 32-KB instruction cache as well as a 32-KB data cache. The 64-bit bus between the cache and memory provides the system with a memory bandwidth of up to 200 MB/s. A 400-MB disk drive is standard with this model with an option to upgrade up to 2 GB of storage. The enhanced Micro Channel provides a throughput of 80 MB/s. The four Micro Channel slots are available for use since the SCSI adapter is integrated onto the system board, along with an Ethernet port.

2.4.7   Model 365 specifics

The 7012 System/6000 Model 365 features a 50-MHz main processor chip. The model comes standard with 16 MB of memory and the option to upgrade it to 128 MB. Both the instruction cache and the data cache on this model are 32 KB in size. A 64-bit-wide memory bus interface allows the system to have a memory bandwidth of up to 200 MB/s for information transfer to and from the memory. The default disk drive on this model is 400 MB, and it can be upgraded to a 2-GB drive if needed. The enhanced implementation of the Micro Channel bus on this machine provides a throughput of 80 MB/s. The single Micro Channel slot that comes with this model is available for use since the SCSI adapter and an Ethernet interface are integrated onto the system board.

2.4.8 Model 370 specifics

The 7012 System/6000 Model 370 features a 62.5-MHz processor chip. On this model the standard memory offered is 32 MB with an option to upgrade it to 256 MB. The cache memory size is 32 KB for the instruction cache and also 32 KB for the data cache. The 64-bit bus between the cache and memory provides the system with a memory bandwidth of up to 200 MB/s. The default hard disk which is 400 MB in size can upgrade to support up to 2 GB of data storage. The enhanced implementation of the Micro Channel supports a bandwidth of up to 80 MB/s. Four slots are available to provide for adapter(s) attachments, since the SCSI interface is integrated onto the planar, along with an Ethernet network interface.

2.4.9 Model 375 specifics

The 7012 System/6000 Model 375 uses a 62.5-MHz chip as its engine. On this model the standard memory offered is 32 MB, with an option to upgrade the memory to 128 MB. A 32-KB instruction cache and a 32-KB data cache is offered on this model. The 64-bit bus between the cache and memory provides the system with a memory bandwidth of up to 200 MB/s. The default hard drive available with this model is 400 MB. It can be upgraded or new drives can be added to increase the total storage capacity of the system to 2 GB. The enhanced Micro Channel provides a throughput of 80 MB/s. The single Micro Channel slot that comes with this model is available for use since the SCSI adapter and an Ethernet interface are integrated onto the system board.

2.4.10 Comparative positioning of desktop models

The processor speeds on the 200 and the 300 series models are shown below in Fig. 2.2. The scalable power within the desktop family illustrates how the configurations vary in terms of performance.

2.5 500 SERIES

The 500 series models have a deskside or, as it is sometimes called, a tower orientation. The mechanical chassis is designed to hold more room. The larger size of the mechanical enclosure allows more main memory, disk storage, and optional components to be housed in it than in the desktop models. The front and rear of the housing contain a row

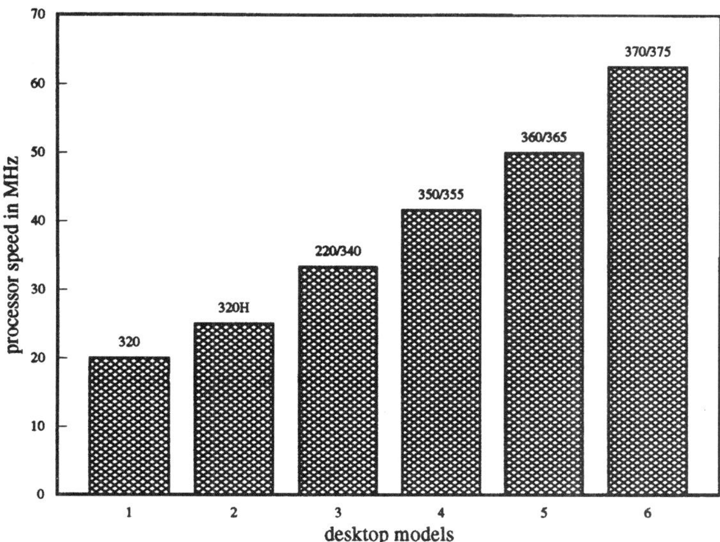

Figure 2.2 Processor speeds on the desktop models.

of vents for cooling the internal components. The front panel contains the key-operated mode switch, the reset button, an LED display, a 3.5-in diskette drive, and the power switch. There is also room in the front to accommodate devices like CD-ROM and 8-mm tape drives. All of the deskside models have more memory card slots and Micro Channel slots than the desktop ones. The model-specific features are described below.

2.5.1 Model 520* specifics

Model 520 uses a 20-MHz processor chip (SGR-2032) and comes standard with 8 MB of main memory on a single card. The memory is upgradable to a maximum of 512 MB by using an appropriate combination of memory cards in its seven available memory adapter slots. In terms of cache, there is an 8-KB instruction cache and a 32-KB data cache. A 64-bit-wide path to the memory allows a maximum permissible data transfer rate of 160 MB/s. The default hard drive available with this model is 400 MB, with an option to upgrade to a total storage capacity of 800 MB. Out of the eight Micro Channel slots provided, one is occupied by the SCSI adapter card.

---

* This model is no longer in regular production.

2.5.2 Model 520H specifics

This 7013 Model 520H features a 25-MHz main processor as its engine. The system comes standard with 16 MB of main memory with an option to upgrade this memory card with a 32- or 64-MB memory card up to a total of 1 GB. The system is configured with an 8-KB instruction cache and a 32-KB data cache. A 64-bit path between the main memory and the data cache allows the system to have a memory bandwidth of up to 200 MB/s. A 400-MB hard drive comes standard with an option to add a 1-GB disk unit, thereby allowing up to a maximum of 7.2 GB of storage. Out of the eight Micro Channel slots, one is occupied by the SCSI adapter.

2.5.3 Model 530* specifics

This model uses a 25-MHz processor (SGR-2564) as its engine and comes standard with 16 MB of main memory installed in two 8-MB cards, replaceable by a pair of 32- or 64-MB memory cards to provide more memory. Further enhancements are possible through six available memory adapter slots provided, up to a maximum of 1 GB. It comes equipped with an 8-KB instruction cache and a 64-KB data cache. A 128-bit path between main memory and the data cache gives a memory bandwidth of up to 400 MB/s. The standard disk drive offered with this model is a 355-MB disk. Seven Micro Channel slots remain available, with one of them being taken up by the SCSI adapter.

2.5.4 Model 530H specifics

Model 530H features a 33-MHz main processor as its engine and comes standard with 32 MB of main memory in two 16-MB memory cards. Cache memory comprises an 8-KB instruction cache and a 64-KB data cache. The memory path between the main memory and data cache is 128 bits wide and provides a memory bandwidth of up to 528 MB/s. In terms of disk drives, a 400-MB drive is offered as a standard option. Of the eight Micro Channel expansion slots, one is occupied by the SCSI adapter.

2.5.5 Model 540* specifics

Model 540 features a 30-MHz main processor (SGR-3064) and offers as standard a 64-MB main memory installed in two 32-MB memory cards. The memory can be extended up to 256 MB. It requires at least two memory cards to support the more efficient 128-bit path between

---

* This model is no longer in regular production.

main memory and data cache. The bandwidth achieved is up to 480 MB/s. In terms of cache, an 8-KB instruction cache and a 64-KB data cache are offered with this model. The disk drive consists of 640 MB of storage as standard. Seven of the eight Micro Channel slots are available for use (with one being used by the SCSI adapter).

2.5.6 Model 550 specifics

The 7013 Model 550 features a 41.6-MHz main processor as its engine and comes standard with 32 MB of memory. Its instruction cache size is 8 KB and data cache is 64 KB. A 128-bit path between main memory and data cache enables the system to achieve up to a maximum permissible bandwidth of 665.6 MB/s. An 800-MB disk drive is offered as standard with options to choose larger-capacity drives. With a SCSI adapter taking up one of the Micro Channel slots, seven more are available for future use.

2.5.7 Model 560 specifics

The 7013 Model 560 has a 50-MHz processor and comes configured with 64 MB of real memory. For cache memory, an 8-KB instruction cache and a 64-KB data cache is offered with this model. A 128-bit-wide path between the main memory and the data cache allows the system to attain a memory bandwidth up to 800 MB/s. An 800-MB disk drive is offered standard with this system. Of the eight Micro Channel expansion slots, one is always occupied by the SCSI adapter.

2.5.8 Model 570 specifics

Model 570 features a 50-MHz processor as its engine and comes standard with 32 MB of main memory in two 16-MB memory cards. Both the instruction cache and the data cache are 32 KB in size. The memory path between the main memory and data cache is 64 bits wide and thus provides a memory bandwidth of up to 400 MB/s. In terms of disk drives, a 400-MB drive is offered as a standard option with upgrade capability to 1 GB internally. On this model, eight Micro Channel expansion slots remain available for use, as the SCSI adapter circuitry is integrated onto the system board. Its 64-bit interface allows notable improvement in overall performance by being able to conduct data transfer at the rate of 80 MB/s.

2.5.9 Model 580 specifics

The 7013 Model 580 uses a processor that operates at 62.5 MHz. The standard memory offered is 64 MB. In terms of cache, it has a 32-KB instruction cache and a 64-KB data cache. Its 128-bit path between the main memory and the data cache allows a maximum memory bandwidth of 1000 MB/s. A standard 2-GB disk drive can be upgraded to support up to 7.2 GB of storage. Like the other 500 series models, this model also features eight Micro Channel expansion slots. A 64-bit interface on the Micro Channel bus allows it to double its bandwidth.

2.5.10   Comparative positioning of deskside models

The processor speeds on the 500 series models are shown in Fig. 2.3. The scalable power within the desktop family illustrates how the configurations vary in terms of performance.

2.6   700 SERIES

The 700 series is regarded as a special-purpose product line. Models in this series are targeted to serve specialized needs. It is typical of models in this series to be custom packaged and fabricated with special-purpose components. Some of the standard features such as the key-operated mode switch, reset button, LED display, 3.5-in diskette drive, and power switch, are likely to remain unaltered.

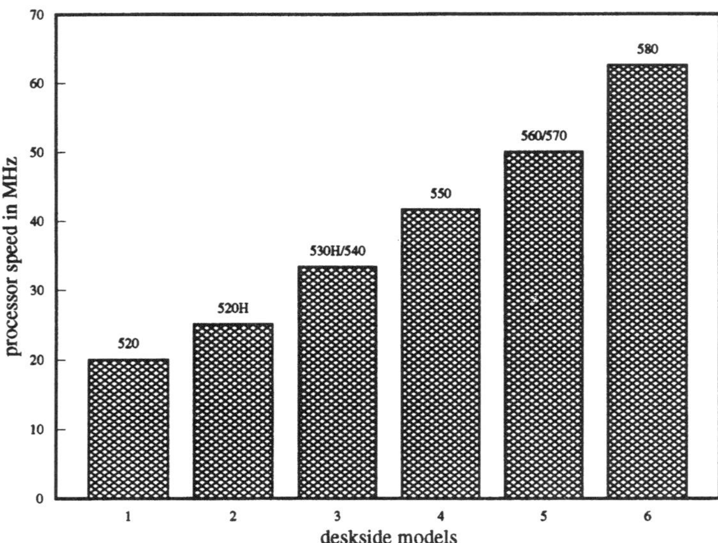

Figure 2.3 Processor speeds on the deskside models.

2.6.1 Model 730* specifics

The 7016 Model 730 has a deskside orientation. The machine is housed in a wide-bodied chassis that is notably wider than the standard towers. The system is based on a 25-MHz processor and comes standard with 16 MB of main memory in two 8-MB memory cards. The base memory can be upgraded with 16-, 32-, and 64-MB memory cards to provide up to 512 MB of real memory. The cache memory consists of 8 KB of instruction cache and 64 KB of data cache. The path to memory is 128 bits wide and yields a maximum bandwidth of 400 MB/s. A 670-MB disk drive is standard with this model with an option to upgrade it to an 857-MB drive in order to provide up to 2571 MB of internal disk storage space. Out of the eight Micro Channel expansion slots in this model, one is dedicated to the SCSI adapter card and one to the graphics subsystem adapter, thus leaving six slots available for use. The principal feature of this model is its support for graphics capability. A graphics subsystem housed in the expanded chassis provides high-end graphics capability, such as 3-D solid modeling hardware, hidden line and surface removal hardware, programmable hardware cursor, PHIGS, and GL support on the graphics adapter accelerators. This specialized circuitry allows creation of near-photo-quality images and full animation. Standard capabilities include a 256-color palette, with optional upgrade to 16.7 million colors in a single image.

2.7 900 SERIES

The 900 series models have a rack-mounted orientation. The rack enclosure in the floor-size models is designed to meet the EIA 310-C standard. The configuration consists of modular drawers. All of the models in this family house the CPU planar, the I/O planar, and the standard I/O planar in the processor drawer of the rack. Other drawers in the rack can accommodate the power distribution unit, disks, tape drives, or an optional battery backup for alternate power supply in case of power failure. The front panel of the floor-standing models contains the key-operated mode switch, the reset button, an LED display, a 3.5-in diskette drive, an internal CD-ROM, and the power switch. There is also ample room to accommodate additional devices like CD-ROM and tape drives. The model-specific features are described below.

---

* This model is no longer in regular production.

2.7.1   Model 930* specifics

The 7015 Model 930 uses a 25-MHz main processor and comes standard with 16 MB of memory, with the option to expand it to 512 MB. An 8-KB instruction cache and a 64-KB data cache is offered as cache memory. The path between the memory and data cache is 128 bits wide, and it allows the machine to achieve a memory bandwidth of 400 MB/s. A 670-MB drive housed in a SCSI drawer is offered standard and can be upgraded to provide up to 2.5 GB of internal storage capacity. An internal 2.3-GB 8-mm tape drive also comes standard with the base configuration. Two more drawers exist for holding additional media devices and a 460-watt power supply comes standard with the machine. With a SCSI adapter taking up one slot, the remaining seven out of the eight Micro Channel slots remain available.

2.7.2   Model 950 specifics

The 7015 Model 950 uses a 41.6-MHz processor as its engine. The system comes standard with 64 MB of memory, with options to expand it to 512 MB. An 8-KB instruction cache and a 64-KB data cache is standard. The path between the memory and data cache is 128 bits wide and allows the machine to achieve a memory bandwidth of 665.6 MB/s. Standard disk storage offered with this model is 857 MB, and it is expandable to 27.4 GB internally. An internal 2.3-GB 8-mm tape drive also comes standard with the base configuration. A pair of extra drawers exists for holding assorted media devices. Other options available in terms of drawers include the expansion racks, async expansion drawer, and half-inch 9-track tape drive drawer. The power supply component provides up to 460 watts of power. A SCSI adapter occupies one slot out of the eight available Micro Channel slots.

2.7.3   Model 970 specifics

The 7015 Model 970 features a 50-MHz processor and comes with 64 MB of base memory, which can be upgraded to a maximum of 1 GB. In terms of cache, this model features a 32-KB instruction cache along with a 64-KB data cache. The 128-bit memory path allows the machine to attain a memory bandwidth up to 800 MB/s. The 1.37 GB of disk space that comes standard can be expanded to 28.8 GB internally. Additional drawers exist for holding additional SCSI devices. An 1170-watt power supply unit ensures availability of adequate power to drive all of the assorted optional components. An internal 2.3-GB 8-mm tape

---

* This model is no longer in regular production.

drive that comes standard with the base configuration is housed in one of the drawers. With a SCSI adapter integrated on the I/O planar board, all of the eight Micro Channel slots remain available.

2.7.4 Model 970B specifics

The 7015 Model 970B employs an upgraded processor chip that runs at 62.5 MHz. The standard 128-MB memory can be expanded to a maximum of 1 GB. The cache memory offered comprises a 32-KB instruction cache and a 64-KB data cache. The maximum permissible memory bandwidth over the 128-bit-wide path is 1 GB/s. In terms of disk storage, four 1-GB SCSI-2 disk drives are provided as a part of the base configuration. This capacity can be expanded up to 28.8 GB internally, if deemed necessary. An 1170-watt power supply unit ensures availability of adequate power to drive all of the assorted optional components. An alternate configuration allows for the use of high-speed serial disk drives using optical channel converter modules. A 5-GB 8-mm tape drive that comes standard with this configuration is housed in the CPU drawer. With one SCSI adapter integrated on the I/O planar and a SCSI-2 adapter taking up one slot, seven out of the eight Micro Channel slots remain available.

2.7.5 Model 980 specifics

The 7015 Model 980 employs a 62.5-MHz processor. The standard 64-MB memory may be expanded to a maximum of 1 GB. The cache memory offered comprises a 32-KB instruction cache and a 64-KB data cache. The maximum permissible memory bandwidth from the 128-bit-wide path is 1 GB/s. In terms of disk storage, 2.74 GB of storage space is provided, with the base configuration using two 1.37-GB drives. This disk capacity can be expanded to 28.8 GB internally. The additional drawers available allow for holding extra SCSI devices. A 5-GB 8-mm tape drive that comes standard with this configuration is housed in the CPU drawer. The system is powered by an 1170-watt power supply. With a SCSI adapter taking up one slot, the remaining seven out of eight Micro Channel slots are available.

2.7.6 Model 980B specifics

The 7015 Model 980B uses a processor running at 62.5 MHz. The standard memory of 128 MB can be expanded to a maximum of 1 GB. The cache memory consists of a 32-KB instruction cache and a 64-KB data cache. A 128-bit path between memory and data cache allows a memory bandwidth of 1 GB/s. Four 1-GB SCSI-2 disk drives provide the base storage configuration. This capacity can be expanded up to 28.8 GB internally. An alternate configuration allows for the use of high-speed serial disk drives using an optical channel converter module. A 5-GB 8-mm tape drive housed in the CPU drawer provides for information backup provision. An 1170-watt power supply is provided. Also, a battery backup for alternate power supply is included as a standard feature of this model. One SCSI adapter is integrated on the planar board and a SCSI-2 adapter occupies one slot. The I/O expansion capability is augmented by the inclusion of a Micro Channel expansion board. This second Micro Channel bus doubles the number of expansion slots to sixteen.

2.7.7 Comparative positioning of rack-mounted models

The processor speeds on the 900 series models are shown in Fig. 2.4. The scalable power within the desktop family illustrates how the configurations vary in terms of performance.

2.8 800 SERIES

The solo member of this family at present is a System/6000-based network data server. The server provides NFS (Network File System) support across local area networks and is targeted to meet the needs of communities where applications require large amounts of on-line data.

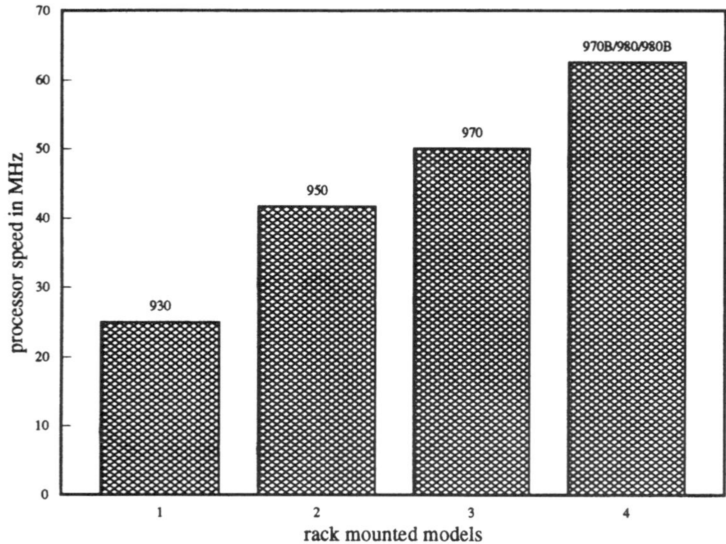

Figure 2.4 Processor speeds on the rack-mounted models.

2.8.1 Model 840 specifics

The 7051 Network Data Server features a scalable asymmetric architecture. The system includes data striping and data mirroring to increase performance and data availability. Increased productivity is also offered through the ability to perform on-line backups without interruption. Together with AIX's ability to dynamically create file space and control mirrored partitions* preemption is not necessary in an operational environment. A Model 340 is used as a host processor. So the basic hardware nomenclature of the processor is the same as that of the Model 340. This model can serve clients on up to eight Ethernet-based LANs. Its I/O-handling capabilities allow up to 20 devices (disks and/or tapes) to be supported. An expansion module called Model 800 is also available for possible future expansions. On its own the network data server can support up to 48 GB of data storage, and if combined with the expansion module the storage can be increased up to 144 GB.

2.9 PARALLEL SYSTEMS

A parallel implementation of multiple System/6000 processor nodes offers a scalable configuration that achieves a new zenith in System/6000's computing coliseum. Designed for a high-end scientific engineering environment and compute-intensive workloads, the parallel system provides an entry into the parallel computing arena using existing RISC technology. Multiple RISC-based processors are tied together using a multistaged, packet-switching, high-speed communications link between processor nodes. This link facilitates a true parallel work environment since its point-to-point communication time is independent of the relative position of the communicating nodes. In order to complement the parallel hardware architecture, an AIX parallel environment is provided (through the use of kernel extensions) as the application interface to optimize switch performance. Parallel debuggers, parallel profilers, and program visualization aids are also provided as a part of the parallel environment.

2.9.1 Model SP1 specifics

The 9076 Scalable Parallel SP1 is a parallel implementation in which multiple System/6000 processors have been tied together. Its basic frame contains eight to sixteen System/6000 processor nodes. Up to four of these physical frames can be connected together to form a

---

* These concepts are covered in detail in Chap. 16.

multinode configuration of 64 processors. Each one of the processors can have 64, 128, or 256 MB of memory. The processors themselves may be diskless or dataless. If dataless, the internal hard disk of 1 or 2 GB provides paging space. The data resides on other file servers and is accessed through NFS and/or FTP facilities. Each frame equipped with a bulk power supply provides fault tolerance capabilities for single-frame power supply failures. The SP1 requires a System/6000 workstation to function as a front-end control unit to manage the multiple nodes. The power of this parallel machine is harnessed by making each node execute one or more serial jobs, or by making multiple nodes handle a massively parallel job. A multistage packet switch supports SP1's interprocessor communications, while load leveler software optimizes utilization by balancing the load among interactive, batch, serial, and parallel jobs. The dual communication links provided over Ethernet use the internal communication for booting and paging, and the external communication for user file access.

2.10 COMPARATIVE CPU AND I/O FEATURES OF MODELS

The processor performance has been compared on a per-series basis for all of the 200, 300, 500, and 900 series families earlier in this chapter. The various processor speeds offered with different models are shown in Fig. 2.5. Table 2.1 shows the comparative I/O features for System/6000 models.

2.11 SUMMARY

This chapter describes the product positioning, packaging, and configurations for individual models in the System/6000 product line. The

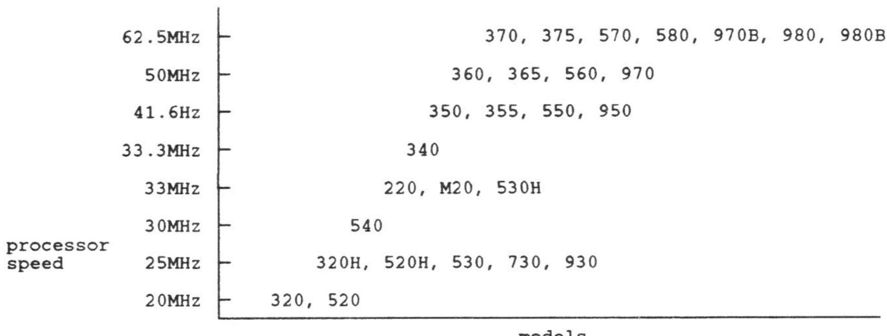

Figure 2.5 Comparative CPU speeds of System/6000 models.

TABLE 2.1   Comparative I/O Features of System/6000 Models

Model	Bus width (bits)	Memory slots	Available I/O slots
220	64	2	2
320H	64	2	3
340	64	2	4
350	64	2	4
355	64	2	1
360	64	2	4
365	64	2	1
370	64	2	4
375	64	2	1
520	64	8	7
520H	64	8	7
530	128	8	7
530H	128	8	7
550	128	8	7
560	128	8	7
570	64	8	8
580	128	8	7
730	128	8	6
930	128	8	7
950	128	8	7
970	128	8	8
970B	128	8	8
980	128	8	8
980B	128	8	16

important fact to recognize is that all of the models are based on a single scalable architecture based on RISC technology. Of the three implementations available for the POWER architecture, the multichip versions (i.e., the RS 1.0 and RS .9) are targeted for the high-end market, while the single-chip version is aimed at the entry-level or low-end marketplace. Over a period of time, new models configured with superior expansion options will continue to refresh the product line. But they are all likely to be based on a derivative of POWER architecture so that backward compatibility is preserved.

Expansion Options

System/6000's versatility enables it to serve in diverse kinds of communities, which makes it indispensable that it be able to support myriad features and expansion options. The computing needs of a rocket launching center are hardly the same as that of a transaction processing shop, so it is essential that an array of expansion options be made available for the machine to serve eclectic environments. A discussion on facilities would be incomplete if the expansion options were left out.

This chapter is not meant to be a product specification sheet, but is intended to introduce the reader to the options available for this machine. Throughout this chapter, 4-digit feature numbers, tagged with individual options, are made available so that one can acquire additional information on that specific unit.

3.1 MEMORY EXPANSION OPTIONS

The single-level storage implementation of the AIX operating system makes the memory a fixed-size address space. This address space comprises memory components of varying speeds. The main components are the cache memory, translation lookaside buffer, system memory, and the disk. The irony inherent in the address space is that its fastest component, cache memory, is smallest in size, and its slowest components, like the disk, are available in abundance. This distribution of components should be obvious for virtually any computer system. After all, the common denominator for a quality machine is not performance, not cost, but cost-versus-performance balance. Since the slower components are available as optional add-ons, one can benefit significantly from choosing the right amount of memory and disk space.

Multifarious options exist for expanding the base memory of the System/6000. Theoretically, one can enhance the system memory capacity of this machine by any amount. However, certain technical differences inside the machine and the components that are marketed prohibit arbitrary interchanges among the different System/6000 models. Although characteristics like error code correction (ECC) to detect/correct are consistent across all the memory cards, the type of memory density varies from card to card.

3.1.1 Memory card specifics

There are numerous types of memory cards available for use with different configurations, as add-on components. The specifics of these memory cards are described here, followed by a card compatibility matrix (Table 3.1) that maps a card to a model.

- The *8-MB SD1 Memory Card* (#4008) provides additional memory in 8-MB increments. Each addition of this feature requires one memory card location in the processor board.

TABLE 3.1   Matrix Showing Support for Different Types of Memory Cards for Available RISC System/6000 Models

Memory card type	PS/2	8-MB SD1	16-MB SD1	32-MB SD1	64-MB HD1	32-MB HD2	8-MB HD3	16-MB HD3	32-MB HD3	64-MB HD3	128-MB HD3
Memory speed (in nanoseconds)	70	80	80	80	80	80	80	80	80	80	80
Model	220	320H 520 520H 530 730 930	320H 520 520H 530 730 930	320H 520 520H 530 730 930	320H 520 520H 530 730 930	540	320H 340 350 360 370 520H 530H 550 950 560 730 930 970	320H 340 350 355 360 365 370 375 520H 530H 550 560 730 930 950 970	320H 340 350 355 360 365 370 375 520H 530H 550 560 730 930 950 970	320H 340 350 355 360 365 370 375 520H 530H 550 560 730 930 950 970	340 350 355 360 365 370 375 550 560 580 950 970 980

- The *16-MB SD1 Memory Card* (#4016) provides additional memory in 16-MB increments. Each addition of this feature requires one memory card location in the processor board.

- The *32-MB HD1 Memory Card* (#4032) provides additional memory in 32-MB increments. Each addition of this feature requires one memory card location in the processor board.

- The *64-MB HD1 Memory Card* (#4035) provides additional memory in 64-MB increments. Each addition of this feature requires one memory card location in the processor board.

- The *32-MB HD2 Memory Card* (#4065) is installed in pairs, using two memory card slots on the processor board. This is necessary to support a 128-bit-wide path between the data cache and main memory.

- The *8-MB HD3 Memory Card* (#4063) is installed in pairs, using two memory card slots on the processor board. This is necessary to support a 128-bit-wide path between the data cache and main memory. Memory is incremented by 16 MB when this addition is implemented.

- The *16-MB HD3 Memory Card* (#4066) is installed in pairs, using two memory card slots on the processor board. This is necessary to support a 128-bit-wide path between the data cache and main memory. Memory is incremented by 32 MB when this addition is implemented.

- The *32-MB HD3 Memory Card* (#4067) is installed in pairs, using two memory card slots on the processor board. This is necessary to support a 128-bit-wide path between the data cache and main memory. Memory is incremented by 64 MB when this addition is implemented.

- The *64-MB HD3 Memory Card* (#4069) is installed in pairs, using two memory card slots on the processor board. This is necessary to support a 128-bit-wide path between the data cache and main memory. Memory is incremented by 128 MB when this addition is implemented.

- The *128-MB HD3 Memory Card* (#4090) is installed in pairs, using two memory card slots on the processor board. This is necessary to support a 128-bit-wide path between the data cache and main memory. Memory is incremented by 256 MB when this addition is implemented.

3.1.2 Memory-model matrix

A memory-versus-model matrix, shown in Fig. 3.1, gives a comparative perspective on the available options.

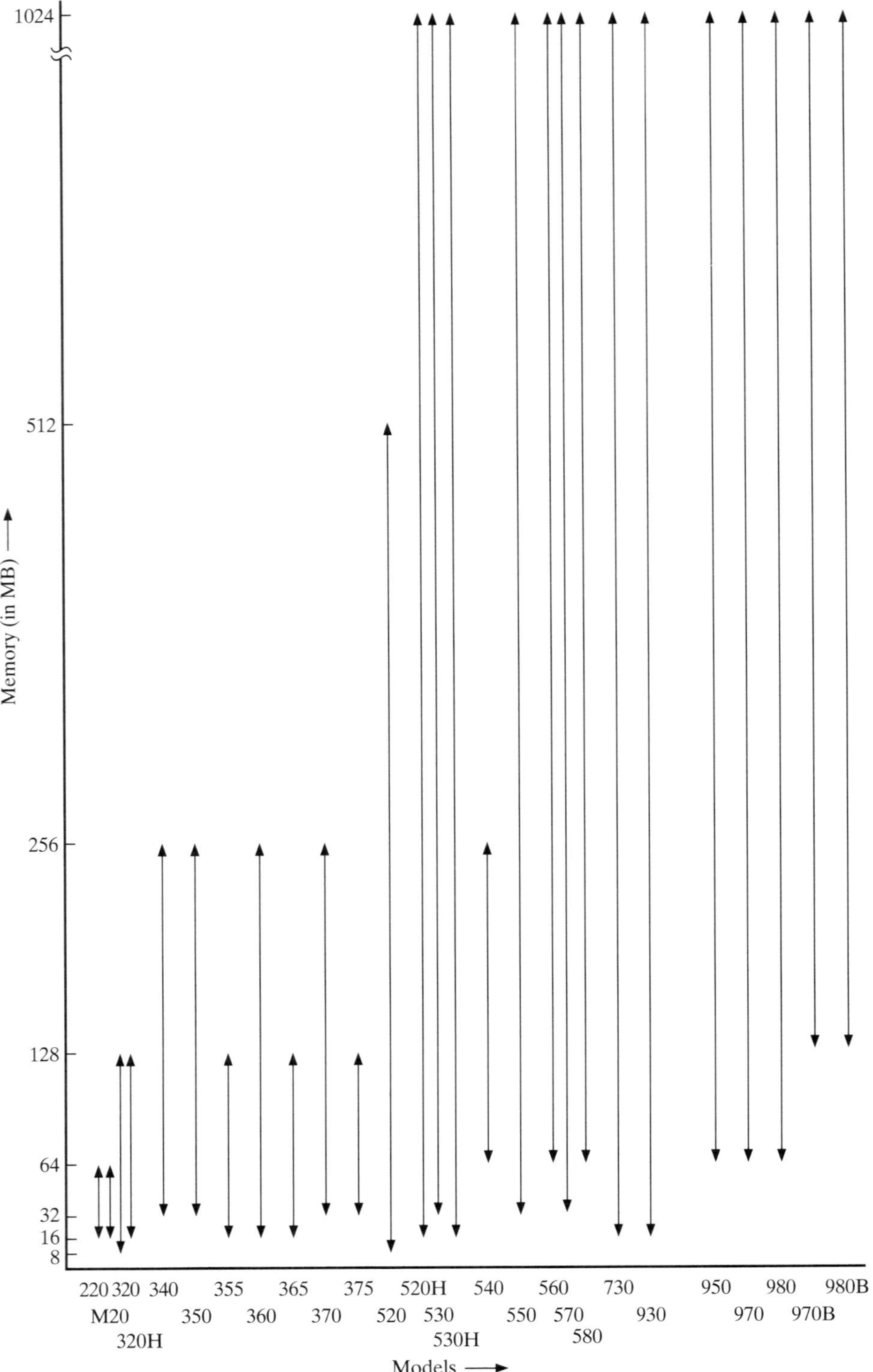

Figure 3.1 Memory ranges for RISC System/6000 models.

3.2   STORAGE MEDIA OPTIONS

Fast processors, like the System/6000 running applications which require a large number of disk drive accesses, are prone to becoming I/O bottlenecks and, in turn, degrade system throughput if the speed and capacity of the drives are inadequate. Although large amounts of memory help to some extent, applications requiring random requests for short records will face disk performance problems. To address this issue, a wide variety of high-performance disk drives of varying capacities and speeds is offered for the System/6000. Also a variety of disk adapters is made available to meet the diversified needs of the System/6000 user base. Industry standard SCSI and SCSI-2 interfaces are available to work with a variety of peripherals. There is also a proprietary serial interface available to meet the needs of high bandwidth, where applicable. The serial interface is able to deliver a command processing rate on the order of 0.5 milliseconds, versus a SCSI interface's ability to do the same in about 4 to 5 milliseconds. A comprehensive list of the currently available disk drives has been summarized in a later part of this section, so that one may evaluate the comparative media transfer rates, bus transfer rate, and access time.

3.2.1   Disk storage

- The *355-MB SCSI Disk Drive* provides an additional 355 MB of internal disk storage. It comes in a 5.25-in form factor providing a data transfer speed of 1.875 MB/s. The interface is provided by a synchronous single-ended SCSI bus.

- The *400-MB SCSI Disk Drive* provides an additional 400 MB of internal disk storage. It comes in a 5.25-in form factor providing a data transfer speed of 2.0 MB/s. The interface is provided by a synchronous single-ended SCSI bus.

- The *640-MB SCSI Disk Drive* provides an additional 640 MB of internal disk storage. It features two 320-MB fixed disks packaged together and requires only one bay. It comes in two 3.5-in drives providing a transfer speed of 2.0 MB/s. The interface is provided by a synchronous single-ended SCSI bus.

- The *670-MB SCSI Disk Drive* provides an additional 670 MB of internal disk storage. It comes in a 5.25-in form factor providing a data transfer speed of 1.875 MB/s. The interface is provided by a synchronous single-ended SCSI bus.

- The *857-MB SCSI Disk Drive* provides an additional 857 MB of internal disk storage. It comes in a 5.25-in form factor providing a data transfer speed of 3.0 MB/s. The interface is provided by a synchronous single-ended SCSI bus.

- The *800-MB SCSI Disk Drive Pair* provides an additional 800 MB of internal disk storage. It features two 400-MB fixed disks packaged together and requires only one bay. It comes as a duplex unit with two 3.5-in drives providing a transfer speed of 2.0 MB/s. The interface is provided by a synchronous single-ended SCSI bus.

- The *1-GB SCSI Disk Drive* provides an additional 1 GB of internal disk storage. It comes in a 3.5-in form factor providing a data transfer speed of 3.0 MB/s. The interface is provided by a synchronous single-ended SCSI bus.

- The *1-GB SCSI-2 Disk Drive* provides an additional 1 GB of SCSI-2 disk drive storage. It comes in a 3.5-in form factor providing a data transfer speed of 3.0 MB/s. The interface is provided by a synchronous single-ended SCSI-2 bus.

- The *1.37-GB SCSI Disk Drive* provides an additional 1.37 GB of internal disk storage. It comes in a 5.25-in form factor providing a data transfer speed of 4.5 MB/s. The interface is provided by a synchronous single-ended SCSI bus.

- The *2.4-GB SCSI-2 Disk Drive* provides an additional 2.41 GB of internal disk storage. It comes in two 5.25-in disk storage units in one package and provides a data transfer speed of 3.0 MB/s. The interface is provided by a synchronous single-ended SCSI-2 bus which has two SCSI addresses. It supports command reordering and back-to-back write operation.

3.2.2 Disk matrix

A comparative feature list of the currently available disk drives is presented in Table 3.2 so that one may evaluate the comparative media transfer rates, bus transfer rate, and access time of the assorted units.

3.2.3 Diskette storage

The following diskette drives are available for use with the System/6000.

- *Internal 5.25-in Diskette Drive.* This particular diskette system is used explicitly with the System/6000 Model 900 series systems. It is installed in the processor drawer and used for information transfer by 5.25-in diskettes.

- *Internal 3.5-in Diskette Drive.* This particular diskette system is used explicitly with the System/6000 Model 220 system and can accommodate up to 2.88 MB of information. It is used for information transfer by 3.5-in diskettes and is a prerequisite for the System/6000 Model 220 hard disk option.

TABLE 3.2   Comparative Features of Available Hard Drives for RISC System/6000

Drive	Media transfer rate (MB/s speed)	Bus transfer rate (MB/s speed)	Access time (milliseconds)
160 MB	1.5	5.0	24.3
400 MB	2.0	5.0	18.0
200 MB (a)	2.0	5.0	18.9
320 MB	2.0	5.0	19.0
355 MB	1.8	5.0	24.3
400 MB	2.0	5.0	18.0
670 MB	1.8	5.0	26.3
857 MB	3.0	5.0	17.2
1.00 GB (a)	3.0	10.0	17.2
1.00 GB	3.0	5.0	16.8
1.37 GB	3.4	5.0	17.6
857 MB (b)	3.0	8.0	17.2
1.07 GB (b)	3.0	8.0	17.2
2.4 GB (a)	3.0	10.0	16.8

NOTE: (a) SCSI-2; (b) Serial.

- *External 5.25-in Diskette Drive.* This 1.2-MB diskette subsystem can be used with any System/6000 model except Model 220 and the 900 series subsystems. It is a self-contained desktop unit attaching to a standard diskette connector by a cable. It is used for exchange of information using 5.25-in diskettes.

3.2.4   CD-ROM storage

The following CD-ROM drives are available for use with the System/6000.

- The *Internal CD-ROM Drive* provides a read-only compact disk drive to support on-line databases. An audio output jack is provided in the front bezel. A media kit containing a test caddy, a disk caddy, and a lens-cleaning device is included. It comes in a 5.25-in half-high form factor with a constant linear velocity (CLV) spiral track technology providing a data transfer rate of 150 KB/s. The interface is provided by a SCSI single-ended asynchronous adapter.

- The *External CD-ROM Drive* is a desktop self-contained package with data transfer rate of 150 KB/s and access time of 380 ns. It can be attached to a SCSI I/O controller via a cable and is supported by all System/6000 models except 900 series subsystems.

- The *650-MB Rewritable Optical Disk Drive* is a stand-alone box attaching to a SCSI-2 port and is capable of read/write operations on optical disks. Capable of accommodating up to 650 MB/s of information, it can transfer data at the rate of 696 KB/s or 4 MB/s over a SCSI bus.

3.2.5 Tape storage

The following tape drives are available for use with the System/6000.

- The *150-MB ¼-in Cartridge Drive* is an internal device used only with the System/6000 Model 900 series. It is installed in the SCSI device drawer through a SCSI I/O controller in ¼-in tape cartridges, each accommodating up to 150 MB of information.

- The *525-MB ¼-in Cartridge Drive* is an external stand-alone deskside unit that can be used by all System/6000 models, except 900 series subsystems, through a SCSI port. There are three current models—Model 1 accommodating 150 MB, Model 11 with 525 MB storage, and Model 12 holding 1.2 GB of information. Thus, multipurpose uses including data transfer and disk backup are feasible.

- The *2.0-GB 4-mm Tape Drive* is an external deskside self-contained unit that can be used with any System/6000 models except the 900 series and connects to a SCSI port via a cable. The primary uses are for disk backup, data archival, and information dissemination. It uses 4-mm tape cartridges that accommodate up to 4 GB in normal mode and 4 to 8 GB with data compression.

- The *5-10-GB 8-mm External Tape Drive* is an external 5.25-in deskside unit compatible with all models of System/6000 except 900 series. There are two models available—Model 1 consists of a cartridge storing up to 2.3 GB and Model 11 accommodates up to 5 GB. Model 11 features a data compression option that allows up to 10 GB on a single cartridge.

- The *.5-in Tape Drawer* is used only with 900 series subsystems. It comes with a SCSI I/O controller that is installed in a Micro Channel slot inside the processor drawer in 900 series subsystems. The built-in tape drive uses standard ½-in 9-track tape reels. A 1-MB memory buffer provides superior performance.

- The *9348 Tape Unit* is a tabletop unit using standard 9-track ½-in tape reels that are automatically loaded and reeled. It is connected to a SCSI port through a cable, has a 1-MB memory buffer, and can continue to store information while it is being positioned. This unique feature improves the performance to a great extent.

- The *2.3-GB Internal 8-mm Tape Drive* provides a high-capacity tape drive for save/restore and archiving functions. It uses 8-mm data cartridges. A media kit containing a test cartridge, a blank data cartridge, and a cleaning cartridge is included. It comes in a 5.25-in form factor with rotating-head, helical scan technology providing a data transfer rate of 245 KB/s. The interface is provided by a SCSI single-ended asynchronous adapter.

TABLE 3.3 Comparative Features of Available Tape Drives for RISC System/6000

	150-MB .25″ cartridge drive	525-MB .25″ cartridge drive	2.0-GB 4-mm tape drive	2.3-MB 8-mm tape drive	5-10-GB 8-mm tape drive	.5-in tape drawer	9348 tape unit
Media	.25″ tape cartridge	.25″ tape cartridge	4-mm tape cartridge	8-mm tape cartridge	8-mm tape cartridge	.5-in tape reels	.5-in tape reels
Data transfer rate (in KB/s)	90	200	183 (normal) 732 (compressed)	245	500 (normal) 1 MB (compressed)	206–768	200–781
Maximum capacity (MB)	150	525	2 GB (normal) 4-8 GB (compressed)	2.3 GB	5 MB (normal) 10 MB (compressed)	Variable	Variable

The comparative media sizes, data transfer rates, and capacities of these tape drives are given in Table 3.3, so that their relative specifications may be evaluated.

3.3 I/O CONTROLLERS

The following I/O controllers are available for use with the System/6000's peripheral devices.

- The *SCSI High-Performance External I/O Controller* conforms to ANSI Doc X3.131-1986 and provides high-performance attachments of single-ended SCSI fixed disk, CD-ROM, and tape devices. Up to seven external SCSI devices can be supported by a single controller card. In each system, a maximum of five controller cards can be attached. It can simultaneously accept multiple commands per device, providing a data rate of 4.0 MB/s in synchronous protocol. It acts as SCSI initiator and provides SCSI parity support. A standard Micro Channel form factor card is supported. The Micro Channel interface consists of a 4-byte (32-bit) bus master, streaming data support, and address and data parity support.

- The *SCSI-2 High-Performance External I/O Controller* provides attachments of single-ended SCSI and SCSI-2 devices. In each system, a maximum of five controller cards can be attached. It can simultaneously accept multiple commands per device, providing a data rate of 10.0 MB/s for SCSI-2 devices and supports command tagged queuing. This feature allows attachment of an IBM 9334 Expansion Unit or up to four external IBM-supported devices with supported cables. It features SCSI parity support. A standard Micro Channel form factor card is supported. The Micro Channel interface consists of a 4-byte (32-bit) bus master, streaming data support, and address and data parity support. Maximum SCSI bus length is 3.75 m for IBM-supported cables and 3.0 m for non-IBM-supported cables.

- The *SCSI High-Performance Internal I/O Controller* conforms to ANSI Doc X3.131-1986 and provides enhancements and additional attachments of internal single-ended SCSI fixed disks and external devices. Up to four SCSI fixed disk devices can be attached internally with a daisy chain cable. Up to a maximum of two external devices may also be included for a total of seven devices. In each system, a maximum of five controller cards can be attached. It can simultaneously accept multiple commands per device, providing a data rate of 4.0 MB/s in synchronous protocol. A standard Micro Channel form factor card is supported. The Micro Channel interface consists of a 4-byte (32-bit) bus master, streaming data support, and address and data parity support. Maximum SCSI bus length is 2.4 m for IBM-supported cables and 3.0 m for non-IBM-supported cables. This controller is intended for use in systems containing six 3.5-in fixed disks to provide optimum performance.

- The *SCSI-2 High-Performance Internal I/O Controller* provides enhancements and additional attachments of internal and external single-ended SCSI and SCSI-2 fixed disks and media devices and supports tagged command queuing. Up to six SCSI fixed disk devices can be attached internally and/or two externally with a daisy chain cable. In each system, a maximum of five controller cards can be attached. It can simultaneously accept multiple commands per device, providing a data rate of 10.0 MB/s in synchronous protocol. A standard Micro Channel form factor card is supported. The Micro Channel interface consists of a 4-byte (32-bit) bus master, streaming data support, and address and data parity support. Maximum SCSI bus length is 2.4 m for IBM-supported cables and 2.4 m for non-IBM-supported cables.

- The *High-Performance Disk Drive Subsystem Adapter* supports attachment of the IBM 9333 Model 500 High-Performance Disk Drive Subsystem. Up to four subsystems can be supported by each adapter. One constraint is that the adapter needs to be installed in one of the first available five slots; slots six, seven and eight are not supported.

3.4   GRAPHICS ADAPTERS AND EXPANSION OPTIONS

The array of graphics adapter offerings can be categorized in two classes: 2-D adapters and 3-D adapters. Listed here is an abridged description of the entry-level, mid-range, and high-end graphics adapters.

3.4.1   Grayscale graphics adapter

Resolution of 1280×1024 is obtained in 256 shades of gray with 16 concurrent shades. It features 4-bit pixels and 16 entries in the lookup table. Each table entry has 8 bits. It utilizes one Micro Channel slot.

3.4.2   Color graphics adapter

In this model, 1280×1024 resolution is obtained in a 16.7-million-color palette with 256 concurrent colors. It uses 8-bit pixels with 256 entries in the lookup table. Each table entry has 24 bits and the adapter utilizes one Micro Channel slot.

3.4.3   3-D graphics adapter

This adapter uses two overlay planes and two window control planes. A 16.7-million-color palette with 256 concurrent colors is provided with 8-bit pixels and 256 entries in the lookup table of 24 bits each. A resolution of 1280×1024 is provided in this model. It can support arbitrarily shaped windows; pan and zoom of graphical images; multiple, colored, local, and infinite lights; and diffuse, ambient, and specular lighting models. The adapter requires two Micro Channel slots for installation.

3.4.4   3-D graphics adapter frame buffer

This adapter provides additional capabilities to the 3-D graphics adapter. It can support up to 16 sets of 256 concurrent colors, 2 additional window control planes, and 2 additional overlay planes.

3.4.5   3-D+ graphics adapter

This is essentially identical to the 3-D graphics adapter. The additional features include 3-D graphics adapter frame buffer upgrade and a 24-bit Z buffer option.

3.4.6   24-bit Z buffer option

This provides a 24-bit Z buffer for the 3-D or 3-D+ graphics adapter for depth queuing, and surface and hidden surface removal. It features 256 colors with 2-D and 3-D graphics. It utilizes two Micro Channel slots.

Graphics expansion options are also available to support the various types of displays. Note that System/6000 Series 900 models do not support any of the graphics options discussed here.

3.4.7   POWER Gt1

This is exclusively used with Model 220 in a special slot in the system board. It is mainly an entry-level adapter for two-dimensional graphics applications. The standard 1280×1024 resolution in black and white can be upgraded to 256 colors using two Gt1 VRAM upgrades.

3.4.8   POWER Gt3

This color display features two on-board processors as its engine, thus allowing faster image creation, animation, and rotation. Two overlay planes allow image overlay and speed up window generation and manipulation. It uses one Micro Channel slot and utilizes a bus master and streaming data procedure.

3.4.9   POWER Gt4 and Gt4x adapters

These are designed for three-dimensional graphics applications and offer double-frame buffers, five-color maps, and a 24-bit Z buffer. Gt4 has two on-board processors for image generation. Two versions of the processors are available—an 8-bit model provides 256 colors and uses two Micro Channel slots, but the 24-bit model uses three Micro Channel slots. Gt4x is a faster version and features six on-board processors, with the rest of the features remaining the same.

3.4.10   POWER GTO

This is a stand-alone box providing the most powerful graphics hardware in the System/6000 family to date. There are two models available. The 8-bit model features 256 colors and provides two frame buffers. Four circuit cards complete the ensemble—a Micro Channel interface card, a graphics processor card, a drawing processor card, and an 8-bit frame buffer card housed in a single frame. The 24-bit model additionally features a shading processor. Any of these models attach to a System/6000 via a GTO accelerator feature.

3.5   ASYNCHRONOUS ADAPTERS

In commercial multiuser environments, UNIX-based systems are subjected to heavy terminal I/O tasks, and the terminal concentrators and terminal drivers often chew up an immense amount of CPU resources. Although users interact with their terminals in a random manner, there is a maximum limit to how much terminal I/O the CPU is able to handle. It is imperative that a terminal concentrator help the CPU lessen its burden. For System/6000 there is a variety of multiport terminal boards offered. They are available in 8-, 16-, and 64-port configurations and can be procured to support either EIA-232 or EIA-422 interfaces. The model options offered currently are:

8-Port EIA-232 Adapter

16-Port EIA-232 Adapter

8-Port EIA-422A Adapter

16-Port EIA-422A Adapter

8-Port MIL-STD 188 Adapter

64-Port Async Controller

The common characteristics of these adapters are described in a comprehensive manner here. The asynchronous adapters occupy one Micro Channel slot and support data rates up to 38.4 KB/s. A 16-byte buffering on transmit and receive lines is available. A single 78-pin connector connects the terminal port box to the adapter. The 8- and 16-port options have DB-25 connectors to attach terminals. Support for EIA-232, EIA-422, and MIL-STD 188 interfaces is available. The connection interfaces for 8- and 16-port adapters are shown in Fig. 3.2.

The 64-port option comes as two components: (1) a 64-port async controller and (2) a 16-port asynchronous concentrator. The controller contains an intelligent controller (an NEC chip) inside it which does the multiplexing. It utilizes async concentrators with a maximum of four concentrators. Distances up to 2500 ft between controller and concentrator are supported. The second component, which is the 16-port async concentrator, is a cigar-box-shaped piece of hardware based on an Intel 80186 processor with 64-KB RAM. It should be noted that there is no support for the DSR (Data Signal Ready) signal and RI (Ring Indicator) signal. Maximum cable lengths of 200 ft and 2500 ft

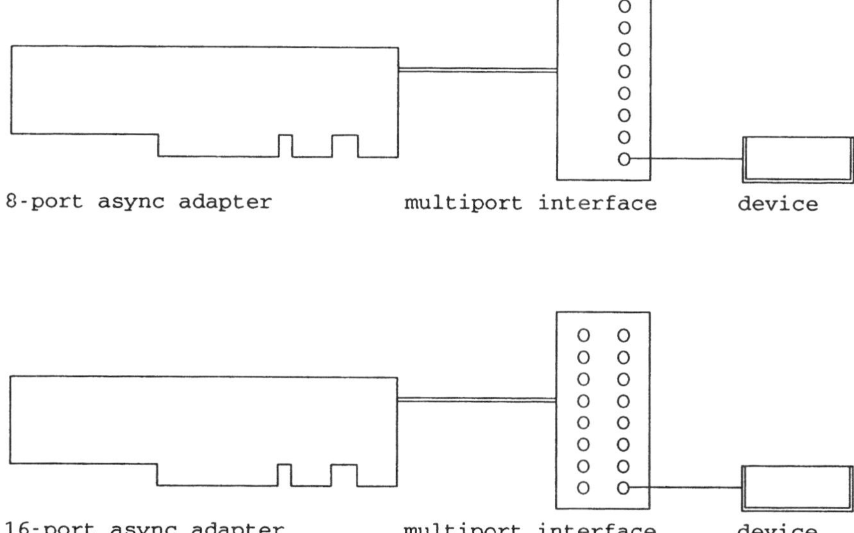

Figure 3.2 Connection interfaces for 8- and 16-port adapters.

are supported from the concentrator to device and controller to concentrator, respectively. Its connection interfaces and configuration layout are shown in Fig. 3.3.

3.6 LAN COMMUNICATION ADAPTERS

The following LAN adapters are available for use with the System/6000.

3.6.1 Ethernet adapter

This conforms to IEEE 802.3 specification standards. This adapter can be attached to a 10-MB/s CSMA/CD (Carrier Sense Multiple Access/ Collision Detection) Ethernet network. It features a 32-bit Cyclic Redundancy Check (CRC) and provides 16-KB RAM for data buffering. A maximum of four adapters per system is supported with an option for on-board transceivers for thin net. It also has the capability to support customer-supplied Ethernet cable—thin, thick, or other.

Ethernet and 802.3 have different frame headers, so direct Ethernet-to-802.3 communication is not possible. Figure 3.4 illustrates the coexistence of Ethernet Type 2 and IEEE 802.3 to show how to connect one kind of network with the other, using an intermediate machine as a gateway.

3.6.2 Token-Ring adapter

This adapter conforms to IEEE 802.5 specification standards and attaches to a 4-MB or 16-MB network. It provides support for data and address parity. A maximum of four adapters per system can be supported. The communication cable is supplied with the adapter.

3.7 WAN COMMUNICATION ADAPTERS

The following WAN adapters are available for use with the System/6000.

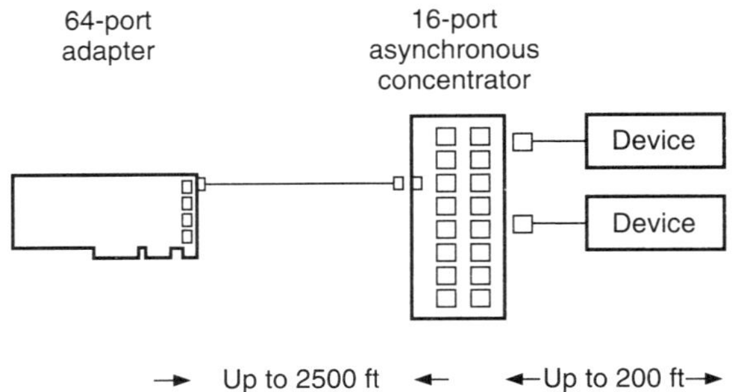

Figure 3.3 64-port async controller concentrator supporting 4×64 devices.

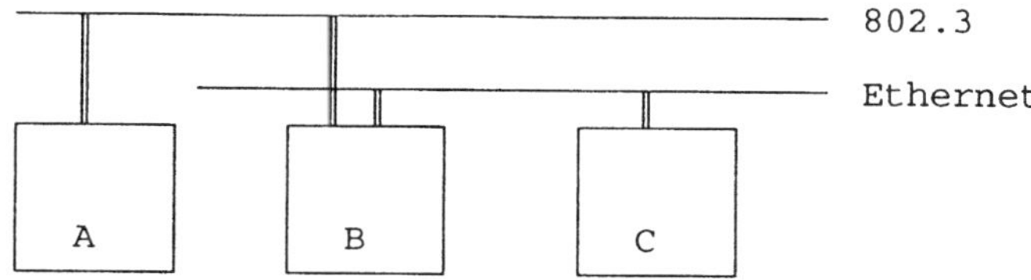

Figure 3.4 Coexistence of 802.3 and Ethernet type 2.

3.7.1 X.25 interface adapter

This adapter attaches to an X.25 serial network and requires 512-KB RAM for data buffering. A single port can support one of three interfaces—an X.21 interface up to 64 KB/s, an EIA-232/V.24 interface up to 19.2 KB/s, and an EIA-232/V.35 up to 64 KB/s.

3.7.2 Multiprotocol adapter

This attaches to synchronous communication networks and supports a cyclic redundancy check (CRC). The base card and daughterboard configuration are as follows. The base card relieves the system processor. The daughter card/fan-out box supports four interfaces—EIA-232D on ports 0 through 3, V.35 on ports 0 and 1, EIA-422A on ports 0 and 2, and X.21 on port 0, as seen in Fig. 3.5.

3.8 HOST ATTACHMENT OPTION

The following host attachments are available for use with the System/6000.

```
Port-specific shared interrupt support
```

Port	232D	422A	V.35	X.21
0	Y	Y	Y	Y
1	Y	N	Y	N
2*	Y	N	N	N
3	Y	N	N	N

```
* Port 2 supports 422A for data only
```

Figure 3.5 Protocol supports on multiport adapter.

3.8.1 3270 connection adapter

This adapter emulates 3278/3279 display stations and supports DFT or CUT modes of connectivity. CUT (Control Unit Terminal) refers to one logical session over a physical line and DFT (Distributed Function Terminal) indicates multiple logical sessions over a physical line.

3.9 MODEMS

The following modems are available for use with the System/6000.

3.9.1 Modems over PST lines

5853 modem.   This is a stand-alone desktop unit attached through an EIA-232D interface and an appropriate cable. It supports full-duplex communication of 2400 bits/s over Public Switched Telephone (PST) lines. Its built-in microprocessor can interpret high-level commands to modem functions and automatically adapt to the appropriate operating mode of the incoming communication packets.

3.9.2 Modems over leased lines

7855 modem.   This model is geared to operate over leased lines in either synchronous or asynchronous protocols. In asynchronous mode, transmission speeds up to 9600 bits/s are supported over voice-grade, public switched lines and up to 19,200 bits/s if data compression is enabled. In synchronous mode, full-duplex transfers of 12,000 bits/s are possible. It uses Enhanced Attention (AT) command sets for modem functions. In the case of a communication failure, it features Switched Network Backup Utility (SNBU) that allows continuation of information transfer. This model is used especially for an irregular but large information transfer.

786X modem.   These models are primarily geared to operate over leased lines. Transmission speeds of 4800 to 19,200 bits/s are featured, depending on the model. They can be used point-to-point or multipoint which allows multiple devices to share a single communications line. They can be manipulated remotely through network management programs, and they feature diagnostic and test functions.

3.9.3 Modems over digital networks

5822 DSU.   This is a modem used over a digital network rather than an analog communication. Digital networks are better suited for transmitting computer information and feature higher speed and reliability. Transmission speeds up to 56,000 bits/s over Digital Data Service networks are supported. It is connected to a System/6000 async port on one side and to the digital network on the other in either a point-to-point or multipoint attachment configuration.

3.10 DISPLAYS AND TERMINALS

The following is a list of displays and terminals that are available for use with the System/6000.

3.10.1 Graphics displays

Graphics displays are primarily used as visual front ends for graphical application packages and are unique in this sense from ASCII terminals or Xstations. There are three main classifications—IBM 6091 Color Displays, IBM 1091-051 Color Displays, and PS/2 Displays.

The IBM 6091 provides high-resolution, full-color images with models ranging from 16- to 23-in screens. It provides 1280×1024 pixel resolution and features shadow mask to improve sharpness of the images.

The IBM 1091-051 is a low-cost alternative to be used with the Model 220 or in an Xstation environment. It has 1280×1024 resolution, providing high-resolution images for scientific/engineering applications.

The PS/2 display is designed to be used with the PS/2 family, but can also be used with some System/6000 systems and Xstations. It features a 19-in screen and white-on-black images consisting of different brightness levels or shades of gray. Attached to a grayscale graphics adapter, it can provide resolution of up to 1280×1024 pixels.

3.10.2 Xstations

Xstations are used to provide low-cost, graphics-capable workstations that can interact with System/6000 or other open systems. Two major Xstation models are currently available: Xstation 120 and Xstation 130.

Xstation 120 comes standard with 512 KB of video memory, 512 KB of system memory (upgradable to 8.5 MB), and 512 KB I/O memory. Standard 640×480 resolution with up to 256 colors out of a 17.6-million-color palette can be expanded to 1280×1024 resolution with 256 colors. It features an 8-MHz processor as its engine. It comes standard with an Ethernet adapter with an option for a Token-Ring network adapter, allowing simultaneous participation in two different networks.

Xstation 130 comes standard with 1 MB of video memory (expandable to 2 MB) and 2 MB of system memory (upgradable to 16.5 MB). The standard 1024×768 resolution with up to 256 colors out of a 17.6-million-color palette can be expanded to 1280×1024 resolution with 256 colors. It features a 12.5-MHz processor as its engine. It comes standard with an Ethernet adapter with an option for a Token-Ring adapter or any other network protocol conforming to Ethernet Version

2 or IEEE 802.3. This allows simultaneous participation in two different networks. Optionally, a dual async adapter can be installed, allowing for two more async ports.

3.10.3 ASCII terminals

ASCII (American Standard Code for Information Interchange) terminals are typically used to provide low-cost interaction with System/6000 in a multiuser environment. They are designed to display alphanumeric text and related symbols and are not capable of full graphics display. Terminals can be used locally through async ports in Micro Channel slots or remotely over communication lines. Three main classifications are discussed here: 3151 terminals, 3164 terminals, and PS/2 terminal emulation. In addition, other workstations may be used with System/6000.

The IBM 3151 family features 14-in monochrome displays with a choice of amber/gold/green on black displays capable of emulating ten types of non-IBM ASCII displays. They display 25 rows of 132 characters with an operator message line on the bottom. Standard interfaces include RS-232 and RS-422.

The IBM 3164 color terminal features screen preservation after a few minutes of inactivity and split-screen capability in addition to the features previously described for the IBM 3151. The standard interface is an EIA-232-C or RS-422-A supporting data rates up to 19,200 bits/s.

A PS/2 can be used as a terminal emulator that allows simultaneous access to multiple System/6000 systems or multiterminal access to a single System/6000 system. This intelligent workstation also provides direct interaction for more complex program-to-program communications.

3.11 PRINTERS AND PLOTTERS

A variety of printers or plotters using diverse technology is supported by this machine. The printing technology on these machines ranges from dot matrix to laser. Most of them are connected using a serial and/or a parallel interface.

3.12 BATTERY BACKUP

Battery backup is used only on System/6000 Series 900 models. It provides 1500 watts of standby power in the event of a power failure and is designed to operate up to three drawers for at least ten minutes. An optional battery backup extender cable can support up to six drawers for this time period. It then performs an automatic shutdown which protects user data and allows for quick recovery on power restoration.

3.13   DIALS AND PROGRAMMABLE KEYBOARD

These are input devices that increase the ease with which a user can manipulate graphical objects. Depending on the model, 8 dials or 32 programmable keys assist in controlling pan, zoom, and rotation of two-dimensional and three-dimensional images. Using a serial attachment feature, these devices can be attached to an async port on a System/6000.

3.14   K-T-S-M: KEYBOARD, TABLET, SPEAKER, MOUSE

Although the keyboard, tablet, speaker, and mouse are separate physical components, their driver interface in the System/6000 is via the same hardware subsystem. Hence, it makes sense to discuss them collectively.

3.14.1   Keyboard

The enhanced keyboard features 101 keys and has an industry-standard layout. The keytops are engraved with U.S. English characters but additional languages are supported by multiple composite keystrokes. The keyboard plugs into a keyboard port provided on all System/6000 models.

3.14.2   Tablet

A tablet eases manipulation of graphical objects. It consists of a flat surface and a six- or four-button cursor or a two-button stylus attached to the standard tablet port. The computer senses the cursor held in the user's hand and responds by moving the display cursor. The stylus is activated by pressing the pen against the flat surface. The tablet also facilitates digitizing a drawing. A tablet can provide resolution of up to 1279 lines per inch.

A digitizer is similar to a tablet and is used for entry of large-scale drawings. It consists of a flat surface and a 16-button cursor that is pressed to digitize points of a drawing placed on the surface. It is attached to a System/6000 via an async port (EIA-232D). The resolution can be defined by the application program (up to 1279 lines per inch) and the output is either in ASCII or binary format.

3.14.3   Speaker

Speaker capability is provided for use with engineering applications as well as for the CD-ROM drive. The speaker is built-in even though the CD-ROM attachment has a headphone jack.

3.14.4 Mouse

The mouse is a useful input device and it augments the keyboard as a means of interacting with System/6000. The user slides the mouse on a desktop to control cursor movement, draw lines, define points, etc., and the system responds depending on the position of the display cursor and the particular button pressed.

3.15 SUMMARY

While not meant to be a product specification sheet, this chapter is intended as a high-level composition to introduce the reader to the options available for this machine. Since it is unlikely that a single person would need every one of the options, knowing what is available broadens the spectrum of knowledge about System/6000's capabilities to support assorted expansion options

Hardware Maintenance and Diagnostics

This chapter describes a set of frequently overlooked aspects of the System/6000. The first aspect is the set of reliability features that is innate to the hardware design of the architecture. Each feature is explained in terms of its functions. The second aspect discusses the boot sequence of the machine while explaining its self-test mechanisms. The third part comprises the troubleshooting guidelines and problem determination techniques in the unlikely event of failures. Available tools and diagnostic components are explained along with the methodology for error analysis.

4.1 MAINTENANCE MODULES

A variety of tools and well-defined procedures exist for the maintenance of the System/6000. They are designed to help diagnose (1) procedural problems such as incorrect setup and wrong device configuration, (2) device problems like adapter malfunctions and disk read errors, and (3) network problems caused by modem breakdown and link deterioration. The complexity of most troubleshooting procedures that are deterministic in nature is such that an average user can handle it. A scientific approach to problem determination and defect isolation makes it possible for the machine's maintenance to be carried out in a structured way.

If the problem is an obvious one, the troubleshooting phase is minimized or often eliminated. Sometimes life may not be that simple and there may be situations where the cause of a system malfunction is not obvious. In order to handle problems that neither get reported by operating system messages nor show up on the system console, an exhaustive set of procedures, called the maintenance analysis procedures (MAPs), exists for troubleshooting ailing systems. These procedures provide a step-by-step methodology to analyze a problem with the machine hardware, and they are intended to be used by a trained person (such as the system administrator or the operator). While MAPs are designed to guide a person through a set of extensive steps in a thorough manner, some devices on the machine may also have their own maintenance documentation. If that is so, the device-specific maintenance steps need to be used prior to running the system diagnostics.

The diagnostic aids translate every machine problem into a 6-digit service request number (SRN), whose left-most three digits indicate the source of the problem while the right-most three digits give the reason code. This SRN is then used to index an extensive list of repair actions which enable the operator to determine whether a repair is to be performed or a part needs to be replaced. At this stage, if a repair is deemed necessary, the service manuals can guide the operator through the steps. If a part needs to be replaced, the SRN number helps determine exactly what is needed by indexing a comprehensive list of failing function codes (FFC) and furnishing the corresponding field replacement unit (FRU) part number for each FFC. Every single component on this machine has been given an FRU number in order to put in place a foolproof strategy for machine hardware maintenance. This multistep approach to problem determination, followed by isolation and rectification, structures the troubleshooting task into a well-defined strategy. For a machine as complex as the System/6000, it is essential that its maintenance strategy be as scientific as its architectural design.

4.2 RAS FEATURES

The concept of reliability, availability, and serviceability (RAS) is important for the robustness of this machine. Several features and functions are incorporated into the design infrastructure of the system hardware. Key RAS features include parity checking, error correction coded memory, bit scattering, memory deallocation, bit steering, and memory scrubbing. Each of the features has a unique role to play in facilitating reliability, aiding availability, and assisting serviceability for the integrity of the machine.

4.2.1 Parity checking

Parity checking is supported on several critical components. The first set consists of CPU arrays (which include the general purpose registers in the execution units and the directory arrays in the two caches). Other components are the processor bus, memory bus, data buses, I/O buses, Micro Channel bus, most adapters, and the SCSI bus.

4.2.2 Error correction code

Error correction codes (ECC) on memory support single-bit error correction and double-bit error detection capabilities. These features are required when a hard error (such as a bit stuck to 0 or 1) is detected which cannot be corrected by mere memory scrubbing.

4.2.3 Bit scattering

Bit scattering is a feature that enables each bit of a 40-bit word* to be distributed across different memory chips, so that a failing bit in a word can be replaced by a spare bit if needed.

4.2.4 Memory scrubbing

Memory scrubbing is an ongoing (configurable) operation on a running system that scans the main memory in a sequential manner. The main memory of the computer is essentially an aggregated set of DRAM memory modules, thus being vulnerable to soft errors. Although these soft errors are correctable, over prolonged periods of time they can be rendered unrecoverable. When such instances do occur, the scrubbing process corrects the single-bit errors in its periodic scans. Without scrubbing, single-bit errors have a chance of turning into double-bit errors, which are uncorrectable.

4.2.5 Bit steering

Bit steering is a memory control function that assists in bypassing hard memory failures by substituting good spare bits for failing bits. Each memory bus line can steer a spare bit into a data or check bit position within the ECC word it receives. Together with the memory

---

* A full word comprises 32 data bits (which we refer to most often), 7 check bits, and 1 spare bit.

scrubbing function, the system uses this bit-steering capability to deal with single-bit errors.

4.2.6 Memory deallocation

Memory deallocation is a scheme that is used to void double-bit aligned errors. In the event of a hard memory error, which cannot be bit-steered, the machine begins to deallocate memory in blocks (up to a certain extent).

All of these RAS features work together in conjunction with the built-in self-test and power-on self-test facilities to provide a reliable work environment.

4.3   BUILT-IN SELF-TEST

The built-in self-test (BIST) takes place when power on the machine is turned on or when a check stop occurs. The participants in this operation are a set of embedded logic in the CPU chips and a resident controller chip on the CPU planar. The process consists of conducting a pseudo-random built-in self-test on the complex chips in a unified manner. A BIST operation comprises the following steps:

1. initializing the logics on the CPU chips

2. initializing the embedded memories on the chips

3. self-testing the memory

4. self-testing the AC and DC logic

5. resetting the hardware for initial program loading

In order for BIST features to work, the hardware of a machine needs to be specially fabricated. In System/6000, each one of the CPU chips contains a special embedded logic called the common on-chip processor (COP). COPs are independent processors and they take up about 3 percent of the CPU chip area. COPs are interconnected by a COP bus, as shown in Fig. 4.1. A bus controller called on-card sequencer (OCS) is used to drive the COP bus. Under normal booting conditions, OCS reads test seed patterns from an OCS EPROM (erasable programmable read-only memory) to control the self-test and reset operations. Any errors detected during this testing phase are recorded in the NVRAM (nonvolatile random access memory). For additional diagnostic and debug purposes, provision is made for an external bus controller called the engineering support processor (ESP) to be employed to handle the COPs. *The ESP is not a part of the System/6000.* It is a

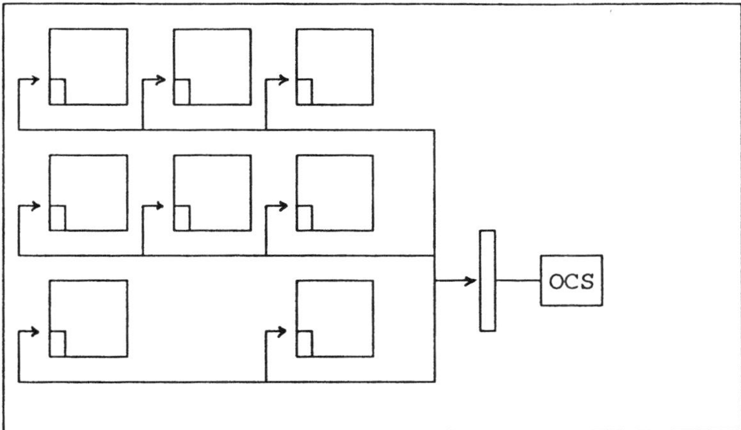

Figure 4.1 Embedded COPs logic in the chips of the CPU planar.

stand-alone workstation used in laboratories that loads, initiates, and monitors test programs. Like OCS, the ESP also implements a full set of COP commands.

The design of BIST is such that it can support parallelism inherently when testing the VLSI chips on the board. As a result of the self-test, not only is a failing chip isolated but also failing embedded memories are identified if present.

4.4 POWER-ON SELF-TEST SEQUENCE

A power-on self-test (POST) phase follows BIST to check out the hardware integrity of the system. The POST code resides in the ROM (read-only memory). The purpose of the POST is to check out the functions needed to boot the machine and the functions that cannot be tested after loading the operating system.

A set of test functions follows the basic POST code, and this sequence is referred to as the extended POST or EPOST. This piece of the test code resides in the boot device rather than in the ROM. Its functional role is similar to that of the POST: in effect, to exercise functions before running the operating system in its normal environment.

There are three control programs worth mentioning here, namely, the initial sequence controller (ISC), the core sequence controller (CSC), and the initial program load controller (IPLC). Their responsibilities and algorithmic sequence of execution are as follows:

ISC

- Perform a CRC (circular redundancy check) on the system ROM.
- If a miscompare error is detected,
  halt the system.
- Examine *check stop count* in NVRAM which is used for cold boot.
- If check stop is nonzero, indicate that a check stop event has occurred and
  halt the system.
- Start RAM POST to determine memory configuration.
- Locate a 1-MB chunk of contiguous error-free memory.
- Construct a bitmapped representation of physical memory.
- If this memory is unavailable,
  halt the system.

CSC

- Conduct the DMA, standard I/O POST, interrupts, SCSI POST, and device presence tests.
- Detect the presence and functionality of devices required for IPL to record their status and information in the IPL control block located in the IPL ROM.

IPLC

- Build a successful boot path by performing a CRC on portions of NVRAM containing the configured boot device selection sequence.*
- Check and validate the boot record on the first device in the list.[†]
- Load the boot record into memory. This record uniquely describes the media, record length and the characteristics of the boot device. With all this information IPLC can now load the boot code into the preallocated 1-MB memory.

Beyond this point the boot sequence is under the control of software, and is characterized by loading of the kernel, initialization of the virtual memory management and I/O subsystems, and creation of processes.

The responsibilities involved in the three control programs make evident the fact that these two phases, BIST and POST, together play

---

* This device list is based on the key switch position and one of two boot lists. For normal boots, the machine maintains a default boot list in ROS and a user boot list in the NVRAM, and for service-mode boots there are separate default and user device lists.

† Typically, the first physical sector of a diskette or disk drive, or the first record of a tape device contains the boot record.

a vital role in the boot sequence of the processor hardware and hand-off of hardware control to the software domain.

4.5   PROCESSOR BOOT

When a machine is powered on, it must go through a specific set of steps before being able to run any software. This set of steps is referred to as the boot sequence and involves verification, setup, and configuration of the machine's hardware. The process consists of a set of events that take place following the power-on reset until the loading of executable code from the boot record. Although we take a pro-

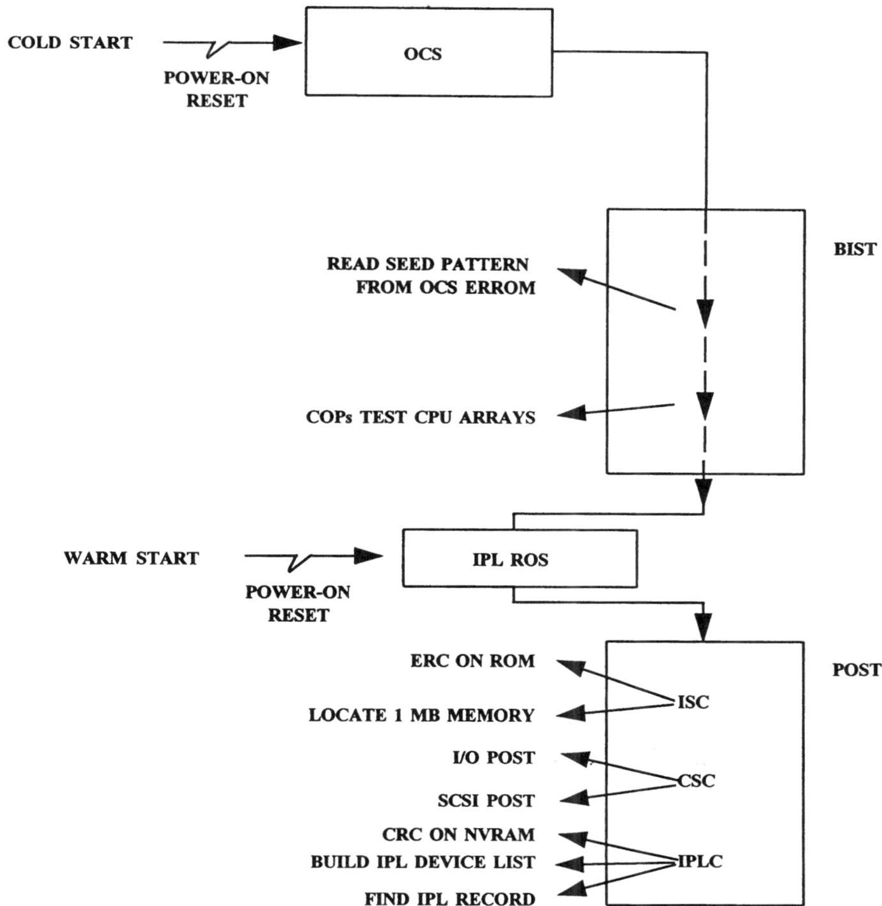

Figure 4.2 Conceptual breakdown of the tasks in the boot sequence of the processor.

cessor's boot sequence for granted in our everyday life, several critical tasks are performed here within a short span of time. The tasks occur in discrete phases, each phase having its own entry and exit criteria for management assurance purposes. A conceptual model of the boot sequence is illustrated in Fig. 4.2, in which its tasks are grouped into functional phases.

The first phase of the boot sequence is called the *hardware initialization phase*. Being the very first phase, it has no predetermined entry criteria. However, it does have rigid exit criteria which require that native instruction code be able to execute on the processor. The tasks in this phase include initialization of cache line entries, TLB (translation lookaside buffer) entries, and the MSR (machine status register). The registers, TLB entries, and the cache directories are also required to have good parity before advancing to the next step.

Upon successful completion of the hardware initialization, the *operations phase* commences. The POWER instructions begin controlling the events from here on. Upon entry to this phase, two triggering events occur back to back; first, a special bit gets set in the MSR to signal a state change and second, a system reset interrupt results to flag the completion of the hardware initialization. Consequently, native code execution begins, and the POST code takes over conducting hardware integrity tests. Its exit criteria include mapping of the main memory to page zero of the functional memory and ensuring that there is enough memory available for the rest of the boot sequence to progress gracefully.

Following the successful completion of POST, a search is begun for the boot device. The boot device is subsequently located and the boot record is loaded off it. One may wonder about the rationale behind the search for this boot device. The reason for this is that boot device contents are always specific to the configuration of individual machines.

The final phase of the boot sequence is marked by the control being passed to the code in the boot record that has recently been loaded from the boot device. From here on, the boot record takes over the responsibilities of loading the software (operating system). The subsequent part of the boot procedure essentially involves loading the AIX kernel and other software components.

Normally a processor boots gracefully. However, if a problem does occur with the system, a well-defined set of problem determination procedures is available to aid in debugging and troubleshooting.

4.6   PROBLEM DETERMINATION

From power-on time until the completion of the operating system boot, the LED panel on the machine continues to rapidly flip through its 3-digit display. It may be difficult for someone to keep up with the code sequences, but it is possible to get an idea of where a machine might be in its boot sequence by observing the most significant digit. In the current generation of the System/6000, a code in the 100s indicates the BIST phase and one in the 200s indicates the POST phase. As the numbers increase, it is an indicator of miscellaneous configuration functions like slot queries, software configuration, etc., being carried out. If an error results at this stage of the game, one should note the error code and report the problem. If no such option is viable, use the following set of steps as a guideline to determine what the error code means.

1. Obtain the entire number by recording the flashing three digits on the LED panel and subsequently pressing the reset button to get the remaining three digits. This 6-digit number gives the service request number (SRN).

2. Cross-reference the SRN code to obtain the corresponding failing function code (FFC).

3. This FFC, in turn, will give a description of the problem that the machine has encountered. Note that this description is often model-specific and may reference a field replacement unit (FRU) number along with the problem description.

Shown in Fig. 4.3 is a graphical summary for the steps involved in translating error codes to descriptive classifications.

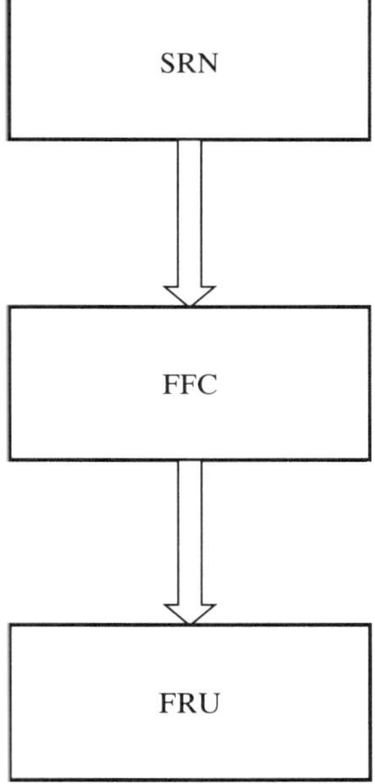

Figure 4.3 Problem resolution flowchart.

4.7 DIAGNOSTIC ENVIRONMENTS

Diagnostics in the current generation of the System/6000 can either be run off the hard drive or used from a diskette. Generally, it is easier to use the set of diagnostics off the machine's hard drive (provided the hard drive is functional!).

There are different environments under which these diagnostics can be run, including a concurrent mode, a maintenance mode, and a stand-alone mode. Almost always, the choice of environment will be context-specific. In other words, the nature of the problem and the component(s) being diagnosed will determine under which environment the diagnostic tests ought to be performed. In the concurrent mode, diagnostic tests may be performed on shared as well as dedicated devices, with AIX running under the normal multiuser environment. Concurrence does not necessarily mean that diagnostics share a device with another application; it merely indicates that the operational system need not be powered down to isolate a defect on the system using concurrent mode. For the maintenance mode diagnostics, the operating system (AIX) does need to be brought into a maintenance mode prior to using the diagnostics. The third diagnostic environment, which is the stand-alone mode, has more stringent requirements, and it requires the processor to be booted in a service mode.*

The command to perform hardware diagnostics can be invoked from the command line by typing *diag* when a problem is suspected. Regardless of which environment is used, a menu-driven interactive user interface provides a structured and modular approach to diagnosing the system.

4.8 DIAGNOSTIC COMPONENTS

The diagnostic components on this machine can be functionally placed into two domains: controller and applications. The program that is invoked to start the diagnostics is referred to as the supervisor. It coordinates the activities between a utility controller for execution of diagnostic utilities and a diagnostic controller for control of diagnostic applications.

The diagnostic controller forms the navigational control base of the diagnostic applications. It orchestrates the overall error scrutiny process by traversing the configuration database on the system. Its additional responsibilities include displaying diagnostic codes, invoking

---

* The mode switch on the chassis selects how the system is to be booted. The possible choices are normal mode, service mode, and secure mode.

selected diagnostic applications, interpreting findings, and reporting SRNs through the 3-digit LED display. Its findings are also logged in a special file which can be viewed using a utility called *diagrpt,* if needed.

Each diagnostic application is a stand-alone test program that is invoked by the controller upon request. It is usually very component-specific—so much so that there is a dedicated application for almost every device and adapter on the system. While some diagnostic applications test a component directly, there is a set of components called application test units (ATU) which is bound into the diagnostic applications. These application test units make use of the device drivers to test a resource. Together, the diagnostic applications and the application test units form the functional component base of the diagnostic subsystem.

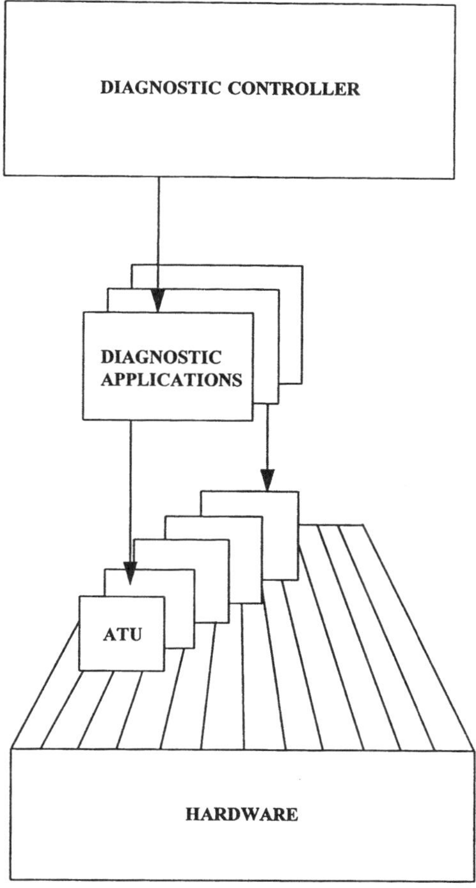

Figure 4.4 Conceptualization of the operational diagnostic process.

In summary, the overall operational structure of the diagnostic process can be thought of as a controller sitting on top of the diagnostic applications invoking applications on an as-needed basis. The result is a modular and effective troubleshooting methodology for a troubled system. A conceptualization of the operational diagnostic process is pictured in Fig. 4.4.

4.9 ERROR LOG

Error logging provides a means of maintaining a chronicle of troubled events on the system. The audit trail kept by the error log simplifies the debugging phase by furnishing information which would otherwise have to be recreated. Some of the reported errors may be temporary and recoverable, while certain errors may require user intervention in order to be corrected. Also, there may be permanent errors that are neither recoverable nor correctable. Regardless of which kind of error the system encounters, running diagnostics results in analysis of these errors, followed by reporting of SRNs to rectify them.

In order to view the error logs rather than analyze them, an error log viewing utility called *errpt* can be run which displays a chronological log of errors. An example of output may look as follows:

```
ERROR_ID TIMESTAMP   T CL RESOURCE_NAME  ERROR_DESCRIPTION

1104AA28 0305193593 T S  SYSPROC        System reset interrupt received
9DBCFDEE 0305193793 T O  errdemon       Error logging turned on
C14C511C 0304125793 T H  scsi0          ADAPTER ERROR
9DBCFDEE 0304112493 T O  errdemon       Error logging turned on
FCA960CE 0301155093 T S  tok0           EXCESSIVE TOKEN-RING ERRORS
E85C5C4C 0223101293 P S  ktsmfns        SOFTWARE PROGRAM ERROR
0F27AAE5 0222172893 P S  SYSPROC        SOFTWARE PROGRAM ABNORMALLY TERMINATED
AEC7B1B0 0222140493 P H  tok0           TOKEN-RING INOPERATIVE
27C1EFFF 0222122993 P H  SYSPROC        Data Storage Interrupt, IOCC
1A660730 0222094093 P S  3270c0         C327 Start error
2BFA76F6 0219171493 T S  SYSPROC        System shutdown by user
9DBCFDEE 0215183493 T O  errdemon       Error logging turned on
192AC071 0215182293 T O  errdemon       Error logging turned off
CBE1D1A5 0215145893 U H  LVDD           Physical volume declared missing
AEC7B1B0 0215132893 P H  tok0           TOKEN RING INOPERATIVE
8564E6B1 0214175893 T H  hdisk0         DISK OPERATION ERROR
FCA960CE 0214164093 T S  tok0           EXCESSIVE TOKEN-RING ERRORS
DD0E4902 0206123793 T H  tok0           PROBLEM RESOLVED
7BDD117A 0206123493 T H  tok0           ADAPTER ERROR
20188DE1 0206123493 P H  tok0           WIRE FAULT
FCA960CE 0206114993 T S  tok0           EXCESSIVE TOKEN-RING ERRORS
DD0E4902 0206113893 T H  tok0           PROBLEM RESOLVED
```

```
7BDD117A 0206113893 T H  tok0        ADAPTER ERROR
20188DE1 0206113893 P H  tok0        WIRE FAULT
8564E6B1 0128115793 T H  hdisk0      DISK OPERATION ERROR
74533D1A 1210221692 U H  SYSIOS      LOSS OF ELECTRICAL POWER
```

4.10   CHECK HANDLER

The check handler provides a means to handle checks that cause a hardware interrupt. Checks may be of several types:

- machine check
- check stop
- data storage interrupt
- external check

The *machine check* can happen because of certain privileged software sequences or a storage fault. The next kind of check handler, *check stop,* can be caused by the same two reasons as before, or because of a processor unit fault. When the check stop does occur, it causes the machine to run BIST again. If the error is processor-related, BIST reports the problem, whereas if it is memory-related, the POST phase reports it. The third type of check, which is referred to as a *data storage interrupt,* is caused by a storage fault occurring due to loading or storing to memory via the I/O space. The fourth kind of check that causes an interrupt is an *external check,* and it may occur because of an uncorrectable storage error during a DMA transfer or a memory scrub operation. All of the checks that cause interrupts get logged in the error log.

4.11   SUMMARY

The maintenance and diagnostic components together with the reliability, availability, and serviceability aspects address a critical quality assurance feature of the System/6000. Although they may be one of the most overlooked and least advertised domains of features, they play a critical role in orchestrating the machine's vital functions.

The maintenance package is characterized by a structured approach to problem determination. The hierarchical procedure of identifying SRNs, indexing them into the corresponding FFC, and eventually resolving the problem using FRUs presents a thorough and reliable approach to machine maintenance. The diagnostic components along with the error-logging utility further aid in troubleshooting and isolating hardware problems.

In addition, an array of RAS features and functions is incorporated into the design infrastructure of the system hardware. Parity checking, error correction coded memory, bit scattering, memory deallocation, bit steering, memory scrubbing, the built-in self-test during cold boot, and the power-on self-test are the key RAS features to know which enable one to augment the technical knowledge of the machine and its diagnostics.

System/6000 Software Subsystem—User's Perspective

Operating Environment

This chapter focuses on the operating environment and primarily on how to get started with the System/6000. The material lays the foundation for the user's perspective of the System/6000 software subsystem. The user's interaction with the software subsystem, i.e., the AIX operating system environment, is described in terms of the computer-human interface and the layout of its files and directories.

In order to feel comfortable with the operating environment one needs to first learn the concepts, then understand the operating system layout, and last but not least, master the basics.

5.1 GETTING STARTED

There are several ways to get started with the System/6000. Which method is best is entirely up to the reader to decide. Some of us get acquainted with computer systems as a part of our academic curriculum, while the rest of us have to pick up the knowledge on our job. One way or the other, if you have been exposed to AIX-like systems already, you can choose the hacker's approach; i.e., simply roll up your sleeves and get started on the keyboard. On the other hand, if you have not had adequate exposure to AIX or UNIX, read through this chapter carefully.

As you read, you may want to try out some examples on your own. At this point it should be mentioned that access to a System/6000 running

AIX is desirable but certainly not a requirement. The concepts and ideas presented here are geared toward a cosmopolitan audience that needs to learn about the software basics with or without access to an AIX system.

5.2 LAYOUT OF PROGRAMS AND UTILITIES

Software is a generalized term given to programs that execute in computers. The word *program* refers to a discrete set of instructions given to the machine to execute. These programs that execute together in a computer system maintain a harmony with each other, thereby providing a structured interface to interact with the system.

The set of programs that executes in a computer can be categorized into two discrete classes. The first class of programs is what the user may have written or acquired. The common term for this class of programs is *application software*. This application software is typically geared to serve the specific needs of the end-users. Examples of application software are word processors that assist in document preparation or databases that maintain on-line information. The second class of programs performs the housekeeping in the machine rather than interacting with end-users directly. These programs manage the execution of the application software and ensure its correct execution, termination, and output. The term used for this class of programs is *system software*. Recognize the fact that this system software is highly specialized and very specific to a certain machine architecture. A piece of system software that formats a diskette on an IBM PC is useless on an Apple computer; the latter will typically have its own format program.

In order to present a conceptual understanding of the layout of the programs and utilities on the System/6000, refer to a conceptual model that resembles a doughnut shown in Fig. 5.1. The hollow core represents the hardware. The outer layer represents the application programs, which can also be user commands. The inner layer depicts the system programs. The insulation between the two layers is provided by a command language interpreter (also referred to as a *shell*) that provides an interface between the user and the system.

In order to provide a more detailed perspective of AIX, consider a sectional view of the doughnut model and view it under magnification. At this level of detail some additional components of the system software can be identified, which exposes much of the mystery about the software subsystem of a machine. In the sectional view (Fig. 5.2), notice that the outermost layer of the figure consists of application programs and utilities that users employ. When invoked, these perform a designated task. Flow of control passes from the user's application pro-

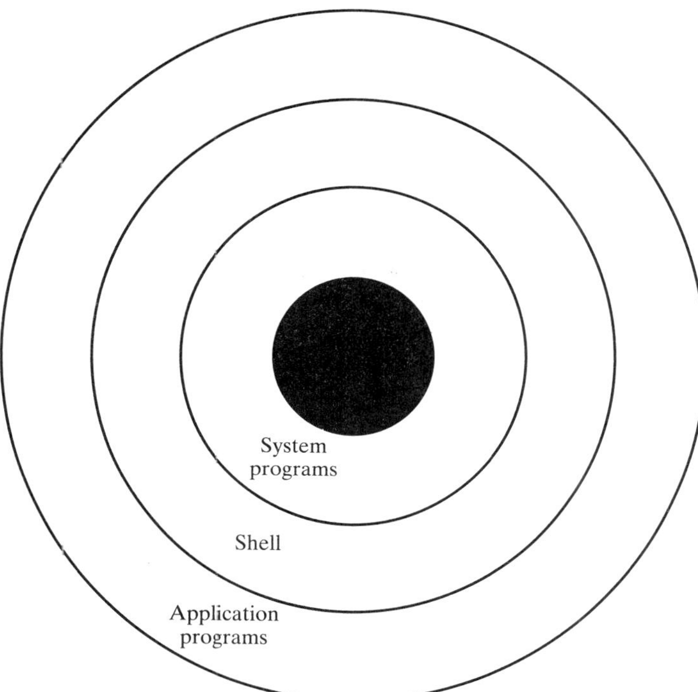

Figure 5.1 Doughnut model.

gram down to the system programs through the shell layer. The vehicles used for transferring control are referred to as *system calls*. Use of system calls is the primary means of requesting information from the operating system and its resources. Details on system calls are covered in Chap. 15.

The third layer in the sectional view of the doughnut model serves as the manager responsible for supervising and scheduling requests from application programs. This layer is referred to as the *kernel*. The kernel services requests and subsequently coordinates with the resources in the machine to schedule access to physical devices for information retrieval or storage, whichever is required.

The fourth level in the sectional view consists of a set of low-level privileged system programs. Once a request has been scheduled by the kernel to access a device, these low-level routines take over the active control. These routines access the physical device (e.g., platters on a hard drive) upon request and send up the retrieved information via the same path on which it was sent down. Needless to say, these low-level routines are highly device-dependent. Collectively, they are referred to

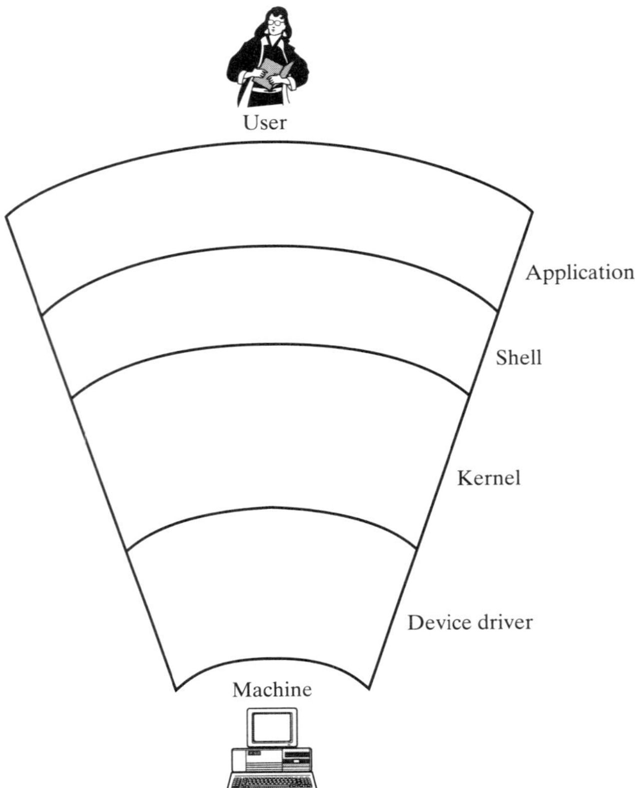

Figure 5.2 Sectional view of the doughnut model.

as *device drivers.* For every device on the system, there is a set of device drivers that are responsible for that physical device and for shielding applications from the hardware specifics of the machine.

In order to review how the layered doughnut model of AIX works from a user's point of view, consider a typical scenario that occurs frequently. What happens when a document is created using a text editor? First, the editor program is invoked by the shell when its name is typed in at the user's command line prompt. Then some new text is typed into it. Thereafter, the text is saved and the editor program is terminated. This may seem like a trivial task to the user, but how do the layers of the doughnut model represent this scenario? To answer the question, visualize the scenario, step by step. Upon initiation of the editor (the application program) by the shell (the command language interpreter), a request to create a document is made to the operating system. Upon granting of this request (from the operating system), new text is added into storage (a buffer in memory) set aside for this task. Each character typed at the terminal gets sent to some device driver (low-level routines) which is responsible for the terminal device I/O. In this way, a document gets created. In order to maintain a focus on the functions of the different layers of the doughnut model, the discussion here has been kept simple. Detailed discussion from a system point of view can be found in Chap. 13 and later chapters.

5.3 AIX DISTRIBUTION TREE

The AIX software distribution is arranged in a hierarchical structure, resembling an inverted tree. Program modules are grouped in directories in this file tree. This logical organization of data and files allows control over the management of multiple directories and files at one time. The basic layout of vital programs has not changed from the standard UNIX file structure upon which AIX is based. But a set of modifications has been made in terms of file organization in order to optimize storage, accommodate enhancements, and comply with standards.

The top-level directory of the file tree is referred to as the *root directory* and is represented by a slash (/) symbol. Every directory under this root directory is considered a subdirectory and may contain files and/or directories.

At the top of the AIX filesystem hierarchy is the system-defined root directory. This root directory contains a set of standard subdirectories. Described below are the names and functions of some of the main directories found under *root*:

bin	contains a set of *bin*ary programs that users employ as commands
dev	holds special files for I/O *dev*ices
etc	contains miscellaneous files for system initialization and system management (the name *etc* being derived from *etc*etera)
export	provides a place for server machines to place binaries and data for diskless client machines
lib	contains common libraries; later releases of AIX have linked */lib* with */usr/lib*
sbin	holds system utilities and files needed to boot the machine
tmp	contains *temp*orary files that may get created by the users or the system itself; typically this directory is purged on a periodic basis
u	contains login directories for the system *u*sers; for compatibility reasons, later releases of AIX have linked */u* with */home*
usr	contains system programs and licensed program products that *usr*s would use

var   serves as a mount point for directories and files which change size, such as things found in the */usr/spool* directory of UNIX or older AIX systems

In addition to these directories, an individual system may also have some additional directories occurring under *root*. It is to be noted that the general convention for system maintenance is to keep the root directory as clean as possible. The standard layout of an AIX file tree, as it appears on the System/6000, is shown in Figs. 5.3, 5.4, and 5.5.

Beneath these directories, one AIX system may vary from the other, depending on the system's options, configuration, and usage. But now,

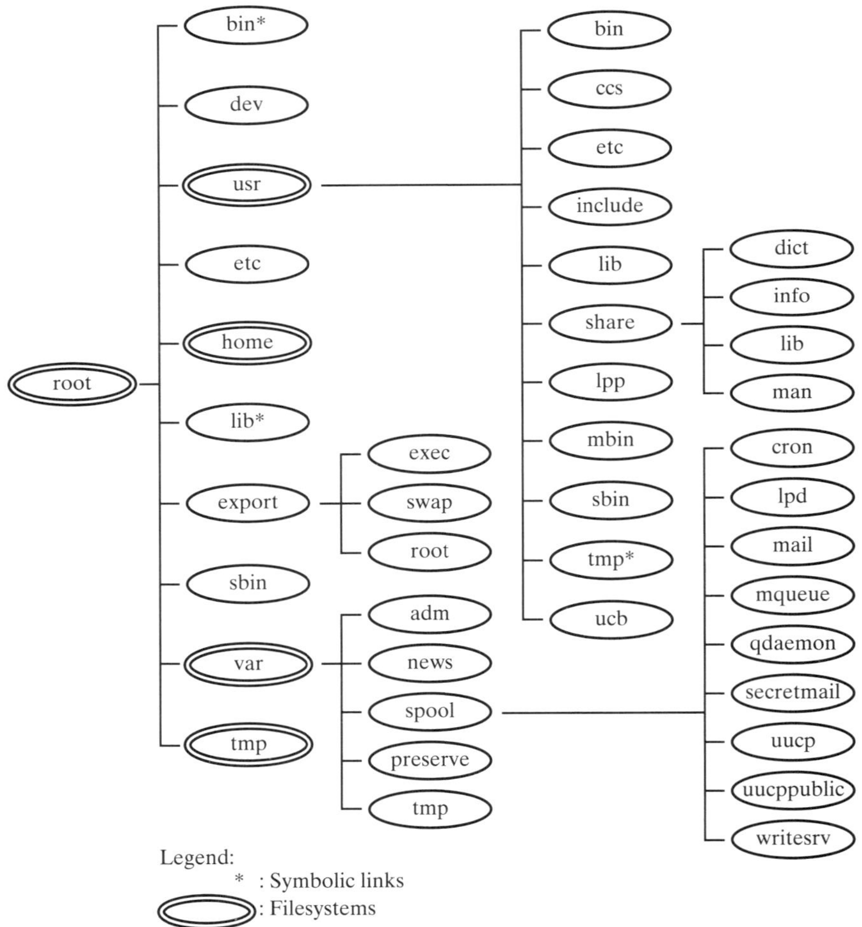

Figure 5.3 AIX file tree (version 3.2).

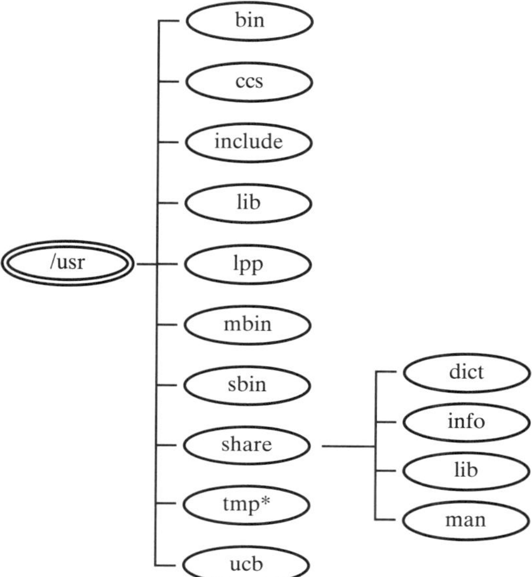

Figure 5.4 *usr* filesystem.

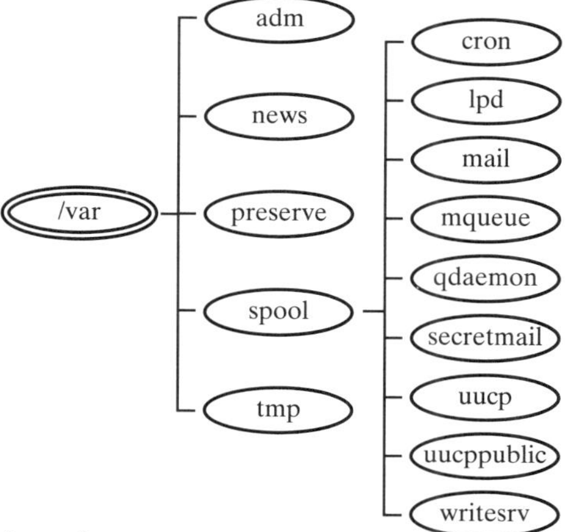

Figure 5.5 *var* filesystem.

having the basic knowledge of the AIX distribution tree and knowing the significance of the relevant directories facilitates navigation within the system.

5.4 NAVIGATING UNDER AIX

One's navigating skills can only be as good as his or her knowledge about the system. Having acquired an overview of the AIX topology, some basic tasks will be reviewed that are needed to get started with the system.

5.4.1 Login/logout procedure

Assuming that a user account has been assigned on the system, the login process involves typing in the account name followed by a password (if any) at the respective prompts. The text for the password will not echo on the screen when it is typed in. This is done in order to secure user passwords from being easily noticed over the shoulder. A typical scenario is given below where a user account name *user1* is typed in, followed by the account's password *Phoenix1*.

```
login: john<cr>
john's Password:     <cr>

$
```

If both the account name and password were typed correctly, access to the system is granted. This stage is identified by the appearance of a command prompt (a dollar sign ($)) following the completion of the login process.

To log out of the system one can either type in *exit* or hit *^D* (control and D-key simultaneously) at the command line prompt.

5.4.2 Renaming and copying files

On System/6000, the method to rename files and copy files can be either straightforward or complex, depending on what is being attempted. For newcomers to UNIX/AIX, these command conventions may appear fuzzy in the beginning, but once the underlying concept of command usage is imbibed, the pieces all fall into place. In order to explain the renaming and copying of files, a set of basic commands is discussed here.

The rename command *mv* (move) can be used to either (1) rename a file or directory, or (2) move files and directories from one directory into another directory. The command accepts two or more arguments, of which the last argument is the target file name or the destination directory as the case may be. Here, it should be noted that a file cannot be moved into itself. Next, consider the simplest case, in which a file named *appendix* is being renamed *apndx.t*.

```
mv appendix apndx.t
```

Note that if a target file named *apndx.t* already existed in that directory, its old contents are replaced with those of *appendix*.

Some other commonly used forms of the *mv* command are illustrated and explained as follows with the help of a file tree. In order to get the optimal benefit from this example, follow the changes in the initial file tree (Fig. 5.6) that occur at every step. Once you are able to identify the respective changes that lead to the final structure of the file tree (Fig. 5.7), you have mastered the basics of the file-renaming convention under AIX.

`mv intro book`	Moves a file into a directory
`mv chap1 temp/ch1`	Moves a file to another directory and gives it a new name

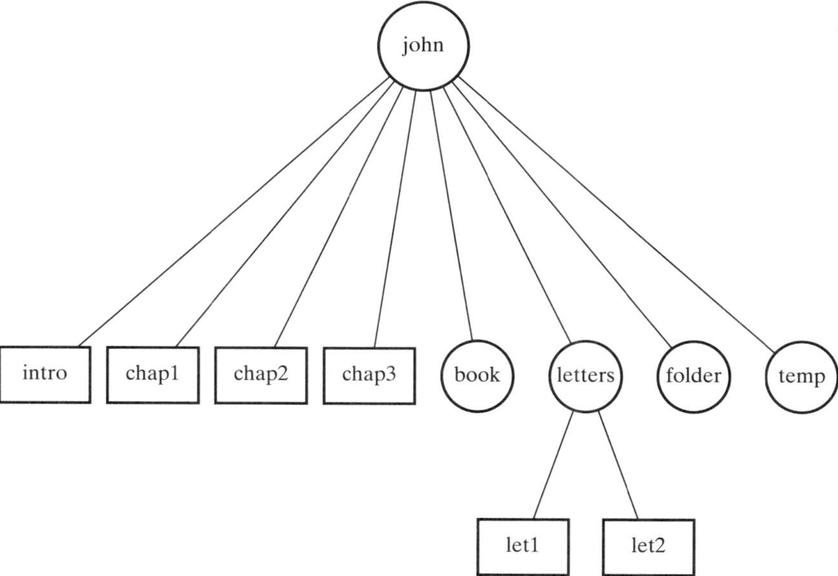

Figure 5.6 Initial file tree as per the example scenario.

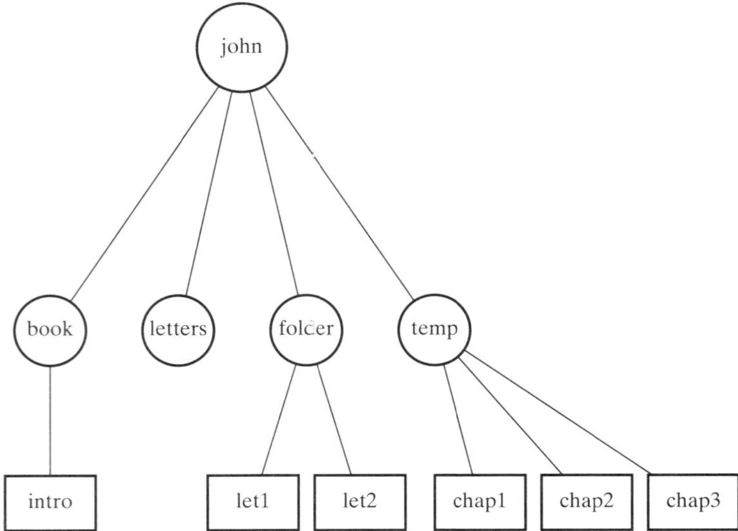

Figure 5.7 Final file tree as per the example scenario.

```
mv letters folder
```
Moves all files and directories under *letters* to the directory named *folder,* if *folder* exists. Otherwise, the directory *letters* is simply renamed *folder.*

```
mv chap2 chap3 temp
```
Moves several files into a directory named *temp.*

The examples depicted how the *mv* command may be used to move files around the system. These examples describe variations of the *mv* command and cover most day-to-day needs.

The *cp* (copy) command works in a way similar to the *mv* command. It copies the source file(s) to the specified target, where the target may be a file or a directory. Again, as in the case of the previously discussed *mv* command, care should be taken to specify destinations. In the following example, if the file *prog.bak* does not already exist, then the *cp* command creates it. But if it does exist, then the *cp* command replaces it with a copy of *prog.c.*

```
$ cp prog.c prog.bak
```

Owing to this nonforgiving nature of the *mv* and *cp* utilities, novice users are advised to use both the commands with the *-i* option that prior to taking the action interactively prompts the user with the name of the old file that will be overwritten.

5.4.3   Moving files between DOS and AIX

AIX provides facilities to allow data to be migrated from and to the DOS world. These utilities not only permit the reading and writing of files in the DOS format but also allow access to DOS directories and formatting of diskettes in the DOS format. To use these utilities, some conflicting conventions between UNIX and DOS had to be resolved. As the backslash character (\) can have special meaning to the AIX operating system, the slash character (/) is used as the delimiter to specify subdirectory names in a DOS path name. For the rest of the functionalities, DOS file-naming conventions are used consistently.

The set of AIX utilities used for moving files between DOS and AIX are described as follows:

dosread	Copies the contents of a DOS file to a specified AIX file
doswrite	Copies the contents of an AIX file to the specified DOS file
dosdir	Displays information about the specified DOS directory
dosformat	Formats a diskette with the DOS format
dosdel	Deletes DOS files

5.4.4   AIX file editors

AIX comes standard with four different editors: *ed, ex, vi,* and *sed.* In addition to these editors a wide variety of other editors may be obtained from commercial or public domain sources.

The *ed* editor is the original editor under UNIX that was developed at Bell Labs and was shipped with the very first distribution of UNIX. The *ed* editor is found on every UNIX and AIX system. Being a line mode editor, *ed* does not get used as often. But situations can arise where *ed* can be a lifesaver by being able to alter files without full-screen terminal support. The *ed* editor works on only one file at a time by copying it into a temporary edit buffer and making changes to that copy. It does not alter the file itself until you exit the editing session.

The *ex* editor was developed at Berkeley. It was the first step toward full-screen editing. Shortly thereafter, the *vi* editor was developed (also at Berkeley). This *vi* editor was built on the primitives of *ed* and *ex.* It provides full-screen editing capabilities, multiple file editing, and many other features. If you were to choose an editor to start with, *vi* should be the obvious choice.

One more editor that is rather specialized in nature comes standard with AIX. It is the *sed* editor. *sed* is a noninteractive, stream-oriented editor that gets used more like a filter than like an actual text editor. The *sed* editor interprets a script that controls the actions performed. You should select *sed* if you need to automate editing actions to be performed on one or more files or to write conversion programs that would be used like filters on input or output data streams.

In addition to the standard AIX text editors, one can acquire commercially available editors. One of the editors worth mentioning here is *emacs*. The *emacs* editor can be obtained through public domain sites on the Internet. This editor is very powerful, as its functionality encompasses everything other editors do, but *emacs* is not easy to use and is not recommended for beginners.

5.5 COMMAND LINE INTERPRETER (SHELL)

A shell, in addition to providing a computer-human interface, offers a variety of tools which may be used to automate many iterative user activities at the keyboard. In order to derive these benefits from the shell, some insight into the shell is required.

5.5.1 Understanding the shell

The shell is exactly what it sounds like; it is a hard casing that provides a private workspace for the user. This private workspace is also referred to as the user's *environment*.

It is best to think of shell commands as filters. As Fig. 5.8 depicts, the commands have a single input, called *standard input* (abbreviated to *stdin*), that accepts characters one at a time. Each shell command also has two outputs, namely, *standard output* (abbreviated to *stdout*) and *standard error* (abbreviated to *stderr*). The typical control flow in a shell command execution involves three discrete phases. The first stage is when data is input from stdin, the second is when the data is acted upon by the shell, and the final phase is the passing of data to stdout. In this way, each shell command acts upon the data that comes in from the stdin stream, and subsequently hands it off to the stdout stream.

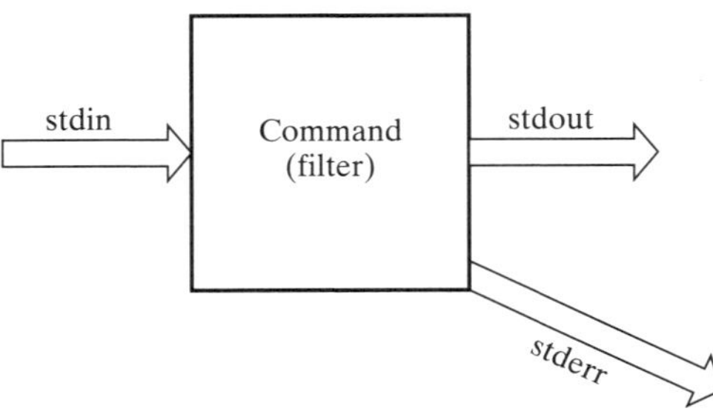

Figure 5.8 Shell filter.

It is possible to alter the default values of stdin, stdout, and stderr by redirecting their input and output streams. The shell recognizes the meaning of the "less than" symbol (<) as the stdin and the "greater than" symbol (>) as the stdout stream. A file name following the < symbol means that it will be used as the stdin for the shell command instead of the keyboard. Similarly, a file name following the > symbol means that it will be used as the stdout stream instead of the screen. In the following example, output of the *ls* (list files) command is being redirected to a file named *reports:*

```
$ ls > reports
```

Sometimes it may be unnecessary to create a file for everything. Occasionally, it is useful to pass the output of one shell command to the input of another. This is done by the use of *pipes*. A pipe is exactly what it sounds like—a conduit to carry data from one command to another (Fig. 5.9). A pipe is used to connect stdout of one command to the stdin of another command. In addition to dealing with temporary files, using a pipe allows two commands to operate synchronously. The shell recognizes the meaning of the vertical bar symbol (|) as the pipe. Consider the following example, where the number of files in a directory is counted using the *ls* command in conjunction with the *wc* (word count) command.

```
$ ls | wc
```

In this way, multiple shell commands can be made to build and process a pipeline of commands. As one gets familiar with the shell and its commands, more complex operations can be performed, thereby helping to increase productivity.

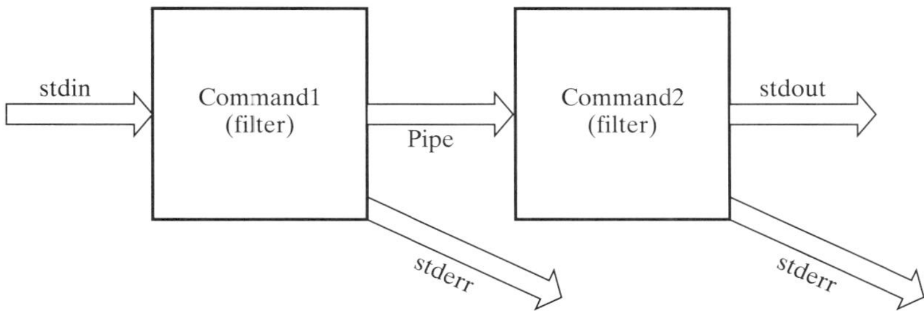

Figure 5.9 Shell pipe.

5.5.2 Customizing your environment

Having understood how a shell works, it is time to delve into the understanding of how the shell finds commands. Most of the shell commands reside in the */bin* directories of the system. The path to these directories is controlled through the user's environment which is defined during the login process. A variable named PATH is available in the environment. It is this PATH variable that actually contains the names of the directories to search for commands and the order in which to search the respective directories. The default initial value assigned to this PATH variable makes the shell search the current directory, */bin*, in the specific order. As a part of customizing the environment it is possible to change the value of the PATH variable to include additional directories. Described here is how to find the default paths, modify the order of the search path, and subsequently add new directories to the search path.

```
$ echo $PATH                Print the content of PATH variable
$ PATH=/usr/bin:/bin::       Reverse the default search path
$ PATH=${PATH}:/other        Add a new search path to the existing path
```

The shell can now automatically traverse the specified directories, looking for a command. If two commands are found with the same name in different directories, the shell will execute the first one it finds.

Recognize the fact that the full path name of a command need not be typed in, if the command resides in a directory that is defined in the search path. This feature of the shell can significantly improve productivity simply by customizing the user environment (the PATH variable in this case).

5.5.3 Choice of command language interpreters

Having obtained an overview of what the shell does for the user, it makes sense to evaluate a preference for one shell over the other. While the basic functionality of the shell remains unchanged, the actual look and feel of a particular shell may vary from those of another shell.

Over the years several shells were developed by enthusiasts in the industry and the universities. The discussion in this section describes the following three shells that AIX provides for day-to-day use:

1. Bourne shell (sh)

2. C shell (csh)

3. Korn shell (ksh)

The first shell, which happens to be the original shell, is called the Bourne shell. It was named for its developer, S. R. Bourne of Bell Labs. The program itself is referred to by *sh*. The Bourne shell is guaranteed to be available on every AIX and UNIX system that you will come across. Despite being around for a long time, it is still the standard shell for use in the industry.

The second shell is the C shell. The program itself is called *csh*. It was so named because its syntax is very much like the C language, as it was developed primarily for the use of C programmers at the University of California at Berkeley. The main contribution to the development of the C shell was made by Bill Joy who was then a graduate student on campus. Being newer than the original Bourne shell, the C shell provides some added functionalities to minimize repetitive typing of commands and to optimize job control. A point to be noted here is the fact that even though the C shell became quite popular in universities, it never was standardized in the industry.

The third and newest of the shells is the Korn shell. The program itself is named *ksh*. It was named after its developer, S. Korn of Bell Labs. In relentless pursuit of standardizing a shell for industrywide use, the Korn shell was shipped with every newer version of UNIX. The Korn shell's success was primarily because it was backwardly compatible with the Bourne shell. (C shell is not.) Thus, all of the existing shell programs that were written in the Bourne shell over the years could be executed under the Korn shell without modification. What made the Korn shell even more attractive was the fact that it also incorporated the best of the C shell features in it, thereby providing a well-paved path for convergence and standardization of this shell as the command language interpreter.

So, which shell is best? There is no right answer for the question, as the choice of a user's shell is purely a subjective matter. Now, which shell should you learn if you were getting started with AIX? The Korn shell would be the preferred choice, as it has become a virtual industry standard and it provides all the features that one needs to interact with the system efficiently. Regardless of which shell is used, the basic purpose served by it remains unchanged. Your shell will continue to provide you with an insulated environment in which to work under AIX. As one gains proficiency with the shell, one would be able to harness its power by using it as a programming tool, in addition to using it as a command line interpreter.

5.6 HELP ACCESS

One of the most useful items to know about is where and how to get assistance on a new system. An introduction to using the System/6000 remains incomplete without a discussion on the help facility. Two kinds of help facilities will be discussed in this section, the first one being the standard facility available on all UNIX machines and the second one being specific to AIX running on the System/6000.

5.6.1   UNIX *man* pages

All UNIX machines are usually shipped with a set of standard manuals for reference. The multivolume reference manuals describe every available option in detail. However, these multivolume manuals are not always the most convenient option for end-users. So, in addition to these manuals, an on-line help facility has also been provided on most UNIX systems. This on-line help facility is referred to as *man* pages, man being short for manual. Man pages are a subset of the standard UNIX documentation and contain synopses of the commands and tools used by users and programmers.

To access the man pages on a specific command you have to type in the *man* command, followed by the name of the command on which help is being sought.

```
$ man who
```

A scrolling screen appears, displaying the text on the usage of the *who* command. (The *who* command displays the currently logged-on users on the system.) At this time one may continue to scroll through the documentation by pressing the space bar or quit out of it at any time by hitting the *q* key.

Thus, it is seen that the man pages on UNIX systems provide a convenient alternative to bulky UNIX manuals for seeking help with petty command syntax, as well as providing a means of accessing information on intricate options for an obscure command.

5.6.2   InfoExplorer facility

In addition to the man pages, AIX on the System/6000 offers a menu-driven tool for information retrieval called InfoExplorer. This facility contains articles, tutorials, and technical references on machine-specific topics. The essential difference between InfoExplorer and the standard UNIX man pages is that instead of being a mere subset of the AIX documentation, the InfoExplorer features the complete set of reference manuals. This on-line access to the entire set of reference manuals (which exceed 20,000 pages) is made possible by the design and implementation of a text retrieval system based on hypertext. Hypertext technology provides a nonsequential method of organizing text in a manner that enables rapid retrieval and efficient storage.

To access the InfoExplorer facility, type in the *info* command and wait for the screen to redraw.

```
$ info
```

To use InfoExplorer simply follow the menu selections. InfoExplorer is easy to use. All of the commands are intuitive in nature. Note that the screen drawing process that occurs is based on the type of terminal being used. In addition to supporting ASCII terminals, the InfoExplorer also provides an interface for X terminals. If using an ASCII terminal, a character-based user interface menu appears which may be operated using the hot-keys that appear in inverse video. If operating in an X environment, the InfoExplorer tool displays an X-based graphical user interface with icons that supports the mouse and other standard X features (as shown in Fig. 5.10).

The superiority of InfoExplorer is emphasized by the fact that in addition to being a completely menu-driven help facility, it offers myriad features. Some of the appealing features include compound word(s) search to locate key words across multiple documents, bookmarks to index selected pages, user notes to tag bookmarks with comments, on-line tutorials for beginners, and a built-in print facility for printing out selected documents.

On System/6000, this hypertext-based InfoExplorer can either be placed on the hard drive or be made available on a removable medium

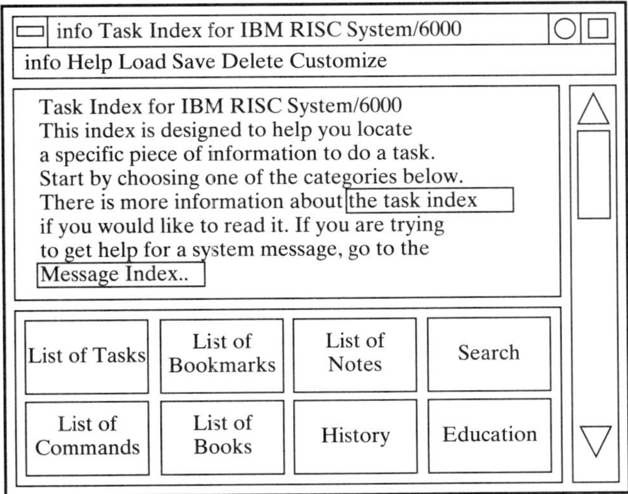

Figure 5.10 InfoExplorer screen. (*Copied with permission from McGraw-Hill U.K.*)

like CD-ROM. The latter is generally preferred (assuming the particular System/6000 model has a CD-ROM drive), as it frees up a significant amount of valuable disk space. It is envisioned that the hypertext technology used in InfoExplorer is likely to become a de facto standard for forthcoming generations of on-line help facilities on automated data processing systems.

5.7 SUMMARY

Some fundamental concepts have been presented in this chapter to establish fundamentals that can be used as building blocks for the understanding of the software subsystem from a user's perspective. The flow of control through the software subsystem is explained from a user's perspective, illustrated by using a multilayered model in which the topmost tier is the user interface and the bottom layer is the interface to the hardware. The layout of the components in the software subsystem is in the form of an inverted tree. Understanding the flow of control and the layout of the software modules enables a user to get started on the system in a more productive way. The learning curve here is purely a function of the amount of time spent moving around the system, trying out the basic utilities such as file copy, edit, etc., and referring to the on-line help facilities to answer queries.

Development Tools

An overview of the most widely used development tools available under AIX is provided in this chapter. The tour starts with a discussion of the C compiler, followed by a discussion of assemblers and debuggers. Source code analysis tools are discussed next, followed by the lexical analyzer, parser generator, and a brief discussion on pattern-matching language. Additional development tools described in this chapter include the macro preprocessor, program module management, and the source code control system.

6.1   C COMPILER

The C compiler (also referred to as the XL C compiler) is an optimizing compiler. This means that in addition to source code optimization, the compiler also performs certain preprocessor and common back-end optimization tasks. The architecture of System/6000 demands that an optimizing compiler be used in order to employ its underlying capabilities intelligently. Together with the RISC-based architecture and the XL optimizing compiler, an efficient computing environment is made possible. This is depicted in Fig. 6.1.

The need for an optimizing compiler depends on the applications to be run. For many general purpose applications, inherent efficiencies will provide a certain level of performance. However, for engineering and scientific applications that process vast amounts of data and tend

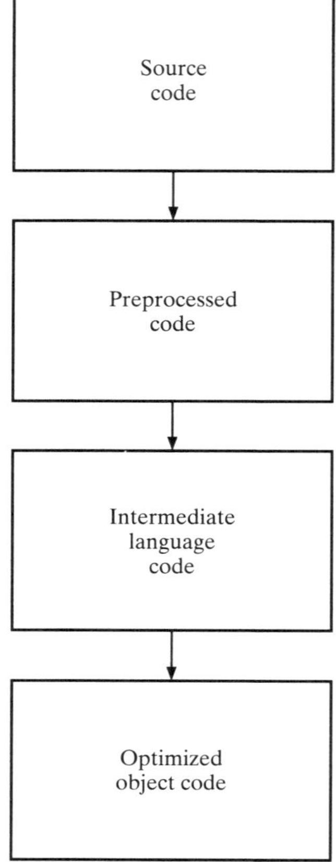

Figure 6.1 Optimized compiler.

to perform repeated operations on each data element, a structured and methodical approach to compile-time optimization is required.

From a programmer's perspective, a program may be executing optimally. But, if tuned properly, even to a minuscule extent, its performance can be doubled or tripled. The implementation of the pipelined execution units in the central electronic complex of the RISC System/6000 is an indicator of the dependency of the sequence of instructions on hardware performance. An instruction dependency between the currently executing instruction and its predecessor can cost precious cycles owing to data unavailability. A tight piece of code fragment spilling outside of the cache boundary can waste several cycles. The former can be controlled (to a certain extent) by implementing an optimized instruction-scheduling algorithm that resequences selected assembly language instructions to minimize idle machine cycles. The latter, however, is likely to require hand-optimization. The optimizing compiler on System/6000 needs a great deal of built-in intelligence to identify potential hotspots during compile time and perform necessary tuning actions.

The instruction-scheduling algorithm in the XL C compiler is its most significant component. In a simplified manner, its operation can be explained as processing the output of the optimizer, constructing a dependency graph for each basic block of the code, and finally arranging the instructions in an order in which they would execute the fastest. This algorithm used in the XL family of compilers is essentially the same.

The XL C compiler uses the *cc, xlc,* and *c89* commands to compile C source files. These commands are essentially the same except for the default language level. For *cc* the default language level is *extended,* whereas for *xlc* and *c89* the default language level is *ansi.* These commands can also process assembler source files and object files. Unless the -*c* option is specified, these commands call the linkage editor to produce a single object file. The input file(s) can be a C language source file (file name with .*c* suffix), preprocessed C source (.*i* suffix), object file (.*o* suffix), and assembler source file (.*s* suffix).

6.2 ASSEMBLER

The assembler used on System/6000 is a two-pass assembler, which alludes to the fact that the assembler makes two passes over a source program. On the first pass, the assembler (1) allocates space for instructions and storage area, (2) assigns the values of constants wherever appropriate, and (3) constructs a symbol table where an entry is made for symbols encountered in the label of statements. The source file is read a line at a time. For every new symbol encountered, an entry is added to the symbol table while assigning the value of the current location counter to the symbol.

Assembly language source code is assembled using the *as* command. The file that *as* reads and assembles ends with a .*s* suffix (by convention). Also, the file that *as* builds as its output is called *a.out.* If no source file is specified, *as* attempts to read and assemble standard input.

The assembler command can also be used to produce an assembler listing. *as* gives a default name to the listing file by replacing the suffix extension of the source file name with a .*lst* extension.

6.3 DEBUGGERS

Under AIX there are four different debuggers available, namely the *adb, dbx, xde* and kernel debug programs. Each of them has specific uses.

adb	debugs executable binary files and examines non-ASCII data files
dbx	allows source level debugging for C, FORTRAN, Pascal, COBOL, and assembly language programs
xde	provides windows for viewing source, context, and variables for application programs
kernel debugger	determines errors in code running in the kernel

6.3.1 adb

adb is a general purpose debugging utility that is used to debug programs. One can examine object files and core files, and also provide a controlled environment for running a program using the *adb* utility.

When processing an executable program file that has been compiled, *adb* requires it to have a symbol table. Without the symbol table, *adb* will not be able to show the value of static, automatic, and external variables of the program. However, executable programs that have been stripped off the symbol table can still be examined for other information.

When no name is specified for the executable program, *adb* looks for the default file named *a.out*. It can also be used for reading core file images that often get created by running an erroneous executable program. One can also use *adb* to examine data files containing non-ASCII data. Yet another use of *adb* is to modify an executable file or a data file by writing directly to memory after running the program. This ability makes *adb* a very powerful utility.

adb can take input from standard input (keyboard) and write to standard output (terminal). One can also enter more than one command by separating each command with a semicolon as a delimiter. Use of expressions, operators, commands, variables, and addresses is supported. However, to use *adb* effectively and set breakpoints at appropriate places in the executable program, one has to be familiar with the assembly language instructions that the C compiler generates. One way to do this is to create an assembly language listing of a C program using the *-S* or *-qlist* flag of the *cc* command and then understand them by consulting the complete instruction set for the RISC System/6000 which has been described in Sec. 9.7.

adb features a set of subcommands for setting breakpoints and examining variables. The common ones are

:r	starts executing the program from the beginning
:b	sets a breakpoint in a program
:k	stops the program being debugged

6.3.2 *dbx* and *xde*

In addition to *adb, dbx* is a full-featured symbolic debugger that comes standard with AIX in addition to *adb*. The tool supports debugging of a program at both source level and assembler-language level. Its source-level debugging features allow debugging of C, Pascal, COBOL, and FORTRAN programs when needed, and its assembler-language-level debug facility enables debugging of executable programs at the machine level. The tool supports all the standard operations such as

- examining object and core files
- providing a controlled environment for running a program
- setting breakpoints at selected statements or running the program one line at a time
- analyzing symbolic variables

Two prerequisites for using *dbx* on an executable file are that it be compiled with a debug flag to contain the symbol table information and that the symbol references not be stripped from the executable file. Usage of *dbx* may be customized by including a set of *dbx* subcommands in a file named *.dbxinit* so that they may execute automatically upon initiation of a debug session.

dbx features a generous set of subcommands for setting breakpoints, tracing program execution, displaying the source file, printing variables and expressions, handling signals, calling procedures, and examining registers during machine-level debugging. Some of the commonly used commands are

run	begins running the application program
step	runs one source line
stepi	runs one source instruction
stop	stops execution of the application program
clear	removes all stops at a given source line
cleari	removes all breakpoints at an address
cont	continues running the program from the current breakpoint until another breakpoint is encountered or the program completes its execution
next	runs the application up to the next source line
nexti	runs the application up to the next source instruction
trace	displays tracing information
where	displays all active procedures and functions
help	displays an on-line list of *dbx* commands
quit	quits *dbx*

There is an X Window interface for *dbx* called *xde* that can be used to debug application programs. *xde* provides an integrated debug environment with X interface that allows viewing of the program's source code, stack traceback, and variables (shown in Figs. 6.2, 6.3, and 6.4).

The same prerequisites for *dbx* apply to *xde,* i.e., an executable file must be compiled with a debug flag to contain the symbol table information and the symbol references must not be stripped from the exe-

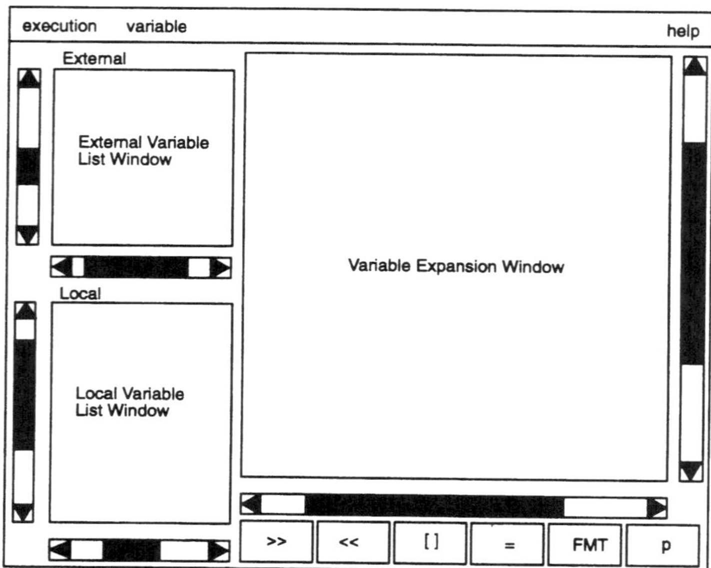

Figure 6.2 XDE variable window. (*Copied with permission from IBM.*)

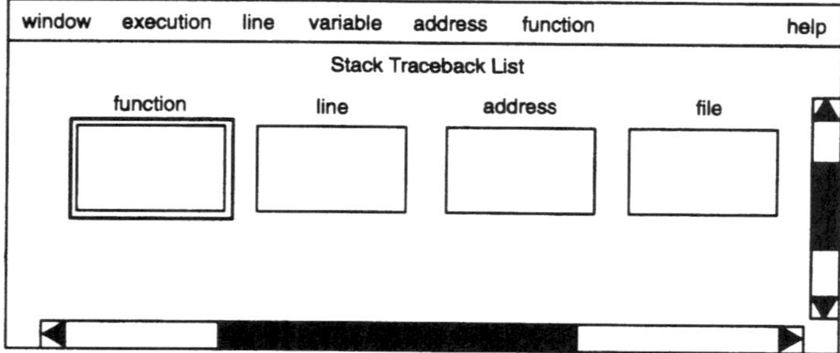

Figure 6.3 XDE context window. (*Copied with permission from IBM.*)

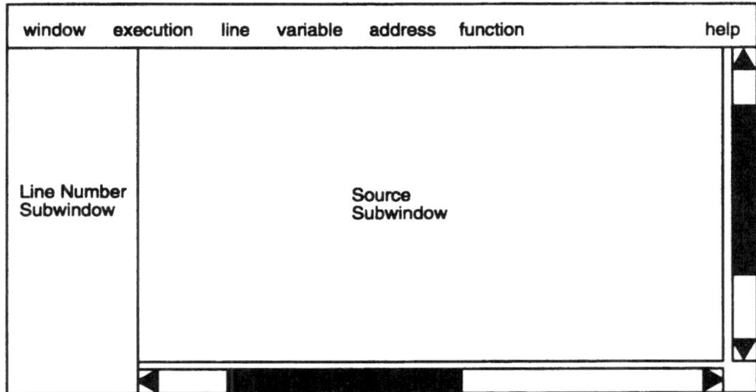

Figure 6.4 XDE file window. (*Copied with permission from IBM.*)

cutable file. The *xde* tool and its X interface may be customized by modifying the *.dbxinit* and/or *.Xdefaults* files which execute automatically upon initiation of a debug session.

The subcommands available in *dbx* appear as objects within pulldown menus in the *xde* environment. Thus, navigating within *xde* windows mostly involves working with buttons and scroll bars.

6.3.3 Kernel debugger

The kernel debug program is used for debugging device drivers and kernel extensions. It provides an efficient mechanism for detecting errors in the code running in the kernel. One of the distinctive features of this debugger is that it disables all external interrupts while it is in operation.

Once loaded, there are two ways to start the debugger. One way is through the use of breakpoints. These breakpoints can be set either by embedding static debugger program traps in the object code or by the explicit use of the debug program *break* command. The second way to start the debugger is through the use of the numeric keypad of the keyboard.* A composite keystroke sequence, resulting in a nonmaskable interrupt from the pressing of the control, left alternate, and the number 4 numeric pad keys simultaneously, starts the kernel debug program. From here on, the user's choice of kernel debugger commands may be entered at the prompt to use the kernel debugger interactively.

---

* The keyboard refers specifically to an asynchronous terminal connected to the system through a serial port. Displays connected through graphics adapter(s) lack support for this kernel debug program in the current implementation.

Note that in addition to a user starting the kernel debugger, it can also be executed as the result of a system crash. If a system crashes (and the debugger is available), the last line of the displayed text will normally describe the cause of the event and an 888 code will flash on the LED display of the processor. At that point, a dump may be taken if desired (using the *quit dump* command) and the system can be rebooted subsequently.

A full set of interactive commands is available for use in the kernel debugger. These commands can be used to set breakpoints, manipulate memory, and perform manipulation of variables and registers. An extensive reference of the commands may be found in the on-line help facility. Some commands are stand-alone, while others accept numeric and string arguments. Limited expression processing can also be performed using the addition, subtraction, multiplication, division, and dereference operators. The program also allows use of variables to represent locations or values that are used repeatedly. Some of the most frequently used commands are

origin	sets the origin of the instruction address register
alter	alters memory
xlate	translates a virtual address to a real address
break	sets a breakpoint
breaks	lists the currently set breakpoints
user	displays a formatted user area
proc	displays the formatted process table
stack	displays a formatted kernel stack trace
drivers	displays the contents of the device driver table
tty	displays the *tty* structure
find	finds a string in memory
sregs	displays segment registers
vmm	displays the virtual memory data structure
help	displays the on-line help commands
quit	ends the debugging session

6.4 SOURCE CODE ANALYSIS TOOLS

Source code analysis tools available under AIX aid in checking the source code for integrity and analyzing the flow of control in the order of their execution. These tools are intended for use by software engineers and programmers to enhance productivity.

6.4.1 *lint*

The *lint* utility checks the source code for coding integrity. The benefit of using *lint* prior to compilation is significant, as it aids in identifying overlooked and trouble-prone code constructs. It also enforces orthodox type-checking rules that help in eliminating possible future bugs. In addition, the *lint* tool also identifies the following

- source code and library incompatibility
- potential problems with variables
- potential problems with functions
- problems with flow control
- legal constructs that may be inefficient
- unused variable and function declarations
- nonportable code

To run *lint,* the user has to supply the source file as an argument to *lint.*

6.4.2 *cflow*

The *cflow* utility generates a flow graph of external references. It is capable of analyzing C assembler as well as object files and can produce a chart of their external references to the standard output.

The input file can be a C language source file (file name with *.c* suffix), a preprocessed C source (*.i* suffix), a *yacc* source file (*.y* suffix), a *lex* source file (*.l* suffix), an object file (*.o* suffix), or an assembler source file (*.s* suffix). Based on the kind of file it is, the contents of the file are sent to the C preprocessor *cpp,* the yacc compiler *yacc,* or the lexical analyzer *lex,* and are subsequently run through the first pass of *lint.* Files suffixed with *.s* are assembled and information is extracted (as in *.o* files) from the symbol table.

The output of all this nontrivial processing is collected, converted into a graph of external references, and subsequently displayed with line numbers and indentation levels to show the flow of control and call sequences of functions and procedures.

6.5 LEXICAL ANALYZER—*lex*

lex is a program-generating tool meant for programmers that produces code to handle *lex*ical processing of character input streams. It accepts high-level, problem-oriented specifications for character string matching. The regular expressions are specified in the source specification to *lex*. The *lex* program generator is a table of regular expressions and corresponding program fragments. The table is translated to a program that reads an input stream, copies the input stream to an output stream, and partitions the inputs into strings that match the given expressions. As each string is recognized, the corresponding program fragment gets executed. This process of expression recognition is done by a deterministic, finite-state automaton generated by *lex*. The program fragments written by the user are executed in the order in which the corresponding regular expressions occur in the input stream.

The *lex* command reads a file or standard input, generates a C language program, and writes it to a file named *lex.yy.c*. This file, *lex.yy.c*, is a compilable C language program, which can be linked with or called from other routines.

6.6   PARSER GENERATOR—*yacc*

The name *yacc* is an acronym for "yet another compiler compiler." It is a general-purpose tool used for imposing structure on the input to programs. A set of specifications (also referred to as the grammar rules) for the input process is prepared by the user describing the input structure, code to be invoked when these rules get recognized, and a low-level routine (the lexical analyzer) to control the basic input. *yacc* then generates a function to parse the input process. This function calls the lexical analyzer to pick up the basic items (referred to as tokens) from the input stream. These tokens are organized according to the input structure rules. When one of these rules has been recognized, the corresponding user code (supplied for this rule as an action) gets invoked. In this way, *yacc* converts a context-free grammar specification into a set of tables for a simple automaton that executes a parsing algorithm.*

The output generated by *yacc* (called *y.tab.c*) needs to be compiled with a C language compiler to produce a function *yyparse*. This function is loaded with the lexical analyzer function *yylex* and the user's main C routine.

6.7   PATTERN-MATCHING LANGUAGE—*awk*

awk is a programming language that makes it possible to handle data manipulations very efficiently. An *awk* program is a sequence of pat-

---

* An LR(1) family of parsing algorithm is produced by *yacc*.

terns and actions that tell what to look for in the input data and what to do when it is found. *awk* searches a set of files for lines matched by any of the patterns; when a matching pattern is found, the corresponding action is performed. A pattern can select lines by combinations of regular expressions and comparison operations on strings, numbers, fields, variables, and array elements. Actions may perform arbitrary processing on selected lines. The action language looks like C, but there are no declarations. Strings and numbers are the built-in data types.

awk scans input files and splits each input line into fields automatically. Because of its automatic nature of input, field splitting, storage management, and initialization, *awk* programs are usually much smaller than they would be in a more conventional language. The same brevity of expression and convenience of operations make *awk* valuable for prototyping larger programs. One starts with a few lines, then refines the program until it does the desired job, experimenting with designs by trying alternatives quickly. Since programs are short, it is easy to get started, and easy to start over when experience suggests a different direction. It is straightforward to translate an *awk* program into another language once the design is right.

awk was originally designed and implemented by the authors of UNIX in 1977, in part as an experiment to see how the UNIX tools *grep* and *sed* could be generalized to deal with numbers as well as text. It was enhanced to a new version made available in 1985. The main feature in new *awk* (available under AIX on System/6000) is the ability for users to define their own functions, support dynamic regular expressions with text substitution and pattern-matching functions, and make use of additional built-in functions and variables.

6.8 ADDITIONAL DEVELOPMENT TOOLS

6.8.1 Macro preprocessor—*m4*

m4 is a macro processor command which is used as a preprocessor for C and other languages for expanding macro definitions. Built-in macros or user-defined macros can be processed using *m4*. It processes each file in the order in which it was specified on the command line. A command reads standard input if a file is not specified or if a minus (–) is specified as a file name. It writes the processed macros to standard output.

m4 reads every alphanumeric token input and determines if the token is the name of a macro; if it is a macro, the name is replaced by its defining text and the resulting string is pushed back onto the input to be rescanned. Macros may also be called with arguments. The arguments are collected and substituted into the right places in the defining text before the defining text is rescanned.

The macro calls have the following syntax:

```
macroname( argument... )
```

A left parenthesis must immediately follow the macro name. If the left parenthesis does not follow the name of a defined macro, the *m4* command reads it as a macro call with no arguments. Macro names consist of ASCII alphabetic letters, digits, and the underscore character (_). Extended characters are not allowed in macro names. The first character cannot be a digit. While collecting arguments, the *m4* command ignores unquoted leading blanks, tabs, and newline characters. Single quotation marks should be used to quote strings. The value of a quoted string is the string with the quotation marks stripped off.

6.8.2 Program modules management—*make*

The *make* program is a useful utility that assists in maintaining up-to-date versions on sets of programs. It simplifies the process of recompiling and relinking programs during software development by allowing the user to record once and for all the specific relationships among files. The *make* command can then be used to automatically perform all the updates. Using this versatile utility, instructions can be combined to create a large program in a single file, macros can be defined to be used within the *make* command description file, and many basic types of files can be created. The *make* command can also be used to create libraries.

make requires a description file called the target file, file names, and a specified set of rules to construct many standard types of files and timestamp the system files. If any parent file was changed more recently than the target file, *make* creates the files affected by the changes, including the target file. The description file contains information on target and parent file name, macro definitions, commands, and user-specified rules to build the target file. Each line in the description file involving the target file is called a dependency line. For example:

```
test:   dependency list 1 ...
        command list 1 ...

    .

    .

    .
test:   dependency list 2 ...
        command list 2 ...
```

The *make* program does not perform any program operations; it simply writes all the steps to build the program, including outputs from lower-level calls to the *make* command. This makes it an extremely powerful and versatile tool for managing a large number of program modules.

6.8.3 Source code control system—SCCS

The source code control system (SCCS) is a complete system of commands that allows specified users to control and maintain an audit trail of changes made to an SCCS file. It allows simultaneous existence of multiple versions of a file and supports multibyte character set (MBCS) characters. It provides a complete system for creating, converting, or changing controls on SCCS files.

An SCCS file is any text file controlled with SCCS commands. An SCCS file is made up of three parts: (1) a delta table, (2) access and tracking flags, and (3) the body of the text. Deltas are changes recorded for each version of a file. Tracking flags are essentially a list of flags with the @ sign which define various accesses and tracking options. The body of an SCCS file contains information about all the versions of the file.

Some commonly used SCCS commands are:

admin	creates an SCCS file or changes an existing SCCS file
cdc	changes the comments associated with delta
comb	combines two or more consecutive deltas in an SCCS file
delta	adds a set of changes (deltas) to the text of an SCCS file
get	gets a specified version of an SCCS file for editing or compiling
rmdel	removes the most recent delta on a branch from an SCCS file
sccs	administrative program for the SCCS system, consisting of a set of pseudo-commands that perform most SCCS services

6.9 SUMMARY

This chapter examined some of the development tools available under AIX, beginning with a discussion of the XL C compiler. The functions of assemblers and debuggers were described. Source code analysis tools were discussed next, followed by introductions to the lexical analyzer and the parser generator, as well as a brief discussion on pattern-matching language. This chapter also looked at the functions of the macro preprocessor, program module management, and the source code control system.

Networking, Interoperability, and Standards

This chapter focuses on three important aspects of the System/6000. It discusses the networking concepts and facilities. It addresses the interoperability options provided with the operating environment of RISC System/6000. Finally, it describes the industry standards that the RISC System/6000 complies with.

7.1 BASIC CONNECTIVITY WITH PEER UNIX MACHINES

Connectivity with peer nodes can be provided using the basic network utilities programs (BNU) that come standard with the AIX regular distribution. BNU comprises a suite of utilities that are used to communicate with peer nodes. BNU is a version of UUCP (UNIX-to-UNIX Copy Program) and is often better known as UUCP in the traditional UNIX communities. It should be noted that although the availability of BNU or UUCP facility predates most networking suites, it still reigns as one of the most widely used means of exchanging files across the Internet. Built in 1976 by Mike Lesk at AT&T Bell Labs, a mere research project became a de facto networking standard by being shipped as a part of the standard software distribution of UNIX Version 7 in 1977. Although less sophisticated in terms of functionality, UUCP provides basic connectivity with peer machines over regular serial lines and does not require any additional network interface hardware.

The three main functions performed by UUCP are the following:

1. Electronic mail

2. Transfer of files to and from remote systems

3. Execution of commands on remote systems

UUCP is a store-and-forward network; that is, requests for mail forwarding, file transfers, or remote execution of commands are not executed immediately, but are spooled for execution when communication is established between the two systems. Depending on how the configuration files have been set up, communication may be established immediately, or it may wait till a later time. Figure 7.1 presents a conceptual view of how UUCP works for forwarding electronic mail.

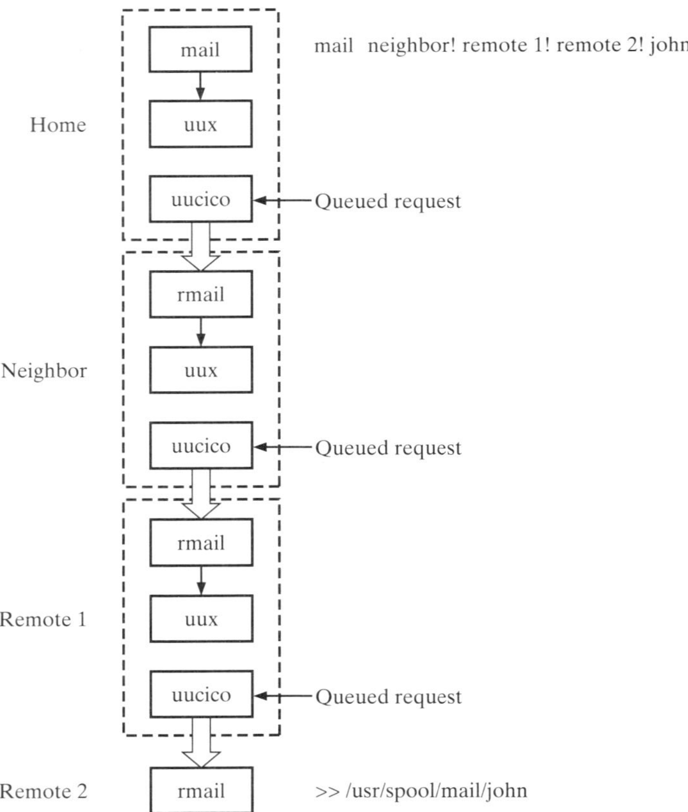

Figure 7.1 UUCP forwarding electronic mails.

Although the suite of programs is referred to as UUCP, the actual *uucp* program only participates in copying files. For mail handling, remote command execution, and other tasks, there are separate stand-alone program files (described later). Perhaps it would have been more appropriate to refer to the UUCP as UU because the name more clearly indicates that UUCP is a collection of many programs, all of which have a name prefixed with the letters *uu*. Referring to this suite of network utilities as BNU eliminates the misleading reference.

UUCP works in multiple steps. When mail is sent, a file transfer command is invoked, or a remote command execution request is issued, two things happen. First, a work file containing logistic information such as the name of the source file, name of the destination file, and command request type (i.e. send file, receive file, or execute file) is created in a spooling directory on the System/6000. The second phase involves starting a command called *uusched* to scan the contents of the work file and subsequently invoking other programs like *uucico,* if needed, to call another system, connect to it, and transfer the data in or out.

Requirements for BNU/UUCP installation are minimal. The simplest hardware requirement only involves using a null-modem serial cable and connecting it between the ports of two machines. A modem will be required at both ends if the connection is being made between two remote machines. There is no additional software requirement as such, but the software needs to be configured to define the machine name(s) to call or connect to, place the phone call (if connecting to a remote machine over a modem), and optionally specify when to call the remote machine to forward files to it and receive incoming files from it.

Once UUCP/BNU is installed and configured, the following commands can be run by any AIX user to log in to remote systems, transfer files, run processes on remote systems, and report the status of jobs and transfers.

Command	Description of the command
uucp	copies file(s) to another AIX/UNIX system running BNU or another version of UUCP
uuencode	encodes a binary file
uudecode	decodes a binary file encoded by the *uuencode* command
uuname	provides information about peer systems accessible to the local system
uupick	completes the transfer of files sent by the *uuto* command
uupoll	forces a call to a remote system so queued jobs can be transferred
uuq	displays the BNU job queue

(Continued)

Command	Description of the command
uusend	sends a file to a remote host that is running BNU or another version of UUCP
uusnap	displays a snapshot summary of the status of BNU
uustat	reports the status of and provides limited control over BNU operations
uuto	copies files to a peer system running BNU or another version of UUCP
uux	runs a command on a remote AIX or UNIX system running BNU or another version of UUCP
ct	dials a remote system and initiates a login process
cu	connects directly or indirectly to another system

These commands provide a diverse repertoire of some of the tasks a network administrator has to perform. Detailed discussion of these commands, their options, and scope are provided in the on-line *man* pages or in the command reference manuals.

7.2 CONNECTIVITY WITH HOST MACHINES

Connectivity with the mainframe world of machines requires use of a software interface so that a user can access applications on the host. The hardware interface requirements are discussed in Chap. 3. The term *emulator* is used in this section to refer to a software application that allows the native system to mimic a terminal session on the host machine. The objective of using an emulator is to provide a transparent interface for a user on the System/6000 to work with applications resident on the host (Fig. 7.2).

There are two primary types of emulators available on the System/6000 to work with host sessions.

- 3278/79 Emulation (EM78)
- 3270 Host Connection Program (HCON)

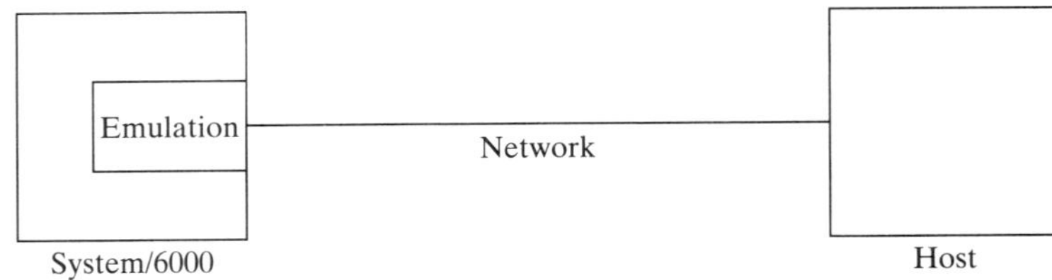

Figure 7.2 Connectivity with host.

The AIX 3278/79 Emulation/6000 program allows a system to emulate a terminal attached to an IBM System/3270 computer. Once the emulator is installed on the local system, it provides the functions of the device being emulated as if one was actually using that device. The *em78* command invokes a 3278/79 session so that one can log into the System 3270 host and use it like a normal host session. File transfer capabilities are supported so that one can upload or download files with automatic format conversion. Either an MVS/TSO host session or a VM/CMS host session can be specified during the transfer process. Keyboard customization is also supported so that specific keys may be mapped to tailor the keyboard to a 3270 session.

The AIX 3270 Host Connection Program/6000 (HCON) allows the local system to emulate a terminal attached to an IBM System/370 host computer. HCON operates in *sessions,* which are periods of interaction with a host computer. A display session is used when emulating a 3278/79 terminal display. Using a display session, one may run commands and applications interactively and/or perform file transfers from and to the host. In the case of file transfers, the file format conversion between ASCII (supported on the System/6000) and EBCDIC (supported on the host) is handled automatically. The HCON as a facility on the System/6000 is only available to registered users. Once registered, a user may have his or her own customized sessions to communicate with different hosts. The recommended method of adding the customized sessions is through the use of the *smit* tool. A variety of display sessions is supported. These display sessions differ primarily in the type of device used to connect to the host computer. The supported display sessions are

- DFT (distributed function terminal) display sessions, which use the 3270 connection adapter in the DFT mode

- SNA stand-alone sessions, that work with SNA services software and need either a multiprotocol adapter, an X.25 adapter, an Ethernet adapter, or a Token-Ring adapter to operate

- HIA (host interface adapter) display session, which uses the mainframe host interface adapter

- TCP/IP display sessions that need either an Ethernet adapter, a Token-Ring adapter, a multiprotocol adapter, an X.25 adapter, or an FDDI adapter to operate

The adapters are mentioned here for completeness only. For details on the individual adapter, refer to Chap. 3, which deals with the expansion options for the System/6000 machine.

7.3 CONNECTIVITY AND ACCESS TO PC-DOS

Using AIX Access for DOS Users (AADU), a product that provides transparent access to the AIX filesystem for PC users through the use of virtual drives, one can use the System/6000's disk space to store PC files. AADU allows DOS PC users to share the AIX/6000 filesystem of the host machine such that no knowledge of the AIX operating system is required. Access to printers on the System/6000 machine is also provided to PC users via network interface drivers. The minimum machine hardware requirements for AADU are 512 KB of physical memory and 1 MB of disk space on a PS/2, AT, or XT class machine that is equipped with an Ethernet, Token-Ring, or asynchronous serial connection. Performance is affected by the amount of memory and disk storage available on the PC. Software requirements call for DOS Version 3.3 or later and Microsoft Windows 3.1 or later. Figure 7.3 shows the connectivity layout of a PC and a RISC System/6000.

Standard AIX file permission modes are used by AADU to protect all the DOS files stored on an AIX system disk. Users can selectively protect files and directories from other users. User management is responsible for evaluation, selection, and implementation of security features, administrative procedures, and communication facilities. Although files are accessible to the users via the virtual drives, recognize that the AIX operating system will not be able to create filenames which include DOS graphic characters or use DOS commands such as *assign, fdisk, format, print, sys, backup, restore, join, tree,* and *share* on the virtual disk.

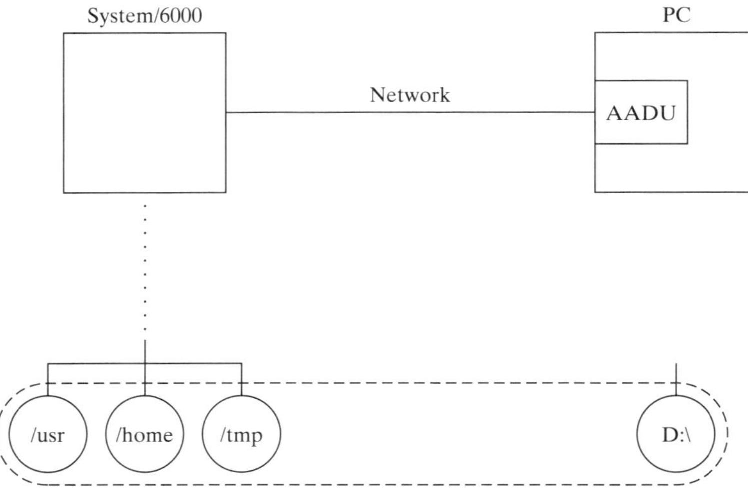

Figure 7.3 Connection with DOS-based PCs.

7.4   OPEN SYSTEMS COMPATIBILITY STANDARDS

The RISC System/6000 hardware and the AIX software running on it integrates a suite of industry standards in its offering. IBM's leadership for setting and defining the trends for industrywide standards at an international level is as old as IBM's existence. Both System/6000 as well as AIX conform to these standards on their own accord, which marks a trend towards the widespread usage of open systems. When hearing about one or more of these standards, it is usually in the form of cryptic jargon or an enigmatic acronym. ISO, ANSI, etc., without a context, will not mean much, but they mean something when there is a connotation to relate to. It is not realistic to condense all the standards into a single volume. Likewise, it is not appropriate to divorce them from the discussion on networking, connectivity, and interoperability. This section describes some of the key standards, their conformance, and their mission.

At the international level, ISO (The International Organization for Standardization) is a nongovernment, independent agency that promotes standardization. Its membership is composed of the national standards bodies of various countries. For example, ANSI (American National Standards Institute) represents the United States, BSI (British Standards Institute) represents Great Britain, and DIN (Deutches Institut für Normung) represents Germany.

ANSI, like all standards groups in the United States, is a voluntary organization and coordinates the activities of the various U.S. representatives to the ISO. ANSI accredits a number of organizations to represent the U.S., depending on the field. In the area of computer operating systems, the IEEE (Institute of Electrical and Electronics Engineers) is the accredited body. The IEEE has over 325,000 members and is organized by subfield into approximately 35 "societies" (e.g., Aerospace and Electronic Systems, Antennas and Propagation, Consumer Electronics, Electromagnetic Compatibility, Information Theory, etc.). Until early 1993, the IEEE's Computer Society designated TCOS (Technical Committee on Operating Systems) as the supervising body over the subcommittee that directed the POSIX (Portable Operating System Interface) effort. In early 1993, this responsibility was transferred to the newly formed PASC (Portable Applications Standards Committee).

7.4.1   POSIX 1003.1 compliance

The POSIX effort is divided into roughly two dozen committees, which are labeled from IEEE POSIX 1003.0 to 1003.19, and are listed at the end of this section. When speaking of POSIX in a generic sense, it usually refers to POSIX 1003.1, which is the system application program interface (API) and is written assuming a C language interface. An effort is currently underway to revise this standard to make it language-independent. The full title of the current standard is ISO/IEC 9945-1: 1990 IEEE Standard 1003.1-1990 Information Technology-Portable Operating System Interface (POSIX) Part 1: System Application Program Interface (API) (C Language). This standard, which most members of the POSIX community call *dot1* (pronounced "dot one") is available from the IEEE Customer Service Department.*

Other major POSIX committees are 1003.2, which deals with commands and utilities, as well as 1003.7, which deals with systems administration. Many of the other working groups are defining applications environment profiles, which specify optional features that can be added to a base standard (such as 1003.1).

7.4.2 POSIX and related committees

A comprehensive list of POSIX and related committees is given here for the reader's reference.

1003.0	POSIX Guide
1003.1	System Interfaces
1003.2	Shell & Utilities
1003.3	Test Methods
1003.4	Real Time
1003.5	ADA Bindings
1003.6	POSIX Security
1003.7	System Administration
1003.8	Transparent File Access—Distribution Services
1003.9	FORTRAN Binding
1003.10	Supercomputing Application Environment Profile
1003.11	Transaction Processing Application Environment Profile
1003.12	Protocol Independent Interfaces
1003.13	Real Time Application Environment Profile (Application Support)
1003.14	Multiprocessing Application Environment Profile (Application Support)
1003.15	Batch Services (Batch Environment Amendment)
1003.16	C Language Binding
1003.17	Directory Service Applications Programming Interface
1003.18	POSIX Platform Application Environment Profile

---

*IEEE Customer Service, 445 Hoes Lane, Piscataway, New Jersey 08854.

1003.19	POSIX ADA Language Interface BDG for Real Time Extensions
1201.1	Windowing Toolkit Applications Programming Interface Window Interface for User and Applications Portability
1201.2	User Interface Driveability Recommended Practice on Driveability
1224.0	X.400 and X.500 Object Management X.400 Mail Services Application Program Interface
1224.1	X.400 Gateway Applications Programming Interface OSI Applications Interface—X.400-Based Electronic Messaging
1238	Common OSI API and FTAM API
1238.1	Dependent Document

7.4.3 FIPS

For those who deal with the U.S. federal government, attention should be paid to the Federal Information Processing Standards (FIPS), which are written by the NIST (National Institute for Standards and Technology) and are available from the National Technical Information Service. The FIPS standards define procurement requirements for the federal government. As of early 1993, the current FIPS standard for POSIX is FIPS 151-1, which specifies, with a few minor changes and clarifications, that the earlier version (POSIX 1003.1-1988) is to be used as the mandated federal standard. FIPS 151-2, which is currently awaiting the signature of the U.S. Secretary of Commerce, cites POSIX 1003.1-1990 as its basis, also with a few minor changes. The differences between the 1988 and 1990 versions of POSIX 1003.1 are relatively minor and largely consist of corrections and clarification.

For those who wish to check their compliance with FIPS 151-1, there is a PCTS (POSIX Compliance Test Suite) that was developed by the NIST (National Institute of Standards and Technology), and can be administered by any one of seven accredited POSIX conformance test laboratories. NIST can supply the names of currently accredited test facilities, as well as information on the current requirements and test procedures.

7.4.4 X/Open

X/Open is an international consortium of hardware vendors, software vendors, and users who have developed the X/Open Portability Guide 3 (XPG3). This is a consensus-based standard and is divided into a base level with extensions. The base level is an extension of POSIX 1003.1. The extensions cover SQL, IPCs, FORTRAN, COBOL, Ada, window management, and numerous other topics. X/Open also has a program of "branding," whereby a product may carry the X/Open seal. Manufacturers who use this seal must meet several requirements that deal with conformance with the XPG3 standard and the testing of the product, and they must guarantee to fix any errors.

AIX's latest version conforms to IEEE POSIX 1003.1-1988, IEEE POSIX 1003.1-1990, FIPS 151-1, and X/Open's XPG3.

7.4.5 Committees involved with standards

Throughout Sec. 7.4, several acronyms have been used to refer to various standards committees. A compiled list of standards groups follows, describing the unabridged forms of the acronyms.

IEEE	Institute of Electrical and Electronics Engineers
IEEE-CS	IEEE Computer Society
POSIX	Portable Operating System Interface
TCOS	Technical Committee on Operating Systems
PASC	Portable Applications Standards Committee
SEC	Sponsor Executive Committee
PMC	Project Management Committee
PSC	Profiles Steering Committee
SCCT	Steering Committee on Conformance Testing
DSSC	Distributed Services Steering Committee
SCWUI	Steering Committee on Windowing User Interfaces
TAG	Technical Advisory Group
SICC	Systems Interface Coordination Committee
TSG1	Technical Study Group 1 (defunct)
SGFS	Special Group on Functional Standards
TFA	Transparent File Access
PCD	POSIX Conformance Document
TPWG	Transaction Processing Working Group
WG15	Working Group 15 (ISO Committee that meets twice a year, and deals with POSIX and computer languages)
SC22	Subcommittee 22 (parent organization over WG15)
SDO	Standards Development Organization
ISO	International Organization for Standards
IEC	International Electrotechnical Commission
BSI	British Standards Institute
DIN	Deutches Institut für Normung
ANSI	American National Standards Institute

7.5 NETWORKING STANDARDS

7.5.1 X Window system

The X Window system (or simply X) is a hardware, vendor-independent, and network-transparent operating environment. It was developed at the Massachusetts Institute of Technology in 1984 as a part of a cooperative effort funded by major computer manufacturers. The goal was to build a network of graphical workstations. The enormous success of this program soon made the X Window system a UNIX-based windowing standard. Today X is available on virtually every workstation in the industry, including AIX.

X has multifaceted benefits to offer. It solves the problem of having a common interface across a heterogeneous range of computers and operating systems. It provides a mechanism upon which one can build different user interface styles. It also addresses the issue of sharing resources among multiple programs. Being operating-system-independent, X encourages the portability of its software to diverse platforms. Hence, X has evolved to be one of the most popular and widely available user interface standards in the workstations arena today.

In terms of facilities, X provides the ability to generate multifont text and graphics in monochrome or in color on a bitmap display. Graphics such as points, lines, arcs, and polygons can be generated in a hierarchy of windows. Each window can be considered a virtual screen and can, in turn, contain subwindows of an arbitrary depth. They may overlap each other and can be moved, resized, or restacked dynamically. Since windows are relatively inexpensive resources, applications utilizing several thousand subwindows are common and are often used to implement user interface components.

The X Window system architecture is based on a simple client-server relationship. The display server is the program that controls and draws the output to the display monitors, tracks client input, and updates the windows accordingly. Clients are application programs that perform specific tasks. Since X is, by design, a distributed environment, its clients and server do not necessarily have to run on the same machine.

The terminology in the world of X may be somewhat misleading to programmers from the traditional host or mainframe environment. The word *server* in this context of X is radically different from the servers in the local area network environments. In fact, it is the reverse. Consider a traditional database environment where the server lives on the remote host and the client application resides locally on the PCs that are attached to it. In X, the server lives on the local workstation, while the clients run on the remote host machines.

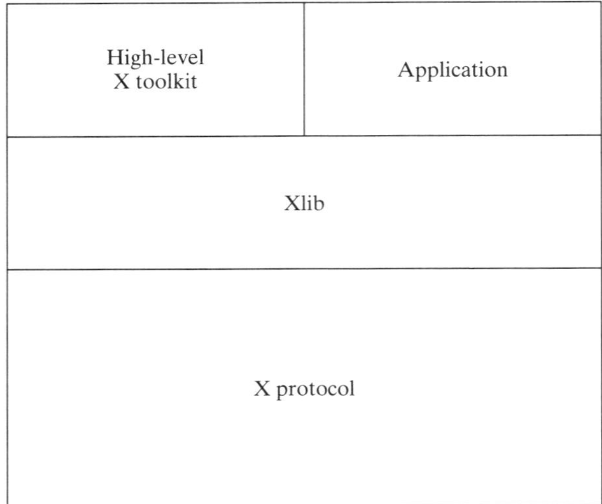

Figure 7.4 X window system.

Although X is fundamentally defined by a network protocol, most application programmers think about it as a graphical user interface (GUI). For ease of use, a higher-level layer is used to abstract the protocol layer and insulate it from programmers building X-based interfaces. This higher-level layer is referred to as the *Xlib* or, more correctly, as the Xlib interface library (refer to Fig. 7.4). This library provides a familiar procedural interface that masks the detail of the protocol-encoding and transport interactions. It also automatically handles the buffering of requests for efficient transport to the server, much as the C language standard I/O library buffers output to minimize system calls. The library also provides a suite of utility functions and primitive constructs that do not directly relate to the protocol, but do, however, aid in building applications.

7.5.2 Trusted computing base

The architecture of AIX addresses the diversified needs of the commercial and governmental, as well as the educational communities, with a single general solution. Keeping in mind the requirements of security policy, accountability, assurance, and documentation, AIX was designed such that it is able to meet the security-related compliance requirements and conformance requirements of POSIX, XPG, and other standards bodies (described earlier in this chapter). The trusted computing base (referred to as TCB from here on) is the aggregation of system mechanisms that enforces and ensures the system's security

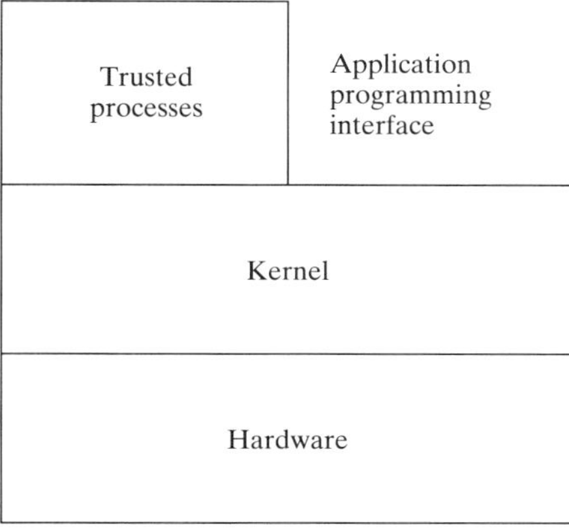

Figure 7.5 Conceptual base of trusted computer base.

policies. (A conceptual view of the TCB boundary is shown in Fig. 7.5.) Selected components from the hardware as well as from the software domains are participants in the TCB's domain base to effectively police its compliance.

The TCB software consists of:

- an operating system kernel that manages the system

- configuration files that control system operation

- programs executed with privilege or access permission to alter the kernel and/or configuration files

The hardware consists of

- a processor that operates in a dual execution mode—system mode and problem mode

The programs running in *problem mode* are functionally independent and can access only limited resources, whereas the programs running in *system mode* are relatively unconstrained. The kernel always runs in system mode and is henceforth considered a part of the TCB. Processes running in problem mode interface to kernel modules through the system call mechanism, causing the processor to change to system mode. However, those processors are part of the TCB only if they run with kernel privilege.

The system state (information indicating the state of the system) consists of a static system state that may be changed only at system start time based on administrative privileges and a dynamic system state that may change at any time based on kernel privileges. The static system state is stored in configuration files such as *$/etc/master$*

and */etc/system*. The dynamic system state is stored in kernel data structures and the state files of trusted programs such as the kernel process table and the */etc/utmp* file. The system security state is the part of the system state that handles security-relevant aspects of the system, the reading or modifying of which can be authorized by administrative or kernel privileges.

All programs that are installed with privilege or invoked by a privileged program are denoted as *trusted programs* (TPs). Additionally, a TP is any process that may alter or read the system security state.

There are three main components in the security policies identified in the AIX operating system. A brief description of them is summarized here.

Access control	Addresses how information resources are created and distributed.
Accountability	Addresses how users are identified on the system and for what actions they are accountable. It can detect actual and potential noncompliance.
Administrative	Addresses issues pertaining to administrative users on the system, provides principle of least privilege, and ensures role separation.

7.5.3 Network file system

Originally developed by Sun Microsystems, Network File System (NFS) has become a de facto networking standard. NFS's biggest asset is that it is independent of hardware, operating systems, and network architectures. This independence was achieved through the use of two sets of protocols:

1. Remote procedure call protocols (better known as RPC protocols)

2. Data-standardizing external data representation (XDR) protocols

In addition to the RPC and XDR, NFS uses the TCP/IP protocol to implement data transmission. NFS requires TCP/IP to be already installed, configured, and operational before NFS can be used. The NFS facility can be started upon request or simply configured to start up when the operating system is booted.

NFS functions are controlled by a set of daemons.* The master daemon associated with NFS is called *inetd*. It is not just for NFS, but it is the master for all other daemons on the system. It essentially triggers

---

* A daemon is a special process under UNIX/AIX systems that can run independently, without any terminal attachment or associated process groups.

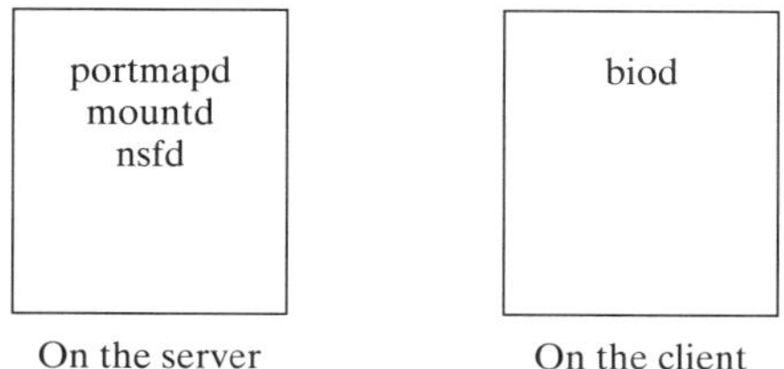

Figure 7.6 Participating daemons in NFS.

the startup of other daemons when and if needed. In addition to the *inetd,* there is a suite of daemons that is associated with NFS, as seen in Fig. 7.6. The list of NFS daemons includes:

portmapd

mountd

nfsd

pcnfsd

biod

The *biod* daemon is required to run on all of the machines that are serving as NFS clients. The *pcnfsd* daemon is needed on the server machine only if a PC's files are mounted. The rest of the daemons run on the server machine.

NFS also supports access control lists (ACLs), which are a separate function handled by an RPC program to exchange information about ACLs between clients and servers.

Mapped files are also supported under NFS on the System/6000-running AIX. This feature allows programs on clients to be accessed as if they were in real memory. Using the *shmat* system call, users can map areas of a file into their address space. As the program reads/writes into this region of memory, the file is read into the memory from the server or updated as needed. Multiple files on the same client can also share data effectively using a mapped file.

Secure NFS is also implemented under AIX. This feature is in addition to the standard UNIX authentication. NFS uses the data encryption standard (DES) and public key cryptography to authenticate users and machines in networks. A DES key is generated from two components: a public key published for general availability and a private key used to encrypt and decrypt data.

The NFS-compatible network lock manager supports file- and record-locking over the network. Local lock requests are handled by the kernel. When a lock is attempted on a remote file on an NFS-mounted directory, the kernel issues a local RPC request to *rpc.lockd,* the network lock

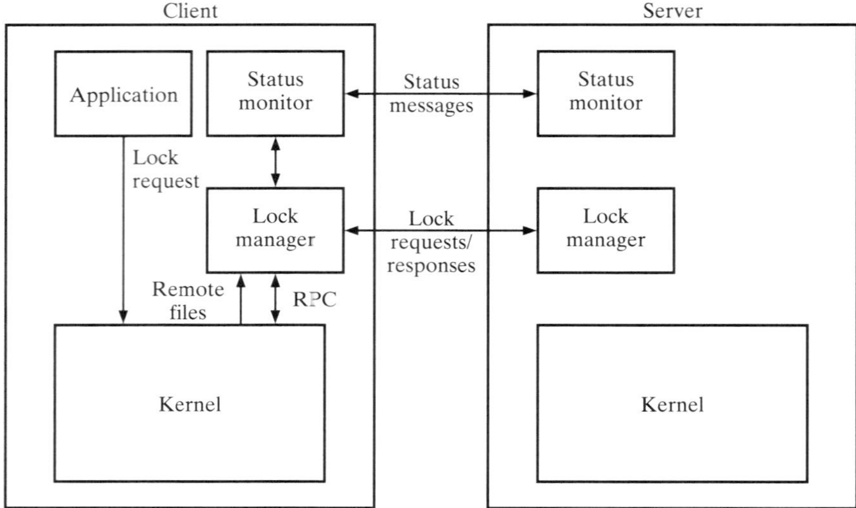

Figure 7.7 NFS lock manager.

daemon, to make a lock request to the network lock manager daemon on the NFS server. The network lock manager contains both the client and server functions. The client services requests from the kernel and sends them to the network server lock manager at the server end, while the server processes lock requests from the network and enforces lock operations in the kernel. Figure 7.7 delineates the coordination between the kernel and the lock manager on individual machines at both ends, while showing the information exchange between the client and the server machines. The status monitor shown in the diagram performs "health-check" duties and keeps a record of relevant failures at the client and the server end, so that the lock information may be recovered if a crash indeed occurs. When a lock request is issued, the kernel ascertains if it is a local request. If so, it processes the lock request itself. If not, it transmits it to the network lock daemon to take necessary actions. This locking system is essentially stateless.

Some of the commonly used commands in NFS are listed here. In order to acquire an understanding of how these commands work, refer to the NFS reference manuals.

Command	**Description of the command**
rusers	displays a list of users currently logged in on remote machines
rup	displays status of a remote host
rpcinfo	reports the status of RPC servers

rpcgen	generates C code to implement an RPC protocol
on	executes commands on remote systems
nfsstat	displays statistics pertaining to the ability of a client/server to receive calls
showmount	displays a list of all clients that have remotely mounted a filesystem
spray	sends a specific number of packets to a host to report performance statistics
rwall	sends a message to all users on the network

7.5.4   High availability for network file system

High Availability for Network File System (HANFS) is an extension to NFS that supports higher availability of data than that provided by a standard NFS configuration. The main feature of HANFS is improved availability of servers through disk impersonation. Data availability is optimized through an option to mirror disks.* It can survive planned outages and failures of the operating system, system planar, adapters, and internal and external disks.

In addition to the NFS daemons, HANFS requires three additional daemons to facilitate in configuration and reconfiguration of the system and of object data manager (ODM) databases. The additional daemons are

hanfsd

hacfgd

hapngd

Hardware configuration required by HANFS comprises a backup server configured with multiple shared volume groups,† which are essentially external disks that are individually connected to a disk adapter of the server on one end and to the backup machine on the other, as seen in Fig. 7.8. There is a rigid requirement on HANFS that both the server and its backup must be POWERstation or POWERserver computers. Like the shared volume groups, there is a redundant configuration of network adapters, too. The server and backup use four network adapters—one each for normal operations, the third to impersonate the server by the backup in case of server failure, and the fourth to impersonate the backup by the server in case of backup failure.

---

* Internal details of disk mirroring is covered in Chap. 16.

† The concept of volume groups is explained in Chap. 16.

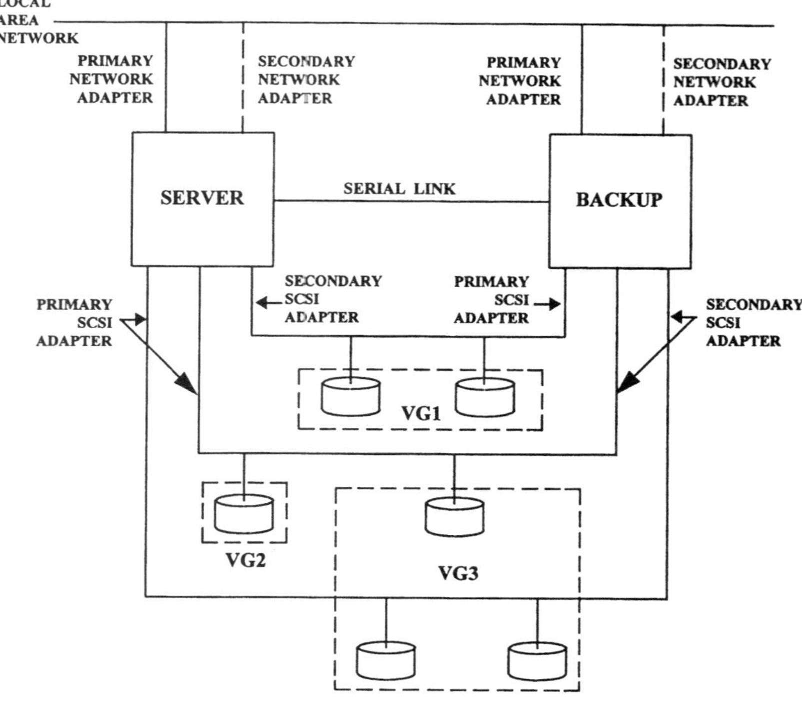

Figure 7.8 Typical high-availability NFS configuration.

7.5.5 Network Information Service

Network Information Service (NIS) is a centralized database service that offers centralized control of networked machines. NIS was formerly known as "Yellow Pages (YP)."

NIS consists of clients and servers, logically grouped together in domains using *maps* (databases), that provide information such as host names or passwords. An NIS server can be thought of as a host providing resources for other computers on the network. An NIS slave is a client that uses the maps to share information. These maps are essentially copies of the data to be shared, stored in a machine-independent standardized form called external data representation (XDR) format. The map files are created using an NIS command called *makedbm*. After creation, each map has two files: a file named *map.key.pag* containing key and value pairs, and a file named *map.key.dir* containing an index for large *.pag* files.

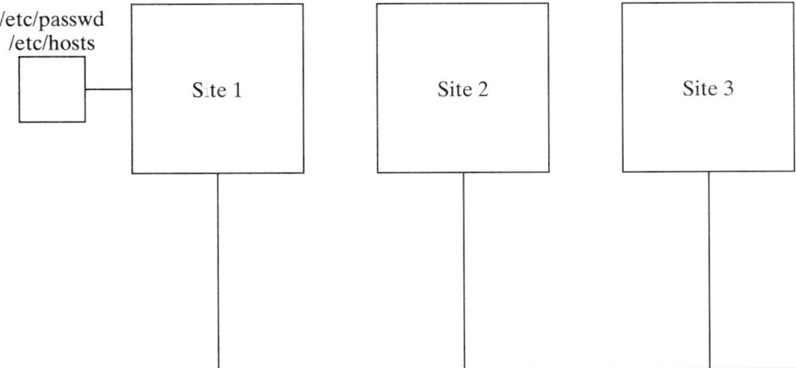

Figure 7.9 NIS: sharing user password and hostname information.

The main benefit of NIS is that it reduces the effort of maintaining repetitive databases of information. It also helps users by making their password, directories, and files available on other systems. Network administration becomes easier and less time-consuming. Figure 7.9 represents typical information stored in NIS database password files and host files whose contents are essentially the same for different nodes on a single network.

A few frequently used NIS commands are listed as follows.

Command	Description of the command
domainname	lists the name of the current NIS domain system for an NIS host
makedbm	creates the NIS database maps
ypbind	enables a client process to connect to a server
ypcat	lists the contents of NIS maps
ypinit	builds and installs NIS maps on an NIS server
ypmatch	displays the values of one or more keys within an NIS map
yppasswd	allows users to change NIS passwords from any NIS host
yppoll	identifies the version of an NIS map on the NIS server
yppush	forces propagation of updated NIS maps from the master server to slave servers
ypserv	looks up information in the local NIS databases
ypset	points the *ypbind* process to a specific server
ypwhich	identifies which machine is the NIS server of an NIS client
ypxfr	transfers an NIS map from an NIS server to a local host

7.5.6 Transmission control protocol/Internet protocol

TCP/IP is a set of communication protocols that specify standards and conventions for routing and interconnecting computer networks. It is a de facto standard for local area networks. It has even proliferated to wide area network environments like the Internet. From a conceptual perspective, TCP and IP are two separate protocol layers. Figure 7.10 shows the protocol stack for TCP/IP. Applications use both the TCP and the IP layers to communicate with the network interface (which is the physical layer).

TCP/IP is a network technology independent of and capable of running on virtually all standard hardware platforms. It supports universal interconnection so that one computer may communicate with any other computer on the same network or another network. TCP/IP can handle a diversity of network-related tasks. Some of the routine uses of TCP/IP are for sending electronic mail, transferring files computer-to-computer, performing remote login, executing commands on a remote machine, printing files on remote systems, and managing a network.

Some of the commonly used TCP/IP commands are listed here, with a short description of each.

Command	Description of the command
finger	displays user information on specified host
ftp	transfers files between hosts
host	resolves a host name
ping	determines status of a network or host
rcp	Copies one or more files between local and remote host, between two remote hosts, or between files at a single remote host

Application
TCP
IP
Link
Physical

Figure 7.10 TCP/IP protocol stack.

rexec	allows a command to be executed on a remote machine
rlogin	logs in to a similar remote host
rsh	executes commands on a foreign host
rwho	displays user information on local area network hosts
telnet (tn)	provides capability for a user to have a remote session on a similar or dissimilar remote host
tftp	provides a minimal file transfer capability to transfer files to and from hosts, provides a stripped set of commands in *ftp*
whois	identifies the owner of a user ID or nickname

One may find multiple sets of commands for remote file transfer, remote command execution, and remote login under AIX and most UNIX systems. This is due to the fact that each set of utilities has descended from the System V and Berkeley domains. TCP/IP is mentioned here for completeness only. To gain an understanding of the protocol suite, refer to the product reference manuals.*

7.5.7 Network computing system

The network computing system (NCS) is a set of tools for distributing computer processing tasks across resources either in a network or several interconnected networks. NCS is an implementation of the network computing architecture, which distributes software applications across networks encompassing a variety of computers and programming environments. Programs based on network computing architecture take advantage of computing resources throughout a network by allocating different parts of each program to be executed on host computers best suited for that task. NCS consists of three major components:

Remote procedure call (RPC) run-time library

Location broker

Network Interface Definition Language (NIDL) compiler

The RPC run-time library and the location broker provide run-time support for network computing. Together, these two components make up what is called the network computing kernel (NCK). The NCK contains all the software required to run a distributed application. The third component, the NIDL compiler, is a tool for developing applications.

The RPC run-time library provides library routines for local programs to execute procedures on remote hosts. These routines transfer

---

* *Communication Concepts and Procedures,* Vol. 2.

requests and responses between clients (the programs calling the procedures) and servers (the programs executing the procedures). When writing a distributed application, a user usually need not employ RPC routines directly. Instead, an interface definition in Network Interface Definition Language can be created and the NIDL compiler can be used to generate the required RPC routines.

The NIDL compiler takes an interface definition written in NIDL as an input. An interface definition specifies the interface between the user and the provider of a service. Once the interface is established, the compiler defines the way in which a client application sees a remote service as well as the way in which a remote server sees requests for its service. From this definition, the NIDL compiler generates client and server stub source code and header files. The client stub program performs the conversion between requests (and responses) that are meaningful to the client and packets that are transmitted (and received) on the network. The server stub program provides similar support for the server. The stub programs produced by an NIDL compiler contain nearly all of the remoteness for a distributed application. They perform data conversions and assembly and disassembly of packets, and they provide interaction with the RPC run-time library. It is much easier to write an interface definition in NIDL than it would be to write the stub code that the NIDL compiler generates from a definition.

The location broker provides information about the network or Internet resources to clients. It maintains a database that contains the identification and locations of objects on a network. Through a client agent, the location broker maintains information about the local brokers that manage information about resources on the local host, the global brokers that manage information about resources on all hosts, and the administrative tools.

Network communications between systems in an NCS environment are handled through the RPC run-time library. It is possible that one program can access different hosts that listen on two different ports or have two different addresses.

RPC Paradigm. The remote procedure calls extend the procedure call mechanism from a single system to a distributed computing environment. The calls distribute the execution of a program among multiple computers in a way that is transparent to the application-level code. Figure 7.11 shows the flow of ordinary local procedure calls between the calling client and the called procedures.

The following is a commonly used set of NCS commands:

Command	**Description of the command**
lb_admin	monitors and administers location broker registrations
libd	manages the information in the local location broker database

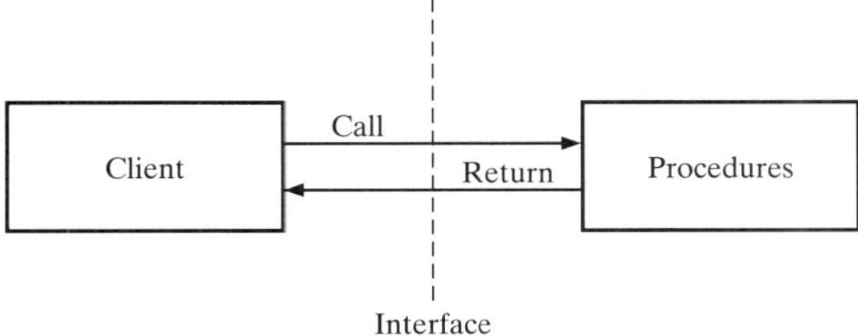

Figure 7.11 NCS single-process procedure call flow.

nidl	compiles program definitions written in NIDL
nrglbd	manages the global location broker database

7.5.8 X.25 communications

X.25 is a communications protocol conforming to international standards that is particularly useful for communicating with diverse computer systems and for applications that access public databases. Both public networks and private networks can be based on X.25 protocol. Public networks are provided on a national basis by the National Post, Telegraph and Telecommunications Authority. Private networks are operated by individual corporations.

X.25 is designed for a form of communication known as packet switching. Figure 7.12 represents a simplified view of how packet switching works. Data is sent in basic entities called frames. There are three main levels in X.25. The first level is the physical or electrical level. The second level is the frame level, also known as the data link or link level. The third level is called the packet level. Packets are sent to the network within the information frames of the second level.

In a packet-switching network, the data to be sent is combined in a packet with addressing and control information. This results in an independent unit that can be sent through any suitable path in the

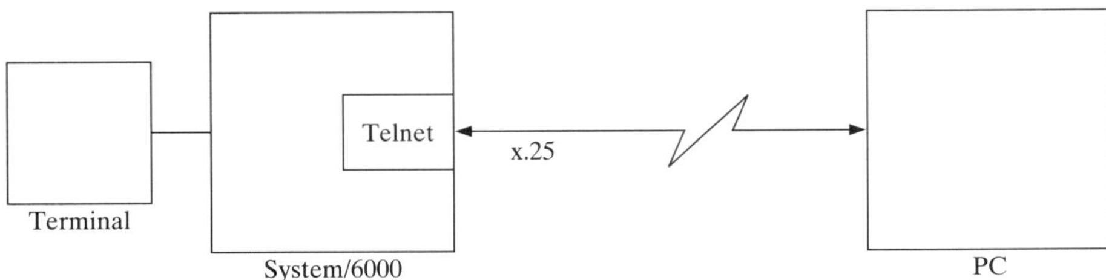

Figure 7.12 X.25 connection.

network. Packets from many different users can share the same network routes and lines. X.25 uses the network user address to route both incoming and outgoing calls to the correct system.

In communication terminology, the computer or workstation that sends and receives data is known as data terminal equipment (DTE). The network equipment that is physically connected to the DTE is the data circuit-terminating equipment (DCE). When a user makes a call to another over the X.25 network, one of the predefined number of logical channels is assigned to the call at each end. Each DTE includes a logical channel number in each packet sent. The number identifies the logical channel that connects the DTE with its DCE. The two logical channel numbers at two ends may be different, but each DTE needs to know only the number it assigned to the channel; it does not need to be aware of the other. When the two logical channels are assigned to a call, a virtual circuit is established from one DTE to the other by DCEs on the network. Each logical channel is either for outgoing calls only, incoming calls only, or two-way calls that are permanently connected. However, once the virtual circuit is established, it is always for two-way communication. The virtual circuit may be either switched or permanent. A switched virtual circuit (SVC) is a virtual circuit that exists only for the duration of the call, acting like a connection over a standard telephone network. A permanent virtual circuit (PVC) is like a leased line that can be established between two addresses to save time in establishing calls. A PVC ties up a logical channel permanently.

Hardware requirements for X.25 on the System/6000 involve the X.25 adapter (described in Chap. 3) that would connect to the X.25 network. The software required is the X.25 interface protocol code, real-time control microcode, applications programming interface, an X.25 device driver, and qualified logical link control (QLLC).

The X.25 commands enable users to use the X.25 network without doing any application programming. Some of the common commands are:

Command	Description of the command
xcomms	starts one of the other commands
xtalk	communicates with other systems and manages address lists for outgoing calls
xroute	manages a routing list for incoming calls
xmanage	displays status information for an X.25 port; connects and disconnects an X.25 port; gets statistics for an X.25 port
xmonitor	monitors the activity on an X.25 port

7.5.9 Simple network management protocol

The simple network management protocol (SNMP) is used by network managers to troubleshoot, locate, and correct problems in a TCP/IP

Internet. SNMP is a protocol used by network hosts to exchange information used in management of networks. SNMP is defined in the following RFCs (request for comments):

RFC 1155   defines the structure of management information

RFC 1157   defines SNMP for creating requests for MIB information and formatting responses

RFC 1213   defines the management information base (MIB)

Network management for SNMP is based on a client-server model. The client agent is run on the local workstation (System/6000 in our case) that needs to be managed, and it is used to contact one or more SNMP server agents that execute on remote machines, usually gateways. The server agent is a process that maintains certain databases for the host. Hosts involved in network management run a monitor process called *xgmon,* that generates requests for MIB information and processes responses.

The management information base (MIB) is a separate standard (from SNMP) that defines the set of variables and the semantics of each variable that SNMP servers maintain. The MIB database contains information pertinent to network management, which may be used to record the traffic statistics, error counts, status of each connected network, etc. There are two MIBs defined at present—MIB-I and MIB-II. A complete reference of these two standards may be found in RFC 1156 and RFC 1213, respectively. MIB-II is essentially a superset of the objects found in MIB-I.

SNMP uses a formal specification language called Abstract Syntax Notation One (ASN.1) to define and specify the format of MIB variable names and messages. ASN.1 defines a hierarchical namespace, so the name of each variable reflects its position in the hierarchy. The point of the ASN.1 hierarchy is to carefully distribute authority to assign names to multiple organizations. The scheme guarantees that although many organizations assign names concurrently, the resulting names are guaranteed to be unique and absolute.

Network management can be passive or active. Passive management basically involves the collection of statistical data so that network activity on each host can be profiled. Active network management, on the other hand, involves the use of a subset of the MIB variables that are designated read-write. The request sent to an SNMP server agent is accepted by the server which performs the specified operations and returns a response to the requester. The SNMP server agent first parses the message sent by the client and translates it to internal form. SNMP then maps the MIB variable specification to the local data item that stores the needed information and then performs the fetch or store operations as requested. An information flow path illustrated in Fig.

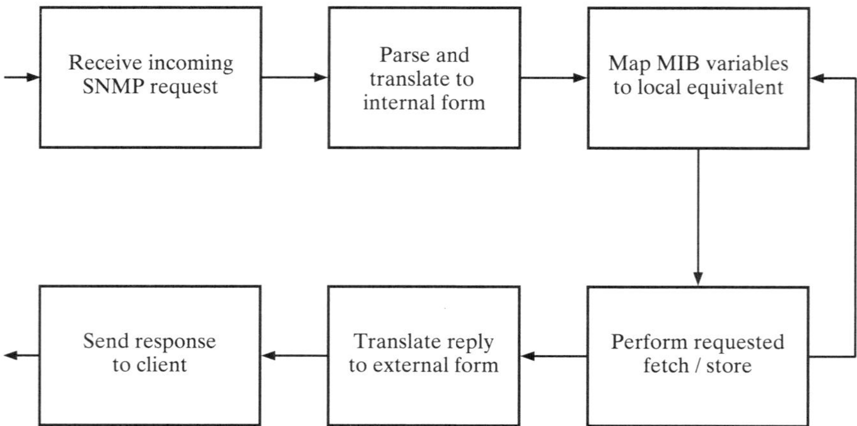

Figure 7.13 Information flow in SNMP.

7.13 shows how SNMP works in general. For fetch operations, SNMP replaces the data area in the message with the new value that it has fetched. If more than one variable value was requested, SNMP fetches the value of each variable and replaces the value with the fetched value in the message. After all the specified operations are completed, the server translates the reply from its internal form to the external form and returns it to the client that requested the values.

7.5.10 Distributed computing environment

The distributed computing environment (DCE) is a standardized approach to distributed computing that enables one to create, use, support, and maintain distributed applications on a diverse network. It allows applications to exploit the potential resources in the network environment and thus improve the performance. There are three basic features of DCE:

1. Remote procedure call (RPC) and presentation services

2. Security services

3. Management services

RPC enables software developers to partition tasks in an application into separate procedure models that can be executed on different systems. It makes use of what are called *threads* to allow multiple sequential flows of execution within a single process. This feature provides better service availability by simultaneously handling multiple clients. The security services ensure against unauthorized access. Management services provide utilities to manage DCE.

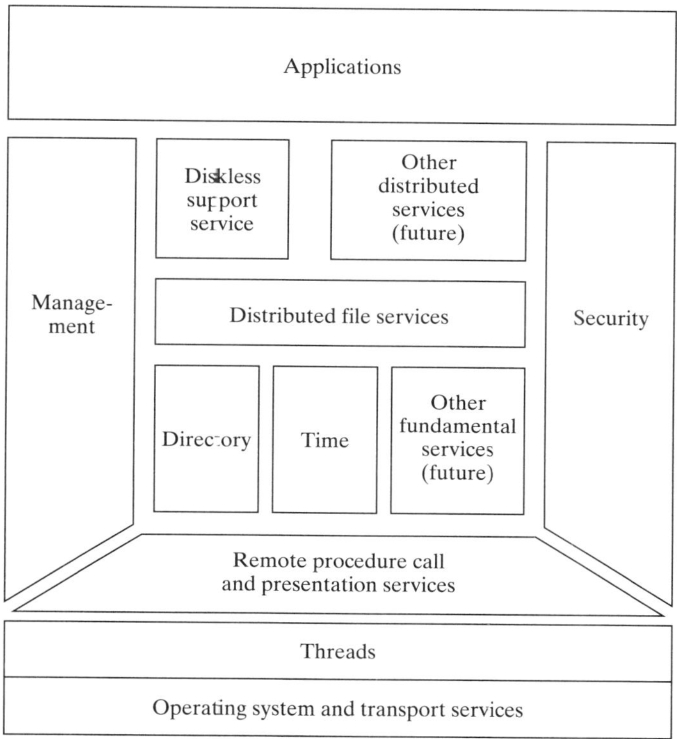

Figure 7.14 Distributed computing environment.

DCE offers a whole suite of services, as seen in Fig. 7.14. The directory service assigns a unique name or attribute to a physical device, making it accessible from any location in the network. Within this paradigm, there are four components:

1. DCE cell directory service (CDS) stores names and attributes within a DCE cell, a group of systems administered as one entity.

2. DCE global directory agent (GDA) is a naming gateway connecting administrative domains through the X.500 worldwide directory service and domain name service (DNS).

3. DCE global directory service (GDS) is used to locate objects in a global environment.

4. X/Open directory service (XDS) defines an application programming interface (API) that can be used to create, delete, modify, or search for directory service calls.

In addition, several other services are available such as time services which provide a consistent view of time. The distributed filesystem offers a consistent and unified view of all files in the distributed system. Diskless support service extends DCE to low-cost, diskless nodes.

A basic architectural difference between DCE and message I/O is to be noted. DCE provides direct dialogue between the client and server application programs through RPCs, unlike message I/O where all interactions between the client and server applications are dependent on the communication service provider.

A DCE software "toolkit" is available on AIX Version 3 for RISC System/6000 and AIX/ESA. DCE is used as a strategic base to build distributed applications, including on-line transaction processing (OLTP) for the AIX environment. Additionally, selected DCE interfaces and protocols are available on certain system application architecture (SAA) platforms.

7.6 SUMMARY

Three separate aspects of the System/6000 are addressed in this chapter. It is shown that in terms of connectivity the System/6000 is able to provide a networking interface to the host world and to DOS-based PCs, as well as to multivendor UNIX machines. The second segment of the discussion revolves around the myriad compatibility standards that are met and exceeded by the System/6000-running AIX. The third part of the discussion introduces the networking and communications standards that are supported by the RISC System/6000.

Owing to the enormity of the information covered in this chapter, the depth of each topic has been limited. A high-level introduction to key topics has been presented with the vision that the reader will recognize it as one of the available facilities on this machine. If needed, the respective reference manuals may be consulted for details like command options, etc. Our focus has remained on introducing the array of functionalities and facilities.

AIX Administration and Tuning

All stand-alone or networked UNIX-based environments require a certain amount of housekeeping and maintenance. These tasks are typically the duties of the system administrator who is entrusted with the operating system upkeep, product upgrades, backups, and other allied duties.

Traditionally, all UNIX systems have had a more or less similar way of doing these tasks. As UNIX evolved we saw a variation in the implementation of these tasks. Very soon there were too many ways of doing the same thing. What was worse, these variations led to diversities, which in turn often caused incompatibilities. In the development phase before the advent of AIX, one of the areas that received a lot of attention in terms of standardization was system administration and management. An entire volume will fall short of describing all the system administration and operating system maintenance methods. One is encouraged to refer to the product documentation for that. The focus of this chapter is twofold—to highlight the essentials of system administration under AIX on this machine and to present some performance management options in light of these concepts and facilities.

8.1 SYSTEM MANAGEMENT INTERFACE

Almost all of the routine system administrative tasks are performed using a common user interface called *smit*. The name *smit* stands for system management interface tool. Unlike user interfaces across miscellaneous tools which are monolithic programs, *smit* offers a layered and standardized interface for the system administrator. It is also able to provide an extendable architecture for commands, methods, and services.

In addition to standardizing the user interface, *smit* insulates the users from complex command syntax and errors. As much as *smit* is designed to look simple, its underlying infrastructure is very complex. A layered structure of *smit* (Fig. 8.1) describes how its basic blocks are laid out. The basic blocks that build *smit*'s layered architecture are first described in a top-down fashion, followed by the details on the user interface options.

In *smit,* the highest-level modules include context-specific user interfaces. The next level consists of high-level commands which are composed of the system management tasks from the administrator's point of view, independent of the operating environment. These commands can be invoked directly from the command line, if needed. The third layer involves methods that apply to objects managed by an object-oriented configuration database. The next level down is a set of low-level facilities, which are invoked by the methods and high-level commands to provide stateless operations. Below this layer are the system management services which include device drivers and subroutines. A flow diagram in Fig. 8.2 shows how the levels interact in a hierarchical manner with the configuration database.

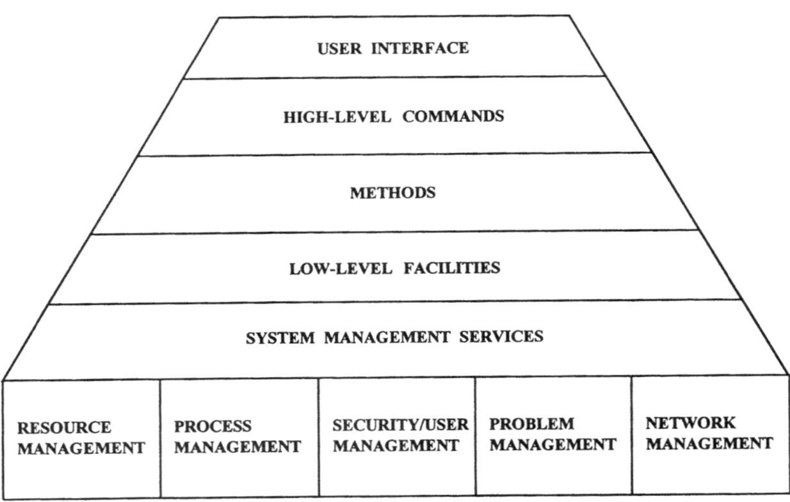

Figure 8.1 Multilayered structure of *smit.*

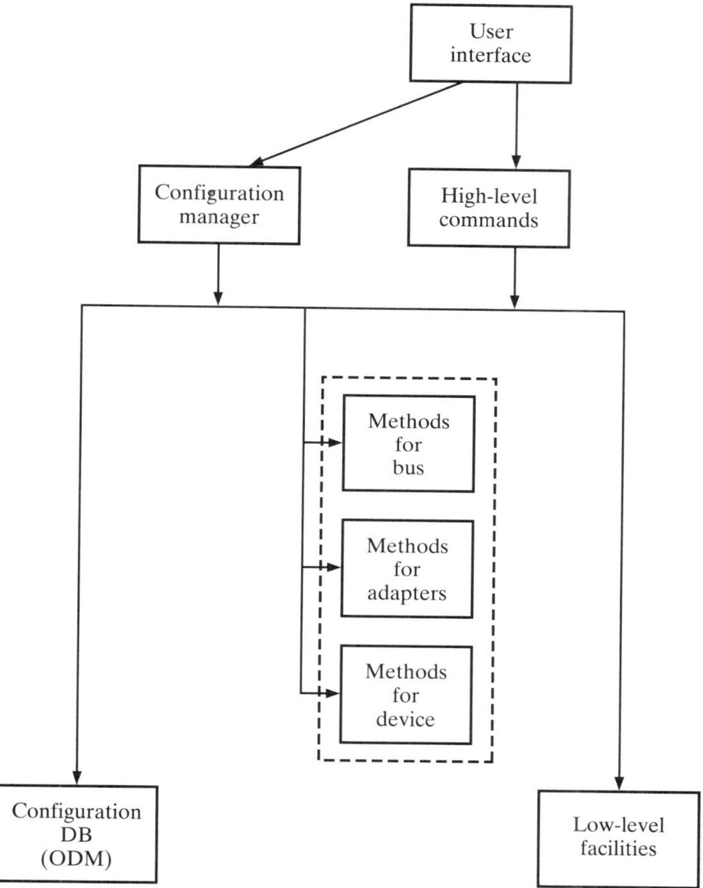

Figure 8.2 Hierarchical interaction of *smit*'s modules with the ODM.

There are three main types of screens in *smit*—menu screens, selector screens, and dialog screens. A menu typically displays a list of choices. A selector may list a set of choices or show a data entry field. A dialog is a terminal menu which comprises data entry fields from which target tasks are constructed and run. The relationship among them is shown in Fig. 8.3.

Although purists may feel at times that accomplishing a task is easier using the old-fashioned way than having to go through the *smit* menus, be advised that much of what is performed via *smit* is also updated in a database on the system. This database concept

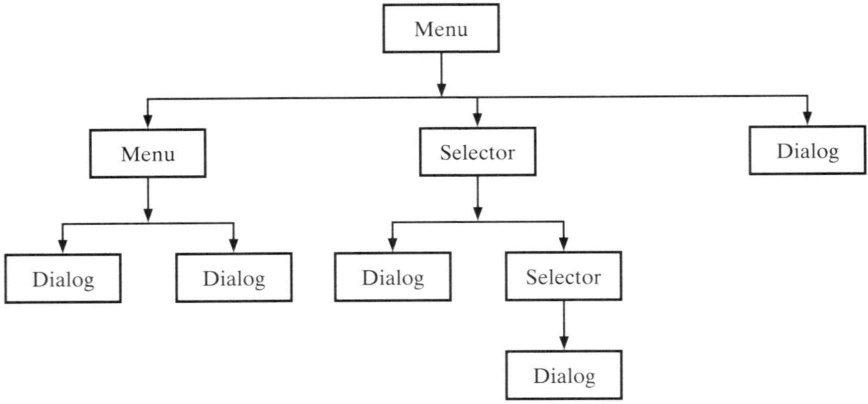

Figure 8.3 Relationship of *smit* menus, selectors, and dialogs.

is new to the UNIX environment. The database stores the device characteristics, setup information, and default values, as well as current configuration states in it. So, bypassing *smit* could render this database out of date.

8.2 OBJECT DATA MANAGER

Having discussed the database in which *smit* stores its information, the database itself needs to be described as a stand-alone entity. It would be a mistake to view this database as a *smit*-specific tool since it can be used to manage data for application programs, too. This database is called the object data manager (ODM). It is by design an object-oriented database.

The ODM supports the concepts of *object classes* and *objects*. An object class is a group of objects with the same definition. An object, a member of a defined object class, is an entity that needs storage and management of data. In fact, an object class is conceptually similar to an array of structures with each object being a structure that is an element of the array. A given object class is also associated with a set of descriptor(s). These descriptors take up values when the object is added to an object class. A suite of ODM-specific commands and subroutines is available as tools and utilities to manage these paradigms. So, if needed, the object descriptors and their associated values can be located and changed in the database using ODM's access methods. An editor (called *odme*) is also available on the system. It can be used as an interactive interface to the ODM functions.

8.3 *smit*-ODM INTERACTION

ODM stores and maintains much of the critical device- and resource-related information on the system. Although the configuration information in its entirety is complex, it can be viewed as a set of predefined and customized information. The predefined information pertains to all the possible devices (and their default configurations) that AIX supports, while the customized information includes the actually installed devices along with their current configurations. In other words, the predefined object class defines what can be there, while the customized object class describes what is actually there. Unlike traditional UNIX, AIX categorizes devices hierarchically, allowing for structured device management. Not only are similar devices clustered under the same functional class but their dependencies with allied devices are also mapped out. The benefit of this is in the degree of control that devices have with one another. This scheme guarantees that a higher-level device like a SCSI adapter always retains a cohesive bond with all its lower-level members such as disk drives and tape drives, and does not get reconfigured or unconfigured by accident. In order to store these device-to-device mappings, the location of devices is also stored by ODM. As a result, the location code becomes handy for identifying paths and dependencies of each device. A typical location code looks as follows:

DD-SS-CC-PP

In it, PP gives the port number,* CC points out the connector location, SS represents the slot in which the adapter is installed, and DD indicates the drawer number.

While using *smit* to install and/or configure devices, one may find that devices are either "available" or "defined" in the ODM database of the system. There is a subtle difference between the two states, which is often confusing. Overall a device may be either usable or unusable on the system, based on its state. And this state is a function of the object classes of the ODM. As seen in the device state transition diagram in Fig. 8.4, a state can be defined, configured, reconfigured (changed), undefined, or unconfigured. When undefined, a device indicates that the entry is in the predefined object class of the ODM, but it is not resident in the customized object class. An unconfigured state

---

* This convention has a slight exception for SCSI devices. The two digits of the PP field identify the SCSI ID number and logical unit number. For example, for a disk drive configured with a SCSI ID of 3 which is attached to an adapter card in slot 4 of the Micro Channel, the locating code would be 00-04-00-30.

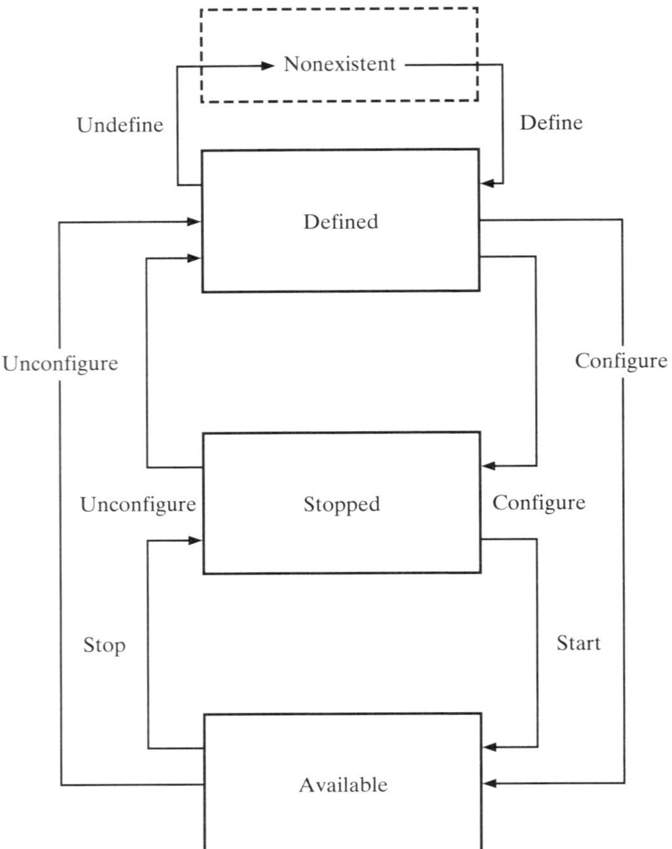

Figure 8.4 Device-state transition diagram.

means that a device's definition has been moved from the "available" to the "defined" state in the customized devices object class. A ,device becomes defined upon detection; this happens when the ODM's device-specific define method is invoked to load a device driver into the running kernel. This is a very powerful statement since it describes the automatic device definition property of the ODM along with the dynamic binding feature of the AIX kernel. This ability of the base kernel to dynamically load kernel extensions sets AIX apart from the other variants of UNIX.

8.4 ADMINISTERING WITH *smit*

The system administrator's day-to-day tasks using *smit* typically include managing user accounts, adding/modifying filesystems, main-

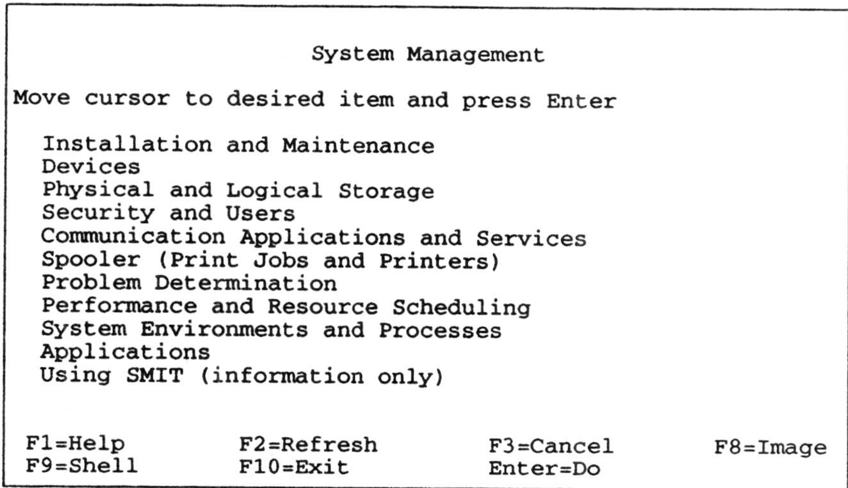

Figure 8.5 Main menu of *smit.*

taining backups, adding new applications, configuring devices (such as terminals and printers), managing networks and communications, and occasionally performing problem determination. The screen-based system administrative interface, *smit,* can be used to do all of these tasks. The main menu in *smit* (Fig. 8.5) displays all the options that one may select. The details on each of the menus can be referenced from the system administrative reference manuals or even from *smit*'s on-line help facility. However, there are a few general conventions in *smit* menus that are worth mentioning here.

Highlighted entries in *smit* indicate user-modified entries. The highlighted entries are in reverse video. Beneath the main *smit* menu there is a set of dialog symbols. The syntax and semantic for each are as follows:

[]	represents a typeable entry field
<>	indicates there is more text to the left (<) or right (>)
*	indicates this field requires a value
+	states that a list of choices is available
X	marks a hexadecimal field
#	marks a numeric field
/	denotes an accessible file name
highlight	means a user-modified entry; a highlighted entry is in reverse video

Beyond these conventions in *smit,* much of it is intuitive. The user interface has been made less error-prone by allowing only those functions that are valid at a specific time to be displayed. Scrollable pop-up windows for context-specific choices further help in restricting the chances of user input errors. Additionally, a command status panel reports completion of each command entered by displaying its status.

Although the user generally remains shielded from the complexity of traditional UNIX operating system administration, it is desirable to possess some knowledge of the operations behind the scene. The following sections explain some of the essential concepts that are specific to AIX running on System/6000.

8.5 USER MANAGEMENT

The creation or removal of user account(s) is pretty straightforward, as the *smit* menus guide the user through the hierarchical selection options in a cohesive manner. The user management option chosen from *smit*'s main menu provides many options, as shown in Fig. 8.6. Although a typical action like adding a new user consists of creating a user home directory, setting the ownerships on that directory, modifying system files to recognize the new user, and updating the ODM database to incorporate the new information, the entire process remains transparent because of the menu-driven user management interface.

Principal files associated with user management are listed here with a brief description of each.

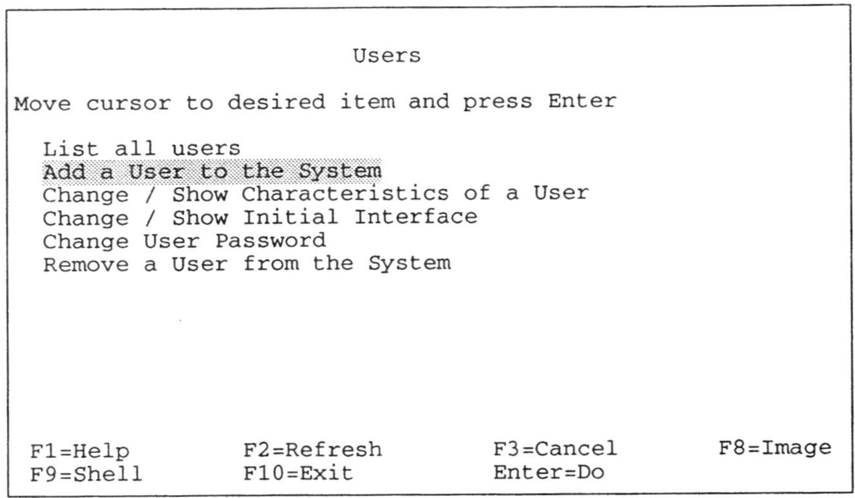

Figure 8.6 User management menu in *smit*.

/etc/security/.ids	contains the sequence numbers used, so that the newly assigned users may get unique *uid* and *gid*
/etc/security/login.cfg	holds rules for password quality, terminal controls, and login herald
/etc/group	contains basic group definitions
/etc/security/group	contains additional group definitions
/etc/passwd	contains basic user account entries as in traditional UNIX systems (except for the password field)
/etc/security/passwd	contains encrypted passwords and timestamp for last update
/etc/passwd.dir	facilitates speedier access to user administration files
/etc/passwd.pag	facilitates speedier access to user administration files
/etc/security/user	holds extended user attributes
/etc/security/environ	holds environmental attributes for users
/etc/security/limits	specifies *fsize* for users
/etc/security/mkuser. default	has all the default for generating a new user
/etc/security/failedlogin	contains an entry for every time a login fails

8.6 SECURITY MANAGEMENT

The first and foremost word of wisdom about security is that no reasonable combination of hardware and software security features will be effective without proper management. Although AIX can provide a higher level of security than traditional UNIX systems, it is best not to use the features any more than is really necessary. From an operational standpoint, security management using *smit* is straightforward. But an understanding of the elements of security helps in comprehending when and how to use the available facilities.

8.6.1 File permission bits

Under AIX, the basic security facility is the same as that of traditional UNIX systems. It makes use of permission bits on files and directories. There are three classifications for file access: *read, write,* and *execute.* A *write* permission allows a user to create or remove a file. A *read* permission allows one to view the contents, while an *execute* permission enables one to execute that file. Associated with these permissions there are three categories of possessions, namely, *owner, group,* and *other.* Each category has its own permission bit. These permission bits can only be altered by the owner of the file. A sample listing of a file with its permission bits is shown as follows, in which the left-most triplet of "rwx" belongs to the owner of the file, the middle refers to the user's group, and the right-most set refers to all others, i.e., the world.

```
714   -rwxrwxrwx  1  root  sys  74091  May 24  09:35  afile
```

Managing data security using permission bits often requires the use of individual commands. A set of frequently used commands is outlined as follows. For options and details, consult the system-specific command reference manuals.

chmod   change permissions on a file

chown   change ownership of a file (requires root privilege)

chgrp   change a file group (requires root privilege)

8.6.2   Access control lists

The additional security feature that AIX offers is called Access Control List (ACL). The concept of ACL is new to the UNIX arena. This feature allows the owner to define access to a file more precisely than what was previously available using the permission bits to grant or deny file access permissions. Using ACL, the basic file permissions can be extended to permit, deny, or specify access modes for specific individuals, groups, or user and group combinations. Specification of an access is conducted using the *permit* keyword, restriction is done using the *deny* keyword, and defining a file access is done using the *specify* keyword. A denial made using ACL cannot be overridden by the permission bits. Note that in order for the access control mechanism to take effect, the keyword *enable* must be specified. The example shown here makes it easier to understand the ACL terminology.

```
attributes: SUID
base permissions:
      owner(karen):    rw-
      group(system):   r-x
            others:    ---
extended permissions:
      enabled
         permit   rw-  u:dnc
         deny     r--  u:john, g:system
         specify  r--  u:jack, g:gateway, g:mail
         permit   rw-  g:finance, g:marketing
```

The first line indicates the attribute which may be SUID (for *setuid*), SGID (for *setgid*), or SVTX (meaning *savetext—sticky bit*). The next four lines describe the base permissions. The first line of the extended permission describes the status as being enabled or disabled. The subsequent lines describe the granting or denial of specific users based upon their group assignments. The last line shows how to permit read/write access to users who belong to both groups.

As stated before, the ACL facility should be used only when and if necessary. A set of common ACL commands is outlined below. For details, consult the system-specific command reference manuals.

aclget   gets the ACL for a file

aclput   sets the ACL for a file

acledit   enables use of an editor to change the ACL for a file

The status of both security modes, i.e., protection by permission bits and protection by access control lists, can be checked by examining the file permissions. The specific bits in a file listing precisely describe not only the security modes, but also all the file characteristics in a nutshell. The summary given in Fig. 8.7 points out all the possible values that a given field can assume. It is strongly recommended that one be able to interpret these fields. Familiarity with all the field types will greatly ease security management responsibilities for a system manager.

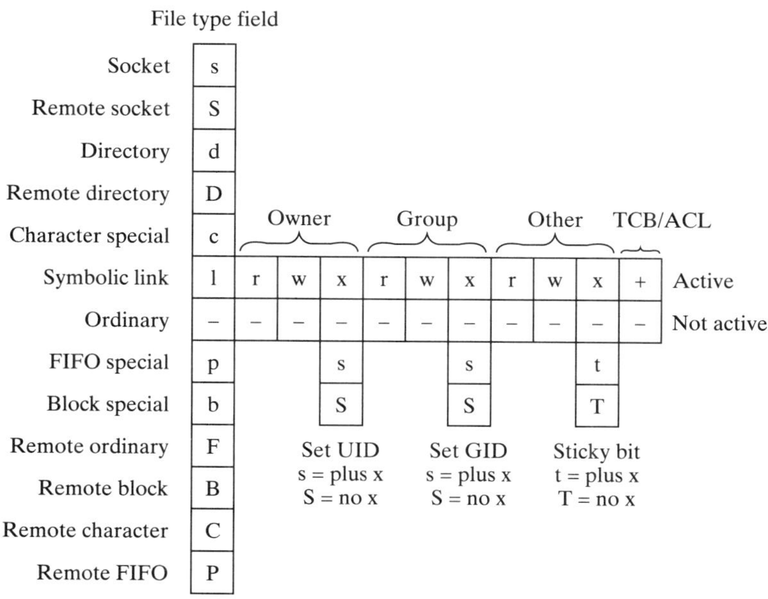

Figure 8.7 Summary of different permission bits.

8.7 FILE MANAGEMENT

AIX on System/6000 supports multiple filesystem types. The native filesystem is referred to as a *journaled file system;* it supports the entire set of AIX file system semantics. There is a support for accessing CD-ROM contents through the normal filesystem interface, which is called the *cdrom filesystem.* The other filesystem type is known as the *NFS filesystem,* which allows files residing on remote machines to be accessed as though they were local files.

8.7.1 Mounting filesystems

A system file called */etc/filesystem* defines and controls the attributes of the different filesystems. All the individual filesystems that form AIX's hierarchical file structure are listed in it. A sample of */etc/filesystem* is displayed at the end of this chapter, illustrating the format of its contents.

If needed, a filesystem may be mounted or dismounted by the system administrator. In addition to using *smit*'s options, the *mount* command can be invoked from the command line to connect the top of an individual filesystem to a designated point on the established file tree. Similarly, an *unmount* (or *umount*) command can be used to disconnect an associated filesystem from a file tree. The requirements to mount and/or unmount filesystems include

1. being the *root*
2. having write permission to the mount point, or
3. being in the *system* group
4. having the specific mount specified in */etc/filesystem* (needed for the mount command)

8.7.2 Backup and restore utilities

In addition to using *smit*'s backup functions, selected files or an entire filesystem may be backed up to a tape or other devices. There are several facilities that can be used for backup and restore functions. A brief description of each is provided:

backup	Copies files or filesystems to tape, diskette, or other files.
restore	Retrieves files that were stored using *backup.*
cpio	Copies files in and out from/to devices.
tar	Archives and restores files from/to devices or other files.

dd	Copies and/or converts files. It is especially suited to I/O on raw physical devices as it allows reading and writing in arbitrary block sizes.
dosread	Reads in a file from PC-DOS media.
doswrite	Writes out a file to PC-DOS media.

The facilities described here are all equivalent from a functional standpoint, i.e., they all backup or restore files. The *dd, tar,* and *cpio* are standard across all UNIX platforms, while others are specific to AIX. So if a file needs to be transferred to a non-AIX platform, one of the standard utilities should be used for the format to be readable.

8.7.3 Maintaining files in a filesystem

A suite of commands and procedures is available for maintaining files on the system. Some of these utilities come standard with all UNIX-based systems, while others are add-ons for AIX. File maintenance, as a task, is relevant for both the system administrator as well as for individual users. But the users are restricted to their own domain as far as being able to carry out the different file management tasks. Commands include the following:

df	Displays available disk space.
du	Identifies disk usage by displaying the number of blocks on a per-file/directory basis.
istat	Shows information about specific files/*inodes.*
fuser	Shows file utilization on a per-process basis.
ncheck	Displays inode number and path name for specified files.
pack	Compresses text files to conserve filesystem space. After compaction the files are renamed with a *.z* suffix.
pcat	Allows one to read compressed text files without having to unpack them.
unpack	Uncompresses *pack*ed file(s).
ff	Lists file information about files in a specified filesystem.
skulker	A shell script that conducts filesystem cleanup. It is especially useful for the removal of aging data files or extraneous core files from the system. If set up to run from the *crontab* by the system administrator, *skulker* will perform its task autonomously, on a periodic basis.
fsck	Detects and repairs filesystem inconsistencies.
dfsck	Similar to *fsck,* but simultaneously checks two filesystems that reside on different drives.

fsdb   This is a filesystem debugging tool which provides a capability to interactively manipulate a filesystem. Remember that a filesystem should be unmounted before one begins to work on it. Repairing a filesystem can include tasks like modifying file allocations, examining or modifying inode entries, adding/ removing physical disk blocks from a directory, etc. As much as this tool can be a lifesaver, its misuse or abuse can prove very costly by destroying a perfectly healthy filesystem.

8.8 APPLICATION MANAGEMENT

Applications may be added to the system and/or updated using *smit*. The application management option chosen from *smit*'s main menu provides multiple options, as shown in Fig. 8.8. When a new application is added under the */usr/lpp* (*lpp* being *l*icensed *p*rogram *p*roducts) directory, the ODM database is also updated to incorporate the new information.

8.9 DEVICE MANAGEMENT

The device management task can comprise a variety of things. The main ones are described here. Although most device management tasks can be performed without *smit,* it is safer to use the *smit* interface whenever possible in order to reduce the risk of errors.

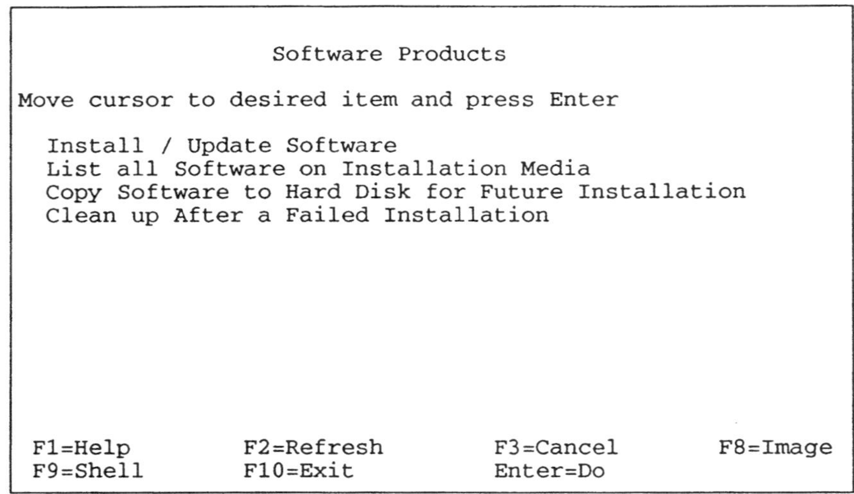

Figure 8.8 Application management menu in *smit*.

8.9.1   Terminal setup

Informing the operating system about a newly connected terminal on the machine involves

1. setting appropriate line disciplines for the port over which data communication will occur
2. marking the terminal port as active in a configuration file
3. updating the ODM database to include this new information
4. starting up an AIX process that begins looking for user input (such as a login) on the newly enabled terminal port

Procedurally, the operation is a lot simpler. The user need not worry about the setup and configuration details, as *smit* takes care of all that. Upon invoking *smit,* the user merely has to traverse through the menus as shown in Fig. 8.9 until the dialog screen appears, and thereafter set the line characteristics.

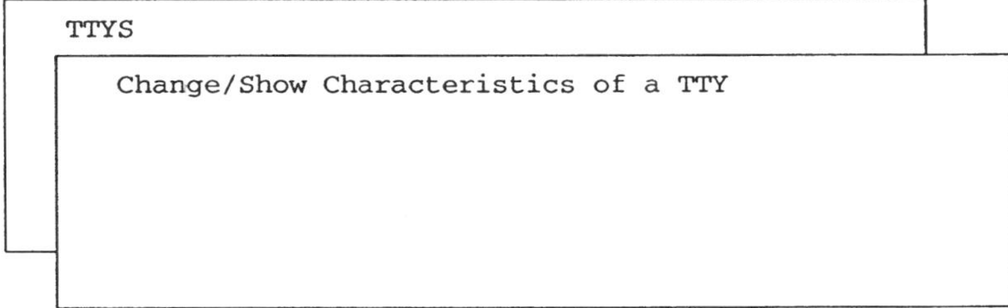

Figure 8.9   Terminal management menu in *smit,* showing its dialog screen.

The example shown in Fig. 8.9 describes adding to the system a new terminal that has an RS-232 interface and is attached to a parent adapter or an async distribution box (refer to Chap. 3). Once configured, it will mean that it has gone through the four steps that are described at the beginning of this section. As far as removing, viewing, or altering a terminal device is concerned, the concept and facilities are essentially the same.

8.9.2 Printer setup

The basic concept of how a file is printed has not changed much since its implementation in the early UNIX systems. From a conceptual perspective, when a job is queued for printing it goes through a spooling mechanism, which handles its own dispatching scheme. By doing so, distinction is made between jobs being queued and jobs waiting to be printed. Because of this, a system administrator is able to alter print priorities, requeue jobs to a different printer in the event of printer breakdown, and preempt jobs from printing, when needed. While the mechanism for submitting, removing, or monitoring a print job has remained the same across all UNIX systems, the commands to perform the tasks have inherited different names based on vendors' implementation. Listed below is an example of three basic printer-related functions along with their vendor-specific command variant. AIX supports all nine variants of the three functions, thus providing some degree of uniformity for those migrating to AIX.

Function	System V	BSD	AIX
Submit a print job	*lp*	*lpr*	*qprt*
Remove a job from the queue	*cancel*	*lprm*	*qcan*
Monitor a queue status	*lpstat*	*lpq*	*qchk*

Despite the underlying concept remaining unchanged, the operational perspective of the printing process is implementation-specific. Consider the most commonly used commands for printing jobs, which are *lp, lpr* and *qprt*. On AIX, these front-end commands hand off the print jobs to a process called *enq* for queueing, which in turn causes a control file describing the request to be written into a special directory called */usr/lpd/qdir*. A special process called *qdaemon* constantly runs on the system, looking for files in the directory */usr/lpd/qdir*, dequeuing them, and running a filter called a *backend* on it. As a result, the file described by the control information is sent to the actual print device. The process is explained in Fig. 8.10.

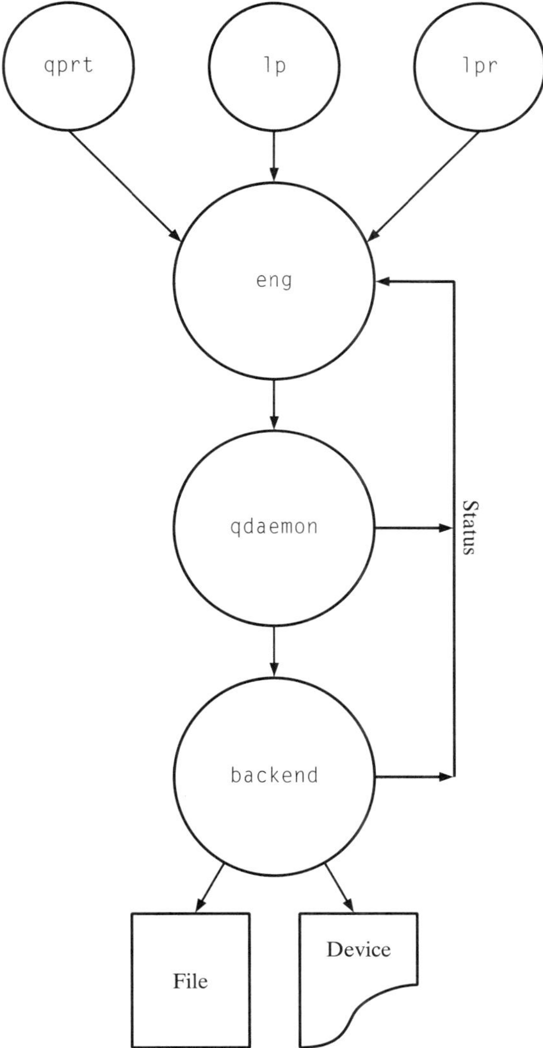

Figure 8.10 Printer queue management.

Printers under AIX can be set up as *real printers* or *virtual printers*. The term *real printer* is used to refer to the piece of hardware that is attached to a serial or parallel port at a unique hardware device address. The interface to it is established through a printer device driver on the system. A *virtual printer* is actually a set of attributes that define a software "view" of a real printer. The data stream (like Postscript or ASCII) is understood by a virtual printer rather than the

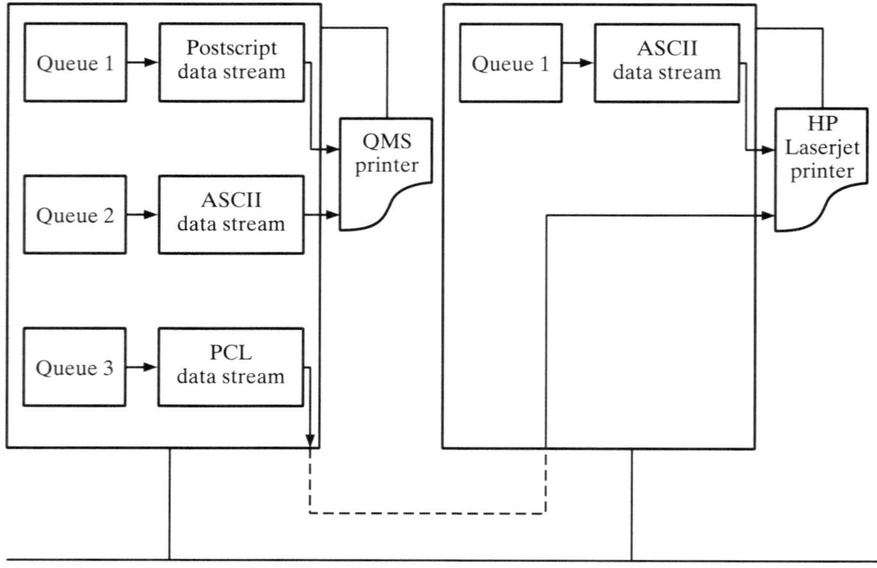

Figure 8.11 Local and remote queue setup in AIX.

printer hardware attached to the computer. Both real and virtual printers may be added on the system using *smit*.

AIX allows management of both local and remote printer queues. *Local queues* refer to printer queues that are affiliated with virtual printers resident on the host machine (refer to Fig. 8.11). *Remote queues* are printer definitions that point to printers on a networked machine. A file called *qconfig* contains all the queue definitions. The first printer in the file is used as the default printer queue for the machine. System administrators can modify these printer queues and alter the default queue by rearranging the stanzas in the *\etc\qconfig* file. Users can also change their default queue by setting up their environment variable to the queue name of their choice.

From a procedural standpoint, printer setup and configuration are straightforward. They consist of a set of steps through the *smit* menus that is essentially similar to that of a terminal. Figure 8.12 shows a sample *smit* screen that prompts for the configuration options.

8.10 NETWORK MANAGEMENT

The main substrate in the communication subsystem that makes the network links work is TCP/IP (Transport Control Protocol/Internet Protocol). The prerequisites for having a host configured on a TCP/IP network are

```
                    Add a Printer/ Plotter

Press <Enter> AFTER making all desired changes

[TOP]
   Printer/Plotter type                osp
   Printer/Plotter interface           rs232
   Description                         Other serial printer
   Parent adapter                      sa2
 * PORT number                         [8]                +
   BAUD rate                           [9600]             +
   PARITY                              [none]             +
   BITS per character                  [8]                +
   Number of STOP BITS                 [1]                +
   XON-XOFF handshaking                yes                +
   Use DTR communication protocol      yes                +
   Printer TIME OUT period             [60]               +#
   STATE to be configured at boot time [available]        +
[MORE...18]


 F1=Help         F2=Refresh      F3=Cancel       F4=List
 F5=Undo         F6=Command      F7=Edit         F8=Image
 F9=Shell        F10=Exit        Enter=Do
```

Figure 8.12 *smit* menu showing option for adding a new printer.

1. availability of a network card in the machine

2. adapter cable for attaching to the network

3. installed TCP/IP software on the host with an assigned IP (Internet Protocol) address

Minimal configuration of a TCP/IP host involves using *smit* to set up (1) hostname, (2) IP address, and (3) type of network interface, as shown in Fig. 8.13. The hostname gives the machine an identity so that other hosts can refer to it by name. The IP address is a 32-bit value that is normally expressed as four 8-bit values, separated by decimal points. The network interface specifies the type of network medium that is being used, i.e., whether it is a Token Ring, X.25, Ethernet, or any other kind of interface.

8.11 PERFORMANCE MANAGEMENT

Performance management is the art of balancing the resources in the computer system in order to derive the optimal performance from it. There are few rigid rules for how to manage performance; however, there is always a tradeoff with every solution. It becomes indispensable that the person administering the system understand all the relevant measures of performance prior to stepping up to tune the system.

In order to best benefit those who have theoretical knowledge of performance as well as those who wish to come up to speed with the

```
                Minimum Configuration & Startup

To delete existing configuration data use further menus

Type or select values in entry fields
Press Enter AFTER making all desired changes

                                            [Entry Fields]
  * HOSTNAME                                [shiva]
  * Internet Address (dotted decimal)       [192.9.200.12]
    Network Masks (dotted decimal)          [255.255.255.0]
  * Network Interface                        en0
    NAMESERVER
         Internet ADDRESS (dotted decimal)  []
         DOMAIN Name                         []
    Default GATEWAY Address                  [192.9.200.1]
         (dotted decimal or symbolic name)
    START TCP/IP daemons Now                 no                    +




F1=Help        F2=Refresh       F3=Cancel        F4=List
F5=Undo        F6=Command       F7=Edit          F8=Image
F9=Shell       F10=Exit         Enter=Do
```

Figure 8.13 A network management menu in *smit* showing minimum configuration for a TCP/IP host.

topic, this section has been organized in three modules. First, the essential concepts of performance engineering theory and principles are explained. Thereafter, available performance-monitoring facilities are described, followed by a discussion of how to fine-tune AIX to best meet user needs.

8.11.1 Theory and principles

The key contributing factors that make performance so important are the orthogonal interests of the person who writes the application program and of the person who manages the resources on which the program runs. As much as a programmer wishes to make use of the maximum amount of resources to run the program as fast as possible, the system administrator worries about how to ration as few resources to serve as many (happy) users as possible.

Although a programmer does not have to know about all the resource details, familiarity with the hardware and software resources on the system and how they work certainly helps in writing a much more effective piece of code which takes maximum advantage of the system's architectural features. The hardware and software resources of System/6000 that can be taken advantage of are described here, followed by a set of metrics that can be used to calibrate code.

Dataflow through the hardware subsystem and the software subsystem may be parallel but are drastically different in nature. Even with their differences, the hardware and the software resources on the system have a common denominator, that is, they both emphasize a hierarchical pyramid of resources. For the hardware subsystem, the most expensive of all resources is the processor pipeline, followed by the cache memories, the TLBs, the real memory, and the hard disk(s), respectively. For the software subsystem, the costliest resource is the process control block where instruction(s) from the currently dispatched program are executing, followed by dispatchable programs, programs in the wait queue, and, last, the executable programs. Recognize that for each of the levels in the hierarchical pyramid (portrayed in Fig. 8.14) the more expensive resources are scarcer than the resources below it. There is room for only one at the top, and as one descends to the lower levels, the abundance increases. For example, a four-stage processor pipeline holds many fewer instructions than a 32-KB instruction cache, which holds many fewer elements than 512 MB of memory, and which in turn can hold a lot less information than a 2-GB disk drive. The other correlation is speed. As one descends down the performance hierarchy ladder, the penalty for access time increases at an exponential rate. For example, time to access an instruction that is in the four-stage pipelined processor takes under four cycles, which is a lot less than that of a 6- to 20-cycle instruction cache access time owing to a "miss," which again is a lot less than a 30- to 40-cycle access time owing to a TLB "miss," which in turn is minuscule as compared to a disk access time of about 15 to 20 milliseconds due to a page fault.*

It ought to be intuitively obvious by now that the trade-off we make in the performance arena is a function of time as well as space. In general, the time required to move from one level of the hierarchy to another consists primarily of the latency of the lower level. In order to best understand the factors that govern this load-balancing game, it is indispensable to intimately understand the impact of each level on program execution.

---

* Here *cycles* are used to denote speed, since the unit is independent of the processor speeds. For a processor running at a specific speed, say 50 MHz, its cycle time is derived as $1000 \div 50 = 20$ nanoseconds. To express the matching speeds of the hardware performance hierarchy, the time required to access an instruction that is in a four-stage pipelined processor will be in the order of 80 nanoseconds, which is a lot less than that of 160 nanoseconds owing to a cache "miss" (using an 8-cycle instruction cache access time), which again is significantly less than 600 nanoseconds owing to a TLB "miss" (using a 30-cycle TLB access time), which in turn is minuscule as compared to a disk access time of 15 milliseconds due to a page fault. Recognize that these values are not rigid, but certainly reflect the order of magnitude for the path lengths involved at the hierarchical stages of access.

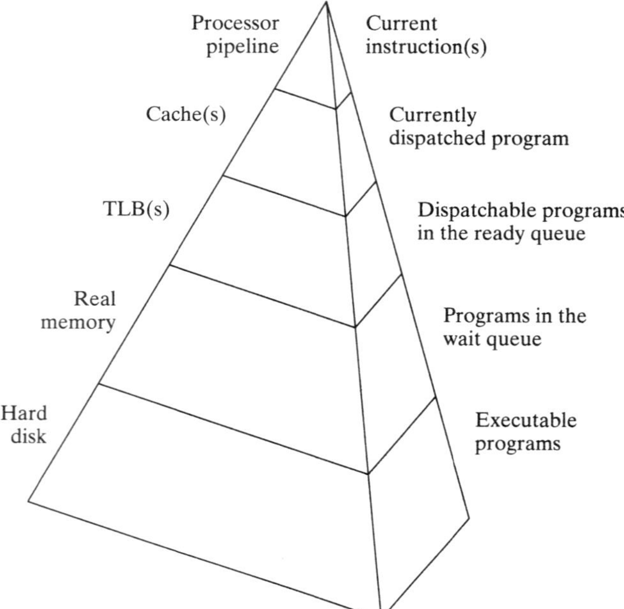

Figure 8.14 Performance pyramid.

The hardware subsystem of the System/6000 has five key components that influence the dynamics of program execution. They are

1. Pipelined processors
2. Instruction and data caches
3. Instruction and data TLBs
4. Real memory
5. Disks

The software subsystem, which is **AIX**, has five fundamental components that influence the dynamics of program execution. They are

1. Current instruction(s)
2. Currently dispatched programs
3. Dispatchable programs
4. Waiting programs
5. Executable programs

The ripple effect of these elements on the hardware and software subsystems shows up in program execution and directly influences the efficiency of execution. To quantify these behaviors, performance measurement metrics are established.

Evaluating a computer system's performance is of interest to a wide spectrum of users. But each perceives the word "performance" differently, based upon the nature of the interaction with the computer. For example, a database system analyst is primarily concerned with the optimal organization of a database. An application programmer is focused on the fastest run-time of software. A system manager looks for a balanced system with fairly shared resources. Despite the diversities of interest, the common premise of concern is performance. Performance metrics fall primarily into two broad categories: external and internal. The external performance metrics are relatively more obvious as they are easier to observe. Some of the common performance metrics are described and explained briefly so that one may measure them using the AIX-based tools.

External metrics:	turnaround time
	elongation time
	response time
	throughput
	capacity
Internal metrics:	CPU utilization
	command processing time
	elapsed time

Turnaround time is defined as the time interval between the instant a program is submitted and the instant its execution ends. For a single program, turnaround time is the difference between S and C, where S is the submission time and C the completion time. Therefore, the mean turnaround time for n programs is given by

$$T_m = \sum_{i=0}^{n} (C_i - S_i)/n$$

where S_i is the submission time for the ith program and C_i is the completion time for the ith program.

Elongation time is defined as the ratio between the observed turnaround time (T_o), and a program's turnaround time (T_p) when it is the only program running on the system. Though the mean turnaround time gives a measure of processing capability, the elongation is often preferred since it is a pure number. The elongation (E) can be expressed by

$$E = T_p/T_o$$

Response time is the interval between the instant of a command input and the beginning of the system response to that specific command. For interactive commands, it is defined as the duration between the instant at which the "send" key of the terminal is being pressed and the instant the terminal starts to output the system response. The variance of response time (rt) is given by a relation

$$\sigma_{rt}^2 = (\Sigma_i \, (R_i - R_m)^2)/(n - 1)$$

where R_m is the mean response time and R_i is the response time of the ith command.

Throughput (V) metric is interpreted as the amount of work done by a system in unit time. The unit of measurement may be expressed in a number of ways. It should be noted that a system's throughput is almost always less than the theoretical value that it claims to provide according to the specifications. A general definition of throughput is

$$V = N_b/T_b$$

where N_b is the number of programs processed during time T_b, the measurement interval. It is to be noted that when benchmarking techniques are used to study performance bottlenecks, N_b corresponds to the number of programs in the workload, and T_b is the total time required for their execution.

Capacity is the claimed value which denotes a system's peak performance rating. A system, when pushed beyond its capacity, results in a saturation phenomenon, causing a reduction in throughput.

CPU utilization is an internal performance measurement metric and is defined as the percentage of the system time during which the CPU is busy. This utilization is then further subdivided into contributions based on the types of CPU activity.

Command processing time (sometimes called the internal command processing time) is another internal metric and is expressed as the time taken by the system to react to an issued command and the instant the CPU starts executing it (not when it starts spewing output, as with response time).

Elapsed time between breakpoints is yet another internal metric that is used frequently by performance analysts in improving the performance of systems. It is quantified as a fraction of the total time for executing critical activities, and is used to identify the source of delays in processing.

All these performance metrics contribute to the global performance of a system. As stated before, there are no rigid rules for measuring performance. However, AIX provides a suite of tools that helps in detecting bottlenecks on the system, and that assists in performance tuning.

8.11.2   Tools and practices

Prior to tuning, one must be able to identify the critical resources on the system that can be tuned, improved, or upgraded, since it is the availability of these resources that determines the performance of a workload on a system. Tools, when used, usually report the availability and utilization of these resources.

It is a common practice to partition the resources into physical resources and logical resources. Physical resources are real components, while the logical resources are programming abstractions. They both have their significance in performance tuning.

Physical resources	**Logical resources**
CPU	Process time slice
Memory	Page frames
	Stacks
	Buffers
	Queues
	Tables
I/O bus	—
Adapters	—
Disk	Logical volumes
	Filesystems
	Files
Network interface	Packets
	Channels

The tools of the trade in performance tuning do one or more of the following: (1) timing, (2) counting, and (3) sampling. Based on how they work, they have been grouped under three categories, i.e., monitoring tools, analysis tools, and tuning tools.

Monitoring tools

iostat.   The tool displays utilization data for CPU, disks, and terminals. The command can be run singly to produce cumulative statistics since the system was booted, or it can be run repetitively to display statistics in real time for successive intervals over a defined duration of time. The report produced can have two types of format: the first type contains terminal-related and CPU statistics, and the second type of report describes disk statistics. Sample output of both types of reports is displayed as follows.

Type 1:

```
tty:    tin     tout    cpu:    % user  % sys   % idle  % iowait
        0.4     30.2            1.4     1.7     96.3    0.6
        3.4      3.6            0.1     2.9     97.0    0.0
        2.3     73.4            1.2     2.0     96.4    0.4
        1.4      1.6            0.2     0.4     99.4    0.0
        0.5    616.6            2.0     7.4     90.1    0.5
        0.5      8.0            0.1     1.0     98.9    0.0
        0.9      0.9            0.2     1.2     95.3    3.3
```

Type 2:

```
Disks:  % tm_act   Kbps   tps   msps   Kb_read    Kb_wrtn
hdisk0    0.0      0.0    0.0            224          0
hdisk1    0.3      3.4    0.2         1713775     165156
hdisk2    0.3      3.2    0.2         1623159     126396
hdisk3    0.4      1.3    0.2          219649     479864
hdisk4    0.1      0.8    0.0          408263      23132
hdisk5    0.0      0.1    0.0           16463      23296
hdisk6    0.0      0.1    0.0           13635      41328
```

netstat. This command is capable of presenting statistics on network and communications activity. It has capabilities to report

1. the active sockets in use

2. contents of network data structures (which are specified in *etc/protocols*) such as TCP, IP, UDP, and ICMP

3. packet traffic (inbound and outbound) distribution for each of the network adapter interfaces configured

4. statistics on participating network device drivers, such as the Ethernet adapter device driver, the Token-Ring adapter device driver, and the X.25 adapter device driver

5. utilization of assigned network memory management routines and size of the page pool being managed by network services

A sample output looks like this.

```
   input    (tr2)   output                input   (Total)    output
 packets errs packets errs colls  packets errs packets errs colls
     157    0       0    0     0    17206    0    4194 3305     0
       0    0       0    0     0      223    0     138  107     0
       0    0       0    0     0      123    0      29   15     0
       0    0       0    0     0      109    0      52   44     0
       0    0       0    0     0       65    0       9    9     0
       0    0       0    0     0       92    0      14   14     0
       0    0       0    0     0       50    0       2    2     0
       0    0       0    0     0       72    0       9    9     0
...
```

The left-hand side of the output displays the statistics on a specific network adapter card (Token-Ring adapter card #2 in this case) and separately reports the number of inbound and outbound packets, along with errors (if any). It should be no surprise that the number of collisions is always zero, since Token-Ring has none! Had the adapter been an Ethernet card, the collision statistics would have been of interest. The right-hand side of the report shows cumulative statistics for all of the adapters, so that one can quantify the amount of traffic on a specific card in relation to the total amount of network traffic affecting the system. Note that the numbers reported by the first line of output are cumulative and the subsequent readings report the delta amount since the last reading. For most of the performance-monitoring tools, this convention is the same.

nfsstat. The *nfsstat* utility is meant for displaying information about the server and client activity, which essentially means the network filesystem (NFS) and the remote procedure calls used by it. The information reported relates to either NFS's server and/or client data, or the server and/or client data used by the remote procedure calls used in NFS.

no. This command displays (and changes) the values of network options, such as socket buffer sizes, low-water marks for the *mbuf* * pools, the amount of memory used in *mbufs,* etc., in the AIX kernel.

ps. The *ps* tool displays *process status*. Its multifarious options allow reporting of information on a variety of system resources on a per-process basis. Some of the key information reported for each process includes (1) CPU usage, (2) approximate memory usage, (3) nice value,[†] (4) number of I/O requests, (5) resident set size, (6) size of the code segment, (7) amount of paging space used, and (8) virtual size of the process.[‡]

A partial output is displayed here.

PID	TTY STAT	TIME	PGIN	SIZE	RSS	LIM	TSIZ	TRS	%CPU	%MEM	COMMAND
0	- S	1:08	6	8	8	xx	0	0	0.0	0.0	swapper
1	- S	1:50	27	148	216	xx	21	32	0.1	1.0	init
514	- R	3274:17	0	12	12	xx	0	0	0.0	0.0	kproc
1599	- S	0:00	0	108	40	32768	2	8	0.0	0.0	biod

---

* *mbuf* (memory buffer) is a data structure in the memory management facility.

[†] In order to interpret the actual nice value for a nonfixed priority process, remember to subtract 40, because 40 is the minimum priority of a normal user process under AIX.

[‡] The value reported is the sum of the paging space used by the process's data segment and the text segment. In general, the text segment remains resident on the filesystem and does not use pages from the paging space.

```
PID   TTY STAT    TIME   PGIN  SIZE  RSS   LIM    TSIZ  TRS  %CPU  %MEM  COMMAND
2808      - S    0:13      9    48   72     xx      1    4   0.0   0.0  syncd
3578      - S    0:00     16   240  324     xx     39   56   0.0   1.0  errdemon
3618      - S    0:01     13   124  184   32768     16   24   0.0   1.0  syslogd
4949  hft/0 S    0:02     31   104  380   32768    303  276   0.0   1.0  ksh
11619     - S    0:00     11    84  140   32768     47   28   0.0   1.0  infod
...
```

sar. *sar* collects and exhibits system accounting reports and is very useful for obtaining an overall view of ongoing system activities and resource usage. It can be used as a display tool to monitor system performance as well as to view captured data from a previous date. Both the sampling interval as well as the granularity can be defined for *sar.* Internally, *sar* calls a process named *sadc* to access system data. Common information reported by *sar* includes (1) CPU utilization, (2) paging activity, (3) disk access, (4) system call frequency, (5) kernel process statistics, (6) request statistics on the run queue and the wait queue, (7) process switching activity, (8) message and semaphore operations, and (9) terminal-related I/O activity.

schedtune. This utility displays (and changes) VMM memory load control parameters and the paging-space-low retry level.

vmstat. This tool monitors real and virtual memory statistics such as page fault activity, process I/O status, and operating system interrupts. In addition, it provides path lengths on disk transfers, system traps, and CPU activity. Like *iostat,* this utility can be run singly or iteratively with a count to produce rate statistics. Common events reported are (1) page ins and page outs which represent the total amount of real I/O by the virtual memory manager (VMM), (2) paging space page ins and paging space page outs that depict the VMM-initiated page ins/outs from/to paging space, (3) address translation faults, (4) device interrupts (related to hardware interrupts), and (5) software interrupts.

A sample out given here describes a few iterations of virtual memory performance statistics.

```
procs   memory            page               faults           cpu
------ ---------- ----------------------- --------------- ----------------
 r  b   avm   fre  re  pi  po  fr   sr  cy   in   sy   cs   us  sy  id  wa
 0  0  11479  113   0   0   1  12   43   0  197  202  115   27   8  63   2
 0  0  11482  153   0   0   5   5   13   0  197  223  132   12   5  80   3
 1  1  11267  438   0   0   0   0    0   0  305  400  248   49  11  31   9
 2  0  11643  120   0   1  31  52  104   0  322  476  252   64  15   4  17
 0  0  11729  124   0   1   0   0    0   0  212  406  147   18  13  69   0
 1  0  11519  667   0   1   1  10   31   0  239  561  194   25  21  47   7
 0  2  11778  125   0   0   5  16   79   0  294  369  226   47  15   7  31
...
```

Analysis tools

acctcom. This accounting tool reads from specific files (usually the */usr/adm/pacct*) and provides accounting information on processes that have been completed. Reporting statistics on the already completed processes is the main difference between this tool and *ps*. Typical information reported includes (1) start time, (2) stop time, (3) CPU utilization, (4) login name of the user who executed the process, (5) the terminal on which the process was executed, and (6) the status of how the process ended.

acctcms. This tool provides accounting information on processes that have been completed, in a manner similar to *acctcom*. The key difference is that this utility combines all the records for identically named processes and reports a combined total for that process name.

accton. This accounting tool works like a toggle switch in enabling and disabling the collection of process accounting statistics.

nulladm. This accounting tool creates a process accounting file with the proper permissions.

filemon. The *filemon* command uses the trace facility to report I/O activity at four separate levels: (1) logical file system, (2) virtual memory segments, (3) logical volumes, and (4) physical volumes. Tracking at the logical file system level yields information on *read, write, open,* and *lseek* system calls. Analyzing the virtual memory system results in availability of physical I/O operations (i.e., paging). Reporting of information at the logical volume level gives I/O statistics on a per-logical-volume basis. Monitoring at the physical volume level allows analysis of physical resource utilization. As such, any combination of levels can be monitored. Normally, this tool runs in the background and monitors filesystem and I/O events in real time. An alternate implementation is to use it like an off-line monitor on previously collected trace files.

fileplace. This command shows the physical or logical placement of the blocks that constitute a file. For more in-depth analysis of file layout, this tool can also be made to report fragmented files within a volume, the indirect block numbers for the file, as well as the file's placement on physical volume blocks. Note that this tool is good for local files only; it does not report information on remote files that may be mounted over NFS filesystems.

gprof. This tool reports flow of control among subroutines of a program and the amount of CPU time consumed by each subroutine. It provides visibility to the sections of the code that are most active and points out spots that require optimization efforts. Two kinds of reports may be generated on a program's run-time behavior: (1) a flat profile showing the CPU time consumption along with frequency of occurrence, on a per-subroutine basis, and (2) a call-graph profile laying out the CPU time consumed by each subroutine plus its child subroutines. The mechanics of how *gprof* works are straightforward. A special library function (called *mcount*) is embedded in the application code when the code is compiled for profiling. This causes a counter to increment each time a parent function calls a child function, which enables tracking the frequency of subroutine calls. A second mechanism (also activated by *gprof*'s compile time option) facilitates sampling of the program's current program counter location each clock tick (every 10 milliseconds) to quantify the time spent in each routine. Another command called *prof* is also available for profiling programs; however, data reported by it is a proper subset of the data available from *gprof*.

lsattr. This utility lists the attributes affecting performance. In addition to displaying the attribute names and their current values, the utility also points out whether they are tunable.

netpmon. This tool uses the trace facility to report network I/O and network-related CPU usage. Normally, this tool runs in the background and monitors network-related system events in real time. An alternate way to use it is as an off-line monitor on previously collected trace files. CPU-related information includes the amount of CPU consumed in network-related events and CPU idle due to network I/O. Device driver I/O-related activities reflect statistics on I/O traffic through Ethernet and Token-Ring device drivers, and queue lengths for transmission I/O. Remote or NFS I/O statistics include remote procedure call requests on a per-process, per-file, per-server basis. Communication interface data includes an inventory of socket-related system calls that have been issued, on a per-protocol (such as TCP, UDP, etc.) basis.

rmap. This utility uses the trace facility to report system calls, process utilization, and I/O events.

rmss. This tool simulates various memory sizes. It temporarily reduces the effective RAM to assess the probable performance of a workload on smaller configurations. Although the tool tends to be optimistic for applications that access too many files, it comes across as a handy stepsaver for scaling memory sizes to study the effect on a workload.

svmon. This tool reports memory status at system, process, and segment levels. It can create four types of reports: global, process, segment, and detailed segment, which are useful for analyzing memory statistics of varying granularities.

time/timex. These tools report elapsed time, user CPU time, and system CPU time used by the execution of a command.

tprof. This utility reports utilization statistics for kernel services, library subroutines, application programs, and even individual lines of source code (of an application program), using the trace facility.

trace. This facility is used for fine-grain analysis and measurement of system events. The tool records a detailed sequence of activities within the system and timestamps it with a granularity in terms of milliseconds. Care should be taken to use this tool sparsely, since a few seconds of data collection can generate several megabytes of data. A sample output displayed as follows gives a flavor for the kind of low-level details that can be analyzed using this tool. Note the detailed chronology of system calls and memory manager faults. This level of detail reveals many types of low-level bottlenecks and aids in debugging complex applications efficiently.

Here is a partial output from *trace:*

```
ID   ELAPSED_SEC   DELTA_MSEC   APPL  SYSCALL  KERNEL    INTERRUPT
001  0.000000000   0.000000                    TRACE ON channel 0
                                                  Fri Apr  9 14:27:34 1993
20F  0.000060160   0.060160                    unlock1 lock addr=11488 lock val=12974 pid=12974
                                                        return addr=152E8
20E  0.000069888   0.009728                    lock1   lock addr=30BE8 lock val=-1 pid=12974
                                                        return addr=88758 flags=0
20F  0.000081920   0.012032                    unlock1 lock addr=30BE8 lock val=12974 pid=12974
                                                        return addr=B5704
104  0.000087040   0.005120     return from system call
101  0.000116224   0.029184     getppid
147  0.000121344   0.005120              GETPPID
104  0.000125696   0.004352     return from getppid [9 usec]
101  0.000142592   0.016896     kill
14E  0.000153600   0.011008              kill: signal SIGUSR1 to process 12461 trace
20E  0.000161536   0.007936              lock1   lock addr=30BE0 lock val=-1 pid=12974
                                                        return addr=36198 flags=0
119  0.000195840   0.034304              KERN_SENDSIGNAL hookdata 0000 000030AD 0000001E
                                         00000000 00000000 00000000
11F  0.000226816   0.030976              set on ready queue trace 12461
11F  0.000258560   0.031744              set on ready queue trace 12974
106  0.000271104   0.012544              dispatch trace 12461
200  0.000283648   0.012544              resume  trace
104  0.000347392   0.063744     return from system call. error EINTR
200  0.000366080   0.018688              resume  trace
200  0.000455168   0.089088              resume  trace
11E  0.000472320   0.017152              issig
101  0.000540928   0.068608     sigreturn
200  0.000669952   0.129024              resume  trace
  .
  .
  .
100  0.001175808   0.039424              DATA ACCESS PAGE FAULT
1B2  0.001203712   0.027904       VMM    pagefault:         V.S=001A.0E43
                                         process_private working_storage
```

```
ID   ELAPSED_SEC  DELTA_MSEC  APPL  SYSCALL  KERNEL    INTERRUPT
1B0  0.001302784  0.099072                   VMM page assign: V.S=001A.0E43 ppage=25F2
                                                  process_private working_storage
1B7  0.001474816  0.172032                   VMM copyparent: V.S=001A.0E43 ppage=25F2
                                                  process_private working_storage
200  0.001499136  0.024320                   resume  trace
 .
 .
 .
```

Tuning tools

Ivedit. This is a tool that can alter the location and attributes of a logical volume.

nice. This utility executes a process with a specified priority level.

no. In addition to being an analysis tool, this command is also used to change (and display) values of network parameters, like *mbufs, lowclust, lowmbufs,* etc., in the running kernel of the System/6000. Extreme care should be taken in using this command since there is no range-checking in the values that one specifies for the kernel-tunable parameters.

renice. This utility is similar to *nice;* it changes the priority of a process.

reorgvg. This utility reorganizes elements of a volume group.

8.11.3   Fine-tuning AIX

The general guideline for fine-tuning AIX is to first identify the workload on the system. Characterizing this workload is often the most time-consuming phase of performance tuning, as it involves queueing effects of network-mounted filesystems and LAN traffic beyond the system's native I/O. Once the workload is defined, a set of objectives is formulated to determine how the results are to be measured. The next step is to identify the "critical" resources that are limiting the system's performance with the help of one or more of the AIX performance-monitoring, analysis, and tuning tools. Having identified the "hot-spots," the subsequent aim is to minimize the workload's "critical" resource requirements, while modifying the allocation of resources to reflect priorities. This allocation and reallocation of resources is what one perceives as performance tuning. The most commonly tuned "critical" resources are the disk drive subsystem, real memory, running processes, and communications I/O.

Disk drives in traditional UNIX systems have always needed periodic attention. Since the logical organization of bytes in a file can be completely different than the physical layout on the disk, data can get fragmented over a period of time. When this occurs, file access results in longer seeks and, as a result, deteriorates I/O performance. The typical remedy for this is to recompact the disks and, if needed, redistribute the frequently accessed components across multiple disk drives. But with AIX, the case is different. AIX on System/6000 implements what are known as *memory mapped I/O* and *I/O pacing* paradigms. The memory-mapped file concept maps files directly in memory and thereby bypasses traditional block I/O and kernel buffers. It alleviates the I/O penalties due to the effect of a file's placement and possible fragmented state on disk. All files are memory-mapped by default. The second paradigm, I/O pacing, prevents I/O-intensive programs from building up long I/O queues. It ensures a fair share of I/O resources for both heavily demanding as well as less demanding programs. If a workload is performing poorly because it constitutes an uneven mix of acutely I/O-bound and lightly I/O-bound tasks, one should look into enabling the I/O pacing option in *smit* by experimenting with the high-water/low-water marks to suitable values (other than the default value of zero which disables the feature).

As far as communications I/O and its fine-tuning is concerned, most of it is a matter of configuration. To communicate across the network, most network protocols use sockets which are made up of smaller memory buffers called *mbufs*. So it is the availability of *mbuf* pools in the network subsystem that governs the performance of the communications I/O. Since the *mbufs* store traffic for inbound and outbound network traffic, having *mbuf* pools of the right size can have a very favorable effect on network performance. At the same time, improper configuration of the *mbuf* pool can impact network and system performance. The key element to tuning *mbufs* is to know how and when to adjust them. Since these *mbuf* pools consist of pinned pieces of virtual memory, they always remain in physical memory and are never paged out. The side effect of this is that the real memory size is reduced. So, to provide the ideal network performance, a minimum number of free buffers is to be maintained in the pools, without degrading network performance. There are options (refer to the *no* command) to specify the minimum number of free buffers for the pool, and to control the amount of memory that is to be allocated for *mbuf* management. When/if the number of buffers in the pool drops below the specified threshold level, the pools are expanded by the same amount.*

---

* The actual task is performed by a kernel process named *netm*.

8.12 SUMMARY

Early UNIX systems like UNIX Version 6 were a lot simpler and required fewer housekeeping chores to add and/or configure devices like printers, terminals, etc. But as the operating system evolved over the years its architectural layout got more complex and so did the sequence of steps for each task. AIX has a standardized system administration interface, *smit,* to handle all the operations. Despite AIX's architecture being significantly more complex than traditional UNIX systems, a generous suite of performance tools enables one to analyze, load-balance, and fine-tune the performance-critical parameters of the kernel in an efficient manner.

A listing of selected files and their partial contents that are relevant to system administration tasks and have been referenced in this chapter are provided here as samples. For factual contents of individual fields and stanzas of these system configuration files, the user's on-site machine should be referenced.

```
/etc/inittab

: @(#)inittab
init:2:initdefault:
brc::sysinit:/etc/brc >/dev/console 2>&1              # Phase 2 of system boot
rc:2:wait:/etc/rc > /dev/console 2>&1                 # Multi-User checks
srcmstr:2:respawn:/etc/srcmstr                        # System Resource
Controller
rctcpip:2:wait:/etc/rc.tcpip > /dev/console 2>&1      # Start TCP/IP daemons
rcnfs:2:wait:/etc/rc.nfs > /dev/console 2>&1          # Start NFS Daemons
cons:0123456789:respawn:/etc/getty /dev/console
piobe:2:once:/bin/rm -f /usr/lpd/pio/flags/*          # Clean up printer flags
files
cron:2:respawn:/etc/cron
qdaemon:2:once:/bin/startsrc -sqdaemon
writesrv:2:once:/bin/startsrc -swritesrv
rcncs:2:wait:sh /etc/rc/ncs
tty0:2:respawn:/etc/getty /dev/tty0
lpd:2:once:startsrc -s lpd
.
.
.
```

```
/etc/environment

# @(#)environment
#
# Searching the current directory last is usually a BIG time saver.
# If /usr/ucb is at the beginning of the PATH the BSD version of
# commands will be found.
#
```

```
PATH=/bin:/usr/bin:/etc:/usr/ucb:/usr/bin/X11:/tools
TZ=EST5EDT
LANG=En_US
LOCPATH=/usr/lib/nls
NLSPATH=/usr/lpp/msg/%L/%N:/usr/lpp/msg/prime/%N

# ODM routines use ODMDIR to determine which objects to operate on
# the default is /etc/objrepos - this is where the device objects
# reside, which are required for hardware configuration

ODMDIR=/etc/objrepos
```

/etc/passwd

```
root:!:0:0::/:/bin/ksh
daemon:!:1:1::/etc:
bin:!:2:2::/bin:
sys:!:3:3::/usr/sys:
adm:!:4:4::/usr/adm:
uucp:!:5:5::/usr/spool/uucppublic:/usr/lib/uucp/uucico
guest:!:100:100::/usr/guest:
lpd:!:104:9::/:
public:!:200:1:Public Logon ID:/u/public:/bin/ksh
andy:!:201:1:Andy Liu:/u/andy:/bin/ksh
chak:!:202:1:Dipto Chakravarty:/u/dipto:/bin/ksh
macneill:!:205:1:Steve MacNeill:/u/macneill:/bin/ksh
barner:!:206:1:Steve Barner:/u/barner:/bin/csh
```

/etc/group

```
system:!:0:root
staff:!:1:andy,dipto,macneill,barner
bin:!:2:root,bin
sys:!:3:root,bin,sys
adm:!:4:bin,adm
uucp:!:5:uucp
mail:!:6:
security:!:7:root
cron:!:8:root
printq:!:9:lpd
audit:!:10:root
```

/etc/filesystems

```
* @(#)filesystems @(#)filesystems
*
* This version of /etc/filesystems assumes that only the root file system
* is created and ready. As new file systems are added, change the check,
* mount, free, log, vol and vfs entries for the appropriate stanza.
*
```

```
/:
        dev        = /dev/hd4
        vfs        = jfs
        log        = /dev/hd8
        mount      = automatic
        check      = true
        vol        = root
        free       = true

/usr:
        dev        = /dev/hd2
        vfs        = jfs
        log        = /dev/hd8
        mount      = automatic
        check      = true
        vol        = /usr
        free       = false

/tmp:
        dev        = /dev/hd3
        vol        = "/tmp"
        mount      = automatic
        check      = true
        free       = false
        vfs        = jfs
        log        = /dev/hd8

/u:
        dev        = /dev/hd1
        vfs        = jfs
        log        = /dev/hd8
        mount      = true
        check      = true
        vol        = /u
        free       = false

/mnt:
        dev        = /dev/hd7
        vol        = "spare"
        mount      = false
        check      = false
        free       = false
        vfs        = jfs
        log        = /dev/hd8

/usr/lpp/info/En_US:
        dev        = /usr/lpp/info/En_US
        vfs        = nfs
        nodename   = r307e9
        mount      = false
        options    = ro,bg,soft,intr
```

/etc/security/login.cfg

```
port:
        sak_enabled = false
        herald = "login:"
```

```
* comma-separated pathnames
        aliases =

defport:
        herald =
"\n\n\n\n\n\n\n\n\n\n\n\n\n\n\n\n\n\n\n\n\n\n\n\rIBM AIX Version 3
for RISC System/6000\n\r(C) Copyrights by IBM and by others 1982,
1990.\n\n\rr310\n\n\rlogin: "

/dev/console:
        sak_enabled = false
        herald =
"\n\n\n\n\n\n\n\n\n\n\n\n\n\n\n\n\n\n\n\n\n\n\n\rIBM AIX Version 3
for RISC System/6000\n\r(C) Copyrights by IBM and by others 1982,
1990.\n\n\rr310\n\n\rConsole Login: "

*auth_method:
*       program =

pw_restrictions:
        maxage = 0
        minage = 0
        minalpha = 0
        minother = 0
        mindiff = 0
        maxrepeats = 8

usw:
        shells = /bin/sh,/bin/bsh,/bin/csh,/bin/ksh
        maxlogins = 0
```

/etc/security/passwd

```
root:
        password = ydZ2kRuNMn1QU
        flags =
        lastupdate = 686603546

daemon:
        password = *

bin:
        password = *
.
.
.
andy:
        password = rG6yzdsOJ9mLo
        lastupdate = 685374568
        flags =

.
.
.
```

```
/etc/security/group

system:
        admin = true

staff:
        admin = false

bin:
        admin = true
.
.
.
usr:
        admin = false



/etc/security/user

default:
            admin = false
            login = true
            su = true
            daemon = true
            rlogin = true
            telnet = true
            subgroups = ALL
            ttys = ALL
            auth1 = SYSTEM
            auth2 = NONE
            tpath = nosak
            umask = 022
            expires = 0

root:
            admin = true
            time_last_login = 708218031
            tty_last_login = pts/0
            host_last_login = r308e9a
            unsuccessful_login_count = 1
            tty_last_unsuccessful_login = pts/1
            time_last_unsuccessful_login = 708221675
            host_last_unsuccessful_login = r87e9a

daemon:
            admin = true
            expires = 0101000070

bin:
            admin = true
            expires = 0101000070

sys:
            admin = true
            expires = 0101000070

adm:
            admin = true
```

```
uucp:
        admin = true
        login = false
        rlogin = false
        telnet = false
        su = true

lpd:
        admin = true
        expires = 0101000070

andy:
        admin = true
        tty_last_unsuccessful_login = pts/9
        unsuccessful_login_count = 0
        time_last_unsuccessful_login = 706901345
        host_last_unsuccessful_login = ruby.com
        time_last_login = 708205182
        tty_last_login = pts/0
        host_last_login = ruby.com
```

/etc/security/limits

```
*
* Sizes are in multiples of blocks, CPU time is in seconds
*
* fsize - maximum file size in blocks
* core  - maximum core file size in blocks
* cpu   - per process CPU time limit in seconds
* data  - maximum data segment size in blocks
* stack - maximum stack segment size in blocks
* rss   - maximum real memory usage in blocks
*

default:
        fsize = 2097151
        core = 2048
        cpu = 3600
        data = 409600
        rss = 65536
        stack = 114688

root:

daemon:

netmail:

bin:

sys:

andy:
        .
        .
        .
```

3

System/6000 Hardware Subsystem—Systems Perspective

Central Electronic Complex

The RISC System/6000 hardware has achieved an exceedingly high level of performance in both commercial and scientific computing areas using an IBM-designed processor as the core of the CPU complex. In this chapter the layout of the central electronic complex that houses the CPU is described in light of its logical view, physical view, and organization. Each of the key components that orchestrates this instruction flow (during program execution) is introduced in terms of its function and respective location within the different parts of the CPU subsystem. The pipelined design of the CPU complex is demystified by tracing the flow of real instructions through each of the CPU's internal pipeline phases.

9.1 OPERATIONAL COMPONENTS

The System/6000 does not have a single microprocessor which can be called the CPU per se. The machine harnesses its power from three separate execution engines, each of which performs dedicated duties. The first of the three execution units is called the *branch processing unit* which processes the branch instructions and dispatches instructions to the floating point and fixed point units. The second processor, the *fixed point unit,* executes fixed-point instructions within the machine. Its other key role is to process the load and store instructions for the floating point unit. This third processor, the *floating point unit,* processes the floating-point instruction stream. Collectively, these three processors are referred to as the *execution units*. Having surveyed the key functions, the positioning of the execution units, along with their interfaces and links, are described in the subsequent sections.

To facilitate the performance of these sophisticated execution units, there is a set of affiliated components as well. These are examined here from a high-level perspective. The first of the affiliated components is the *storage control unit* (also called the memory management unit) and the second is the cache memory. The former serves as the central system controller through which the CPU-bound, memory-bound, and I/O-bound communications are arbitrated. It is sometimes easier to view this storage control unit as a bridge or an address-mapping structure. The latter component, the cache memory, can consist of a separate *instruction cache unit* to manage the instruction stream and a *data cache unit* to store data references, or as a combined *data-instruction cache structure* depending on the implementation of the POWER chip. Detailed descriptions of their internal schematics are explained in later chapters.

The following is a list of the core components of the central electronic complex just described, along with their appropriate abbreviated forms that have been used to describe the components in this chapter and in subsequent chapters.

BPU	branch processing unit
FXU	fixed point unit
FPU	floating point unit
ICU	instruction cache unit
DCU	data cache unit
SCU	storage control unit

The three execution units, namely the BPU, FXU, and FPU, together comprise the core of the central electronic complex. The three functional units—the ICU, DCU, and SCU—together aid in the execution and transfer of information inside the central electronic complex subsystem. *Note that the use of the terms ICU and/or DCU in the current and subsequent chapters will implicitly mean that we are referring to the full-scale POWER architecture that features dedicated instruction and data cache.* It is important to point out that the POWER architecture available today has several variations of its chips with not only a wide range of clock speeds but also a variety of implementations.

9.2 POWER CHIP IMPLEMENTATIONS

The central electronic complex (CEC) of the RISC System/6000, which is based on the IBM-developed scalable POWER architecture, is the nucleus of all the offerings. But the different implementations of the POWER chip set may display small variations in design aspects of the CEC's affiliated components (for example, cache size). Currently, there are three implementations of the POWER architecture. They are referred to by the following names:

- RS 1.0

- RS .9

- RSC

The RS 1.0 features the full-scale POWER architecture. The RS .9 chip set implements a cost-reduced version of the POWER architecture targeted for low-end systems. It features a smaller data cache and a less wide memory bus. The third variant, called the RSC, is a single-chip implementation of the POWER architecture that features a combined data and instruction cache, designed to meet the needs of the entry-level systems.

9.3 LOGICAL VIEW

A logical perspective of the central electronic complex can be best understood through the mutual interactions of the individual components. Figure 9.1 shows the interaction of the execution units, along with their links to the functional units. Instructions flow from the main memory to the BPU, via the I-cache. The BPU processes the branch instructions in the incoming stream and dispatches the fixed-point and floating-point instructions to the FXU and FPU. Together, the three execution units orchestrate the code execution for the System/6000. The components with double-line borders in Fig. 9.1 represent the execution units, while the ones with single-line borders indicate the functional units. The solid lines interconnecting the execution units and the functional units represent the flow of control. At this point, the flow of information from main memory to the execution units (via the cache) should be conceptually clear. Having understood the operational role of the execution and the functional units, we are now ready to look at the physical perspective of the central electronic complex as it appears on the planar board inside the actual machine.

9.4 PHYSICAL CHARACTERISTICS

The physical layout of the boards and planars is discussed in this section, with emphasis on the different configurations of the system currently available. The purpose of this discussion is to present a comprehensive overview of the main components of the central electronic complex; for any intricate details and variations between indi-

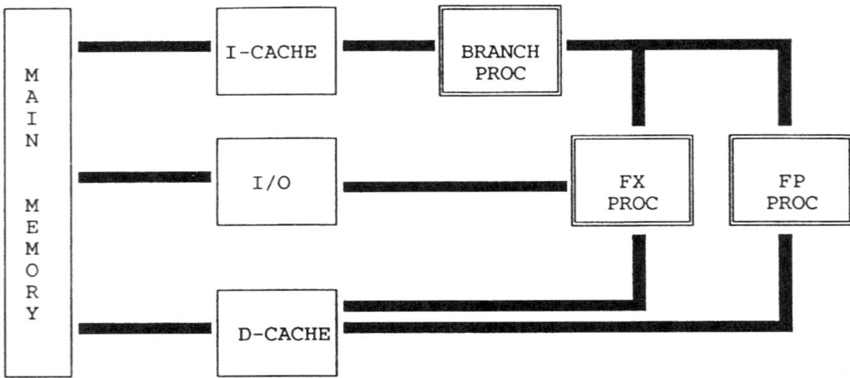

Figure 9.1 Logical view of the central electronic complex.

vidual models, the current version of the Hardware Technical Reference Manual for the specific model should be consulted.

The hardware electronics and circuitry related to the central electronic complex are laid out on three different planars for this machine: (1) the CPU planar, (2) the I/O planar, and (3) the standard I/O planar. Direct benefits of this modular design are maintainability, serviceability, and scalability. The components on each of the three planars are described in detail in the subsequent paragraphs and their physical layout is shown in Fig. 9.2.

9.4.1 CPU planar

Figure 9.2 illustrates how the operational units are all laid out on the CPU planar. The fixed point unit and floating point unit components have been implemented as individual chips, located adjacent to each other. The next component, the data cache unit, takes up more than one chip. The number of physical D-cache chips on the planar varies, depending on which specific model you are dealing with. Figure 9.3 shows the four D-cache chips as they appear on some of the models. For the data cache structure, only the data part is contained within the DCU chip; the cache directory part is embedded in the fixed point unit. Some of the models have only two of the four D-cache chips, the specific layout of which also appears in Fig. 9.3. In addition, there is a third implementation, in which all of the operational unit chips are integrated on a single multichip module, as shown in Fig. 9.4. Therefore, there are external differences among the planars of different models and configurations. But even though one model may seem different when viewed externally, the actual underlying POWER architecture and circuitry essentially remain the same as what is dis-

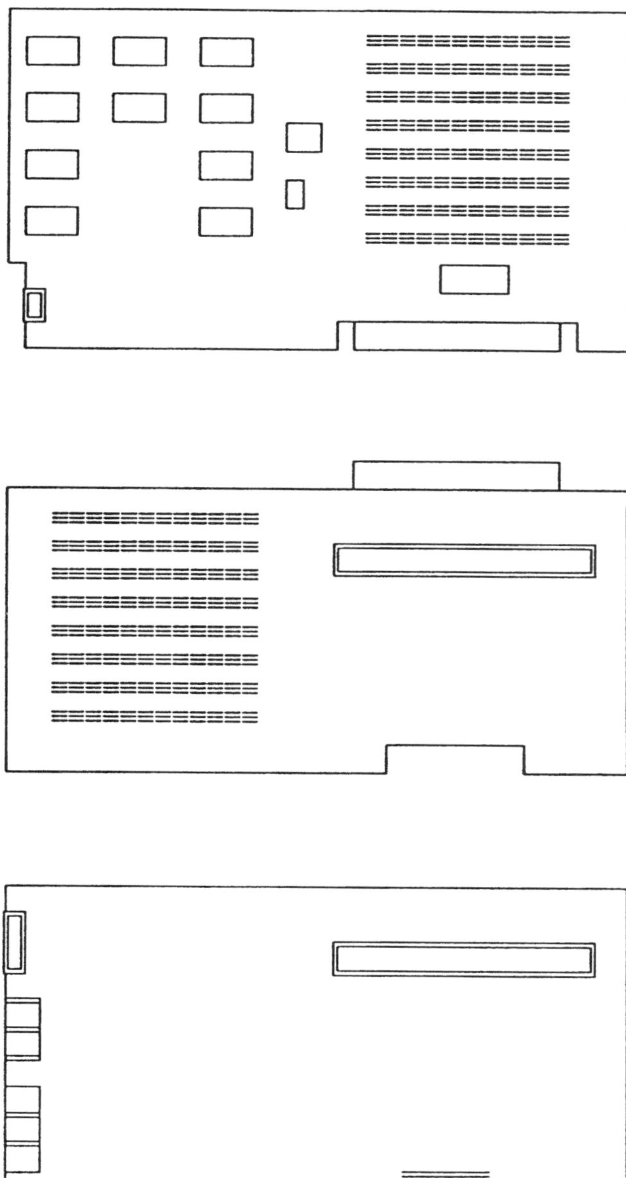

Figure 9.2 CPU planar, I/O planar, and standard I/O planar boards.

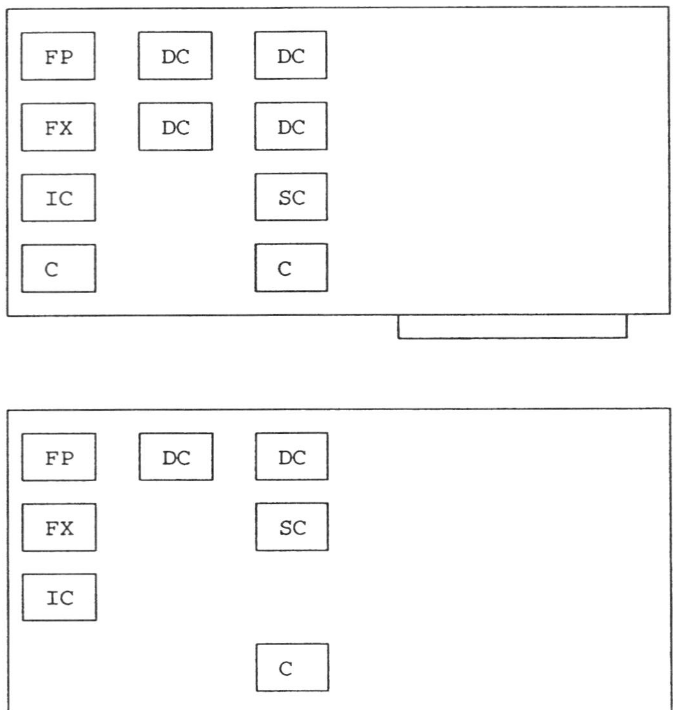

Figure 9.3 Physical view of the central electronic complex as seen on an RS 1.0 planar (top) and an RS .9 planar (bottom). Actual chips identified on the CPU planar are:

FP = floating point unit
FX = fixed point unit
DC = data cache unit
IC = instruction cache
SC = storage control unit

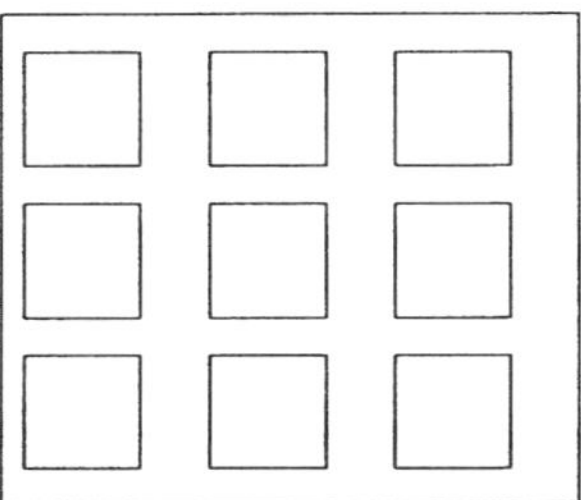

Figure 9.4 Physical layout of the processor chip sets on the RSC planar.

cussed here. The next component for discussion is the instruction cache, which is integrated into a single physical chip together with the branch processing unit. The last of the key components on the CPU planar is the storage control unit which serves as the central system controller to arbitrate the CPU-bound, memory-bound, and I/O-bound communications.

In addition to these operational units, the CPU planar also houses a few accessory elements. Though they do not form the core of the central electronic complex, they still have some significant roles to play. These accessory components include the memory expansion slots which are used for addition of extra memory beyond the current configuration of the system. Also included on this planar is a special socket called an engineering support processor (ESP) port, which, though seldom used, plays a vital role in debugging the System/6000 CPU by loading test programs and monitoring them interactively. Typical use of this ESP port is in manufacturing or laboratory environments. The process is performed by connecting a separate stand-alone workstation to the System/6000 via the ESP port.

9.4.2   I/O planar

The I/O planar, which is the second of the three planars, connects to the CPU planar via a massive 278-pin in-line connector. Besides providing the interface for the CPU planar to communicate with the I/O feature boards and the standard I/O planar, this I/O planar provides the capability to customize the System/6000 family of machines to meet unique customer requirements.

Two of the main components of this planar are discussed here in terms of their specific functions and features. Additional components of this planar are described thereafter. First, the planar houses the I/O adapter slots for the system that is used by the Micro Channel cards. These I/O slots allow end-users to configure and customize their System/6000 systems appropriately. The second component is less familiar to us; it is called the on-card sequencer (OCS). Essentially, it is a microcontroller (an 8-bit 8051 microchip) that has a small on-chip ROM and an on-chip RAM. Its primary task is to initialize the processor complex at boot time and carry out a self-test to verify proper operation of the modules located on the planar. There are three additional modules in the I/O planar. They include the nonvolatile RAM (referred to as NVRAM) for configuration, the operator panel interface for error display, and the real-time clock for time-of-day functions. The NVRAM stores vital system information which may be required for the system boot process (commonly referred to as initial program load or IPL). The NVRAM unit, which is 32 KB in size, normally derives its power from the system power supply. When the system is powered off, the NVRAM remains powered by a battery (this battery itself is not located on the I/O planar). The operator panel interface, which is another module on the I/O planar, displays error codes through the light-emitting diodes (LED). The next module, which is the clock, provides the time-of-day (TOD) functions. This clock chip is a nonvolatile, fast-access (90 nanoseconds cycle time) clock which uses a National Semiconductor DP8570 timer clock peripheral device.* Like the NVRAM, this clock also remains powered by battery while the system is powered off. In fact, it is the same battery unit that provides power to both the NVRAM and the TOD clock. Specific locations of the individual components can be found by referencing the I/O planar diagram in Fig. 9.2.

9.4.3 Standard I/O planar

The standard I/O planar connects to the I/O planar through a common interface connector, as shown in Fig. 9.2. This board fits underneath the I/O planar and contains the interfaces and connectors to mouse, keyboard, tablet, diskette, parallel port, and two serial ports. Each of these items is discussed in detail here, highlighting their layout, capabilities, and design elements.

The circular 6-pin mouse connector provides the interface between the Micro Channel and the mouse itself. The adapter accepts mouse commands from the host and sends them serially to the mouse using a clock and data interface. Conversely, the adapter accepts serial mouse data and passes it to the host by way of an interrupt or polling. The component has a complex implementation. For the keyboard, tablet, and speaker connectors on the planar, there is a single adapter interface which uses a programmed 8051 microcontroller. This keyboard/tablet/speaker adapter provides a bidirectional interface to the I/O channel through a programmable chip (actually an 82C55 peripheral interface). Externally, both of these interfaces look distinct. The keyboard connector resembles the 6-pin circular mouse connector. The tablet connector, though circular in shape, has an 8-pin interface. The succeeding component, i.e., the D-shaped 25-pin parallel port interface, need not be restricted just to parallel printing devices. Being a bidirectional port, it allows attachment of various devices that transfer 8 bits of parallel data at the standard TTL level. The ensuing components are the two serial ports that use 10-pin in-line connectors. Each

---

* This clock chip is used on the multichip implementations only.

port uses a 16550 Universal Asynchronous Receiver/Transmitter (UART) module for data communication. Typically, one would use one of these ports to attach an ASCII console to the System/6000 system. The subsequent component is a diskette connector, which is the last item for discussion here. The connector uses an 8473 floppy disk controller and is capable of supporting a 3.5-in as well as a 5.25-in diskette drive. Together, all of these components on the standard I/O planar provide a central part for attachment of assorted I/O devices.

9.5 ORGANIZATION OF FUNCTIONAL UNITS

Having identified the operational components and acquired an understanding of the logical and physical layout of the central electronic complex of System/6000, we will now delve into its organizational aspects.

As program execution begins by fetching instructions from memory, it would be logical to start with the description of the memory bus. The memory bus is four words (one word is 32 bits) wide and serves as the interface between the I-cache and the main memory. The path leading from the ICU/BPU chip to each of the floating-point and fixed-point execution units is two words wide. A one-word data bus runs between the FXU and the D-cache, while a two-word data bus exists between the FPU and the DCU. These wide buses together provide a high bandwidth for this system. Refer to Fig. 9.5 for a block diagram of the standard System/6000 processor chip sets. Each line represents a one-word-wide path and the arrowhead indicates the direction of the instruction/data flow. In addition to this standard CPU described here, there is a variation available as well. Adhering to the design objectives of the POWER product family to use a common chip set with scalable performance and varying cost, an alternate CPU configuration is available with two DCUs instead of four.

Figure 9.6 illustrates the layout of a cost-reduced version of the same processor chip sets which is used in the low-end or entry-level systems. Note that on these models the memory interface is half as wide; therefore, some of the bit-scattering features which are applicable for the full-size CPU do not apply here. Because of the reduced width of the memory bus, a minimum of one memory card is needed (instead of the usual two) for its base configuration. The details about hardware configuration requirements are covered in Chap. 2. As is evident from Fig. 9.6, the DCU sends the data to reload the I-cache over the SIO bus instead of a dedicated I-cache reload bus. Also, notice that the fixed-point and floating-point buses are dotted together, while interfacing with the DCU.

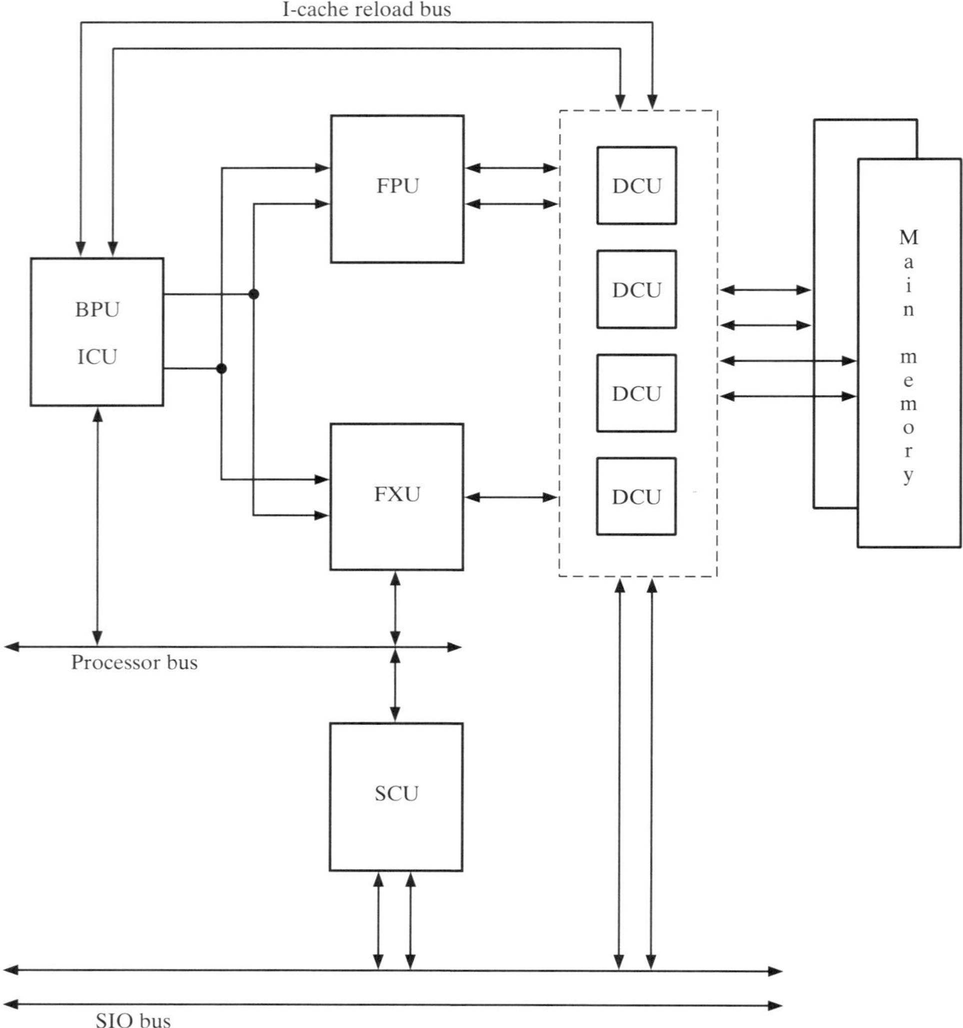

Figure 9.5 Block diagram of the standard processor chip sets (RS 1.0 implementation).

9.6 INSTRUCTION MIX IN SYSTEM/6000

The instruction set architecture of the machine consists of a total of 184 instructions. This large instruction set is contrary to the classic definition of the RISC systems (such as Berkeley RISC I, Berkeley RISC II, and IBM 801 that had as few as 39, 55, and 120 instructions respectively, as referred to in Chap. 1). The availability of indepen-

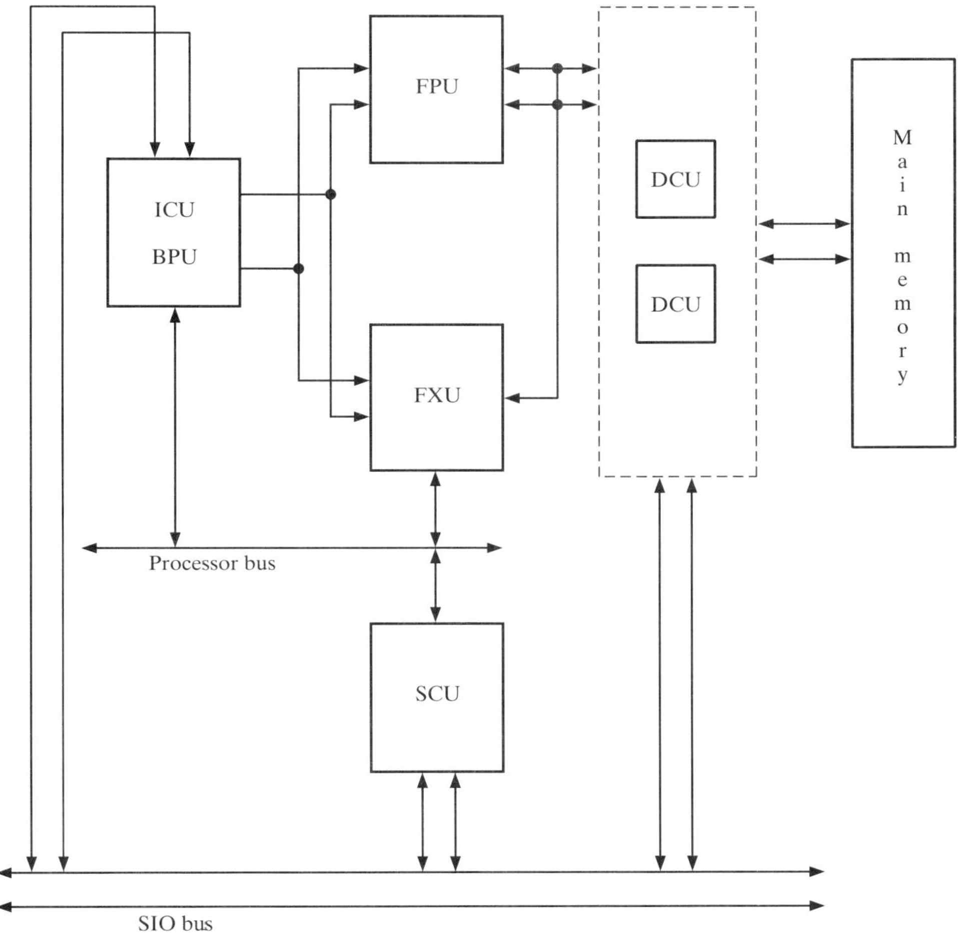

Figure 9.6 Block diagram of the cost-reduced processor chip sets (RS .9 implementation).

dent execution units in the System/6000 that are capable of concurrent execution of instructions justifies a large instruction set so rich that the machine can execute multiple instructions in a single clock cycle. This *superscalar* implementation, i.e., the ability to process multiple instructions in a single clock cycle, has thus become a distinctive architectural feature of the System/6000's central electronic complex.

Recognize that the performance leverage is in making optimal trade-offs between instruction set functionality (the power of each instruction) and the clock cycles per instruction. Hence, the design goal focuses on optimal functions per instruction. First, the cycles per instruction are minimized (using simplified instructions). Second, the path length is reduced as much as possible. As the overall program execution time is really the number of instructions executed (path length), each using the given number of clock cycles that the architecture supports, while the cycle time is fixed for the given architecture, the performance metric of program execution time can be expressed as a product of (1) path length, (2) cycles per instruction, and (3) the cycle time. All three variables contribute equally to the overall performance of the system. Note that variables (1) and (2), i.e., the path length (PL) and cycles per instruction (CPI), can be controlled, while the third one, cycle time, will remain constant for a given architecture. Minimizing the first two variables augments the overall performance metric. Understanding that this performance leverage is in making optimal trade-offs between instruction set functionality and cycles per instruction, you will be able to appreciate how the POWER architecture is defined with as much function per instruction as possible. This results in a parallelism among three independent execution units of this machine, i.e., the BPU, FXU, and FPU. The compilers harness the capabilities of the machine to handle multiple operations per cycle.

Having addressed the performance-oriented design considerations for the instruction set, the instruction mix is described in terms of how the different instructions have been distributed across the three different execution units. The FXU instruction set of the POWER architecture adds up to a total of 134 individual instructions. This set is composed of 79 arithmetic and logical instructions and 55 data reference instructions. The FPU instruction set and the BPU instruction set account for the remaining 184 instructions.

The first set of 79 arithmetic and logical operations for the FXU can be further broken down for survey purposes into subgroups. The first group consists of 24 arithmetic instructions that consist of (1) 14 add/subtract instructions, (2) 5 multiply/divide instructions, and (3) 5 instructions for maximum, minimum, and absolute value. Each of them contains an overflow enable bit. (The ones dealing with unsigned values do not set the overflow bit.) The second group consists of logical instructions that provide bitwise Boolean operations; there are 16 of them. The third group of instructions includes rotate, shift, and mask instructions, of which there are 26 total. Finally, there is the fourth group of 13 instructions that transfer information between the FXU and the BPU. This group consists of 13 instructions which can be further categorized into (1) 4 fixed-point compare instructions (that set individual fields of a rather important register called the condition register that is covered in detail in Chap. 11), (2) 2 trap instructions (that compare two values and force the BPU to take a precise interrupt), and (3) 7 other transfer instructions.

The second set of 55 data reference instructions is essentially for both FXU as well as FPU data load/stores. Out of the total set there are 13 floating-point arithmetic instructions that perform add, subtract, multiply, divide, round-to-single, and register move operations. There are 6 instructions to control, save, and restore the FPSCR. Also, there are 2 floating-point compare instructions that compare two FPRs (floating point registers). Finally, there is a family of unique multiply-add instructions (A * B + C) that uses a fused logic to execute the multiplication and addition operations atomically for three variables. Some of the variations supported for this multiply-add instruction are shown here, using pseudo-assembly language constructs:

multiply-add:	frt = fra * frc + frb
multiply-subtract:	frt = fra * frc − frb
negative multiply-add:	frt = −(fra * frc + frb)
negative multiply-subtract:	frt = −(fra * frc − frb)

This assortment of instructions, including the data reference, arithmetic, and logical instructions, makes up the rich instruction set of the machine.

9.7 POWER INSTRUCTION SET

A complete set of instructions is presented in Table 9.1 for reference.

9.8 PIPELINED INSTRUCTION EXECUTION

Instruction execution in the System/6000 takes place in a way different from the classical machines that normally executed one instruction at a time with a program counter pointing to the current instruction being executed. A pipelined architecture of the three execution units of System/6000 adds a new set of complexities to the instruction execution mechanism, while yielding a high degree of performance. It is legitimate to ask why this new design has been embraced, despite its complexities. The most significant benefit of pipelining is that it provides a way to start a new task before an existing one has been completed. Hence the completion rate of an instruction is not dependent on the total processing time, but rather on how soon a new instruction can be introduced in the pipeline.

Handling of "bubbles" in the pipeline, resulting from indeterminant branch outcomes, adds yet another degree of complexity. When the execution (or processing) stage lies idle on a particular cycle (that is, when the idleness is due to the lack of available input rather than to a poten-

TABLE 9.1   POWER Instruction Set

Command	Mnemonic	Opcode	Extended Opcode
Add	a	31	10
Absolute	abs	31	360
Add Extended	ae	31	138
Add Immediate	ai	12	
Add Immediate and Record	ai.	13	
Add to Minus One Extended	ame	31	234
AND	and	31	28
AND with Complement	andc	31	60
AND Immediate Lower	andil.	28	
AND Immediate Upper	andiu.	29	
Add to Zero Extended	aze	31	202
Branch	b	18	
Branch Conditional	bc	16	
Branch Conditional to Count Register	bcc	19	528
Branch Conditional Register	bcr	19	16
Compute Address Lower	cal	14	
Compute Address Upper	cau	15	
Compute Address	cax	31	266
Cache Line Compute Size	clcs	31	531
Cache Line Flush	clf	31	118
Cache Line Invalidate	cli	31	502
Compare	cmp	31	0
Compare Immediate	cmpi	11	
Compare Logical	cmpl	31	32
Compare Logical Immediate	cmpli	10	
Count Leading Zeroes	cntlz	31	26
Condition Register AND	crand	19	257
Condition Register AND with Complement	crandc	19	129
Condition Register Equivalent	creqv	19	289
Condition Register NAND	cmand	19	225
Condition Register NOR	cmor	19	33
Condition Register OR	cror	19	449
Condition Register OR with Complement	crorc	19	417
Condition Register XOR	crxor	19	193
Data Cache Line Store	dclst	31	630
Data Cache Line Set to Zero	dclz	31	1014
Data Cache Synchronize	dcs	31	598
Divide	div	31	331
Divide Short	divs	31	363
Difference or Zero	doz	31	264
Difference or Zero Immediate	dozi	09	
Equivalent	eqv	31	284
Extend Sign	exts	31	922
Floating Add	fa	63	21
Floating Absolute Value	fabs	63	264
Floating Compare Ordered	fcmpo	63	32
Floating Compare Unordered	fcmpu	63	0
Floating Divide	fd	63	18
Floating Multiply	fm	63	25
Floating Multiply Add	fma	63	29
Floating Move Register	fmr	63	72
Floating Multiply Subtract	fms	63	28

TABLE 9.1   POWER Instruction Set (*Continued*)

Command	Mnemonic	Opcode	Extended Opcode
Negative Absolute Value	fnabs	63	136
Floating Negate	fneg	63	40
Floating Negative Multiply Add	fnma	63	31
Floating Negative Multiply Subtract	fnms	63	30
Floating Round to Single Precision	frsp	63	12
Floating Subtract	fs	63	20
Instruction Cache Synchronize	ics	19	150
Load	l	32	
Load Byte Reverse Indexed	lbrx	31	534
Load Byte and Zero	lbz	34	
Load Byte and Zero with Update	lbzu	35	
Load Byte and Zero with Update Indexed	lbzux	31	119
Load Byte and Zero Indexed	lbzx	31	87
Load Floating Point Double	lfd	50	
Load Floating Point Double with Update	lfdu	51	
Load Floating Point Double with Update Indexed	lfdux	31	631
Load Floating Point Double Indexed	lfdx	31	599
Load Floating Point Single	lfs	48	
Load Floating Point Single with Update	lfsu	49	
Load Floating Point Single with Update Indexed	lfsux	31	567
Load Floating Point Single Indexed	lfsx	31	535
Load Half Algebraic	lha	42	
Load Half Algebraic with Update	lhau	43	
Load Half Algebraic with Update Indexed	lhaux	31	375
Load Half Algebraic Indexed	lhax	31	343
Load Half Byte Reverse Indexed	lhbrx	31	790
Load Half and Zero	lhz	40	
Load Half and Zero with Update	lhzu	41	
Load Half and Zero with Update Indexed	lhzux	31	311
Load Half and Zero Indexed	lhzx	31	279
Load Multiple	lm	46	
Load String and Compare Bytes Indexed	lscbx	31	277
Load String Immediate	lsi	31	597
Load String Indexed	lsx	31	533
Load with Update	lu	33	
Load with Update Indexed	lux	31	55
Load Indexed	lx	31	23
Mask Generate	maskq	31	29
Mask Insert from Register	maskir	31	541
Move Condition Register Field	mcrf	19	0
Move to Condition Register from FPSCR	mcrfs	63	64
Move to Condition Register from XER	mcrxr	31	512
Move from Condition Register From XER	mfcr	31	19
Move from FPSCR	mffs	63	583
Move from Machine State Register	mfmsr	31	83
Move from Special Purpose Register	mfspr	31	339
Move from Segment Register	mfsr	31	595
Move from Segment Register Indirect	mfsri	31	627
Move to Condition Register Fields	mtcrf	31	144
Move to FPSCR Bit 0	mtfsb0	63	70

(Continued)

TABLE 9.1   POWER Instruction Set (*Continued*)

Command	Mnemonic	Opcode	Extended Opcode
Move to FPSCR Bit 1	mtfsb1	63	38
Move to FPSCR Fields	mtfsf	63	711
Move to FPSCR Field Immediate	mtfsfi	63	134
Move to Machine State Register	mtmsr	31	146
Move to Special Purpose Register	mtspr	31	467
Move to Segment Register	mtsr	31	210
Move to Segment Register Indirect	mtsri	31	242
Multiply	mul	31	107
Multiply Immediate	muli	07	
Multiply Short	muls	31	235
Negative Absolute	nabs	31	488
NAND	nand	31	476
Negate	neg	31	104
NOR	nor	31	124
OR	or	31	444
OR with Complement	orc	31	412
OR Immediate Lower	oril	24	
OR Immediate Upper	oriu	25	
Real Address Compute	rac	31	818
Return from Interrupt	rfi	19	50
Return from SVC	rfsvc	19	82
Rotate Left Immediate Then Mask Insert	rlimi	20	
Rotate Left Immediate Then AND with Mask	rlinmlux	21	
Rotate Left Then Mask Insert	rlmi	22	
Rotate Left Then AND with Mask	rinmq	23	
Rotate Right and Insert Bit	rrib	31	537
Subtract from	sf	31	8
Subtract from Extended	sfe	31	136
Subtract from Immediate	sfi	08	
Subtract from Minus One Extended	sfme	31	232
Subtract from Zero Extended	sfze	31	200
Shift Left	sl	31	24
Shift Left Extended	sle	31	153
Shift Left Extended with MQ	sleq	31	217
Shift Left Immediate with MQ	sliq	31	184
Shift Left Long Immediate with MQ	slliq	31	248
Shift Left Long with MQ	sllq	31	216
Shift Left with MQ	slq	31	152
Shift Right	sr	31	536
Shift Right Algebraic	sra	31	792
Shift Right Algebraic Immediate	srai	31	824
Shift Right Algebraic Immediate with MQ	sraiq	31	952
Shift Right Algebraic with MQ	sraq	31	920
Shift Right Extended	sre	31	665
Shift Right Extended Algebraic	srea	31	921
Shift Right Extended with MQ	sreq	31	729
Shift Right Immediate with MQ	sriq	31	696
Shift Right Long Immediate with MQ	srliq	31	760
Shift Right Long with MQ	srlq	31	728
Shift Right with MQ	srq	31	664
Store	st	36	
Store Byte	stb	38	

TABLE 9.1   POWER Instruction Set (*Continued*)

Command	Mnemonic	Opcode	Extended Opcode
Store Byte Reverse Indexed	stbrx	31	662
Store Byte with Update	stbu	39	
Store Byte with Update Indexed	stbux	31	247
Store Byte Indexed	stbx	31	215
Store Floating Point Double	stfd	54	
Store Floating Point Double with Update	stfdu	55	
Store Floating Point Double with Update Indexed	stfdux	31	759
Store Floating Point Double Indexed	stfdx	31	727
Store Floating Point Single	stfs	52	
Store Floating Point Single with Update	stfsu	53	
Store Floating Point Single with Update Indexed	stfsux	31	695
Store Floating Point Single Indexed	stfsx	31	663
Store Half	sth	44	
Store Half Byte Reverse Indexed	sthbrx	31	918
Store Half with Update	sthu	45	
Store Half with Update Indexed	sthux	31	439
Store Half Indexed	sthx	31	407
Store Multiple	stm	47	
Store String Immediate	stsi	31	725
Store String Indexed	stsx	31	661
Store with Update	stu	37	
Store with Update Indexed	stux	31	183
Store Indexed	stx	31	151
Supervisor Call	svc	17	
Trap	t	31	4
Trap Immediate	ti	03	
TLB Invalidate Entry	tlbi	31	306
XOR	xor	31	316
XOR Immediate Lower	xoril	26	
XOR Immediate Upper	xoriu	27	

tial future collision), the idleness eventually propagates through the entire pipeline and deteriorates the overall pipeline efficiency. Several methods to deal with bubbles in a pipeline are available. Some of the standard techniques such as delayed branching, branch prediction, branch history, and decode history have been described in the discussion of pipelined implementation in Chap. 1. After careful evaluation of several techniques to deal with bubbles in the pipelines, the branch prediction method was found to be most suitable, given the architectural traits of this machine.

The branch prediction technique used in the System/6000 is a way to sustain high performance in which the branch target is guessed in advance and the instructions in the pipeline are marked provisionally. After the outcome has been resolved, the temporarily tagged results are made permanent if the guessed outcome is true. These tentative results are purged if the guessed outcome is false, and the operations in progress are all canceled. The algorithm looks as follows:

```
guess branch outcome
proceed on that path
    .

    .

    .
if prediction correct
    < no bubbles in the pipeline >
if prediction incorrect
    partially executed instruction canceled
    < bubble left in the pipeline >
```

It is obvious that this technique is very effective when the guesses are correct most of the time. In programming language constructs like FOR and DO/WHILE loops, an assumption is made that a branch, when encountered, is not taken. The availability of a unique branch-and-count instruction in the System/6000's instruction set makes the task of counting the loop iteration easy. This implies that for a FOR or DO/WHILE loop of 100 iterations, all but the last iteration will succeed, thereby yielding a 99:1 success ratio. For IF/THEN constructs, the outcome has a 50:50 chance of succeeding. In real-life, instruction mixes usually consist of three different types of branches: (1) unconditional, (2) loop-closing, and (3) forward branches. With each of the three branches occurring in equivalent proportions, it is imperative that the unconditional branches occur $\frac{1}{3}$ of the time, the loop closing branches occur $\frac{1}{3}$ of the time, and the forward branches occur for the remaining $\frac{1}{3}$ of the time. As the probability of the forward branches not taken is 0.5, the total likelihood of predicting the branches correctly is $\frac{1}{3} + \frac{1}{3} + (\frac{1}{2} * \frac{1}{3}) = \frac{5}{6}$. So, only $\frac{1}{6}$ of the branches (taken conditionals) may waste cycles and cause bubbles in the pipeline.

Having seen the "why" aspect of the pipelined instruction execution in the System/6000, it is time to examine the "how" aspect of the pipelined implementation. The cycle-by-cycle progress of each of the execution units' pipelines will now be investigated. Each of the three execution units has a different number of pipeline stages. The BPU has the shortest pipeline, followed by the FXU and the FPU. The most significant benefit of pipelining—its ability to start a new task before an existing one has been completed—is achieved through regulating the flow of instructions through these pipelines in the optimal way.

9.8.1 Two-stage ICU pipeline

The ICU pipeline consists of two stages, namely, an instruction fetch stage and an instruction dispatch stage. As a function of the first stage,

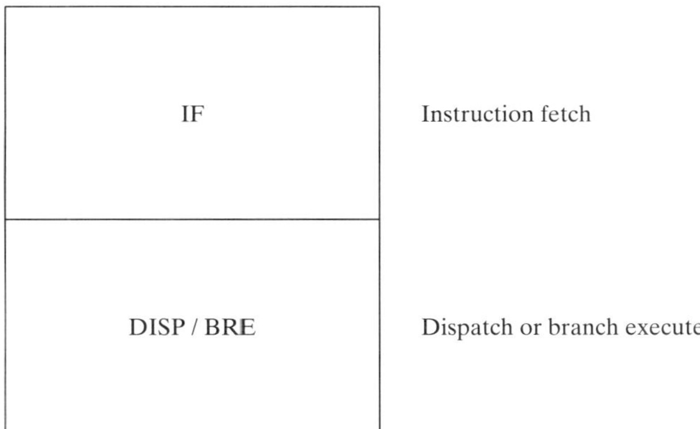

Figure 9.7 Stages of the ICU pipeline.

up to four instructions can be fetched (from the instruction cache) in one clock cycle. The second stage, as depicted by Fig. 9.7, is instruction-dependent. If the instruction encountered happens to be a branch instruction, it gets executed instantly. On the other hand, if it turns out to be a fixed-point or floating-point instruction, it is dispatched to one of the two execution units.

9.8.2 Four-stage FXU pipeline

Figure 9.8 represents the individual stages of the FXU pipeline. During the first stage, fixed-point instructions are decoded (i.e., examined before execution). In the second stage, the instructions are executed. If, instead of being a regular fixed-point instruction, the instruction is a load or store instruction, several things happen: its address is generated, segment registers are accessed to acquire its virtual address, and TLBs (translation lookaside buffers) and the data cache are searched (in parallel). A hit/miss outcome for the cache directory access is known by the end of this stage. The occurrence of the third stage is contingent upon the data item being found in the cache. If data is found, the cache is accessed and the data is returned to FXU or FPU, as the case may be. In the fourth and final stage, the result of the load or store instructions is written to the FXU's registers (also called the register file). If the results were derived from fixed-point instructions, the register file would have been written to in the previous cycle, i.e., the cache access cycle.

9.8.3 Six-stage FPU pipeline

The six-stage pipeline for the FPU, as depicted in Fig. 9.9, is the deepest of all the pipelines. Its first stage consists of a pre-decode cycle

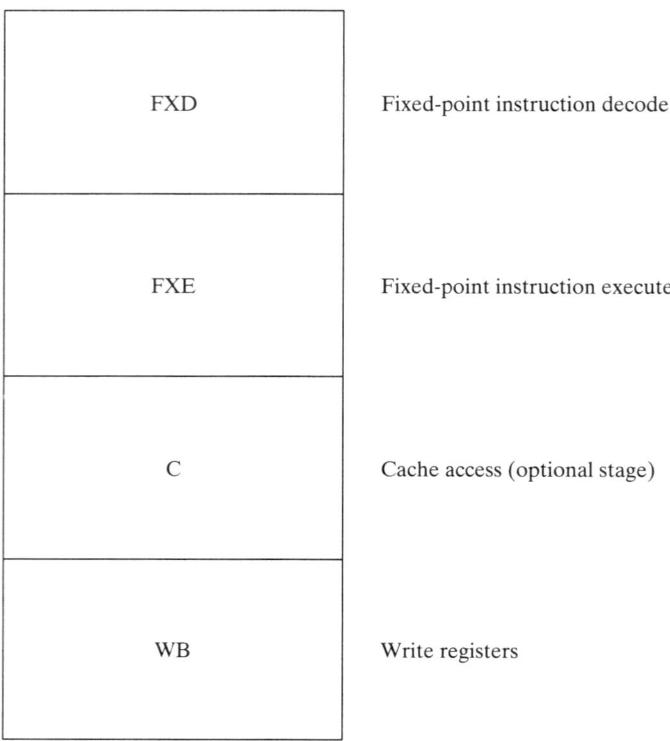

Figure 9.8 Stages of the FXU pipeline.

where instructions are pre-decoded in preparation for register remapping. In the remap stage, the floating-point registers are mapped to the physical registers. The floating-point decode stage examines the registers. The next two stages denote the first and the second phases of the multiply-add pipeline. The sixth and final stage involves writing back results to the floating-point registers.

9.8.4 Instruction flow through the pipelines

In order to best understand the operations of the three execution units and how they orchestrate the complex flow of instruction inside the CPU, consider the following pseudo-assembly code fragment:

```
loop:     lfdu fp8, x(i)
          fma fp10, fp8, fp2, fp3
          lfdu fp9, y(i)
          fma fp11, fp9, fp2, fp4
```

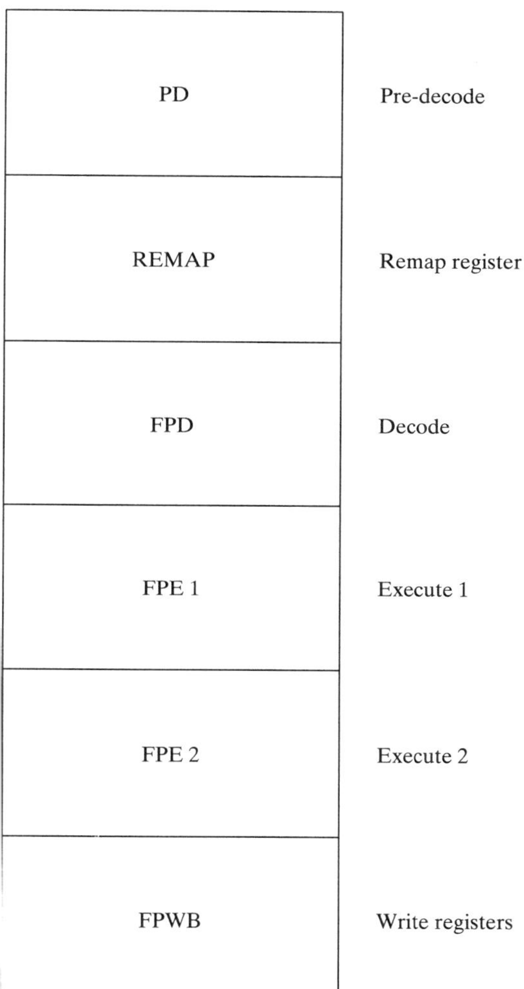

Figure 9.9 Stages of the FPU pipeline.

```
fma  fp12, fp9, fp1, fp10
stfd fp12, x(i)
fma  fp13, fp8, fp0, fp11
stfd fp13, y(i)
bct  loop
```

Cycle-by-cycle execution of the instruction stream is depicted in Fig. 9.10, illustrating the three pipelines for the three execution units. All of the pipeline stages are shown in rows, along with the clock cycles

	1	2	3	4	5	6	7	8	9
IF	lfdu8 fma lfdu9 fma	fma stfd fma stfd	bct		lfdu8 fma lfdu9 fma	fma stfd fma stfd	bct		
Disp/BRE		lfdu8 fma	lfdu9 fma	fma stfd	fma stfd bct	lfdu8 fma	lfdu9 fma		
FXD			lfdu8 fma	lfdu9 fma	fma stfd	fma stfd	lfdu8 fma	lfdu9 fma	fma stfd
FXE				lfdu8	lfdu9	stfd	stfd	lfdu8	lfdu9
C					lfdu8	lfdu9			lfdu8
WB									
PD			lfdu8 fma	lfdu9 fma	fma stfd	fma stfd	lfdu8 fma	lfdu9 fma	fma stfd
Remap				lfdu8 fma	lfdu9 fma	fma stfd	fma stfd	lfdu8 fma	lfdu9 fma
FPD					fma	fma	fma	fma	fma
FPE1						fma	fma	fma	fma
FPE2							fma	fma	fma
FPWB								fma	fma

Figure 9.10 Cycle-by-cycle execution of the instruction through the pipeline stages.

across the columns. Described here is a detailed insight into what happens as the clock cycle ticks away.

Cycle 1:	BPU	Fetches the first four instructions from the I-cache.
	FXU	Idle
	FPU	Idle
Cycle 2:	BPU	Dispatches two out of the four instructions to FXU and FPU. An additional event includes fetching four more instructions from the I-cache.
	FXU	Idle
	FPU	Idle

Cycle 3:   BPU   Dispatches the remaining two of the four instructions that were brought in during cycle 1 to the FXU and FPU. An additional event includes fetching the remaining instruction over the I-cache interface.

FXU   Decodes the load instruction (despite the fact that it is a floating-point load).* An additional event includes discarding the multiply-add instruction (since it happens to be a floating-point instruction).

FPU   Pre-decodes the multiply-add instruction. An additional event includes discarding the load instruction (since it is an instruction for the FXU to handle).

Cycle 4:   BPU   Dispatches two out of the four instructions that were brought in during cycle 2 to FXU and FPU. The fetch stage is idle.

FXU   Executes the load instruction to generate an address. Additional events include decoding the load instruction and discarding the multiply-add instruction from the incoming instruction pair.

FPU   Remaps the floating-point load and the multiply-add instruction. An additional event includes pre-decoding the next incoming instruction pair.

Cycle 5:   BPU   Executes the branch instruction. Additional events include dispatching the remaining two out of the four instructions brought in during cycle 2 to FXU and FPU, while fetching four more new instructions from the I-cache, as a result of the next iteration of the loop.

FXU   The load instruction accesses the D-cache. Additional events include executing the second load instruction to generate an address, and decoding the store instruction (despite the fact that it is a floating-point store),* while discarding the multiply-add instruction.

FPU   Decodes the first multiply-add instruction after the remap stage. Additional events include remapping the second pair of floating-point load and multiply-add instructions, while pre-decoding the third incoming instruction pair.

Cycle 6:   BPU   Dispatches two out of the four instructions to FXU and FPU again, while fetching four more instructions from the I-cache.

---

* FXU conducts the load and store for fixed-point as well as floating-point instructions.

	FXU	The second load instruction accesses the D-cache. Additional events include executing the store instruction to generate an address, and decoding the second store instruction, while discarding the multiply-add instruction.
	FPU	Executes the first phase of the first multiply-add instruction. Three additional events include decoding the second multiply-add instruction after the remap stage, thus ensuring that required registers are free;* remapping the third instruction pair; and pre-decoding the fourth incoming instruction pair.
Cycle 7:	BPU	Dispatches the remaining two instructions that were brought in during cycle 5 to FXU and FPU. An additional event includes fetching the remaining instruction over the I-cache interface.
	FXU	Nothing accesses the D-cache in this cycle. Events include executing the second store instruction to generate an address, and decoding the subsequent instruction pair.
	FPU	Executes the second phase of the first multiply-add instruction. Four additional events include starting the first phase of execution for the second multiply-add instruction, decoding the third multiply-add instruction, remapping the fourth instruction pair, and pre-decoding the subsequent incoming instructions.
Cycle 8:	BPU	Dispatches two out of the four instructions that were brought in during cycle 6 to the FXU and FPU. The fetch stage remains idle.
	FXU	Nothing accesses the D-cache in this cycle. Events include executing the first load instruction (from the second iteration of the loop) to generate an address, and decoding the incoming instruction pair.
	FPU	Writes back the results of the floating-point arithmetic to the FPU register file. Five additional events include continuing through the second phase of the multiply-add operation for the first multiply-add instruction, starting the first phase of execution for the second multiply-add instruction, decoding the fourth multiply-add instruction, remapping the fifth instruction pair, and pre-decoding the subsequent incoming instructions.
Cycle 9:	BPU	Similar to cycle 5.
	FXU	Similar to cycle 5.

---

* The principle of the register remap mechanism is explained in detail in Chap. 12.

FPU   Similar to cycle 5 (except for the fact that the last three stages of the six-stage FPU pipeline, i.e., the two execution stages of the multiply-add operation and the write-back stage of the floating-point register file, remain active).

An analysis of this cycle-by-cycle execution of the instruction stream reveals several interesting observations. Observe from the pipeline diagram of Fig. 9.10 that the deepest of the pipelines were kept 100 percent busy. The next noteworthy phenomenon is that the branch instructions caused no additional bubbles in the pipelines. The third point to be noted is that the final stage of the FXU pipeline, which is the register-file write-back stage, has remained empty. The explanation for this is the fact that the instructions being processed were all floating-point loads; hence, there is no scope for a write-back to the register file. Also recognize that when data is produced in cycle 10 (not shown in the illustration), the store will get written to the D-cache at the first free cache cycle. Among the finer observations, from cycle 2 onward it can be seen that the instruction pairs are dispatched to both the FXU as well as to the FPU simultaneously. The redundant instruction merely gets discarded upon reaching the decode stage. Although redundant, this instruction does inform one execution unit about its synchronization point with respect to the other execution unit. In this way, the FXU and the FPU can stay informed about each other's progress. (Additional details about synchronization mechanics are discussed in Chap. 11.)

9.9   SUMMARY

The presence of multiple operational components does not allow a microprocessor to be called the CPU for this machine. The operational components are collectively referred to as the central electronic complex (CEC). Its three execution units, namely the BPU, FXU, and FPU, facilitate the actual code execution, with the allied components such as the cache memories and the storage control unit ensuring timely availability of the data and instructions. From a physical implementation view, there is no single motherboard; instead, the components are assembled across three independent planars.

With regard to the instruction set, the POWER architecture supports a total of 184 instructions. A complete list of instructions has been included for reader reference. Note that almost all of the instructions are implemented in hardware. Hence, the instructions execute faster. The detailed tour of the three execution units of the central electronic complex described the pipelined layout of the execution units and the superscalar implementation of the central electronic complex.

A description of the execution unit's functions and the pipelined stages is presented here.

BPU functions:

- Processes branches in the instruction stream
- Dispatches instructions to the floating-point and fixed-point units

FXU functions:

- Processes all fixed-point instructions
- Also processes the load and store instructions for the floating-point unit

FPU function:

- Processes all floating-point instructions

BPU stages:

1. Instructions are fetched from I-cache
2. Instructions executed/dispatched

FXU stages:

1. Instructions are decoded and register file gets accessed for operands
2. Instructions get executed
3. If applicable, the D-cache is accessed
4. Register file gets written

FPU stages:

1. Instructions are pre-decoded for remapping
2. FP registers are mapped to physical registers
3. FP registers get read
4. Executes the multiply and add operations
5. Register file gets written

Cache Memory Organization

Cache memories are high-speed memories that are used to reference nonresident parts of an executing program before accessing the main memory of the computer. Research studies and statistics have shown that there is a strong tendency for the memory accesses to be clustered around small regions of memory over a short period of time. Hence, a fast access to reference-selected regions of memory that are frequently used is deemed desirable. This is where the significance of a cache comes in. Cache memory implementation has become standard in all modern computers, as it facilitates a way to conduct a rapid access to information without losing precious machine cycles to go to the main memory. As the speeds of modern computers have continued to increase, larger and faster cache memories have become necessary. A concept of multiple levels of cache memories (such as primary and secondary) have also been introduced in modern workstations so that multiple tiers of caches may be accessed before resorting to the main memory.

10.1 COMPARISON OF CACHE AND VIRTUAL MEMORY

Cache memory is functionally equivalent to the virtual memory of a computer. A conceptual positioning of the processor, cache memory, and main memory in Fig. 10.1 illustrates how the cache is located physically closer to the processor for optimal access. Upon the generation of an

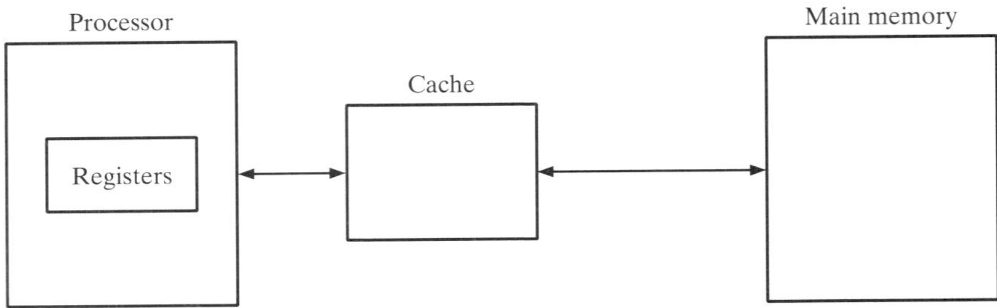

Figure 10.1 A conceptual positioning of the processor, cache, and main memory.

address reference, a lookup is first made in the cache; if the cache query turns out to be negative, then the request is presented to the main memory of the computer. In effect, the cache serves as a lookup table for information retrieval, as much as the main memory does. They both rely on the correlation properties observed in the sequence of address references. Their sole difference is in the implementation. Cache implementations are radically different from virtual memory implementations because of the speed requirements. The speed of accessing a cache is typically on the order of magnitude of ten or more times faster than that of a memory access. To achieve this exceedingly high access speed, cache memory is implemented in hardware, while virtual memory is implemented in software. Generally, cache memory is a lot smaller in size than the main memory. Its size is generally a cost-performance tradeoff, since it happens to be lot more expensive than conventional memory. A summary of the comparison between cache and virtual memory as discussed here is shown in Fig. 10.2.

Data is referenced in a similar fashion by the cache as well as the main memory. When an item available in the virtual memory is not found in the main memory, we refer to the phenomenon as a *page fault,* which subsequently results in fetching nonresident pages from the disk. In a similar way, when an item is not found in the cache memory, we say that a *cache miss* has occurred. If we look at the flow of control, or the footprint, of referencing nonresident data at the time of program execution, we observe multiple levels of indexing. When a CPU requests an instruction or data, the first level of access occurs in the cache memory. If the item is found in the cache, then the event is referred to as a *cache hit.* If the item is absent, a cache miss occurs. As a result, the main memory is now searched as a second level of access. If the item still remains missing, a page fault occurs, resulting in a subsequent access to the auxiliary (or disk memory) of the computer. Using this procedure of multiple levels of referencing, programs are executed in an orderly and efficient manner.

Criteria	Cache	Virtual memory
Item not found	Cache miss	Page fault (PF)
Miss /PF	Access main memory	Access disk
Miss /PF time	Short (e.g., 30 ns)	Long (e.g., 300 ns)
Miss /PF processing	In hardware	In software
Block /page size	Small (e.g., 128 bytes)	Large (e.g., 4 KB)

Figure 10.2 Comparison of cache and virtual memory.

10.2 PERFORMANCE IMPLICATIONS

The effect on performance of cache memory and virtual memory varies significantly. A comparative study of the two yields interesting inference. With regard to cache misses, the fast memory is cache and the slow memory is main memory; as far as page faults are concerned, the fast memory is main memory and the slow memory is the auxiliary disk memory (also called paging space). Although cache misses may be costly, their access time remains minuscule compared to a page fault. So, one would always prefer a cache miss over a page fault. Second, it makes sense to have a bigger-size cache memory which minimizes the chance of cache misses and increases the probability of cache hits. Third, it likewise makes sense to separate the cache memory area into instructions and data areas, which minimizes selection conflicts. In order to understand the implications of these design enhancements to a cache memory for improving the overall performance of the executing programs, the actual layout of a generic cache needs to be studied.

10.3 CACHE DESIGN BASICS

The typical implementation of a cache memory consists of a partitioned *set* of *lines,* where each set contains one or more lines. Lines (sometimes referred to as *blocks*) are the basic units of transfer between the cache itself and the main memory. Figure 10.3 shows an example of a

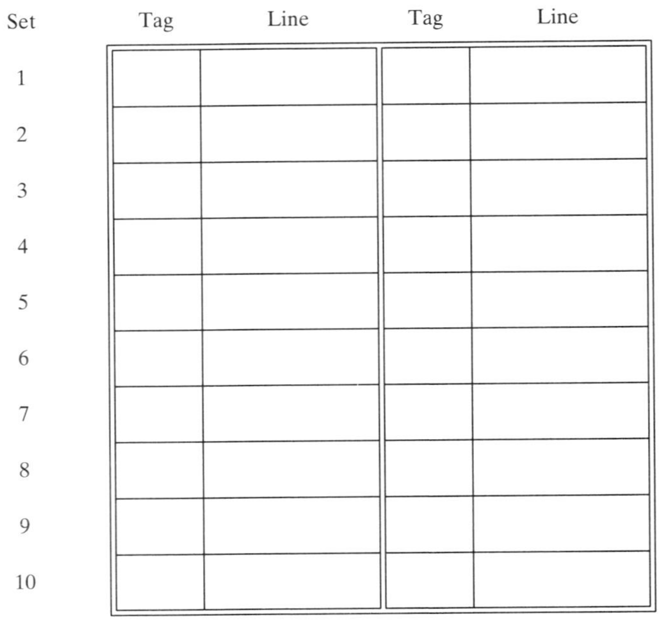

Set   Tag   Line   Tag   Line

1

2

3

4

5

6

7

8

9

10

Figure 10.3 Organization of a two-way set-associative cache with 10 sets.

classic cache memory, where the cache has been partitioned two ways and has 10 sets. These types of caches are commonly referred to as being *set-associative*. To restate the parameters that explain a cache design comprehensively, the first one is the number of sets (N) in a cache. The second parameter is the associativity of the cache (K) that determines how many lines are present in a set. The third parameter is the size of a cache line (L), which explains how many bytes there are in a line. Henceforth, the total number of bytes in a cache is the product of L, K, and N.

$$\text{Cache size} = L \times K \times N$$

It is rather common to find a set-associative type of cache memory implementation in present-day workstations. In this scheme, each address gets mapped to a particular set by means of an address translation operation. The address itself is partitioned for conducting a cache search, as shown in Fig. 10.4. Designated bits in the address are used to (1) index the reference into the tag for the line selector, (2) determine the set number to get to the specific set, and (3) use the offset to access a specific datum. Since a given tag only matches a particular set, the entire cache does not get searched in entirety; only that

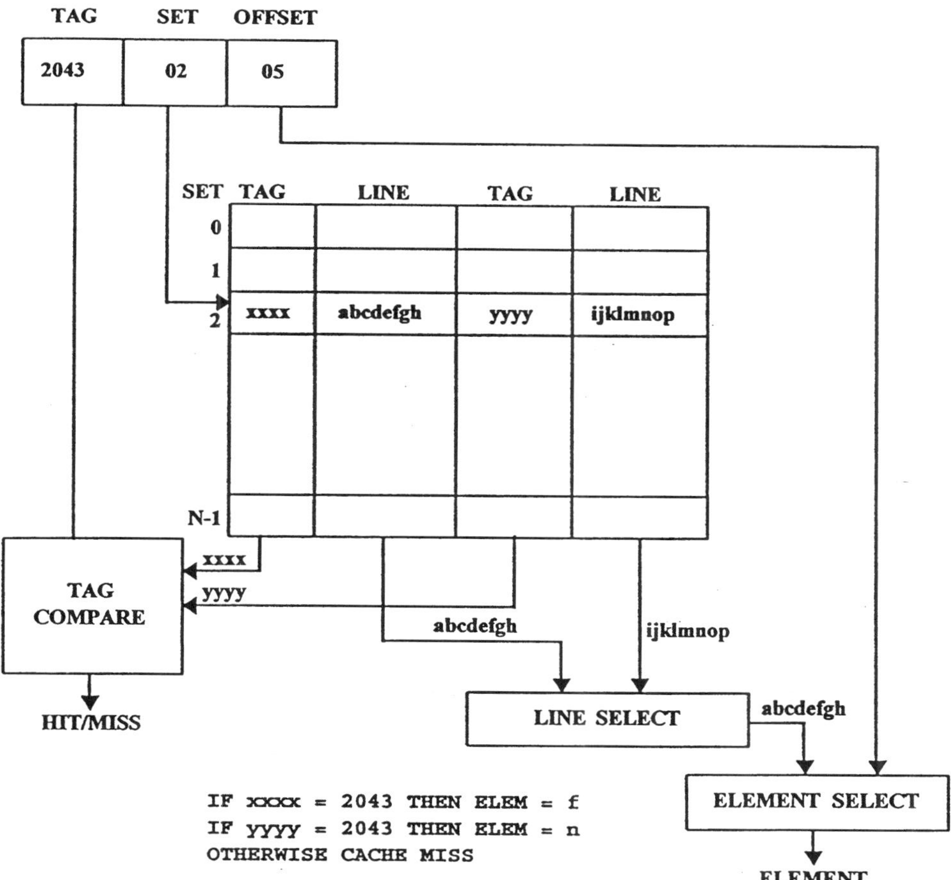

Figure 10.4 Data access mechanism in a two-way set-associative cache. Breakdown of a cache referencing address field where designated bits are used to (1) index into the tag for the line selector, (2) determine the set number to get the specific set, and (3) use the offset to access a specific datum.

set to which the address is mapped gets searched for the reference. If you were to consider the search for the address reference shown in Fig. 10.4, the search occurs by simultaneously searching both the cache directory entries. The data in the lines is also read concurrently. Thereafter, both of the directory entries are matched with the tag reference, using a set of comparator logic circuits as shown in Fig. 10.5; the results are subsequently multiplexed through an OR gate to determine a hit or a miss.

On current systems with virtual memory as well as set-associative cache, the address translation step prior to lookup becomes slightly more complex. The virtual page number from the virtual address ref-

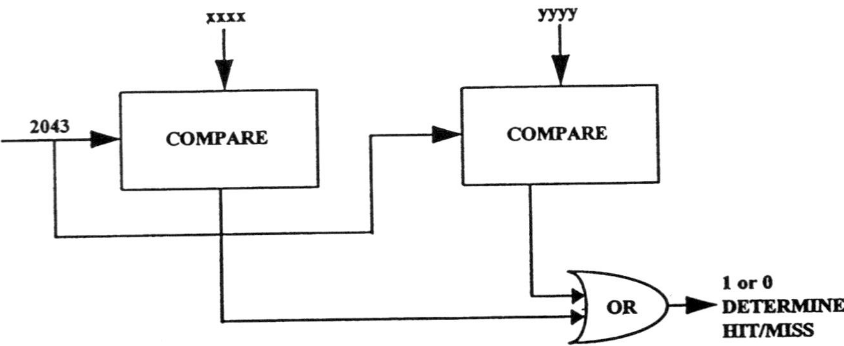

Figure 10.5 Comparator logic that is used to match cache directory entries with tag references.

erence must first be translated to a real page number. This operation is performed with the help of an intermediate structure called the translation lookaside buffer (TLB). Figure 10.6 shows where the TLB interface is present. Once the real page number has been generated, the comparison step for tag references with the directory entries remains the same as before.

The design of cache memories can be an area of research by itself. The rationale for cache designs and analysis for cache efficiency is beyond the scope of this book. A set of basic concepts is covered here, in terms of the design philosophies behind the cache memory of the System/6000. As one cannot accurately model the workloads for various types of cache layouts, there is a need to stay focused on achieving an acceptable degree of performance. We rely on good judgment and trial-and-error results of cache simulators to determine the optimal layout of a cache memory. If we were to consider the variable parameters for a cache, there are only three:

1. Number of sets

2. Associativity of the cache

3. Size of the cache line

Generally, for short lines, increasing the line length decreases the miss ratio (probability of a miss), since a miss fetches more useful data into the cache. Conversely, for long lines, increasing the line length increases the miss ratio, since a miss results in fetching long lines with unnecessary data that replace the useful data in the cache. In other words, we find that for short lines, line length is inversely proportional to the miss ratio; whereas, for long lines, line length is directly proportional to the miss ratio.

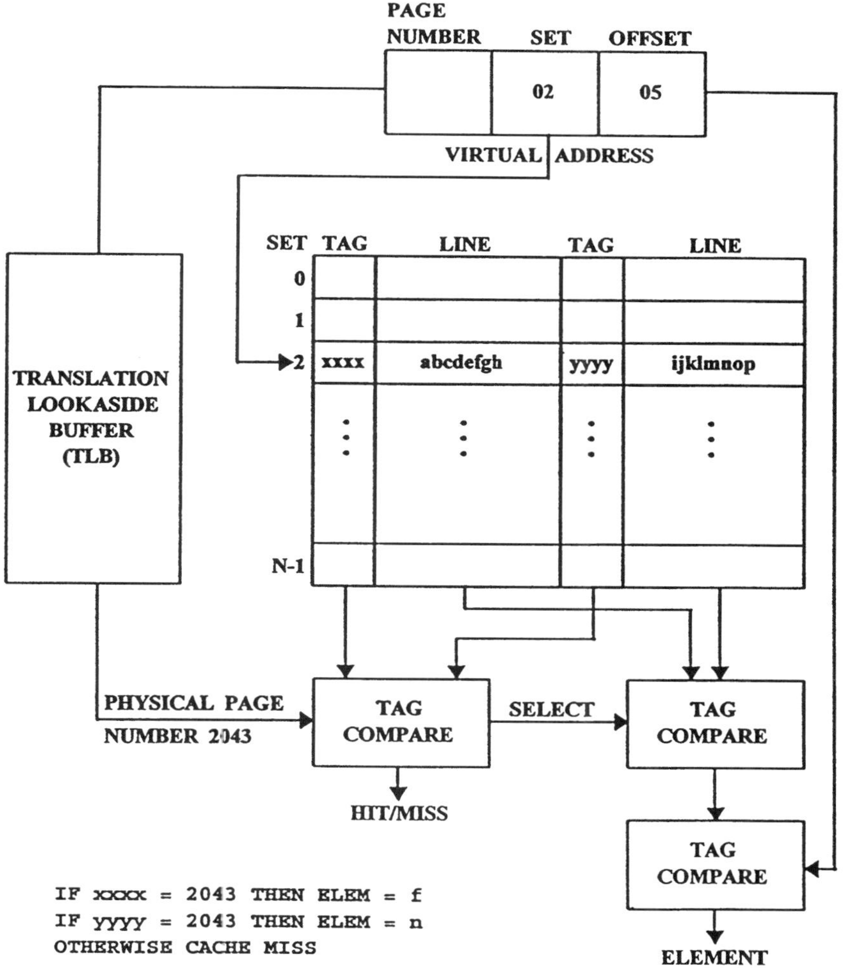

Figure 10.6 Organization of a two-way set-associative cache with virtual memory.

$$\text{for short lines, line length} \propto \frac{1}{\text{miss ratio}}$$

$$\text{for long lines, line length} \propto \text{miss ratio}$$

We infer that if we were to plot a graph for cache-miss ratio versus the cache-line length, there would be a well-defined optimal point in the graph, as represented by Fig. 10.7. By tweaking any one of the three parameters alone, the effectiveness of the cache cannot be achieved. It is the sum total effect of the line length that needs to

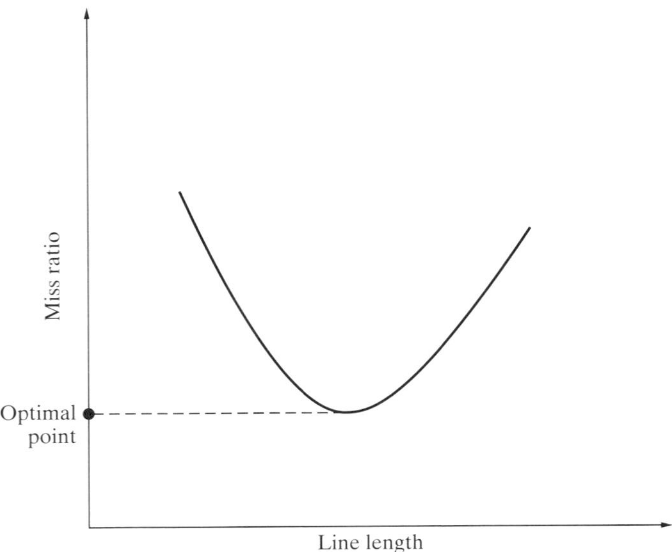

Figure 10.7 Graph for cache-miss ratio versus the cache-line length.

be reduced. System/6000 is able to achieve this performance boost by reducing the effect of its cache line length by implementing a *fetch bypass* technique to load its line while sending the item to the CPU in parallel, thereby bypassing the cache. This results in a saving of one clock cycle, thus boosting performance.

Performance implications in cache memory layout discussed in the previous section indicate that we always prefer a cache miss over a page fault during a program execution. This implicitly states that a larger cache size is preferable whenever possible. As cache memory is expensive, this criterion ends up being a cost-performance factor rather than a feature for a given machine. The System/6000 happens to provide a generous cache size for effective execution of programs. The other performance implication, i.e., separating the cache memory area for instructions and data to minimize selection conflicts, has been addressed in System/6000 by supplying a dedicated instruction and a dedicated data cache. The size of the data cache can be 64 KB or 32 KB and the size of the instruction cache can be 32 KB or 8 KB, based on individual models. Associated with each of the caches, there is a set of TLBs: an I-TLB (32 entries with a two-way associativity) and a D-TLB (128 entries with a two-way associativity).

10.4   I-CACHE ORGANIZATION

The instruction cache unit (ICU) is located on the same physical chip as the branch processing unit (BPU) in System/6000. The integrated design of this chip is achieved through embedding more than 200,000 logic and 550,000 memory transistors into a single silicon die that measures about 10.7 mm^2 in size and is equipped with 252 signal pins.

10.4.1   I-cache layout

In light of the cache design basics reviewed in Sec. 10.3, the I-cache of the System/6000 is described here to explain its design layout. It is a two-way set-associative cache, consisting of 64 sets. This layout gives the I-cache a total of 128 lines. As there are 64 bytes per line, the total cache size adds up to 8 KB. Figure 10.8 explains the breakdown of set and line mapping in further detail. A line size any larger than 64 bytes would have increased the miss ratio in a cache of this size (according to simulation studies) and also would have resulted in longer than eight cycles to reload the cache line following a miss (since the instruction reload bus is only two instructions wide). For models configured with a bigger I-cache, the number of sets has been increased to 256, thereby further increasing the already generous size of the I-cache to 32 KB. As far as the various interfaces to I-cache are concerned, it has a two-word interface to the main memory from where instructions are brought in, a two-word interface to both the FXU and the FPU, and a one-word interface to a processor bus that is a common connector for the FXU, SCU, and ICU.

To comprehend how this I-cache works, some of its functional layout needs to be understood. The I-cache has a directory part and an array part. The directory part contains real address bits, while the array part contains the instructions. Specific bits in the real address, which is

I-cache organization :

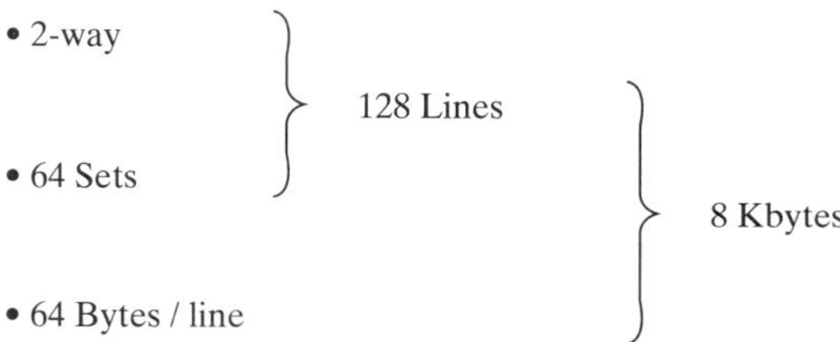

Figure 10.8 Description of the I-cache in terms of its sets and lines.

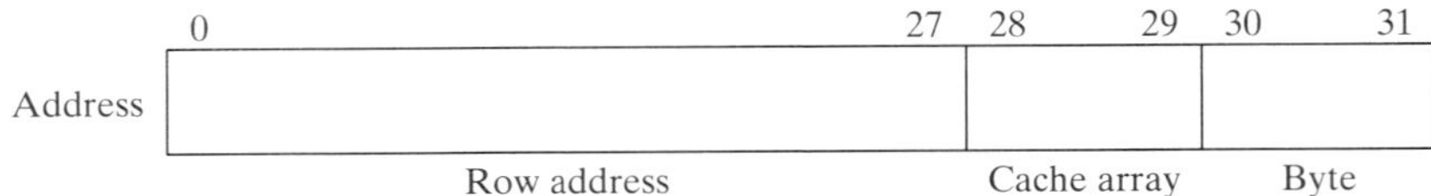

Figure 10.9 I-cache showing row and array mappings.

32 bits long, denotes the row and the array an address maps to. The row address field is 28 bits and the cache array address field is 2 bits, as shown in Fig. 10.9. The cache array part is further split into four independently addressable subarrays to contain the instructions along with tag bits that specify the instruction type. The instructions remain interleaved between the cache arrays. The following table illustrates exactly how this instruction interleaving scheme is mapped across each array.

Cache array	Address index	Address representation (in binary)
Array 0	0xx	00xx
Array 1	1xx	01xx
Array 2	2xx	10xx
Array 3	3xx	11xx

Array 0 contains instructions whose four low-order address bits are 00xx. Similarly, array 1, array 2, and array 3 contain instructions whose four low-order address bits are 01xx, 10xx, and 11xx, respectively. This design of the I-cache is shown in Fig. 10.10 to display the resultant storage order of instructions in the four cache arrays. As the interleaved instructions i_0, i_1, i_2, and i_3 from cells A0, A1, A2, and A3 in Fig. 10.10 are aligned across a quadword (16-byte) boundary, fetching all of them in one cycle poses no problem. But, in order to fetch a set of instructions that are laid across two contiguous rows as effectively, some additional complexity has to be added to the array part of the I-cache. A *row-incrementation logic,* added to the cache arrays, helps in

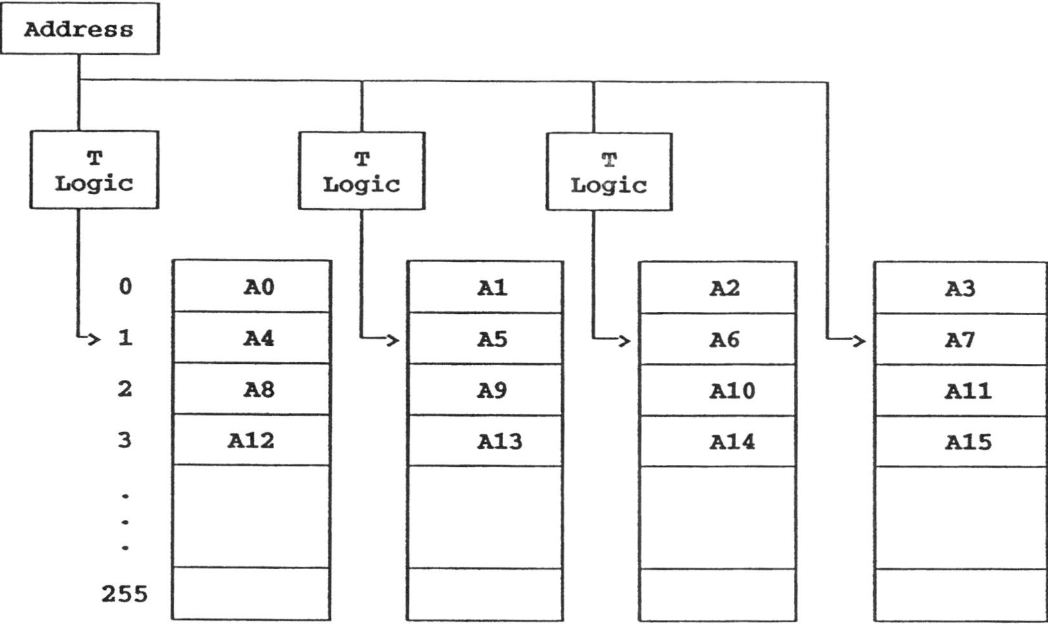

Figure 10.10 I-cache showing the four arrays and row-increment logic.

facilitating performance by saving cycles. Using this row-incrementation mechanism in the cache arrays, a set of four instructions such as i_1, i_2, i_3, and i_4 from cells A1, A2, A3, and A4 gets fetched despite two contiguous cache rows getting crossed, as shown in Fig. 10.10. But how about fetching instructions such as i_{13}, i_{14}, i_{15}, and i_{16} that occur across two cache lines? Having seen how to fetch instructions aligned across quadword boundaries and row boundaries, we now examine how cache line boundaries have been dealt with in the System/6000's cache design scheme. The cache directory part is sectioned into an even and an odd compartment so that the I-cache is able to fetch four instructions even if two cache lines got crossed in the process of accessing the instructions. Together with this even-odd directory split implementation and the row-incrementation mechanism, four instructions get fetched despite two contiguous cache lines being crossed. Figure 10.11 displays the even-odd split directory scheme that is used to extend the basic design of Fig. 10.10.

10.4.2 I-cache operation

Unlike most of its competition, the System/6000's I-cache is capable of fetching instructions across two lines in the same cycle. With 16

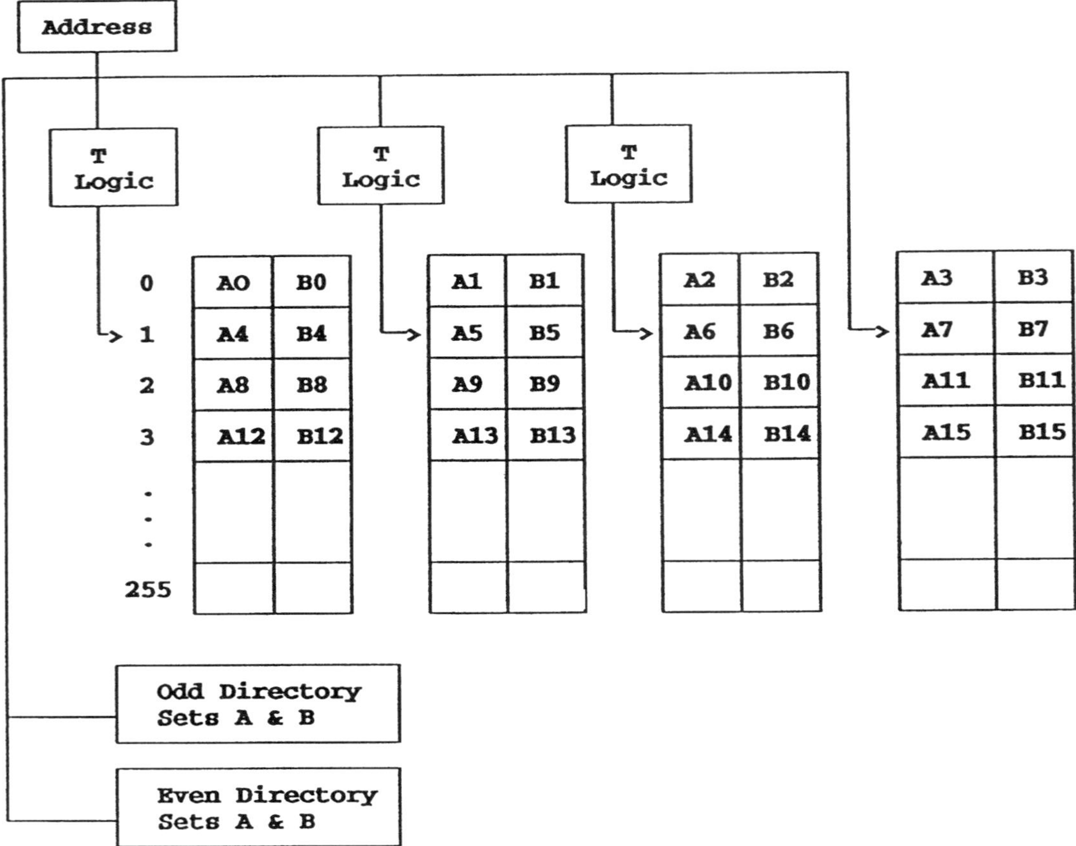

Figure 10.11 I-cache showing the even-odd split directory organization with row-increment logic.

instructions being accommodated in a single cache line, the operational aspect is reviewed for all the possible situations.

For case 1, consider fetching instructions i_0 through i_3, which happen to be aligned on a quadword boundary. All of the four cache arrays are accessed using the same row address in a straightforward way.

For case 2, accessing instructions across rows is slightly complex. Instructions i_1 through i_4 present the arrays 1, 2, and 3 with the same row address. The fourth cell, array 0, is accessed using the row-incrementor logic, which was described in detail in the previous section.

For case 3, the fetching of instructions spanning two cache lines is more complex. Accessing these instructions across two cache lines implies that they both belong to the same virtual memory page. As in case 2, the same row address is used for instructions i_{13} through i_{15}. But the fourth instruction, i_{16}, is obtained by incrementing the row address for array 0. Although a total of eight instructions is accessed from the four cache arrays as a side effect of the cache directory being split into even and odd compartments, a late-select operation is performed to filter out the four correct instructions each time.

After all this, even if a cache miss should occur, it is overlapped with the execution of fixed-point and floating-point instructions, thereby ensuring that no cycle is wasted. The resulting I-cache miss is forwarded to the SCU. As a result, an I-cache reload request is transmitted. The reload takes place from the main memory at the rate of two instructions at a time. Since it takes eight cycles to reload an I-cache line, a concurrent operation also takes place at this instant in which the two instructions that are in the process of being fetched are bypassed into a set of structures called the instruction buffers with the intent of being stored temporarily.

10.4.3 Instruction buffers

The instruction buffers consist of two separate buffers that are located on the ICU itself. The main function of these instruction buffers is to hold instruction fetches from the I-cache before dispatching to the FXU and the FPU. Their significance comes into play when a branch is encountered in the instruction stream.

The first type of instruction buffer is referred to as a *sequential buffer*. These buffers hold up to eight instructions. The second type of buffer is called a *target buffer* and can accommodate up to four instructions. The function of the sequential buffer is to store the normally fetched instructions, while the target buffer stores the prefetched targets of branch instructions. The basic algorithm of the instruction buffers operation is as follows:

```
if branch instruction encountered
      T-buffer <- instructions (4)

if branch taken
      S-buffer <- T-buffer
else
      T-buffer <- NIL
```

Normally, four instructions at a time are brought into the sequential buffer of the ICU for temporary parking until the ICU pipeline can begin processing the information. Although four instructions are fetched on every clock cycle, the second stage of the ICU pipeline processes only two instructions per cycle. Depending on the instruction type, it either executes the instruction by removing it from the buffer, or dispatches it to the FXU and FPU using the two instruction buses. Many of the details about the ICU pipeline were discussed in Chap. 9. Here, it will be sufficient to state that the four instructions fetched in one cycle remain stored in the sequential buffer until ICU's dispatch/execute stage is able to operate on them, pair by pair.

Normal processing continues for a sequential instruction stream. It is when a branch instruction is encountered that use of a target buffer becomes relevant. Upon encountering a branch instruction, the target buffer holds the prefetched target of the branch instruction. If the branch outcome turns out to be true, i.e., if a branch is taken, the target buffer contents get written into the sequential buffer; otherwise, the target buffer contents are purged. The process is made more evident through the use of an example, in which a generic instruction stream, i_1, i_2, i_3, . . . , has been considered for step-by-step trace and discussion.

Figure 10.12 displays the representative instruction stream and shows the state of the initial step where the first cycle has resulted in fetching instructions i_1 through i_4 into the sequential buffer. Step 2 results in fetching four more instructions, i_5 through i_8, into the remaining part of the sequential buffer, as shown in Fig. 10.13. Step 3 fetches the next set of instructions, i_9 through i_{11}, into the sequential buffer by overwriting the old information, as seen in Fig. 10.14. Notice that each of the recent sets of four instructions has a branch instruction in it. The next cycle, which is Step 4, loads the target buffer with instructions that execute if the branch is taken. Figure 10.15 depicts the state of the buffers in Step 4. Now either of two things can happen when the branch instruction is actually executed. If the branch is taken, then the content of the target buffer gets written into the sequential buffer, as shown in Fig. 10.16 as Step 5a. But, if the branch is not taken, the target buffer is purged, represented in Fig. 10.17 as Step 5b.

10.4.4   I-cache performance gains

In the design of the I-cache, a set-associative design was chosen, since it delivers a significant performance gain over a direct-mapped cache.* Regarding its associativity alternatives, a two-way design offers a

---

* A direct-mapped cache has only one line per set. For any given candidate address, there is only one line that may contain the reference.

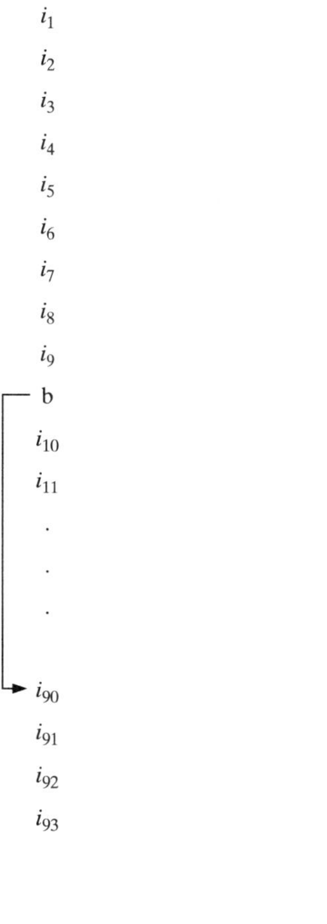

Step 1

i_1	i_2	i_3	i_4		

Sequential buffer

Target buffer

Figure 10.12 Step 1: instruction buffer operation.

marginally smaller degree of performance over a four-way design, thus making it an appropriate cost-performance choice. This efficient design of the 8-KB I-cache normally offers a miss ratio of less than 2 percent. Even when a cache miss occurs during program execution, it is overlapped with the execution of the fixed-point and floating-point instructions in the instruction stream, thereby not wasting any cycles. In order to further conserve cycles, a fetch bypass technique is used with special buffers (called instruction buffers) to load its line while sending the item to the execution units in parallel.

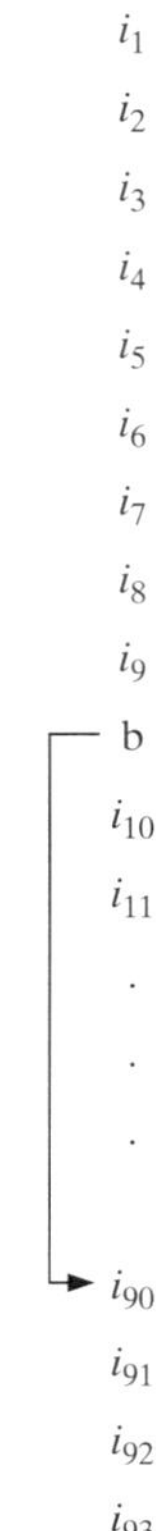

Step 2

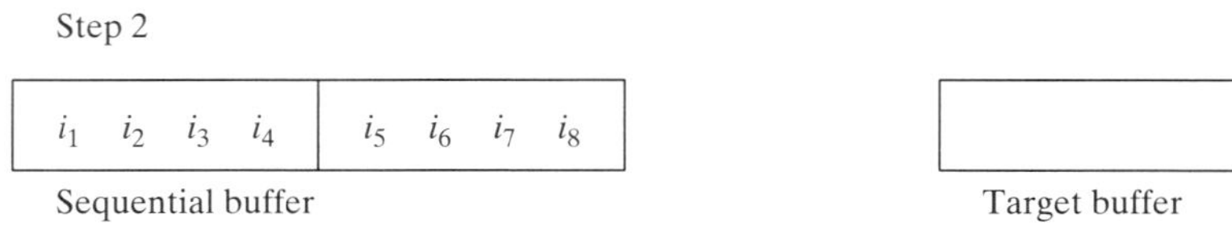

Sequential buffer   Target buffer

Figure 10.13 Step 2: instruction buffer operation.

10.5 D-CACHE ORGANIZATION

A set of four separate chips makes up the data cache unit (DCU). The design was achieved through embedding about 16,000 logic and 1130 transistor devices into four separate silicon dies, each of which measures about 11.3 mm^2 in size.

10.5.1 D-cache layout

The layout of the data cache is discussed in light of cache design basics and the I-cache schematic described in the previous sections. The

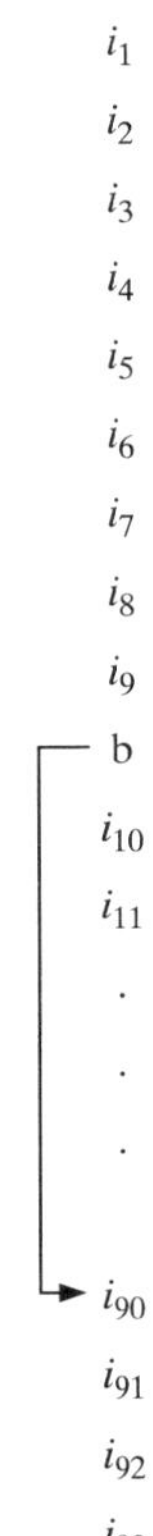

Step 3

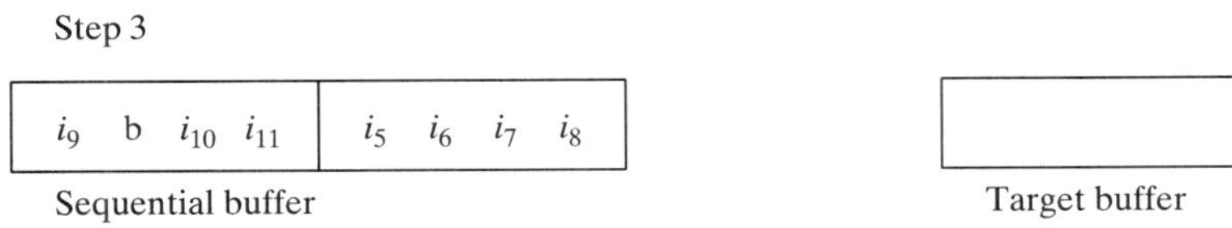

Sequential buffer   Target buffer

Figure 10.14 Step 3: instruction buffer operation.

D-cache is a four-way set-associative cache, consisting of 128 sets. This blueprint gives the D-cache a total of 512 lines. With 128 bytes per line, the total cache size adds up to 64 KB. Figure 10.18 explains the breakdown of set and line mapping.

Although we discuss the D-cache layout in full-scale POWER architecture in detail, it should be noted that there are some implementational variations in the D-cache size found in some of the scaled-down implementations of the POWER chips. For example, in the cost-reduced version of the POWER chip implementation (referred to as the RS .9 chip set) the D-cache is half the size and features 64 sets instead

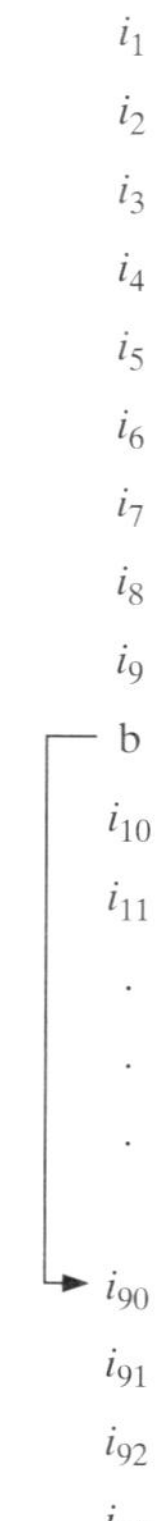

Step 4

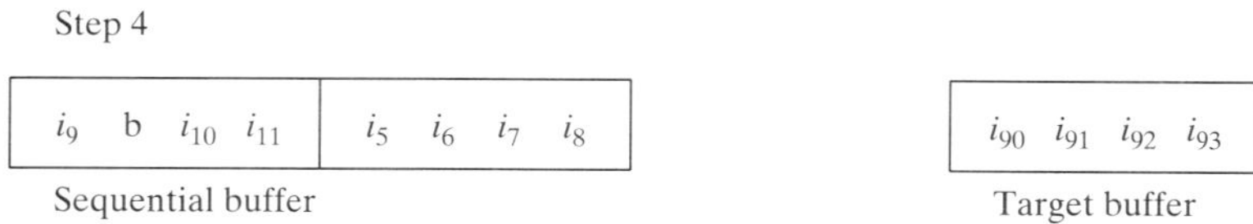

i_9	b	i_{10}	i_{11}	i_5	i_6	i_7	i_8

Sequential buffer

i_{90}	i_{91}	i_{92}	i_{93}

Target buffer

Figure 10.15 Step 4: instruction buffer operation.

of 128. Therefore, its size is 32 KB in total. Similar exception holds for the single-chip implementation of the POWER chip (called RSC).

Like the I-cache, the D-cache also has a directory part and an array part. The directory part that contains address bits is located on the FXU chip rather than on the D-cache chips.

As far as the cache interfaces are concerned, the D-cache has a two-word interface to the FPU bus, a one-word interface to the FXU bus, a two-word interface to the I/O control unit, a four-word interface to the main memory, and a two-word interface to the I-cache reload bus, as

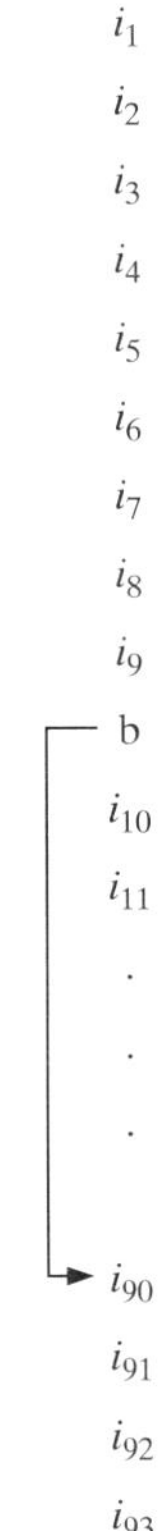

i_1
i_2
i_3
i_4
i_5
i_6
i_7
i_8
i_9
b
i_{10}
i_{11}
.
.
.
i_{90}
i_{91}
i_{92}
i_{93}

Step 5a: branch taken

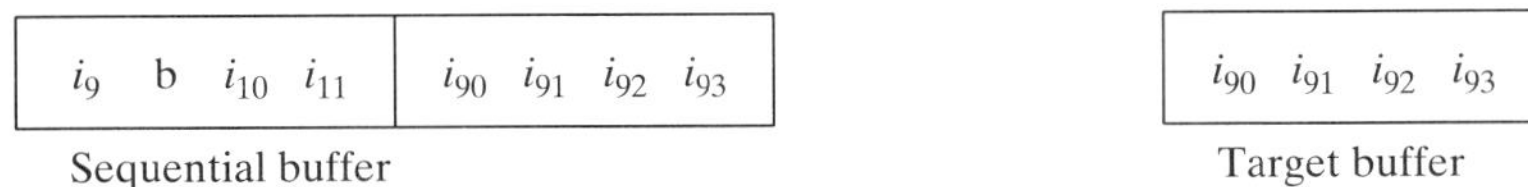

Sequential buffer   Target buffer

Figure 10.16 Step 5a: instruction buffer operation.

shown in Fig. 10.19. Although the I-cache reload memory interface is located on the D-cache chips, it is not a part of the D-cache. All instruction reloads bypass the D-cache while being streamed from the memory to the I-cache. Note that for the cost-reduced implementations of the CPU planars, the D-cache interface appears somewhat different. Its two-word interface to the I-cache reload bus is connected via the common SIO bus (instead of a dedicated interface, as in the case of the standard CPU planar). Second, the two-word FPU interface is dotted with the one-word FXU interface (unlike two decoupled

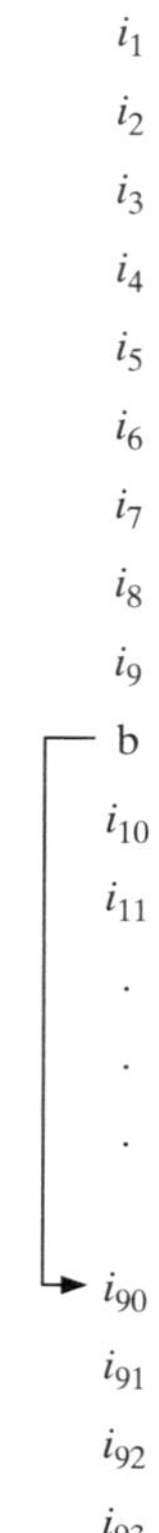

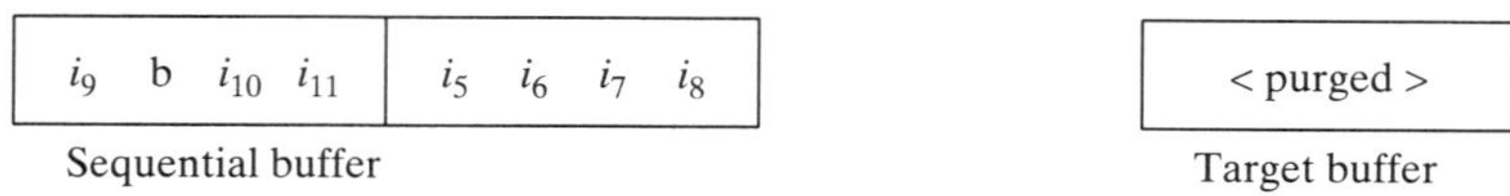

Step 5*b*: branch not taken

i_9 b i_{10} i_{11}	i_5 i_6 i_7 i_8		< purged >
Sequential buffer			Target buffer

Figure 10.17 Step 5*b:* instruction buffer operation.

interfaces in the case of the standard CPU planar). Third, the two-word interface to the I/O control unit is through the common SIO bus. Furthermore, the interface to the main memory is only two words wide. So, analysis of the D-cache interfaces found on the two types of CPU planars can lead one to infer that the peak level of data flow performance for I/O-bound workloads will vary to some extent for the two different implementations of the POWER chip. Although no striking loss of performance has been observed, some difference in benchmark

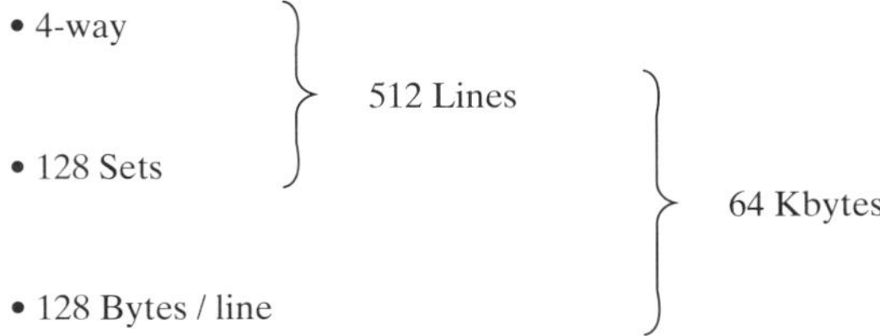

Figure 10.18 Description of the D-cache in terms
of its sets and lines.

results is quite likely since there is some performance loss due to contention on the SIO bus and additional delays for reloading instruction cache data over the SIO bus.

10.5.2 D-cache operation

System/6000's D-cache processes data using a buffering scheme to and from the cache directory. This implementation has been done to service cache misses more efficiently, while making optimal use of the four-word-wide, high-bandwidth memory bus.

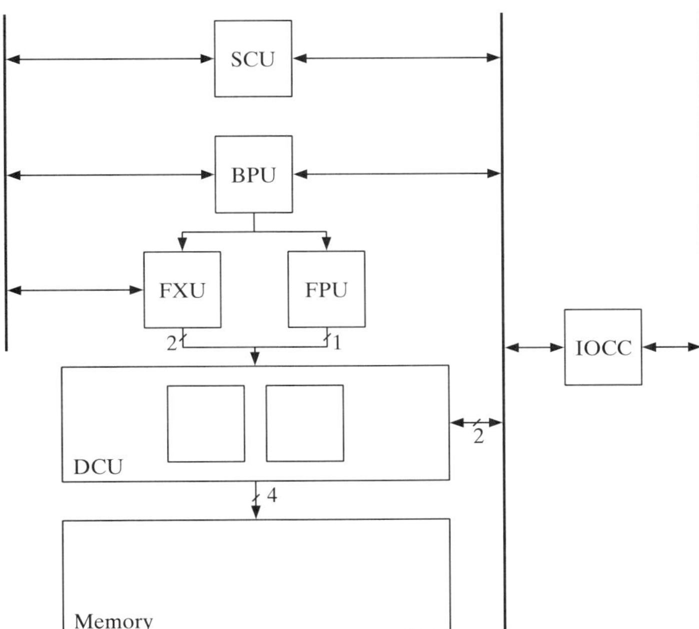

Figure 10.19 D-cache interfaces (RS .9 implementation shown).

When a D-cache miss results in a memory access, causing a cache line to be replaced, it becomes imperative that the data fetched be stored in some temporary place until all the memory transfers have been completed. In fact, to load a D-cache line, eight memory transfers are conducted, each transferring 16 bytes per cycle. Recognize here that a cache miss implies that two memory operations take place concurrently. First, the new cache line should be loaded from memory, and second, a dirty line (i.e., one that has been changed) should be stored in memory. This phenomenon is made possible with the help of two buffers, namely a cache reload buffer and store-back buffer. Their positioning and control flow is illustrated in Fig. 10.20. The function of the cache reload buffer is to hold the data as it is returned from memory. Data is queued up in the cache reload buffer until a full line has been filled, before being unloaded into the D-cache arrays. The function of the store-back buffer is to hold the dirty line discarded from the D-cache to make room for a new line, before unloading the data to memory. So, judging from an operational perspective, two things happen simultaneously: while the cache reload buffer is being loaded from memory, data from the D-cache array is transferred into the store-back buffer. This benefits us by using only a single cycle to perform both the operations, i.e., loading the buffer and dispatching to memory.

In the event of a cache miss, the first quadword from memory will contain the requested data. If a request is made for a data word that is not in the first quadword of a line, the data will be fetched until the end of the line is reached and then wrap around the line to fetch the remaining words till a complete line gets loaded. Figure 10.21 exemplifies this *wraparound load* mechanism. This first quadword is loaded into the cache reload buffer in parallel, while being returned to the requester using the fetch bypass technique. Should a second data word be required before the line gets loaded into the cache array, it can be accessed from the cache reload buffer.

10.5.3 D-cache performance gains

Beyond the layout of the 4-way set-associative D-cache itself, several of its functional implementations facilitate performance gains. First, buffered data to and from the D-cache guarantees faster servicing of cache misses and more effective usage of the wide four-word memory bandwidth. Second, the wraparound load feature saves cycles in the loading of data words that are not in the first quadword of a line. Furthermore, replacement of a dirty line is handled efficiently by carrying out the load and store operations in parallel with the help of the cache reload buffer and the store-back buffer. Perhaps the most inconspicuous and unobtrusive feature of the D-cache is its two diverse imple-

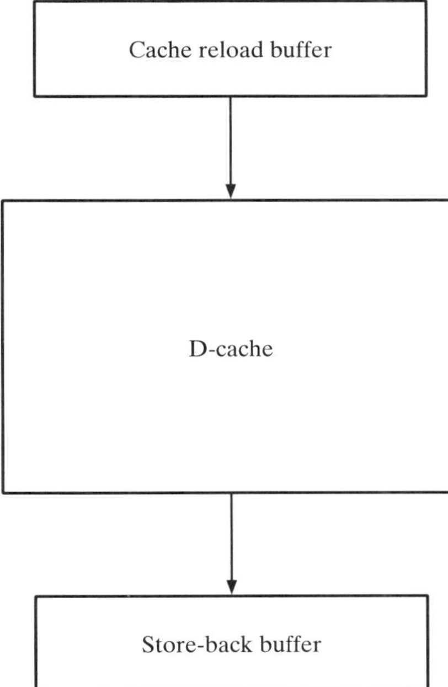

Figure 10.20 Conceptual positioning of the cache reload buffer and store-back buffer with respect to the D-cache.

mentations of a standard and a cost-reduced planar. The two different design points make use of the same chips without a discernible difference in efficiency. The two variants of the D-cache—(1) 64-byte lines in a 32-KB-size cache implemented on two data cache chips, and (2) 128-byte lines in a 64-KB-size cache implemented on four D-cache chips—being fully compatible, not only offer comparable performance, but also a modular upgrade path in the System/6000 product family.

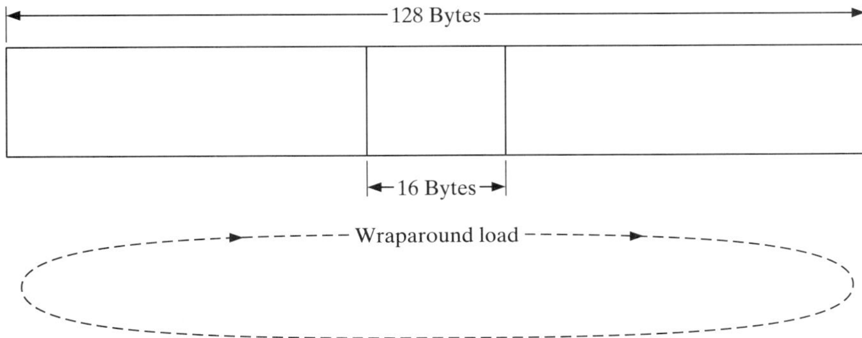

Figure 10.21 Wraparound load operation in D-cache.

10.6 SUMMARY

Cache memory has become an integral component of modern-day machines as it facilitates a way to conduct rapid access to nonresident parts of executing programs. Although functionally similar to virtual memory, cache is implemented in hardware. Current RISC-based architectures have taken the performance threshold of cache memory even higher by achieving minimal selection conflicts between data and instruction streams of an executing program. Separating the instructions from the data stream of a cache has augmented its already fast access time even more than ever before. The separate I-cache and D-cache on the System/6000 are organized as dedicated units.* Each of them has been further modified in its own way to aid the underlying architectural dependencies. The I-cache implements an augmented instruction access scheme by modifying its arrays to fetch instructions around quadword boundaries and by modifying its directory to facilitate fetching of instructions around row boundaries. The D-cache has been designed in such a way that it is able to cope with the high demands of the execution units (FXU and FPU), while meeting the scalable requirements of the workstation industry.

As the speed of modern machines continues to increase, the need for cache memories will grow. Faster SRAM technologies will evolve. Soon, secondary and tertiary cache memories will be anticipated in the System/6000 product line, as well as in other commercially available machines.

---

* The RSC implementation is an exception.

Execution Units

An architecture like the System/6000 that makes use of multiple execution units to perform its instruction execution has to be able to simultaneously process several instructions in a single clock cycle. This implies that several instructions must be fetched in each cycle, too. Orchestrating this task of fetching as well as executing multiple instructions adds a substantial amount of complexity to the architectural design of the system. Since there are three different implementations of the POWER architecture (pointed out at the beginning of Chap. 2) offered with different models of the RISC System/6000 computer, there are likely to be some minor implementation-specific differences. However, the underlying functions of how the execution units of the POWER architecture work remain unchanged.

In this chapter, each of the three execution units is examined. Wherever necessary, additional details about the design rationales are pointed out so that the user is able to appreciate the complex orchestration of the instruction and data flow through the heart of the execution units.

11.1 BRANCH PROCESSING UNIT ARCHITECTURE

The benefit of having a separate branch processing unit (BPU) is that it minimizes the pipeline penalty caused by branch instructions. The function served by the BPU is the fetching of instructions from the I-cache* and the forwarding of instructions to the FXU and FPU.

11.1.1 General organization

The BPU is integrated on the same physical chip with the ICU. It contains several special registers. First there is a link register (LR) that contains the return address from subroutine and supervisory system calls. A set link bit in the branch instruction causes the next instruction address to be placed in the Link Register. The second register is called the count register (CTR), which is used for counting loop iterations. Most present-day machines that do not have this special feature treat loop iterations as conditional branches. But on the System/6000, all enumerated loops are closed with a *bct* or branch-and-count assembly language instruction, causing the CTR to decrement by one each time, and branching on the resulting value. This naturally augments the performance level for code execution by a significant extent. The third register, the condition register (CR), is best known for its contribution to reducing the cost of compare-and-branch penalty. This CR is explored in further detail in the forthcoming sections.

In addition to these registers, there is a set of privileged registers that is not visible to the application programmers. One such register is the machine state register (MSR) that contains system states like user/supervisory mode, interrupt enable/disable mode, and address relocate on/off status. There is another set of important registers called the save and restore register (SRR). The SRR0 and SRR1 save the old value of MSR and the address of the interrupted instruction in the event of an interrupt. Upon returning from the interrupt, they restore the MSR value and resume execution from the interrupted instruction.

Bus interfaces to the BPU are the same as those to the ICU, since both are integrated on the same physical chip. There is an interface to the main memory from which instructions are fetched, a two-word instruction dispatch bus to both of the FXU and FPU where non-branching instructions get forwarded, and a one-word interface to a processor bus that is a common connector for the FXU and SCU chips.

11.1.2 Pipeline stages

The ICU/BPU pipeline includes two stages, namely, a *fetch* stage and a *dispatch/execute* stage. The first stage fetches up to four instructions in

---

* Any reference to an I-cache (ICU) or D-cache (DCU) implies that the reference is being made to a multichip implementation. For the single-chip implementation, RSC, there is a combined cache that handles both instructions and data.

one cycle. The second stage's behavior is instruction-dependent. If the instruction encountered happens to be a branch instruction, it gets executed instantly. On the other hand, if the instruction happens to be a fixed-point or floating-point instruction, it simply gets dispatched to the two execution units. The BPU is able to carry out this instruction-forwarding operation (using address generation and address translation) until a situation with data dependency arises. When a data dependency occurs, the BPU is in need of data from the FXU that is not yet available. In order to address this problem, the design of BPU has been implemented in a way that it is capable of fetching four instructions in every cycle (one branch operation, one each for the FXU and the FPU, and one condition register operation), thereby being in a position to assert an upcoming branch before the FXU or the FPU knows about it.

11.1.3 Branch handling with condition registers

The significance of a condition register can be best understood in terms of a sample instruction stream. Shown in Fig. 11.1 is a high-level language pseudo-code construct and its assembly language equivalent. This code poses no problem on classical machines that have only one execution unit in them. As all of the instructions get sequentially executed by the single CPU, dealing with assignment statements and compare statements poses no predicament. But how about a computer with multiple independent execution units? On a machine like the System/6000, the integer compare instruction in this code fragment gets executed by the FXU, while the branch instruction gets to be executed by the BPU. This adds an additional complexity. To add to this imbroglio of separate execution units, we also have to assure the proper sequence of the two instruction executions. This is where the need for an instruction synchronization scheme comes in. The basic concept is to set a bit upon encountering a compare instruction, and reset (i.e., clear) the bit upon executing the corresponding branch instruction. It is essential to understand that the set and the clear operations are being performed by two independent execution units, as seen in Fig. 11.2. The bit in the condition register is set by the FXU upon its execution of the compare instruction. When the ICU dispatches a compare instruction to the FXU, it tags the condition register as having a pending update. If a subsequent branch is encountered before the update is complete, the branch is held off until the update is done. This is a form of scoreboarding.

The idea is now extended to a situation with compound Boolean expressions. Figure 11.3 shows an assembly language code fragment that will be generated for a compound Boolean logic in a high-level lan-

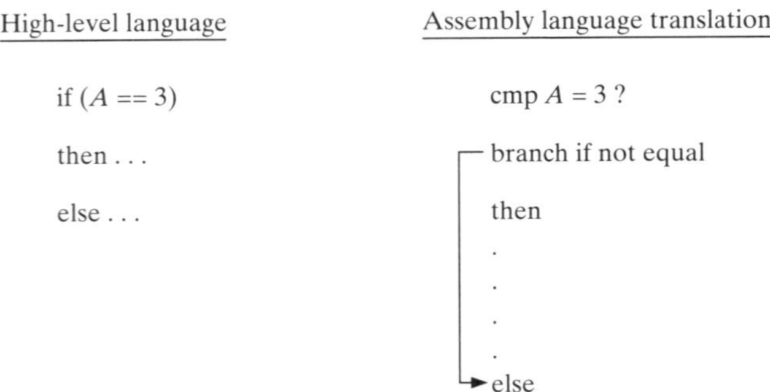

Figure 11.1 An IF statement construct in a high-level language and its assembly language equivalent.

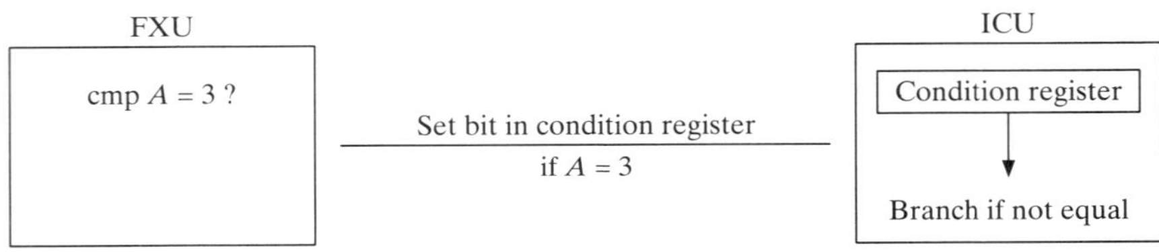

Figure 11.2 Mechanism behind a condition register operation.

guage, on classical machines. It is seen that the resulting assembly code treats the Boolean logic as multiple IF-THEN-ELSE constructs, implying that there are multiple pairs of branch-and-compare instructions. The transfer of control indicated in Fig. 11.3 shows where each of the branch instructions would jump to if all of the corresponding compare operations were to fall through. Once again on the System/6000, the assembly language code generated for this same high-level instruction fragment would be quite different. As seen in Fig. 11.4, multiple branches are replaced with a single branch. Each of the Boolean comparisons, i.e., *cmp A = 3* and *cmp B = 4,* sets a bit in $B0$ and $B1$, respectively. Thereafter, results of these cells are AND-ed using a condition register operation (*crand*) to evaluate the outcome of the total expression and to allow the branch to be taken as per the evaluated result.

Having understood the operational concepts we now describe the actual physical implementation of the condition register. There are eight fields in the 32-bit condition register. Each of the eight fields comprises four bits that hold the status of compare operations. The hardware implements interlock bits to ensure a sequential execution mode transparent to the programmers, gets set if an instruction is being dispatched to the FXU or FPU, and sets a field in the condition register.

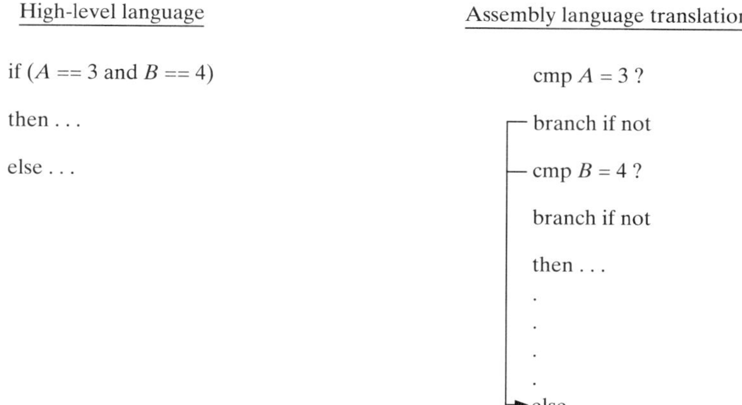

Figure 11.3 Assembly language output of a compound Boolean logic written in a high-level language on a classical machine.

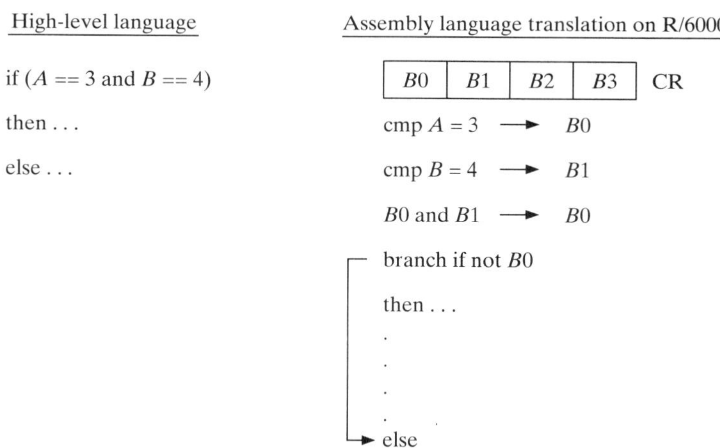

Figure 11.4 Assembly language output of a compound Boolean logic written in a high-level language on System/6000.

All subsequent instructions attempting to read or set this field remain in the instruction buffers. Eventually the FXU (or FPU as the case may be) ends up executing this instruction and notifies the BPU, via its bus interface, to reset the field's interlock bit. Since instructions setting the condition register fields are subject to conditional scheduling (thus cancelable), any corresponding interlock bits set by the instructions can be reset. Note that these interlock bits cannot be misused easily since the software has no control over them. However, it is helpful to know how these locking bits have been implemented. The fields in the condition register are paired up for locking purposes, as shown in Fig. 11.5. For example, if an instruction happens to set field 0, the BPU will internally lock up the field 0 as well as field 4. Similarly, remaining bits like bit 1 and bit 5, bit 2 and bit 6, and bit 3 and bit 7 are also affected. Thus, it is seen that this implementation allows four outstanding operations to the condition register to be maintained at any given time. This "pairing" was a cost-performance tradeoff.*

11.1.4 Instruction dispatching

As discussed earlier, as many as four instructions may be dispatched or scheduled in one cycle on this machine. To achieve this number it is essential that two instructions get executed by the BPU and one gets executed by each of the FXU and FPU, respectively. However, the ability to execute four instructions per cycle also requires the instructions to be in a specific order. The ideal combination of instructions is not likely to occur most of the time, as instructions in an instruction mix are not completely independent of one another. In real-life workloads, there are delays and hold-offs between instructions that occur because of off-chip communication and the pipelined nature of the execution units. For instance, execution of a load instruction results in a one-cycle delay as the data must be fetched from D-cache (and D-cache array is not on the FXU chip). Similarly, execution of a floating-point instruction results in a delay if the outcome of one instruction is needed by the very next one.†

In order to maintain a view of a sequential instruction, the FXU and the FPU each decode one instruction per cycle, while remaining synchronized with the help of a synchronization counter (explained in Sec. 11.2.4). However, the actual scheduling of instructions becomes the key to optimizing the power of this machine. Not only does the scheduling algorithm have to be extremely smart in terms of arranging instructions for the fastest execution, but also the hardware logic itself should be able to deal with preemptive interrupts among the three execution units.

11.2 INTERRUPT HANDLING

Occurrence of interrupts in classical machines is not a new concept, as the program counter is able to maintain a pointer to the precise loca-

---

* The more granularity is implemented, the better the performance will be, leading to a more costly and complex implementation.

† Execution of a single floating-point instruction takes two cycles to complete.

Register number	Condition register field number	Interlock bit
0	000	0
4	100	
1	001	1
5	101	
2	010	2
6	110	
3	011	3
7	111	

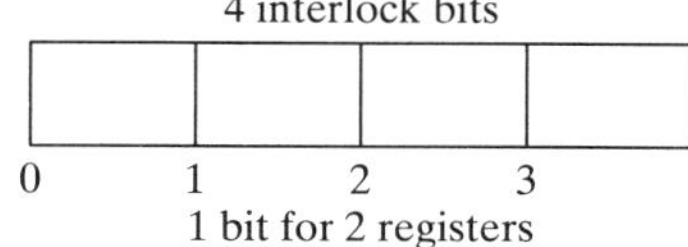

Figure 11.5 Condition register locking mechanism for fields 0 and 4, 1 and 5, 2 and 6, and 3 and 7.

tion of the instruction stream. But on the System/6000 there is no program counter per se. With three separate independent execution units, processing a single instruction stream makes recovering from interrupts not a simple task. Therefore, numerous schemes are used to address this issue. Before describing these strategies and methods, we present the interrupt handling problem in a little more detail.

11.2.1 Precise/imprecise interrupts

If an interrupt, which is a temporary suspension of the normal sequence of program execution, leaves the machine's program counter pointing to a specific instruction up to which all instructions in the instruction stream have completed execution and no subsequent instructions have modified the registers, it is referred to as a *precise interrupt*. Handling of precise interrupts poses no problem since it is feasible to resume execution of the CPU from where it left off (example shown in Fig. 11.6). But occurrence of an interrupt on a system with multiple execution units results in a fragmented state, giving rise to *imprecise interrupts*. As different instructions get executed by different (and independent) execution units on this machine, the instruction

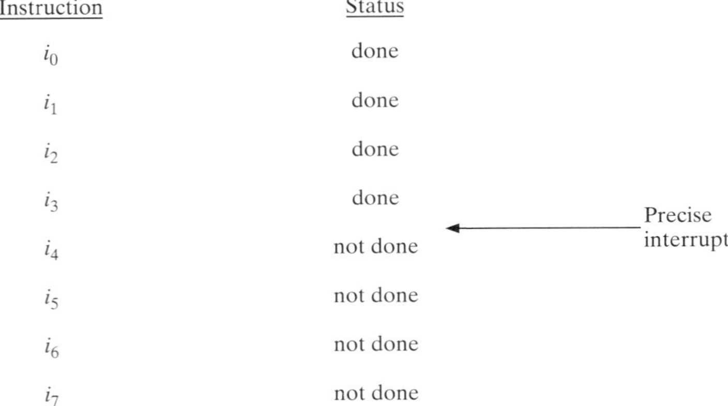

Figure 11.6 Instruction stream showing precise interrupts.

stream is left fragmented, as seen in Fig. 11.7. Imprecise interrupts require the architecture to provide a means for reconstructing the instruction stream around the point of the interrupt so that the post-interrupt processing code can recreate the sequential state of the machine. Due to the pipeline complexity of the machine organization, architecting a method for handling interrupts in an imprecise manner gets costly and complex. So, heterogeneous strategies to address this issue have been used after taking a closer look at different factors that cause interrupts.

Unlike precise interrupts which allow their resume points to remain well-defined, factors causing imprecise interrupts have to be scrutinized on an individual basis. External interrupts caused by events such as the responses of I/O devices can be handled, as they are yet to

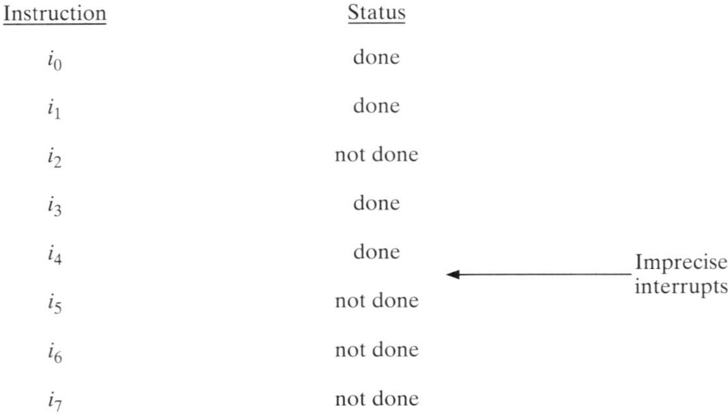

Figure 11.7 Instruction stream showing imprecise interrupts.

start their processes. By stopping their instruction dispatches and subsequently allowing the pipelines to drain, we ensure that the instruction streams do not stay fragmented. But internal interrupts caused by instances like page faults, floating-point exceptions, or overflows cannot be preempted. Since an instruction causing the page fault may not be complete, it becomes imperative that it either be able to recover from the fragmented state or be able to generate a precise interrupt. The scheme for generating precise interrupts for the interrupt-causing phenomena vary, based on which of the two out of three execution units is involved in the interaction. Listed here are some possible types of events along with execution units that are involved in the imprecise interrupt-causing interactions.

Execution Units	**Event Type**
BPU ↔ FXU	branch and condition register logic instructions
BPU ↔ FPU	floating-point exceptions (i.e., when FP precise interrupts are enabled)
FXU ↔ FPU	load and store instructions

11.2.2 BPU-FXU interaction

A functional perspective of the scheme reveals that in the interaction between the BPU and the FXU a fragmented state is permitted following an interrupt. Subsequently, the instructions in question, i.e., branch and condition register logic instructions, are canceled by restoring registers to reflect their original state. As exhibited by the pipelined structure of the execution units, instructions are processed by the BPU and its registers well before reaching the FXU. Therefore, a load operation causing a page fault several cycles later in the FXU will have no apparent way but to undo the already scheduled instructions.

To better understand the BPU-FXU interaction, study a case in which three instructions—(1) a load, (2) a condition register operation, and (3) a branch—that are being dispatched as a part of the instruction stream happen within the same cycle. Upon tracing these instructions individually, we see that the load instruction itself is forwarded to the FXU for execution, with its address getting recorded on the stack. For the condition register operation, the value of the condition register field is modified and its old value is saved on its backup stack. Finally, for the branch instruction, the value of the link register is updated*

---

* A variant of the branch instruction, branch-and-link, sets the link bit; in other words, it makes bit 31 equal to 1, while placing the effective address of the instruction following the branch instruction into the link register of the BPU.

and its old value is saved on its backup stack. As a side effect of these updates, a set of status bits also gets set. When the load generates an interrupt later, the status bits cause the link register and the condition register to be restored from their stack to erase any changes to the machine state. Although scheduled instructions are canceled and precious cycles are lost, the scheme assures the integrity of the global instruction stream.

11.2.3 BPU-FPU interaction

The data flow implementation between the BPU and the FPU is straightforward. Floating-point exceptions cause no interrupts on the System/6000 in its normal mode of program execution. As much as exceptions are natural and perhaps an expected consequence of floating point operations, their handling does not always yield the desired results. This is so because exception-handling rules are described by the generic IEEE specifications. But it is the underlying hardware (POWER RISC System/6000 in our case) that implements the recovery mechanism logic. The simplest way to recover from a floating-point exception is to generate a floating-point interrupt for the failing instruction whenever there is a floating-point exception that is not defaulted.* But this implies that all instructions after a floating-point instruction must remain conditional until it is known that no exception is possible on that instruction. Also, the floating-point instructions that take several cycles to complete will not be able to determine the exception until their last cycle. So, in effect, this would serialize the floating-point instructions. The net result of this implementation of a floating-point interrupt is to penalize the overall floating-point performance of the machine, if it were to be implemented for normal program execution. Keeping these performance penalties in mind, the recovery method from floating-point exceptions was formulated along the lines of setting an inspection flag test code (at compile time) to indicate its location, rather than generating an interrupt to report its occurrence at run-time. As a result, program execution continues until the end of the program or subroutine before the floating-point exception is reported. The obvious advantage of this implementation is that there is no loss of speed owing to floating-point exception recognition. The disadvantage is that the exact location of the floating-point-exception-causing code is not reported. It is to be noted that this strategy to get around floating-point exceptions requires both the compiler as well as the linker to support this feature.

---

* Default exception handling is defined by the IEEE standard.

In order to complement the *normal mode* of program execution in which floating-point exceptions are merely pointed out, but not before the program has gone well beyond that point, the System/6000 supports a *synchronize mode* in which an interrupt can be generated upon identifying the failing instruction. The machine executes programs in a serial manner, rather than the normally executed overlapped manner. This synchronize mode is only used for debugging purposes, essentially in algorithms where pinpointing the precise location of a floating-point exception is necessary. Needless to say, the speed of instruction execution is greatly reduced in the synchronize mode.

11.2.4 FXU-FPU interaction

In order to adhere to the independent processing abilities and parallel processing needs of the two execution units, it was necessary to devise a synchronization scheme that supports overlapped execution without disrupting the integrity of the instruction flow. Additional goals consisted of allowing the FXU to run ahead and feed data into the FPU, allowing the FPU to run ahead of the FXU in the event of a burst of floating-point instructions, as well as maintaining precise interrupts. The instruction-synchronization scheme to undertake this process is implemented at two different design levels. At the first level, the extent to which one execution unit may run ahead of the other is regulated. The scheme is implemented as a special-purpose counter, known as the FXU-FPU Synchronization Counter (FFSC); its function is to track the runahead of one execution unit over the other, while reporting the relative progress. Its possible values are interpreted as follows:

+'ve (up to +6)	=>	FPU ahead of the FXU
−'ve (down to −2)	=>	FXU ahead of the FPU
0	=>	Both synchronized

At a second level, accidental execution of interruptable instructions by the FPU is conservatively controlled. This scheme is implemented as a hardware latch, known as the interruptable instruction latch (IIL); its function is to ensure that the FPU does not execute past an interruptable instruction. The mechanism consists of controlling the decode phase of the FPU. Recall that it is the FXU that performs the load and store for the floating-point instructions. When the FPU is executing past the FXU and it encounters a page faulting instruction, it sets the IIL and thereafter waits for the FXU to ramp up. As long as this IIL remains set, no floating-point instruction is allowed to be decoded. When the FXU ramps up, it does know (from the status of the IIL) that the FPU is waiting on it. The FXU either executes the page-faulting instruction that the FPU was waiting on, or it confirms that this inter-ruptable instruction had not caused an interrupt. Thereafter, the FXU promptly resets the IIL so that the FPU can continue execution (until the occurrence of the next page-faulting instruction).

Figure 11.8 displays the FXU-FPU synchronization logic, which essentially is a partial view of the FXU and FPU pipelines. The implementation consists of two of the FXU stages, namely, the decode and execute, and three of the FPU stages, which are pre-decode, remap, and decode. Also associated with this logic is a set of buffers. The first

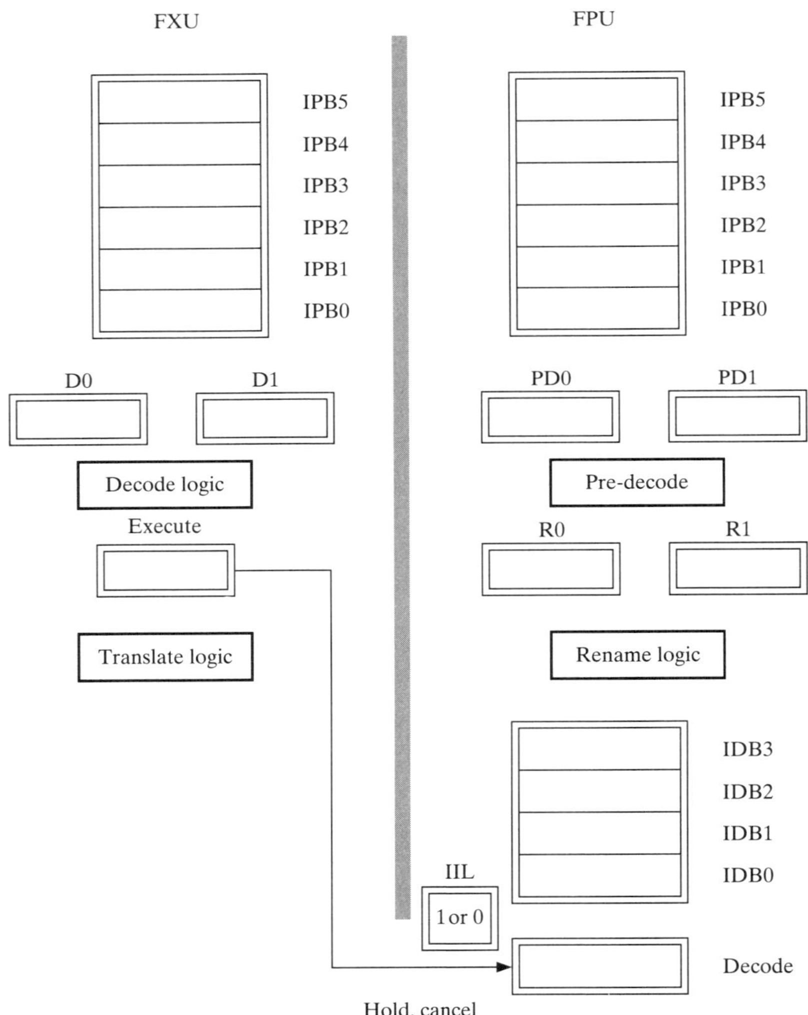

Figure 11.8 FXU-FPU synchronization mechanism.

one is called the instruction prefetch buffers (IPB), which allow the BPU to run ahead of the FXU and FPU, while feeding data into them. The second set of buffers is the instruction decode buffers (IDB), whose task is to allow the FXU to run ahead and feed data to the FPU. The registers present are a set of decode registers (D0, D1), pre-decode registers (PD0, PD1), and remap registers (also called rename registers) (R0, R1). The operation is similar to what was described before. A flag in IIL gets set by the FPU when it encounters an interruptable instruction, thereby preventing any further loading into the FPU. When the FXU ramps up, it knows that the interruptable instruction has not executed yet. It executes this instruction and resets (or clears) the IIL promptly. Now FPU continues with its normal instruction execution sequence again. So the IIL continues to be set and reset, when interruptable instructions like *load* and *store* occur.

Using this scheme, the three execution units interact with one another, displaying a significant degree of parallelism, concurrence, and synchronization. All three of the tasks—(1) the interaction of branch instructions with condition register logic instructions, (2) the handling of floating-point exceptions, and (3) the coordination of load/store instructions—are carefully orchestrated to achieve perfect harmony. Whatever little impact on performance is incurred is all due to the complex design scheme of the POWER instruction set of the System/6000 processor. In this way, all three of the execution units and their three-way communication with one another are taken care of, thus guaranteeing generation of precise interrupts wherever necessary.

11.2.5   Branch instruction processing

While dispatching instructions from the ICU to the FXU and FPU, in many instances the BPU of the System/6000 is able to provide an uninterrupted instruction stream, thereby making it devoid of branch penalties. As the branches appear invisible to the execution units in terms of cost, they are often referred to as *zero-cycle* branches.

These zero-cycle branches occur in case of (1) unconditional branches, (2) loop-closing branches (DO I=1,N), and (3) not-taken conditional branches. The fourth kind, which is the taken conditional branches, is not a zero-cycle branch and can consequently result in a delay, depending upon the distance between the compare and the branch instruction(s) in the instruction stream. Statistical research has shown that the three main types of branches, which are (1) unconditional, (2) loop closing, and (3) forward branches, occur in equivalent proportions in the instruction streams of real-life workloads. Thus it is imperative that the unconditional branches occur $\frac{1}{3}$ of the time, the loop closing branches occur ⅓ of the time, and the forward branches occur for the remaining ⅓ of the time. As the probability of the untaken forward branches is ½, the total likelihood of correctly predicting the branches is ⅓ + ⅓ + (½ * ⅓) = ⅚. So, only ⅙ of the branches (taken conditionals) may cause delays by wasting cycles. The length of this delay depends upon the distance between the compare and the branch instructions. This compare-conditional branch pair produces a three-cycle delay if they occur back-to-back. A two-cycle delay is caused when there is one instruction in between; a one-cycle delay results when there are two instructions in between; finally, a "zero"-cycle delay results when there are three or more instructions in between the compare-conditional branch pair. So, the strategy adopted by the compilers is to introduce one or more instructions between the compare-conditional branch pair (in order to "cover" the delay) whenever possible. This is easier said than done, because reordering of instructions without disrupting data dependency is not a simple task. The compiler not only needs to be intelligent enough to identify an independent instruction, but it also should be able to interleave these independent instructions within the basic blocks. Using instruction-scheduling algorithms in highly optimizing compilers, run-time delays in compiled code can be reduced for pipeline machine architectures that allow increased throughput by overlapping instruction execution.

11.3 FIXED POINT UNIT ARCHITECTURE

The role of the fixed point unit (FXU) is to process all the fixed-point instructions and also execute the floating-point load and store instructions. It plays a vital role in the multiunit orchestration by undertaking the instruction synchronization in the overlapped execution of fixed-point and floating-point instructions and by coordinating the data synchronization by generating the addresses for the floating-point instructions.

11.3.1 General organization

The FXU comprises several registers and specialized components, each of which contributes to its performance-crafted design. The first component consists of 32 general-purpose registers (hereafter referred to as GPRs), and these may be used by general programs for assists. Second, there is a set of segment registers (SR), which aid in address translation. Subsequently, there is a set of special-purpose registers. A data address register (DAR) specifies the address of storage access that caused a data storage or alignment interrupt.* Another register, data storage interrupt status register (DSISR), defines the actual cause of the data storage or alignment interrupt. Also, there is an exception register (XER) which deals with the carry and overflow flags, and contains byte count and comparison byte used by string instructions. In addition, there are two more registers which are present in the RS 1.0 and RS .9 implementations of the POWER architecture. The first one is called the transaction identifier register (TID) which holds the transaction ID of the currently executing process in the system. The second one is a multiplier-quotient register (MQ), which is used by multiply, divide, and extended shift instructions, and also as temporary storage by store string instructions.

Among the key components of the FXU is the arithmetic logic unit (ALU), which is used for arithmetic and logic operations. The next component is called the fixed-point multiply/divide unit, and it is used in conjunction with the ALU. The data translation lookaside buffer (D-TLB) works together with the segment registers (SRs) to aid in address translation, page protection, and data locking. It should be noted here that the page table lookups for D-TLB and the instruction translation lookside buffer (I-TLB) reloads and page table updates are all performed by the FXU hardware. The FXU chip also contains the directory part of the D-cache. The address generation task and D-cache controls for both fixed- and floating-point load/store instructions, as well as cache operations, are performed by the FXU. In addition, there is a store buffer (SB) in the FXU that is used to hold the data and address of a single fixed-point store instruction while waiting to write it into the D-cache. Consequently, the fixed- and floating-point loads can get ahead of the fixed-point stores, and the FXU and FPU can obtain the data they need sooner. But it should be noted here that the instructions are not executed out of order; only the D-cache access is made out of order (to save cycles).

The architecture supports handling of misaligned operands, for both string and nonstring instructions. This support for nonstring instructions can be best explained using an example. Consider a case where a full-word (4 bytes) on an odd half-word (2 bytes) boundary or an odd byte boundary is misaligned. Figure 11.9 explains the full-word and half-word boundaries across an 8-byte grid for convenience. In this case of the POWER architecture, the hardware handles all fixed-point

---

* A *data storage interrupt* is a hardware interrupt that occurs because of a nontranslatable virtual-address access, a storage-protection violation, an access denial owing to data locking, or an I/O exception condition. An *alignment interrupt* is another type of hardware interrupt that is raised when the effective address generated by a load or a store violates a storage boundary.

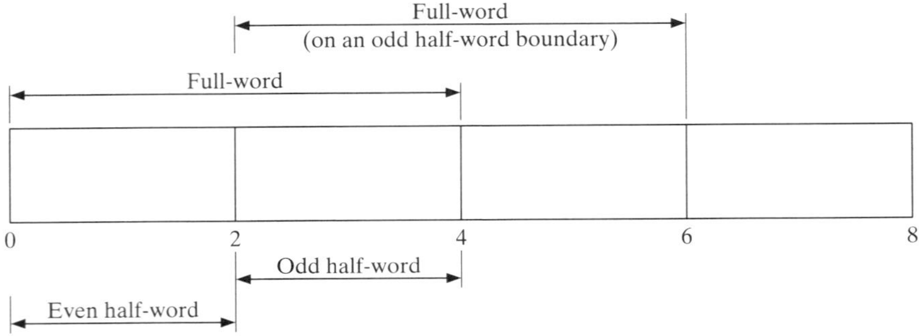

Figure 11.9 Types of word boundaries.

storage accesses (except load/store multiple, which generates alignment interrupts). The hardware also handles double-word floating-point storage access to odd word addresses. All other forms of unaligned floating-point storage accesses generate alignment interrupt (the reference completes in software). Misaligned operands for string instructions are handled through a special hardware called the string subunit (SS), located on the FXU. It is able to transfer strings at the maximum permissible rate allowed by the processor-cache bandwidth, which happens to be 32 bits for the FXU.

11.3.2 Pipeline stages

The pipeline stages in the FXU may be viewed as either a three-stage or a four-stage process, depending on whether the D-cache is being accessed for that specific iteration. During the first stage, fixed-point instructions are decoded (i.e., examined before execution). In the second stage, the instructions are executed. Now instead of being a regular fixed-point instruction, if this particular instruction happens to be a load or store instruction, several things happen back to back: its address is generated, segment registers are accessed to acquire its virtual address, and TLBs and the D-cache are searched (in parallel). A hit/miss outcome for the cache directory access is known by the end of this stage. The occurrence of the third stage, which is the cache access stage, is contingent upon the data item being found in the cache. If data is found, the cache is accessed and data is returned to FXU or FPU, as the case may be. In the fourth and final stage, termed the write-back stage, the result of load or store instructions is written to the FXU GPRs, assuming that they were derived from fixed-point instructions that accessed the D-cache in the previous cycle, i.e., the cache access cycle. A detailed layout of the FXU is given in Fig. 11.10 to illustrate each of the pipelining phases in detail.

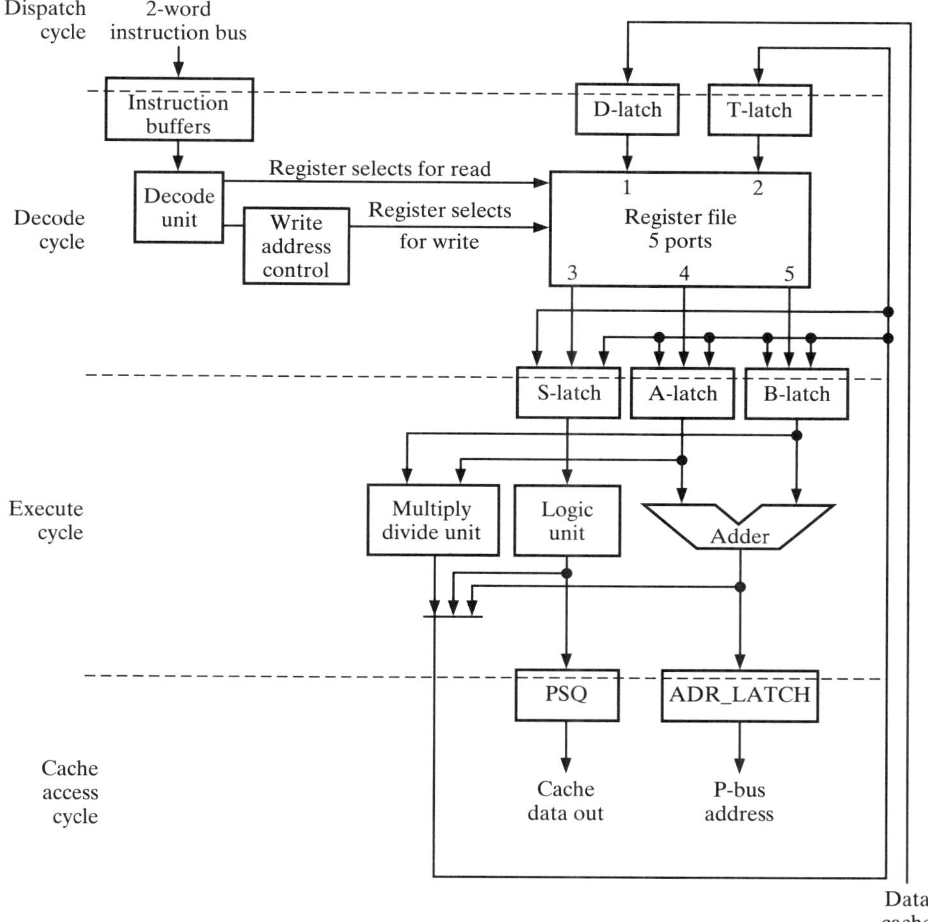

Figure 11.10 Organization and pipelining of the FXU.

11.3.3 FXU-FPU data synchronization

Earlier in this chapter, Sec. 11.2.4 explained the instruction synchronization scheme for the FXU and FPU, in which both execute the floating-point load and store instructions in a synchronous manner. Here we study the data synchronization mechanism for the FXU and FPU. The FXU generates the effective addresses, while the FPU provides the data. The addresses generated by the FXU are held in a stack called the pending store queue (PSQ). In this way, the FXU is able to continue its execution without waiting for the data part to become available. When the FPU is able to supply the data (which may be several cycles later), the actual write operation to the data cache is performed. In this way, the PSQ assists in performance enhancement of the overall instruction flow by allowing the FXU to go ahead without waiting for the floating-point data.

The problem arises when loads bypass stores in this situation. Since the wrong (old) data may get fetched in this case, a workaround is needed. The scheme used by the System/6000 is to refrain from executing a load if there is a conflicting store present in the PSQ at that instant. The load address is compared against all the addresses in the PSQ; if a match is found, the load is detained until the store gets removed from PSQ.

11.3.4 Data translation lookaside buffers

The data translation lookaside buffer (D-TLB) is a fancy name for a cache. It is used to translate virtual addresses to real addresses. The concept of translating a virtual address to a real address is a multi-stage process. It consists of, first, using the effective address to index into segment registers to obtain a segment ID for a virtual page number. Thereafter, this virtual page index is used to search the D-TLB and the page frame table to acquire the real address.

Figure 11.11 illustrates the steps involved in the process of translating the virtual address into a real address. Out of the 32 bits of the virtual address, 4 bits (0–3) are used to index into the segment registers. A 24-bit segment ID, when grouped with 16 additional bits (4–19) of the original effective address, yields a 40-bit virtual page number. This, in turn, is indexed into the TLB to yield a 20-bit real page number. When the offset (i.e., the remaining 12 bits, 20–31) from the effective address is added to this, we end up with the corresponding real page number.

Having discussed the purpose of the D-TLB, it is time to look at its physical implementation. The TLB has a set-associative implementation, similar to that of the D-cache. Not only does this implementation increase the component's hit-ratio, but it also simplifies the design point. The D-TLB is two-way set-associative with 64 sets, thus resulting in its ability to contain mapping for 512 KB. As seen in Fig. 11.12, each entry in the D-TLB maps to one page* of the virtual memory.

The mechanism of D-TLB access is explained in Fig. 11.13. The basic timing starts with the access during the execution cycle. During the first half of the execute cycle, the 32-bit effective address is generated

---

* The size of one page on the System/6000 is 4 KB.

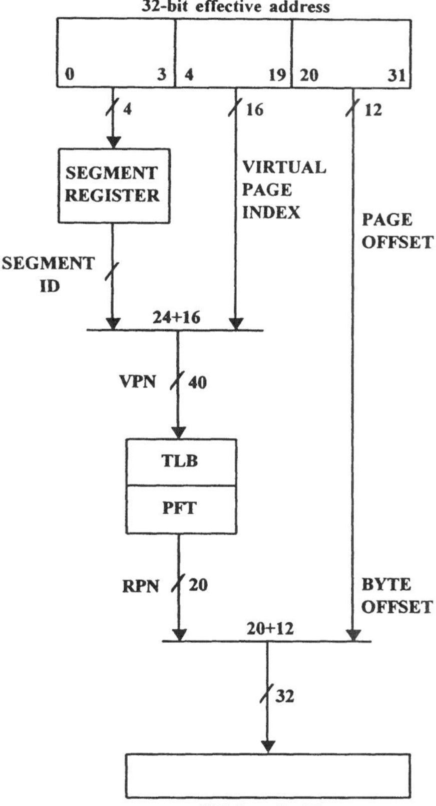

Figure 11.11 Process of virtual address translation to real address.

first. The second event to occur is the sending of the cache address to the D-cache chips containing the directory arrays; this occurs in the form of 14 bits getting sent (with the upper 7 bits setting the line and the lower 7 bits containing the bytes). The second half of the execute cycle starts with accessing the segment registers and using the scheme explained in Fig. 11.11, to obtain the virtual page number. The subsequent event to occur is the D-TLB search. Actually, the D-TLB and the D-cache are searched in parallel. As a result, the hit-or-miss outcome is known by the end of the execute cycle.

During the D-cache directory access, the 32-bit address format that is interpreted by the cache is quite different than the address interpreted by the virtual memory. The cache uses 18 bits for the tag, 7 bits for the set number, and 7 bits for the byte in line, whereas the virtual memory uses 20 bits to represent the real page number and 12 bits to represent the byte offset in the page. An interface dia-

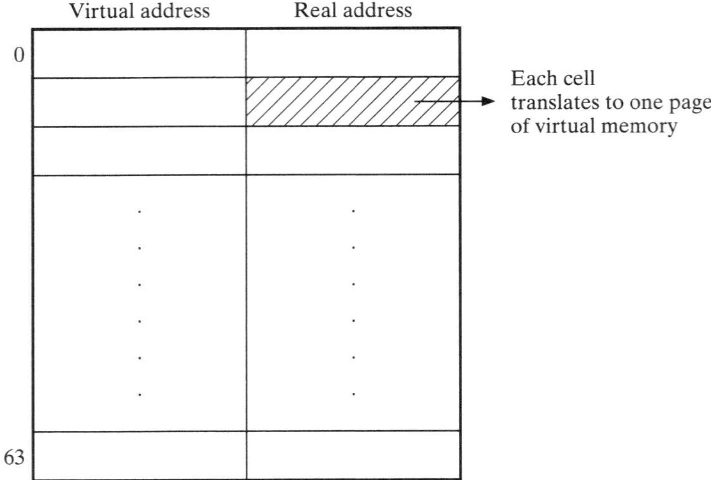

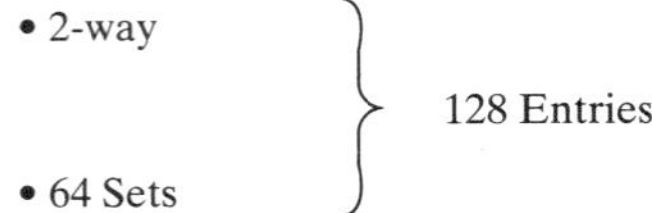

Figure 11.12 Description of two-way set-associative D-TLB.

gram given in Fig. 11.14 interprets the address representations from the two perspectives.

11.4 FLOATING POINT UNIT ARCHITECTURE

The role of the floating point unit (FPU) is to execute the floating-point instructions in the instruction stream. The FPU of this machine complies to the IEEE floating-point standards. Unlike most floating-point coprocessor chips, this FPU is tightly coupled with the FXU. The FPU is able to achieve a dramatic degree of concurrence by being able to handle two separate task-pairs simultaneously. The design of the FPU enables it to exploit (1) floating-point load operations in parallel with floating-point arithmetic operations, and (2) floating-point multiply operations pipelined with floating-point add operations. The other distinctive feature about the FPU is its ability to deliver a higher degree of accuracy beyond the capabilities of other currently available IEEE-compatible double-precision floating point units.

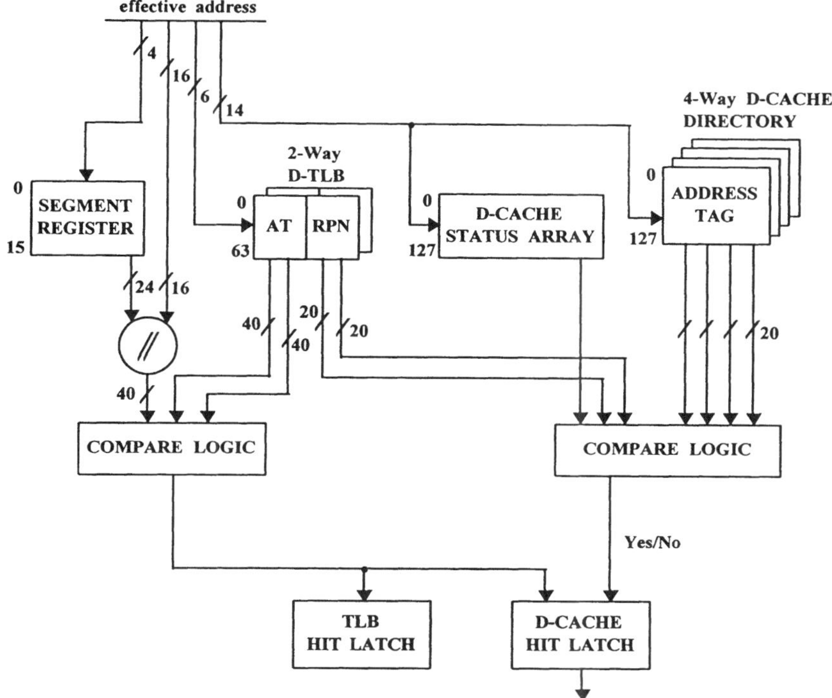

Figure 11.13 Mechanism of D-TLB and D-cache directory access.

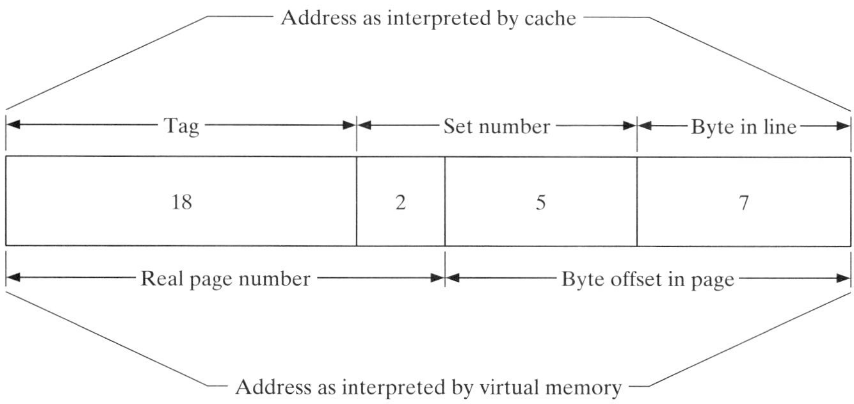

Figure 11.14 Address interpretations by cache and virtual memory.

In this section, the general organization of the FPU is first described. Thereafter, the key concepts of the FPU's underlying components are explained. Finally, the implementation of the FPU pipeline is described to aggregate the concepts under one roof.

11.4.1 General organization

The FPU includes a set of registers and dedicated elements, each contributing to the overall performance-crafted design of the execution unit. The first group of components consists of a set of general purpose registers called the floating-point registers (FPRs). These are used as source and destination operands for all the arithmetic floating-point operations and their results. There are 32 FPRs available for use by instructions. Each FPR is 64 bits in size and thus is able to deliver double precision results, with the only exception being in the case of load and store operations, because they are handled by the FXU. The next key component of the FPU is a special register called the floating-point status and control register (FPSCR). It handles floating-point exceptions and records status resulting from the floating-point operations, which are required by the IEEE 754 standard. The FPSCR is 32 bits in size, with bits 0–19 being status bits and the remaining bits 20–31 used as control bits.

Representation for a floating-point number consists of a signed exponent and a signed significand. The quantity expressed by this number is the product of the significand and the number 2^{exponent}. Encodings are provided in the data format to represent finite numeric values, $\pm$infinity, and values which are not a number.

11.4.2 Pipeline stages

The six-stage pipeline for the FPU happens to be the deepest of all the pipelines on this machine's processor complex. Its first stage consists of a pre-decode cycle where instructions are pre-decoded in preparation for register remapping. In the next stage, which is the remap stage, the floating-point registers are mapped to the physical registers. The third stage, the floating-point decode stage, consists of examining registers and fetching source operands. The next two stages, execute-1 and execute-2, denote the first and the second phases of the multiply-add pipeline. The sixth and final stage, which is the write-back stage, involves results getting written back to the FPRs. The physical implementation of the actual pipeline is covered later in this section.

11.4.3 Multiply-add subunit

Probably the most distinctive feature of the FPU is its multiply-add fused subunit (MAF). Its key significance comes into play when working with dot products in matrix operations. The multiply and accumulate operation in matrix manipulations, which is in the general form of $(A \times C) + B$, is performed as an atomic step using this MAF. Since it takes a single clock cycle to execute the operation, there is a direct saving of one clock cycle for every occurrence of this instruction. Being a frequent operation in the floating point computations, the MAF results in a dramatic performance benefit.

The motivation for MAF evolved from the fact that dot products happen to be the most frequently executed floating-point operations. An optimization in its fundamental level, which consists of a multiply and an accumulate (or add) function, was implemented by fusing the two. The design yielded a significant performance gain.

The defining feature of the multiply-add primitive is its ability to process the accumulate operation of $(A \times C) + B$ as an indivisible step. The basic concept of multiplying two operands and subsequently adding its product to a third operand remains the same on the MAF implementation. However, its execution takes place under the envelope of a single instruction. Four operands are needed with the MAF instruction. Some permutations of the MAF primitive are:

MAF primitive	Operation	Instruction syntax
Multiply-Add	$t1 = a \times c + b$	*fma* fp1, fp10, fp11, fp12
Multiply-Subtract	$t2 = a \times c - b$	*fma* fp2, fp10, fp11, fp12

The first column lists the different permutations; the second column represents the corresponding operations performed with three representative source values (a, b, and c) assigned to respective targets $t1$, $t2$, $t3$, and $t4$. The third column provides the assembly language syntax of the MAF instruction, *fma*, with its parameters. (Note: FPRs 1, 2, 3, and 4 represent the targets, while FPRs 10, 11, and 12 indicate the source values.)

The implementation of the multiply-add primitive involves fusing the multiply and add operations, while eliminating the intermediate rounding and making use of additional hardware logic to predict the number of leading zeros in advance. Before being able to describe the System/6000's implementation, it is necessary to review the classical way of processing floating-point operations in a computer system. In general, a floating-point multiply consists of adding the exponents, multiplying the significands, and subsequently normalizing and rounding the result. Similarly, a floating-point add consists of calculating the difference of the exponents, aligning the significand with the smaller exponent by the same amount as that of the difference, adding up the two significands and using the larger exponent as the resultant exponent, and normalizing and rounding the result. Note that multiplication turns out to be simpler than addition. A comparative table given in Fig. 11.15 summarizes the sequence of steps involved in the case of a floating-point multiply and a floating-point add operation. In MAF, by collapsing both operations into a single instruction, the normalization and rounding of the multiplication operation are discarded and the partial result is routed to the adder's input port. Not only does the fusing of the multiply and add operations result in saving extra cycles, but it also reduces the amount of dataflow logic that would have been required for the second normalization and rounding for the multiply operation result. The second immediate benefit is a reduction in internal busing, since the hardware only has to implement the circuit for four ports into and out of the MAF, as compared to six ports in the case of the classical approach. The third advantage in this implementation is the extra accuracy gained by the elimination of one normalizer. Figure 11.16 elucidates the implementation of the MAF while comparing it to a classical multiplier and adder.

<u>Classical FP Multiply</u>	<u>Classical FP Add</u>
1) Add exponents	1) Subtract exponents
2) Multiply significands	2) Shift significand with smaller exponent to right by the difference of exponents.
3) Normalize	3) Add significands. Larger exponent is the exponent of the result.
4) Round	4) Normalize
	5) Round

Figure 11.15 Comparison of steps involved in a floating-point multiplication and a floating-point addition.

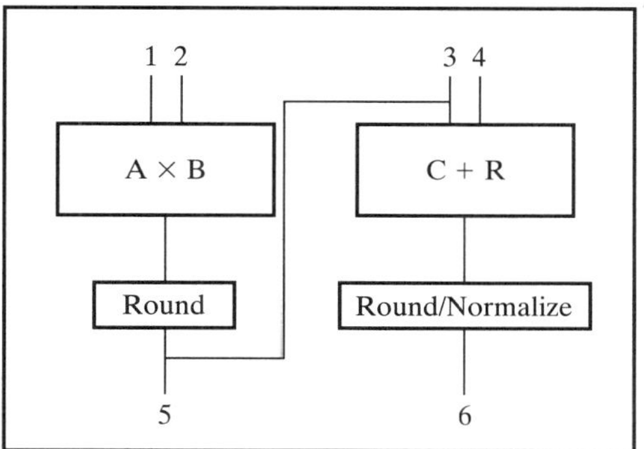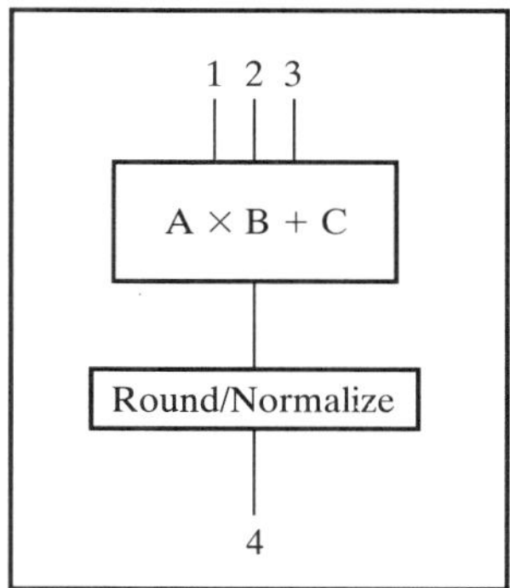

Figure 11.16 Implementation of a classical multiplier and adder, versus MAF implementation.

11.4.4 Leading zero anticipator

A hardware logic called the leading zero anticipator (LZA) is present in the FPU to aid in predicting the number of leading zeros on the output port of the adder, thereby enabling the normalization of the final result to be completed within the same cycle. Since it operates in parallel with the adder, the shift amount needed for normalization is available when the addition completes. The design of the LZA is described in detail in the works of Hokenek and Montoye (1989).

11.4.5 Normalization

The process of normalization is used as a means of referencing a number to a fixed radix point. The process is done in two phases. The first phase consists of using a hexadecimal shifter to traverse the leading zeros, starting from the decimal point. The zeros are scanned in groups of fours until quadruplets are exhausted. Subsequently, the second phase of the normalization process kicks in, using a binary shifter to scan and shift the remaining zeros and adjusting the exponent accordingly. In an example like 0.000000000011, the hexadecimal shifter moves the first set of zeros, after which the binary shifter eliminates the remaining two zeros. Its operation is presented in Fig. 11.17. After the completion of the binary normalization (and rounding), the result either gets written to registers or is fed back into the pipeline.

11.4.6 Data bypass

Data bypass is an implementation to deal with instruction dependencies in an instruction stream. The FPU provides a data bypass provision for dependent operations in two different forms. Both cases are

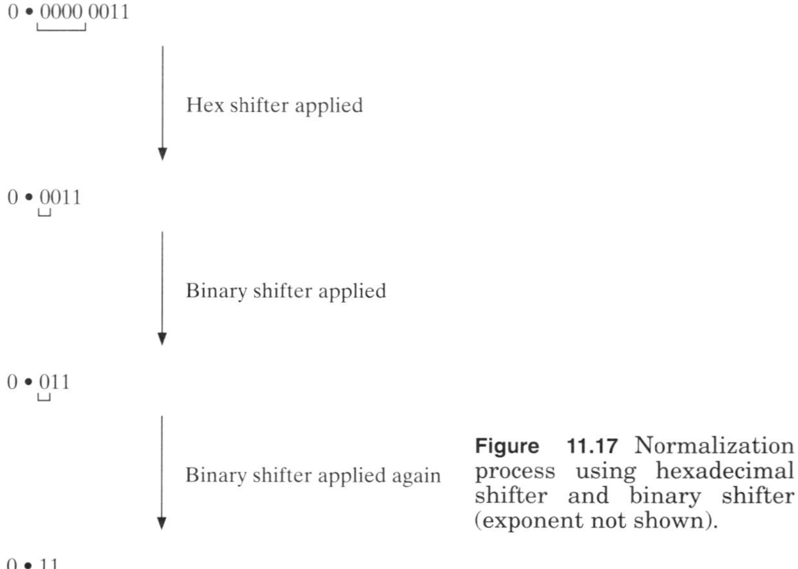

Figure   11.17 Normalization process using hexadecimal shifter and binary shifter (exponent not shown).

explained using simplified examples. For the first case, consider the following example:

$$I_1: \quad \boldsymbol{r1} = r2 + r3$$
$$I_2: \quad r4 = \boldsymbol{r1} * r5$$

In the above code fragment, the second instruction, I_2, depends on the result of the first one, with the exact source operand dependency being shown in boldface. Without data bypass, the second instruction waits in decode stage for two cycles: in cycle 1, the first instruction completes, and in cycle 2, its result is written in r4. But with data bypass, the second instruction waits in decode stage for only one cycle, which is for the first instruction to finish. The result is obtained directly from the pipeline output. For the second case, consider the following example:

$$I_1: \quad \boldsymbol{r1} = r2 + r3$$
$$J: \quad \text{independent}$$
$$I_2: \quad r4 = \boldsymbol{r1} * r5$$

In this code fragment, an independent instruction, J, has been introduced. The third instruction, I_2, depends on the result of the first instruction, I_1, with the source operand dependency for $r1$ shown in bold. Without data bypass, the third instruction would have had to wait in decode stage for one cycle, i.e., until the result is written in $r4$. But with data bypass, the third instruction does not wait at all. The result is obtained directly from the pipeline output.

11.4.7   Register remapping

The concept of register remapping (also known as register renaming) results from the need to keep the pipeline full and devoid of any stalling owing to the unavailability of load instructions. Load instructions are allowed to go ahead and execute, by creating an illusion that the content of the FPR has been overwritten by allowing a load to complete before the previous instruction has accessed it. This trick is achieved by having a pool of free physical registers available beyond the advertised number of 32 FPRs. It so happens that there are six additional registers available in the FPU for our remapping purpose!* The actual implementation of the register remap structure is extremely complex. Hence, the process of architected registers (used in instructions) getting mapped to physical registers is best explained with the use of an example, rather than by describing the process generically.

Before starting with the example, the register remap structure needs to be introduced. The first component is the remap structure which is a map table (MT) containing one entry per each of the 32 architected registers, each entry being 6 bits wide. The second member is a set called free list (FL) which holds the extra (initially unassigned) physical registers. The subsequent element is the pending target store queue (PTSQ) that contains physical registers which have been removed from the map table (due to a new remapping) but are still used by instructions that have not passed the decode stage yet. A head (H) and a tail (T) pointer in the PTSQ maintain it as a circular queue. Other components are the pending store queue (PSQ) that holds addresses generated by the FXU and the instruction decode buffers (IDB) which assist the FXU to run ahead and feed data to the FPU. Last, there is a pair of remap registers (R0 and R1), containing an opcode field, a target-register field, and source-register fields.

The example code fragment listed here will be used to trace through the register remap scheme. Note that *what* this code does is not as relevant as *how* the code gets handled by the remap structure.

```
fa      fp3,    fp2,    fp1     ;floating add
lfd     fp3                     ;load fp3
fm      fp6,    fp3,    fp1     ;floating multiply. uses fp3.
fs      fp2,    fp6,    fp2     ;floating subtract. uses fp6.
```

---

* In total, there are 40 registers in the FPU. Thirty-two registers are available for programmers. Six additional ones are used for remapping. The remaining two registers are dedicated to the floating-point divide operation.

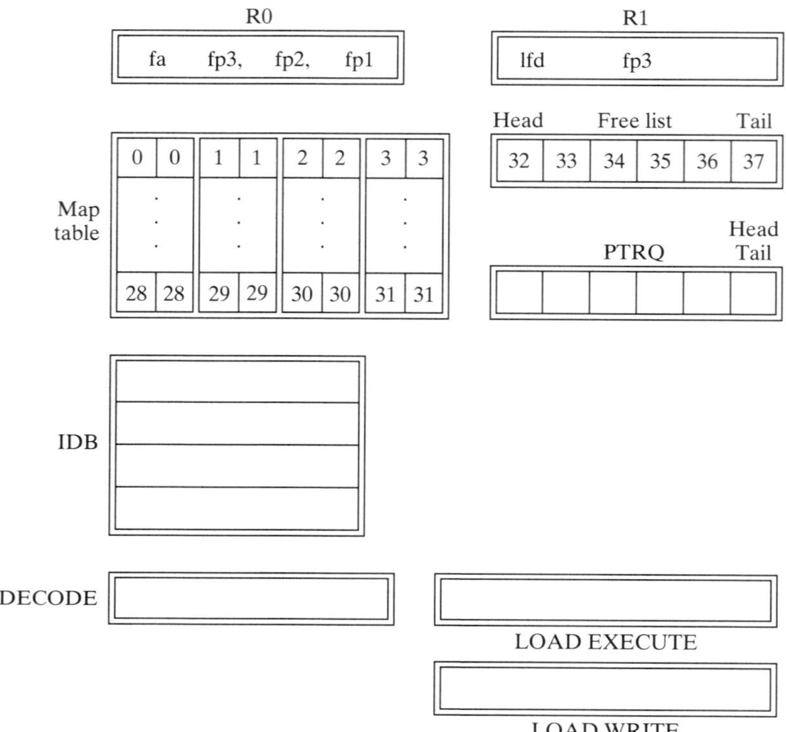

Figure 11.18 Register remap structure in its initial stage, cycle 1.

In cycle 1, the first pair of instructions is brought into the remap registers, R0 and R1, as shown in Fig. 11.18. Cycle 2 results in (1) dispatching the *fa* from R0 to the decoder for further processing, (2) forwarding the *lfd* from R1 to the load execute stage, and (3) fetching the next pair of instructions into R0 and R1. Notice that *fa* in the decode stage uses pr3, pr2, and pr1 (pr*n* being a convention to represent physical register) instead of using the originally specified fp3, fp2, and fp1 registers. Now the *lfd,* finding pr3 to be in use upon attempting to remap its corresponding physical register, borrows pr32 from the free pool, FL (causing the head pointer of the FL to shift to the next consecutive register, pr33). As a result, the index for pr3 ends up in the PTSQ. The state of the remap structure after completing cycle 2 is depicted in Fig. 11.19. Cycle 3 consists of (1) dispatching *fm* from R0 to the decode stage, (2) queuing *fs* up in the IDB (until *fm* releases the decode stage), (3) completion of the load write stage for the *lfd,* and (4) return of the physical register pr32 to the free list and clean-up of the PTSQ. The state after completing cycle 3 is shown in Fig. 11.20. Cycle 4 con-

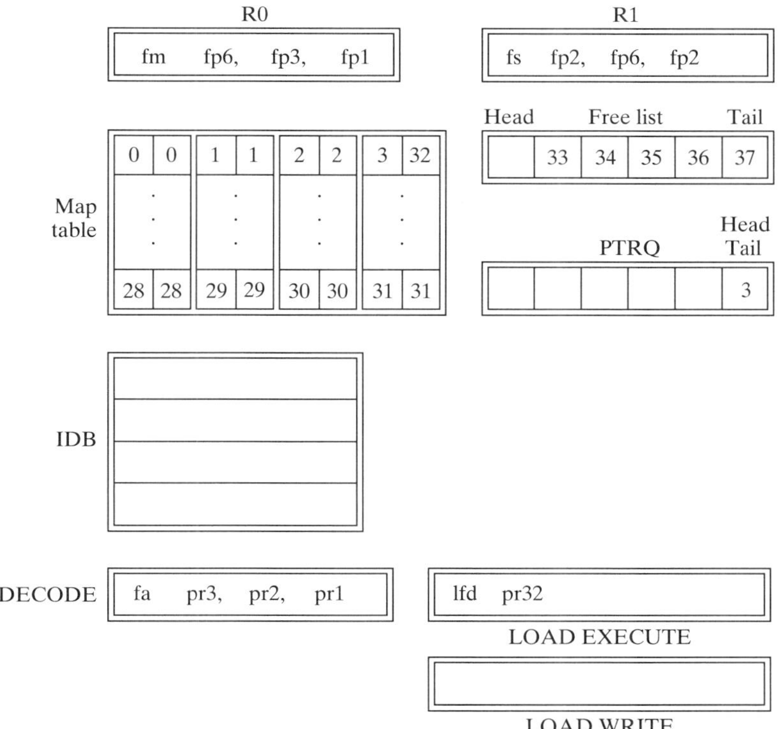

Figure 11.19 Register remap structure in cycle 2. *Note:* (1) register fp3 renamed to physical register pr32, and (2) physical register pr3 is in PTRQ.

cludes the instruction processing by dispatching the queued *fs* from the IDB to the decode stage, which is now freed. The *fs* subtract operation is held in decode for one cycle until the result of the previous instruction is made available. Cycle 4 is represented in Fig. 11.21. Tracing the code fragment through the diagrams of the four stages yields the best understanding of the register remap mechanism.

11.4.8 Pipeline implementation

The FPU pipeline receives instructions from the ICU over the instruction bus interface at the rate of two per cycle. A pool of six buffers is provided between the instruction bus and the pre-decode stage to maximize the usage of the instruction bus and deal with queuing. After processing, the FPU pipeline transfers data to the DCU over the data bus located between the FPU and the DCU. A set of four buffers, referred to as the floating-point store queue (FPSQ), is provided here to

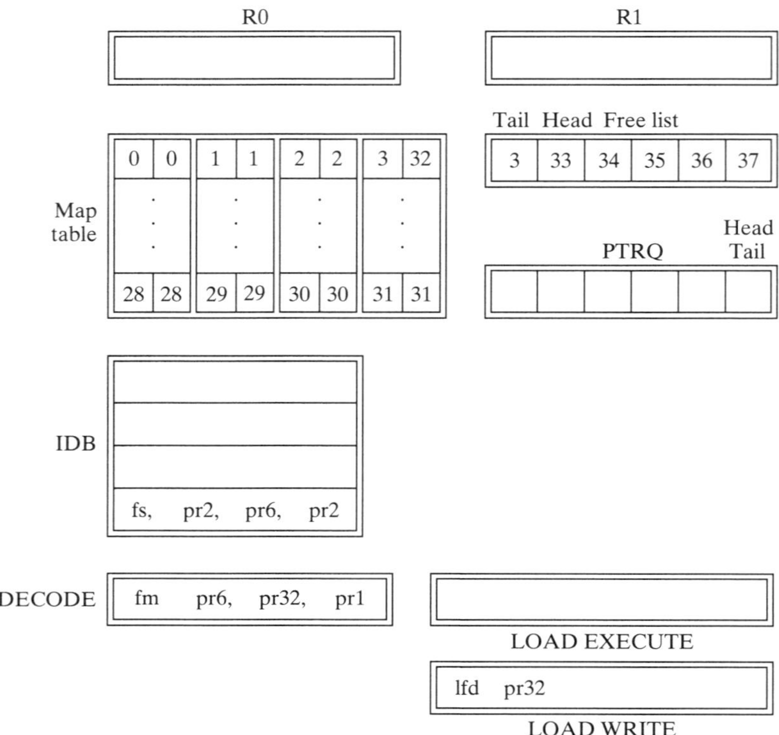

Figure 11.20 Register remap structure in cycle 3. *Note:* Physical register pr3 returned to free list.

allow store instructions to queue up while waiting for free cycles on the FPU data bus to forward data to the DCU. In this way, the FXU and FPU pipelines remain free to execute their subsequent instructions, pretending that the store instruction is completed.

The complete instruction pipeline stages of the FPU are shown in Fig. 11.22 along with a partial view of the FXU that is involved in the load/store task. The instructions from the ICU are brought into a set of six instruction buffers as instruction dispatch overruns. In the pre-decode stage, a pair of instructions gets processed every cycle. Based on whether they are fixed-point instructions or floating-point instructions, they either get discarded or forwarded. The remap stage is also capable of processing two instructions per cycle. In this stage, the architecting registers get remapped to the physical registers. From the decode stage onward, the processing rate of two instructions per cycle is reduced to one instruction per cycle. To deal with this overrun, a set of four decode buffers is implemented. Operands are accessed either

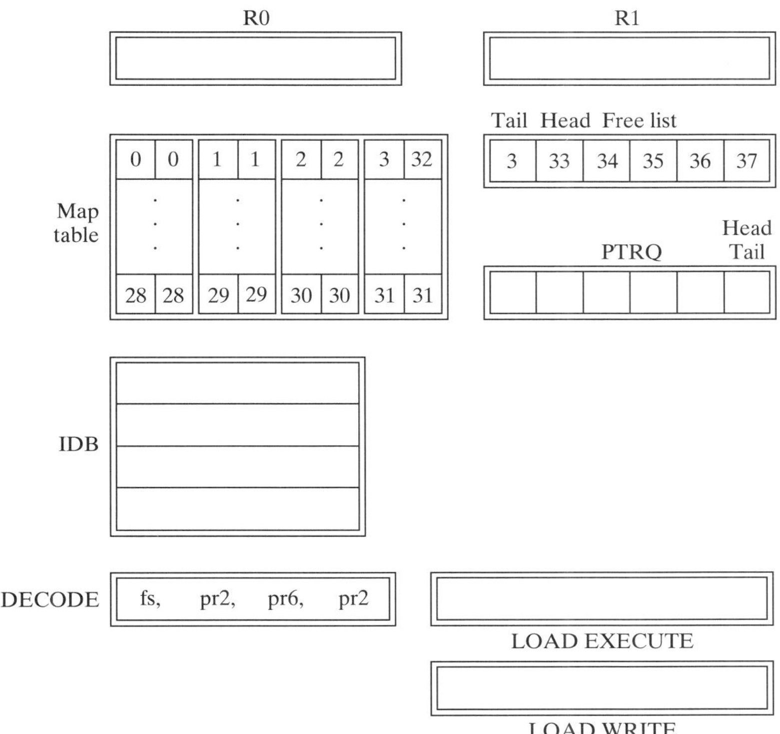

Figure 11.21 Register remap structure in cycle 4. *Note:* Subtract instruction held in decode for one cycle while waiting for the result of previous instruction.

from the registers or from the output of the FPU pipeline using one of the bypass mechanisms. The next stage, which is multiply or execute-1 (the first of the two execute stages) involves manipulation of A and C from the originally described $(A \times C) + B$ construct. The 53-bit significands of A and C are multiplied together to produce a 106-bit significand product. The exponent of A is then added to the exponent of C, followed by computing a difference with the adjusted exponent of the operand B, which was obtained by subtracting 53 from the exponent and left-shifting the significand of B by 53 bits. The amount of right-shift made by significand B is dependent upon the difference between the exponent of B and exponent of $(A \times C)$. The left-shifting of the significand B by 53 bits results in an effective 159-bit aligned significand. The add, which marks the second execution stage, causes the 159-bit significand B to be added to the 106-bit significand of $(A \times C)$. Both remain right-justified. With the LZA working in parallel at this stage

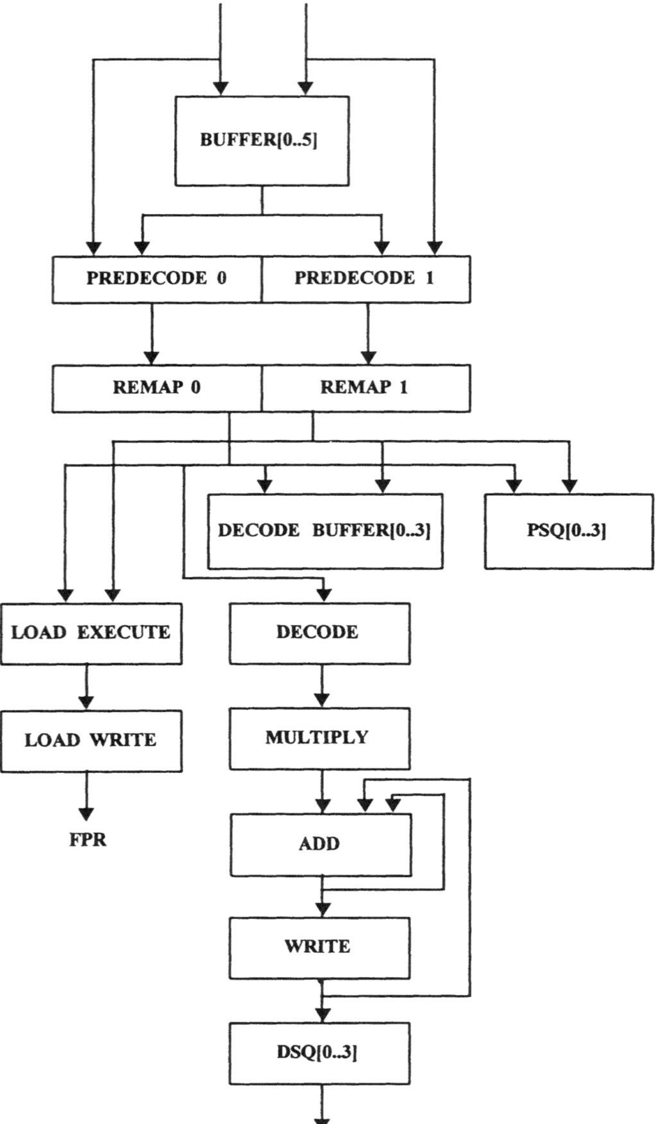

Figure 11.22 The FPU instruction pipeline implementation.

of the game, the number of leading zeros at the output of the adder can be predicted. The hexadecimal shifter operates during this stage to do its work. In the write stage, the binary shifter kicks in to complete its task of normalization; subsequently, the value is rounded and written into the FPRs.

11.4.9 IEEE exceptions

The specifications in the IEEE Standard for Binary Floating-point Arithmetic, ANSI/IEEE Std. 754, describe several types of exceptions that can occur in floating-point computations. The document also describes how these exceptions should be dealt with. The hardware architecture of the FPU deals with some of these specifications, such as overflow, underflow, divide by zero, etc., in the prescribed manner. Other exceptions like square root, integer conversion, etc., are left for the software to implement.

11.5 SUMMARY

The POWER architecture with its superscalar design and independent execution units achieves a pinnacle in terms of performance-crafted design. The high-bandwidth interfaces between the dedicated cache memories enable the machine to achieve a significant degree of concurrency and parallelism. The ability to simultaneously process (and fetch) several instructions in a single clock cycle without sacrificing performance makes the System/6000 even more attractive. In fact, the mention of the fused multiply-add instruction to leapfrog ahead of the competitive offerings is most appropriate here. With its inclusion in the POWER instruction set, up to five operations in a single clock cycle are made possible. The three execution units which orchestrate the program execution are contributors in their own rights. The BPU minimizes the pipeline penalty caused by branch instructions. The FXU processes all the fixed-point instructions and also conducts the loads and stores for floating-point instructions. The FPU remains involved with execution of the floating-point instructions at the maximum permissible rate. Aggregated here are the principal registers belonging to each of the three execution units:

FXU	BPU	FPU
GPRs	LR	FPRs (64-bit)
SR	CR	FPSCR
TID	CTR	
MQ	MSR	
DAR	SRR	
DSISR		
XER		

All of them have been discussed in detail in this chapter, along with the internal design of the execution units.

Memory and I/O Subsystem

The overall processing capabilities of a CPU complex are only as good as its input/output subsystem. The case is the same for the System/6000, where the high-performance central electronic complex is complemented by a high-speed memory I/O subsystem for feeding data into the CPU and an efficient device I/O subsystem for handling data output from the CPU.

This chapter is organized into three parts. The first part discusses the layout of the I/O subsystem that surrounds the CPU subcomplex, i.e., the memory interface, the storage control unit (SCU), the system I/O (SIO) bus, and, eventually, the I/O channel controller (IOCC). The second part of this chapter discusses the Micro Channel bus which is the interface between the IOCC and the peripheral devices. The key concepts and features of the Micro Channel interface definition are covered here. The third segment describes the SCSI (less popularly known as the small computer system interface) subsystem in detail. Principal features of the SCSI protocol are covered, describing its attachment to the Micro Channel bus, discussing its supporting features, and explaining the handshaking protocol.

12.1 LAYOUT OF FUNCTIONAL UNITS

The memory chips are located on memory cards that plug into the CPU planar's dedicated slots (refer to Fig. 9.2). Each memory card has eight sockets for SIMMs (single in-line memory modules), where SIMMs of appropriate densities may be installed. In an effort to keep this information generic so that it may be applicable to variable densities of DRAMs, no specific sizes of SIMMs are being discussed. The System/6000 product line was originally introduced in 1990 with 1-Mbit and 4-Mbit DRAMs. As technology evolves we will see the advent of 16-Mbit, 64-Mbit, 128-Mbit, and higher-density chips. With provision for eight SIMM sockets per memory card and eight memory cards per processor, one can always calculate the maximum permissible physical memory for the System/6000. With regard to the interfaces, the memory cards implement a four-way-interleaved design using a pair of multiplexing data buffer chips and a single control chip, as seen in Fig. 12.1. As a result, two words of data per machine cycle can be provided from each of the memory cards. These cards support buffering for up to 16 words of write data. The cards themselves are compatible with standard SIMM packages for DRAM chips so that they can interpret read-write signals from/to the memory bus. The bus interface from the memory to the DCU is four words wide. This interface also connects the memory to the ICU. A bit-scattering feature is implemented on this bus to ensure that no more than one bit of a 40-bit word is stored in an individual DRAM. A point to be noted here is that this memory bus is only two words wide on the cost-reduced version of the CPU board that uses only two DCUs (refer to Fig. 9.6) and lacks the bit-scattering feature.

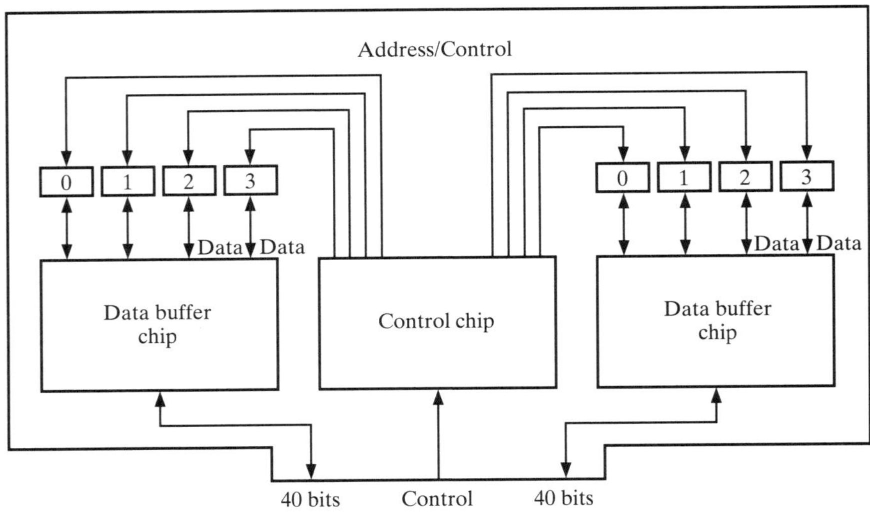

Figure 12.1 Interleaved memory card.

The SCU is located on the CPU planar and has several important functions to perform. Its role can be expressed in a nutshell as the central orchestrator for the coordination of information transfer between the CPU subcomplex and the I/O subcomplex. There are two interfaces for this component. The chip interfaces with the execution units in the CPU subcomplex via a dedicated processor bus. Its interface with the I/O subsystem is through another bus, called the system I/O bus (referred to as the SIO bus from here on).

The SIO bus interfaces with the IOCC. The IOCC, in turn, interfaces with the Micro Channel bus at its other end. The principal function of this IOCC is to move data between the memory subsystem and the device(s) attached to the adapters on the Micro Channel bus. A view from the global perspective of the hardware architectural layout depicts this IOCC to be a conceptual barrier between two domains, namely, (1) the CPU and memory complex and (2) the I/O device and storage complex. Figure 12.2 further illustrates the concept.

12.2   SCU-MEMORY INTERACTION

The SCU interacts with the main memory to arbitrate the communications between the execution units and I/O. It generates the control signals for the memory upon receipt of I-cache reload, D-cache reload, and D-cache store-back requests. Furthermore, it acts as the bus master for the memory bus and the SIO bus, while providing a data path for I/O load/store operations between the execution units and the I/O device.

12.2.1   Memory interface

Memory organization on this architecture is software-configurable. Its base addresses are held in the SCU. In the SCU there are sixteen memory configurable registers (MCRs), which are used to map the physical memory of the machine to its system address space. Each MCR is composed of two parts, the bank size and the bank base address ("bank" refers to contiguous physical memory). The bank size code refers to the physical memory size, while the base address indicates the real starting address.

When analyzed, a single unit of memory transfer on the System/6000 shows that a quadword (64 bytes) is the basic unit of a transfer. Figure 12.3 portrays a typical memory-write scenario along with the main timing signals that conduct this transfer. Note that the actual transfer timing will depend upon the particular implementation of the memory card. But in general, a single memory-read transfer operation

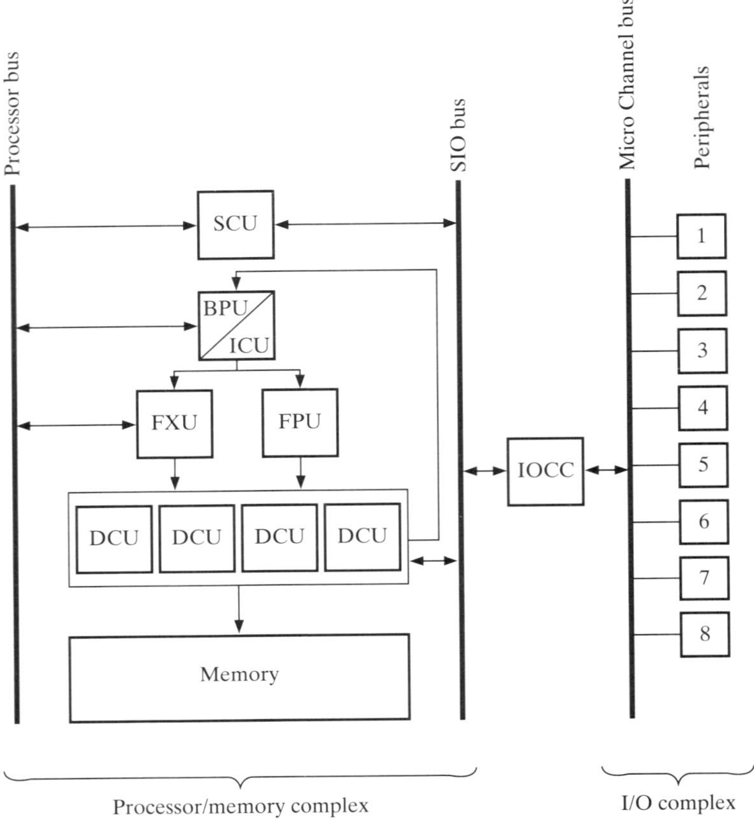

Figure 12.2 Positioning of the memory, SCU, and IOCC.

requires six cycles* for address and control setup and access of memory before an actual transfer of data takes place. When a transfer happens, it is performed in units of quadwords (16 bytes). So, a total of ten cycles (four cycles for four quadword transfers and six cycles for setup overhead) are needed to perform a single transfer operation. Figure 12.3 shows the four quadword transfers. Upon extending this concept of a single unit of transfer to a real situation, it can be seen how successive memory read/write operations work off the same memory card as well as across a different memory card.

A memory request buffering is implemented by augmenting the memory bus utilization. The memory interface is allowed to keep two

---

* The 6 cycles will vary depending on the speed of the processor and the speed of the DRAM.

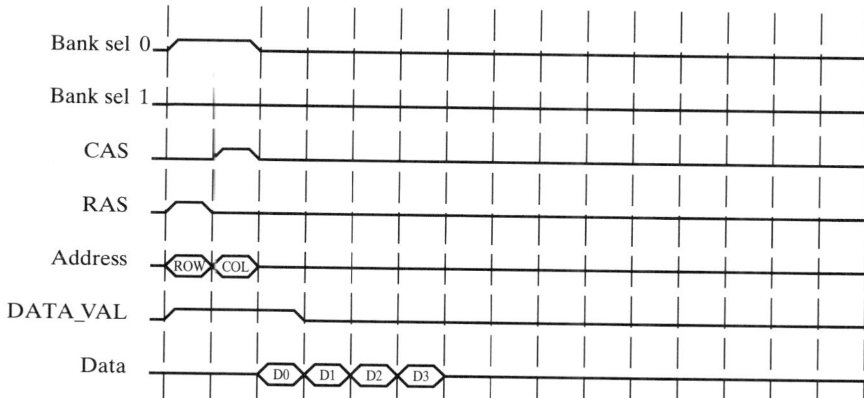

Figure 12.3 Timing diagram for a single memory-write operation.

memory requests pending at any given time. The card starts processing the second request while the first is being completed. If these requests happen to be on different cards, the memory requests happen concurrently. Now, because the memory-to-cache interface is four words (128 bytes) wide, minimal delay is necessary in loading the cache line with two quadword transfers (2×64-bytes $= 128$ bytes). This calls for an ability to perform two quadword transfers back-to-back. In a situation with two read or write requests, Figs. 12.4 and 12.5 characterize how the transfer operation will progress (1) when it is issued from different cards, and (2) when it is off the same card.

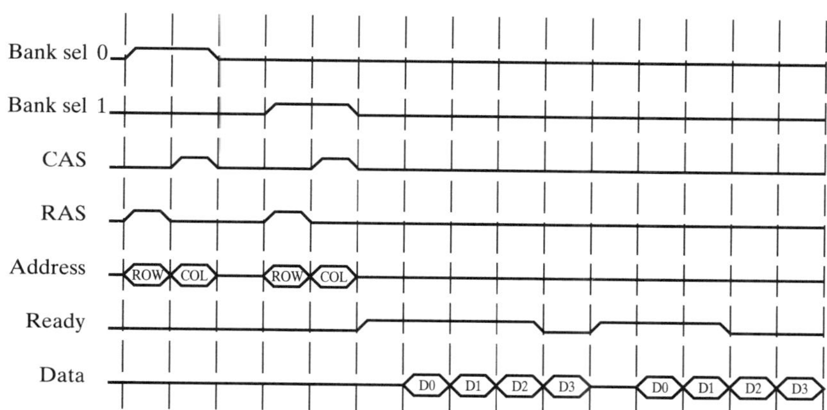

Figure 12.4 Timing diagram for a pair of memory-read operations from two separate cards.

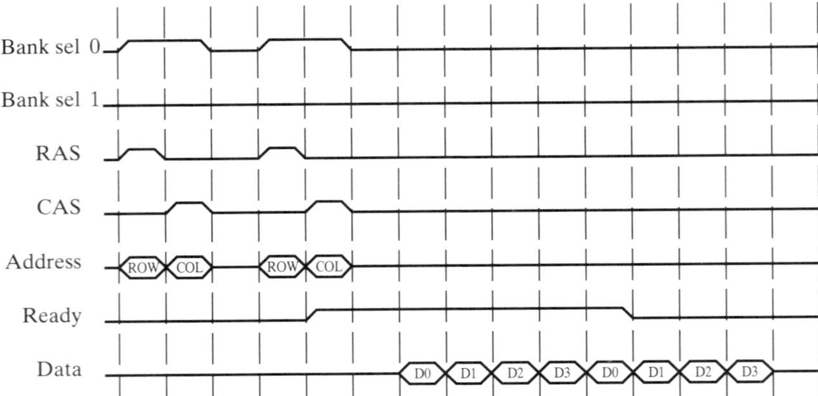

Figure 12.5 Timing diagram for a pair of memory-read operations from a single card.

A pair of quadword transfers for memory-read operations from two different memory cards indicates that there are two memory banks involved in the process. In the timing diagram of Fig. 12.4, which depicts a pair of quadword transfers for a read operation, the first two signals are issued by the SCU to select the banks. The SCU issues two more signals to select the row and the column cells of the memory. After the address of the memory cell has been resolved, a ready signal is issued to the SCU by the memory card to initiate the read transfer. The next signal is the data signal and it consists of the data arriving from the memory bank in quadwords. Note that for a write operation, the process of issuing a ready signal would have been the same, except for the fact that the ready signal would have been issued to the memory card rather than the SCU. Also, the data would have appeared from the SCU into the memory bank. The overall process can be outlined in 15 cycles, with 6 cycles taken for the overhead to include bank, row, and column selections, 4 cycles used to transfer the data to the first memory card, and 5 cycles used to write data to the second card.

Two quadword transfers for memory-read operations to the same memory card differ slightly. The read operation commencing from the same memory card implies that it would have the same row address, as conceptualized within a memory cell model in Fig. 12.6. After the bank, row, and column selection signals have been issued (by the SCU), the ready signal is sent to indicate the initiation of data transfer. The subsequent signal is the data signal itself and it consists of the data arriving from the memory bank, quadwords at a time. Note that for a write operation the direction of the dataflow would have been opposite. Having the same row address implies that the data is being read from the

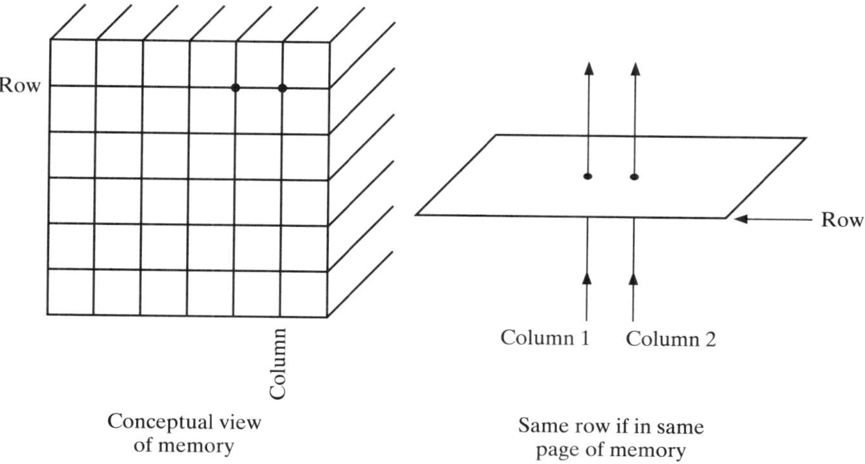

Figure 12.6 Concept of the machine's memory as a three-dimensional entity, to access the same row address when reading from the same memory card.

same page of the memory. If this is so, the memory card places the DRAMs into a page mode, so that multiple transfers can occur by merely changing the column address. In this way, data is transferred in a continuous burst across the memory bus, as seen in Fig. 12.5. Note that with access to different memory pages, a gap would have arisen between the data for two transfers. The overall process in this case can be outlined in 14 cycles, with 6 cycles in overhead, 4 cycles for the first quadword, and 4 cycles for the second quadword.

In order to extend the performance level of the memory architecture, an early data-ready mechanism is implemented such that the data-ready signal gets issued before the data is actually valid on the bus. In the case of write operations, the SCU issues this signal, whereas in the case of read operations, the SCU receives this signal (from the memory card). This early data-ready signal is actually issued two cycles earlier, as seen in Fig. 12.4. In this implementation, there is no additional latency as both the SCU and the memory cards are able to predict when there will be data ready to transfer to the bus. This ability to issue a ready signal before a unit of data is valid on the bus gains us a couple of precious cycles in each transfer.

12.2.2 Memory bus

Implementation of a self-arbitrating memory bus was necessitated in order to eliminate the overhead for arbitration and additional signals. The arbitration itself was required so that only one device may drive the bus at any given time. There is no bus master in the memory bus.

However, there is a criterion that all memory requests must be completed in the order issued. To deal with this, a queue is maintained for arbitrating for the memory bus, and each device keeps track of the pending requests. The general rules for arbitration are (1) there cannot be more than two uncompleted requests on the bus, (2) each memory card needs to keep track of its requests and pending requests of other memory cards, and (3) there needs to be a dead cycle on the data bus between transfer from different cards to prevent contention. It should also be noted that out of all other buses in the architecture of this machine, only the memory bus is self-arbitrating.

12.2.3 Memory operational functions

The memory bus may be requested by a functional unit to perform assorted functions. Memory request arbitration consists of the SCU arbitrating among three disjointed types of memory requests. The first of the three types of memory requests involves the processor bus directly, and it entails operational requests with the processor bus for reading the memory for cache misses or storing data from DCU to memory. The second type of memory arbitration request consists of performing direct memory access (DMA) read/write operations to memory. The third type of memory arbitration request consists of scrubbing the memory to correct/detect errors.

Zooming in on the first of the three memory requests results in some interesting findings. Recall that the I-cache path to the memory is via the D-cache. So, when an I-cache miss occurs, the ICU sends a request to the SCU over the processor bus. The SCU in turn accesses the memory to load the pertinent data into the DCU,* from which it promptly gets transferred to the ICU. In general, this transfer occurs over the I-cache reload bus. But on the machine models equipped with the half-size D-cache on the CPU planar, the SIO bus takes it upon itself to conduct the transfer.

12.2.4 Memory control functions

While carrying out all its operational tasks, the memory bus also has to conduct numerous control functions so that the likelihood of errors remains minimal on a running system.

Memory scrubbing is one of such tasks that requires mentioning while discussing the facilities and architecture of this machine. It can

---

* Actually, this piece of datum is loaded into the cache reload buffer (CRB) of the DCU, the steps for which are covered in Chap. 10.

be defined as an ongoing process that scans the DRAM-based main memory sequentially on an operational system. The main memory of the computer, being essentially an aggregated set of DRAM memory modules, remains vulnerable to soft errors. Although soft errors are correctable, over a prolonged period of time they can be rendered unrecoverable. So the scrubbing process is periodically used to correct single-bit errors. Without scrubbing, single-bit errors may turn into 2-bit errors, which are uncorrectable. This memory-scrubbing feature is built into the hardware. However, it is controlled by software. Software oversees the periodicity of this event by treating it as a low-priority but essential task. This implies that whenever there is a higher-priority memory transfer, the scrubbing sequence would have to be interrupted. Software drives the memory scrubbing process with the help of three registers that supply its starting address, ending address, and the scrub rate. The algorithm for a single memory scrub operation is as follows:

```
read cache line to detect error
if error found
     write to cache line to correct the error
     read cache line again to verify the correction
advance to next cache line address
```

When a hard error (such as a bit stuck to 0 or 1) is detected it cannot be corrected by memory scrubbing. Error detection and correction logic is implemented to deal with hard errors on the system. Each word that DCU receives from the memory interface is made up of 40 bits. Out of the 40 bits, 32 are data bits which we refer to most often, 7 are check bits, and 1 is a spare bit. Each word is encoded using an error-correction scheme (a modified Hamming code) prior to a memory-write operation. Similarly, each word is checked for errors following a memory-read operation. The error-correction code allows single-bit errors to be corrected and 2-bit errors to be detected. Upon correcting a faulty bit, the address of the corrected bit is written to a register. The operating system reads this register and the failing address to isolate the failure to a particular memory bit.

Bit-steering is another of the memory control functions that assists in bypassing hard memory failures by substituting good spare bits for failing bits. Each DCU can steer a spare bit into any data or check-bit position within the ECC word it receives. The bit-steering information is kept in a set of registers called the bit-steering configuration registers (BSCR). These BSCRs are reprogrammed every time the system is turned on. Together with the memory-scrubbing function, the system uses this bit-steering capability to deal with single-bit errors.

Diagnostic programmed I/O to check the extra bits in memory is required owing to the implementation of the error correction and detection logic. The SCU arbitrates for the memory bus to conduct programmed I/O to the memory for conducting diagnostics during the boot time. It tests (1) the ECC code generator and (2) the error correction/detection logic. I/O load/store commands give software direct address to main memory (bypassing the cache) by mapping the full memory address into local I/O space. Data is transferred in blocks of 20 words (16 words of data and 4 words of ECC check and spare bits). Testing of the ECC code generator is done by sending data patterns into the D-cache, having the ECC code generator produce ECC codes, flushing data from D-cache to main memory, and subsequently using I/O load commands to read data (bypassing D-cache) for verifying the check bits by comparing them to known values. Testing of the error correction and detection logic is done by using I/O store commands to store data and ECC bits directly into memory (bypassing D-cache), and thereafter loading data into GPRs using load commands. Single-bit errors return corrected data, while the double-bit errors result in a system error.

12.2.5 System I/O bus

The system I/O (SIO) bus lies between the main memory and the IOCC. Figure 12.7 shows its positioning in relation to the other buses on the system. From a physical standpoint, this bus is made up of a 72-bit multiplexed address and data interface, along with a 9-bit control interface. The primary function of the SIO bus is to connect the SCU and the DCU to the I/O units. The SIO bus is often referred to as the communiqué channel, for it is used for communications between the processor complex (through the DCU), memory subsystem (through the SCU), and I/O control units. The key features of the bus include processor I/O load/store capability, support for direct memory access (DMA) transfers, and I/O-interrupt-requests-handling capacity. During SIO bus arbitration, the SCU remains as the bus master. Control of

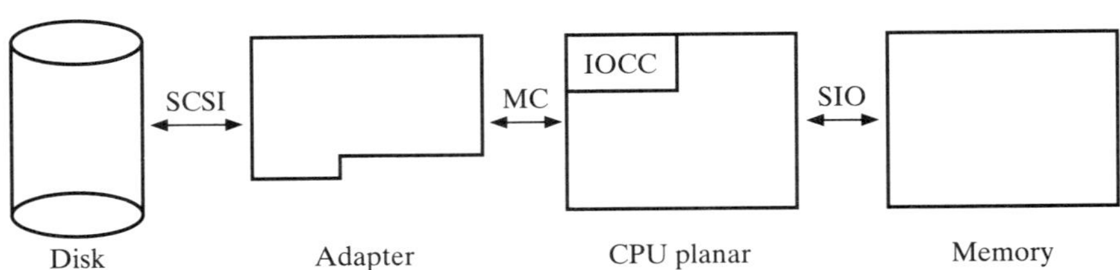

Figure 12.7 Placement of the SIO bus and positioning of components taking part in a DMA operation.

the SIO bus is acquired by activating one of its dedicated bus request signals and persistently holding the signal active until a dedicated bus is granted. Once the bus is granted, the I/O control unit is able to place either an I/O load/store, a DMA operation, or an interrupt request on the bus. The SIO arbitration logic alternates between the two requesters (which are the FXU for the I/O load/stores and the IOCC for the DMA, I/O load replies, and I/O interrupts), with FXU having the highest priority while granting the bus. It makes sense for the FXU to have the highest priority since it needs short bursts to conduct I/O operations like loads and stores. Performance of this already high bandwidth SIO bus is further increased by its ability to handle over-lapped arbitrations. Having separate arbitration lines from bus controls allows the SIO bus to conduct continuous data transfers, thereby bringing about a very high transfer rate. The bandwidth of the SIO bus is compared to those of the Micro Channel and SCSI buses later on in this chapter.

12.2.6   I/O channel controller

The I/O channel controller (IOCC) is connected on one end to the SIO bus and on the other end to the Micro Channel bus. The SIO bus is a relatively higher-speed bus with an interface that is 2 words (64 bits) wide running at the processor's clock frequency which can range anywhere from 50 to 16 ns (16 ns being for the fastest commercially announced processor). On the other hand, the Micro Channel is 32/64 bits wide, with a cycle time of 200 ns (for a basic transfer). Because of these speed differences, several speed-matching buffers are provided as we transit from the processor subcomplex to the I/O subcomplex of the machine. This synapse formed by the IOCC between the two buses establishes the rules for proper arbitrations. During actual information transfers, it also functions like a gateway by bridging the two domains. Figure 12.2 shows the IOCC's logical placement in relation to the relevant functional components on the system.

Before describing the internals of the IOCC, some memory-related terms need to be explained in this context. *Virtual memory* is a term used for the large address space that contains the logical system objects (like programs and data), each of which is allocated a unique address label. *System memory* refers to the physical memory of the machine. *Bus memory* is the memory that logically resides on the I/O bus. Unlike the 80x86 PC family I/O buses, which use disjoint address spaces for bus memory and I/O devices, the System/6000 maps both together. A distinction is made by way of an address decode. If the address is at or above 64 KB, the bus memory gets referenced, whereas if it is below 64 KB, the control registers in the I/O devices get referenced.

There are 16 independent I/O channels in the IOCC. Associated with them are 16 channel status registers (CSRs) for controlling the I/O channels and a set of 16 IOCC buffers,* each controlled by a buffer control register (BCR). In addition, there are a set of specialized registers,† like the IOCC configuration register (IOCC-CR), that play a vital role in coordinating the address mapping through the control of TCW RAM. Though they are normally only read or written by ROM, it is possible to manipulate them through the use of privileged load/store instructions under special circumstances. IOCC's facilities map the virtual address of the Micro Channel address space to the system memory's real address space using a translation mechanism. This translation of a virtual page number (VPN) to a real page number (RPN) is carried out by a component called translation control word (TCW) which is similar to that of the system translation table in the software world. Each of its (32-bit) entries maps to a 4-KB page in the Micro Channel address space. The TCW table's size can vary from 96 KB to 4 MB, depending on the size of the memory used for the TCW table.‡ With its maximum permissible size of 4 MB and each entry able to map to a 4-KB page, the maximum addressable bus memory space comes out to be 4 GB. The organization of the TCW is illustrated in Fig. 12.8.

Having described the characteristics of the IOCC, it is appropriate to explain its operational functions. The primary function of the IOCC is to transfer data between processor or system memory and adapters on the Micro Channel bus. This transfer of data can be of two types. If the processor is directly involved in transferring the data from/to adapter(s) using I/O load/store operations, the process is referred to as a *PIO transfer.* When an adapter itself transfers data from/to the system memory using direct memory access, the event is called a *DMA transfer.* Figure 12.9 shows a DMA transfer occurring between memory and a bus master adapter. Figure 12.10 shows a PIO transfer taking place between the FXU GPRs and an adapter.

DMA I/O transfer modes may be of two types: (1) bus master mode and (2) slave mode. Bus master mode refers to data transfers using intelligent adapters which are capable of gaining control of the Micro

---

* Not available in the models which feature the single-chip implementation of the POWER processor.

† Models with the single-chip implementation feature a TCW/Tag Anchor address register.

‡ The TCW RAM is attached to the IOCC for models with the multichip implementation, and it is in the system memory for models with the single-chip implementation.

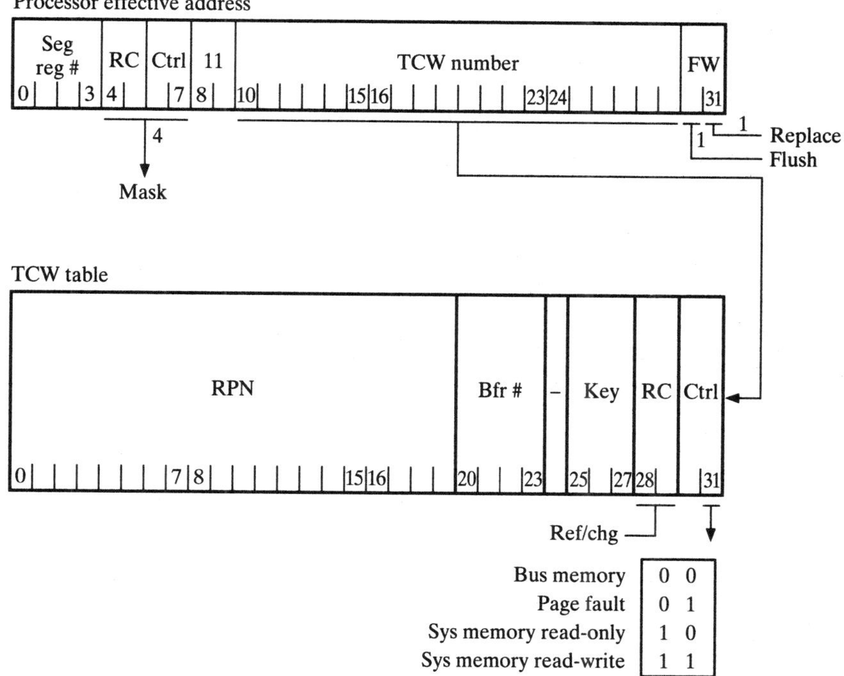

Figure 12.8 Organization of TCW.

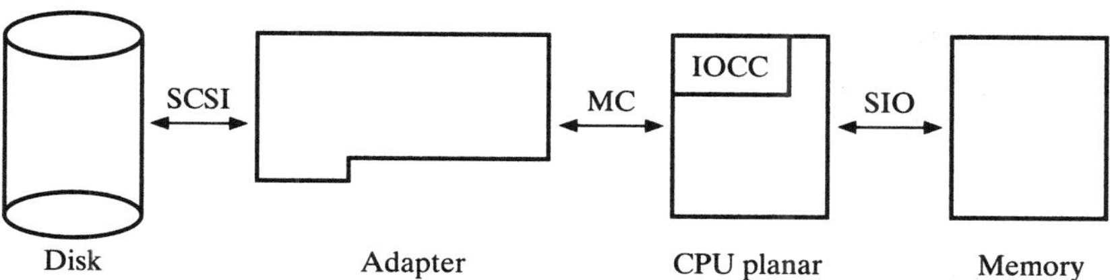

Figure 12.9 Positioning of components taking part in a DMA operation.

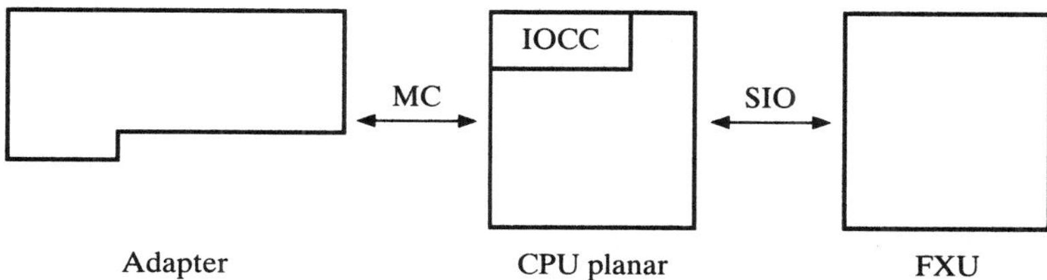

Figure 12.10 Positioning of components taking part in a PIO operation.

Channel bus by themselves. The slave mode alludes to transfer of data using adapters that need the DMA controller in the IOCC to provide control.

In the bus master mode, the bus master supplies the memory address and controls the transfer. The process involves translating the bus memory address space into system address space using a multistage mapping process. The bus memory address is divided into 4-KB pages. This 32-bit bus memory address is decomposed into a 20-bit page number, a 6-bit I/O address, and a 6-bit offset, as seen in Fig. 12.11. The first step consists of loading the mapping information into the TCW table (a copy of working TCW entries is kept in the IOCC's buffer control registers for faster access). This lookup yields a 20-bit real address. The second step consists of combining this real address with the 6-bit I/O address to yield a 26-bit bus master address in the system memory. This identifies a 64-byte buffer in real memory to transfer data from the I/O buffer. With 16 separate 64-byte buffers in the IOCC,* I/O devices can accumulate data at their own pace, thus reducing system contention. If a coherency problem arises because the processor and the I/O device share the memory section, load/store operations can be redirected by software through I/O buffers.[†]

In the slave mode, the transfer operation requires involvement of the DMA controller in the IOCC or another bus master component. The controlling elements in this type of a transfer are called *tags*.[‡] Each tag is essentially a 64-bit unit of data that contains information such as the address, the data length, and the address of the next tag. Tags are organized as a heap in a special 32-KB memory called the tag table, which can be updated on a demand basis. So, with 64 bits per tag, 4096 separate entries are possible in a 32-KB tag table. Since a single tag can reach one page of memory, chaining of these tags allows a way to handle larger logical buffers. Whenever a page boundary is crossed, the DMA controller automatically fetches the tag containing the matching information for the subsequent page and reloads the DMA slave control registers for that channel. The transfer operation uses a multistage process. During transfers between a DMA slave and system memory the data remains temporarily stored in the IOCC until the DMA controller is able to generate sequential read/write cycles to perform the data transfer. The data is transferred in chunks of 64-byte blocks to and from system memory, thereby helping to optimize performance.

---

* Absent in the models with single-chip implementation.

[†] In models featuring the single-chip implementation, hardware is responsible for keeping coherency.

[‡] TCWs are used in place of tags in the single-chip implementation.

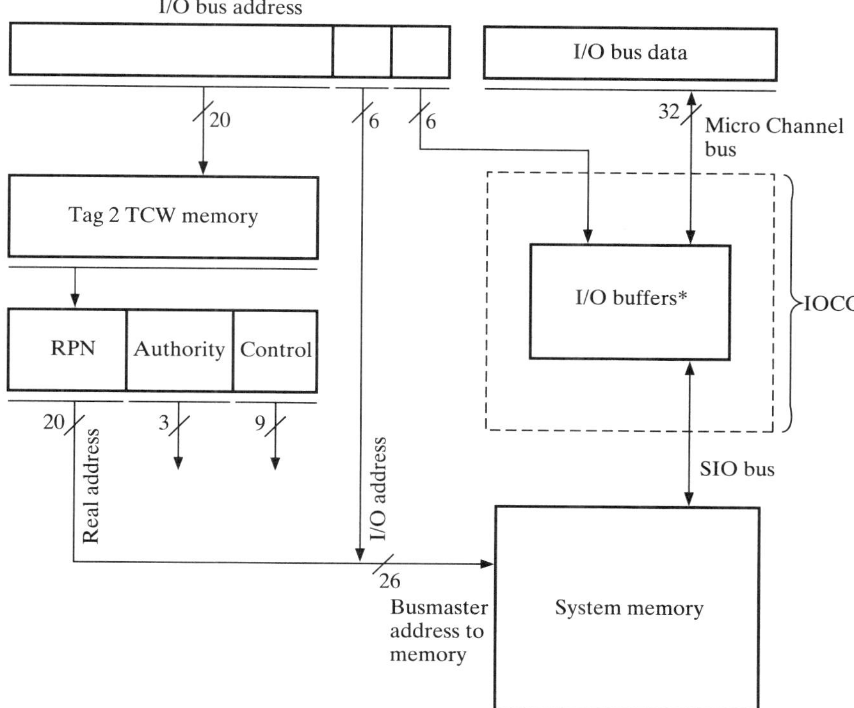

* Buffers absent from RSC implementation (Models 220, 230, M20).

Figure 12.11 Busmaster-system memory operation.

PIO mode operation (as seen in Fig. 12.12) consists of generating an I/O address from an effective address. A GPR in the FXU generates a 32-bit effective address, including four bits that are used to select a segment register. This segment register provides the control bits. It also determines (using one of the control bits called the *type bit*) whether the address is to be treated as an I/O operation or as a memory operation. The address generation process is completed by concatenating the original effective address with the four extant bits from the segment registers.

As processor speeds increase, the I/O and memory interfaces must keep up with the higher demands. Beyond the current design of the I/O subsystem and memory interfaces for the System/6000, improvements can be made to push its current capabilities further. More I/O buses, larger caches, and faster I/O devices attached to the SIO bus are some of the obvious artifacts that can be enhanced and tuned to meet the evolving demands of the industry in the future. For now, the current capabilities of the memory and SIO buses remain adequate to handle workload-intensive tasks efficiently.

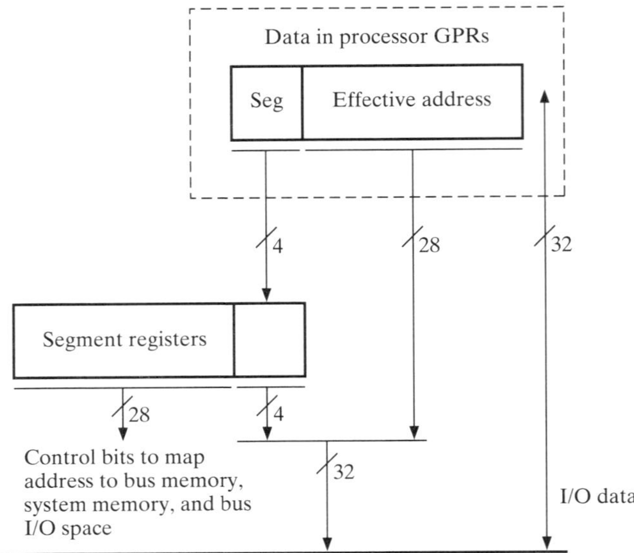

Figure 12.12 Mechanism involved in a PIO operation.

12.3 MICRO CHANNEL IN SYSTEM/6000

The Micro Channel bus on this machine has implemented several new features to augment its already versatile capabilities. The I/O structure of the machine showing the Micro Channel bus and components associated with it is shown in Fig. 12.13. In addition to an overview of the bus architecture, the Micro Channel interface definition features that are supported in this machine are discussed in this section.

12.3.1 Overview of the interface definition

Micro Channel is an I/O bus, originally designed for the IBM PS/2 product line in 1987. Since then it has been used in other computers like the IBM 800 System, the IBM 9371, the IBM 3172 LAN attachment controller, and now the IBM RISC System/6000. The purpose of the Micro Channel bus, simply stated, is to provide a medium for transfer of data. Its architecture comprises mechanical, electrical, and logical descriptions of the bus that provide the rules by which the machine and its associated peripheral components can communicate in a homogeneous manner. Being generic yet versatile, the Micro Channel bus can be used in different ways on different systems. For example, PS/2 machines use the Micro Channel bus as a common bus to connect the I/O peripherals and additional system memory, whereas

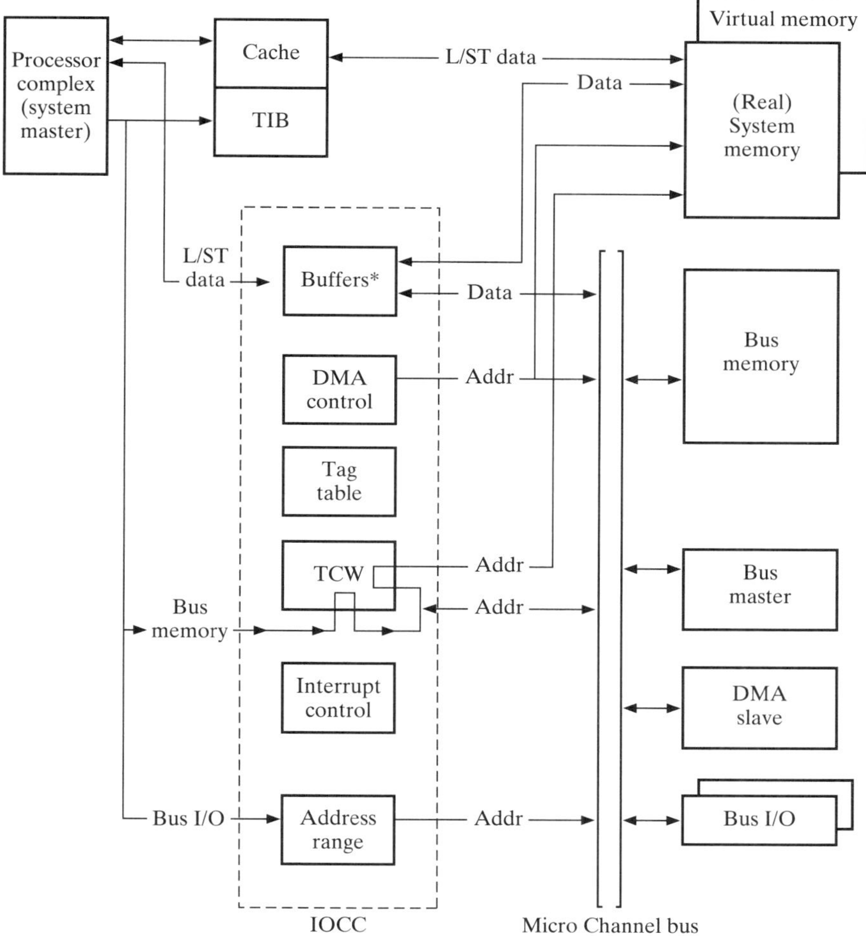

* Buffers absent in RSC implementation (Models 220, M20).

Figure 12.13 I/O structure of the System/6000 showing the Micro Channel bus, the IOCC, and allied components.

the System/6000 only connects the I/O peripherals, keeping the memory disjoint.

Key features of the bus include a decentralized, self-resolving bus arbitration mechanism, with up to 16 priority levels. It also has a DMA controller that can service devices attached to the bus. Regarding transfer of data, a single-cycle or multiple-cycle (burst) transfer capability is available. Eleven level-sensitive interrupt levels also exist. Beyond the basic transfer capabilities, the Micro Channel bus on the System/6000 also supports a streaming data transfer feature and synchronous exception handling, as well as address and data parity for increased reliability.

12.3.2 Bus bandwidth

The bandwidth of the bus varies based on the type of transfer modes. The Micro Channel bus specifications always had the varying levels of bandwidth, as per the specifications shown in Fig. 12.14. However, specific implementations were made available with different computer product lines over a period of time. Since the introduction of Micro Channel in 1987, the evolutionary process has come a long way. Basic transfer and streaming data transfer are the two main modes in Micro Channel architecture. In the basic transfer mode, the Micro Channel bus uses a 32-bit data path to transfer data at the rate of 20 MB/s, using a data cycle time of 200 ns. In the streaming data transfer mode, using a 32-bit data path, the bus is capable of delivering 40 MB of data per second with a cycle time of 100 ns. This capability of achieving a 40-MB/s throughput was announced with the System/6000 product line. If a 64-bit data path is used, an 80-MB/s data transfer rate can be derived from the bus, using a 100-ns data cycle time. This capability was made available with selected high-end models in 1992, and is described later in this chapter. The Micro Channel bus itself is capable of achieving an even higher level of performance. With a 64-bit data path and using a data cycle time of 50 ns, a data transfer rate of up to 160 MB/s can be achieved. Figure 12.15 summarizes the different performance levels that have been achieved to date.

12.3.3 Bus characteristics

The physical characteristics of the Micro Channel bus are best described as a backbone with up to eight connectors for attachment of adapters. Although these connectors are 32-bit, they can still support 16-bit adapters, if needed. The Micro Channel bus interfaces with the

Transfer mode	Data path	Data cycle	Bandwith
Basic	32-bit	200 ns	20 MB/s
Streaming	32-bit	100 ns	40 MB/s
Streaming	64-bit	100 ns	80 MB/s
Streaming	64-bit	50 ns	160 MB/s

Figure 12.14 Different Micro Channel bandwidths.

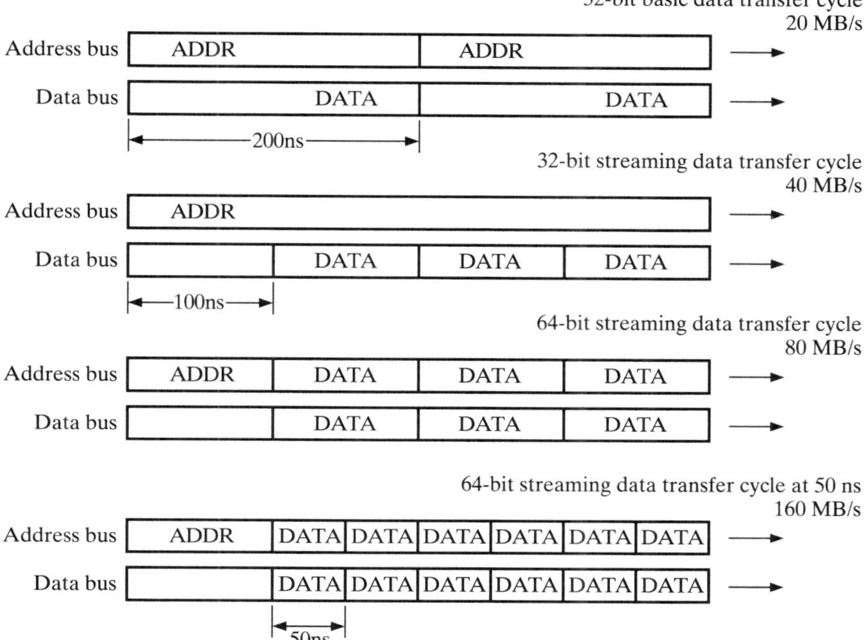

Figure 12.15 Micro Channel performance levels.

internal components of the computer through the IOCC and communicates with the peripheral components through the adapter slots. The maximum permissible number of connectors on a single Micro Channel bus is eight. Regarding the length of the bus itself, there are no defined specifications. However, the recommended length in the currently available implementations is no more than a few feet. With regard to extendability, it is feasible to have more than one Micro Channel bus in a machine.

The logical structure of the Micro Channel can best be described in terms of its layout into six distinct buses, rather than as a single bus. They are as follows:

- address bus
- data bus
- arbitration bus
- control bus
- interrupt bus
- power distribution bus

The job of the address bus is to send out a signal to the I/O port or memory address that is selected for an operation. The data bus is used to pass data between devices on the Micro Channel bus. The arbitration bus is used to determine who controls the bus. The control bus is utilized for signaling between devices on the Micro Channel bus. The role of the interrupt bus is to send out interrupts. The power distribution bus supplies power to the Micro Channel connectors.

12.3.4 Data representation

Micro Channel architecture orders bytes in a 32-bit word from right to left for data management purposes. This scheme is better known as the *Little Endian* mode and its arrangement is illustrated in Fig. 12.16. System/6000, like most IBM computers, uses a left-to-right numbering scheme for data storage, which is referred to as the *Big Endian* mode. This arrangement of bytes in the 32-bit words is reversed on the machine's internal bus versus the Micro Channel bus. So, this notion shouldn't spring any surprises when dealing with data stream off the internal bus and the Micro Channel bus, or when writing an assembly language code to manipulate data on the System/6000. Each byte is reordered in the IOCC and mapped from one mode to another as it passes between the processor's internal bus and the machine's Micro Channel bus. Figure 12.17 shows the byte-by-byte mapping for a 32-bit word.

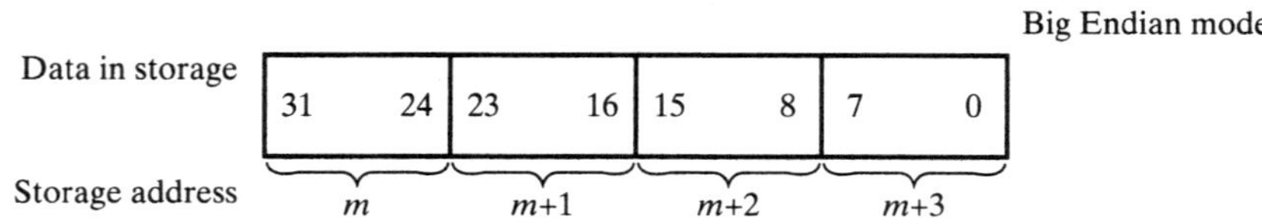

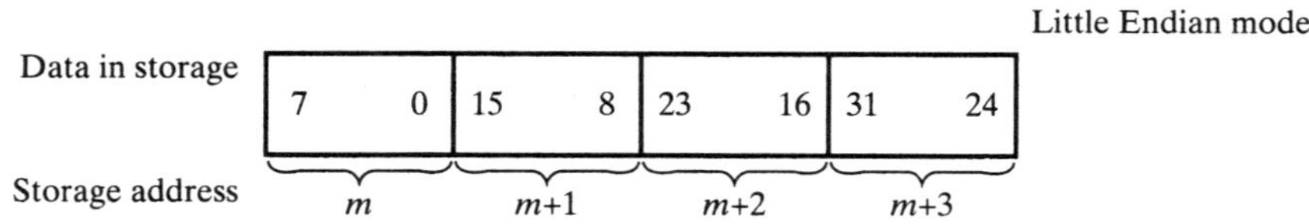

Figure 12.16 Little Endian and Big Endian modes of data representation.

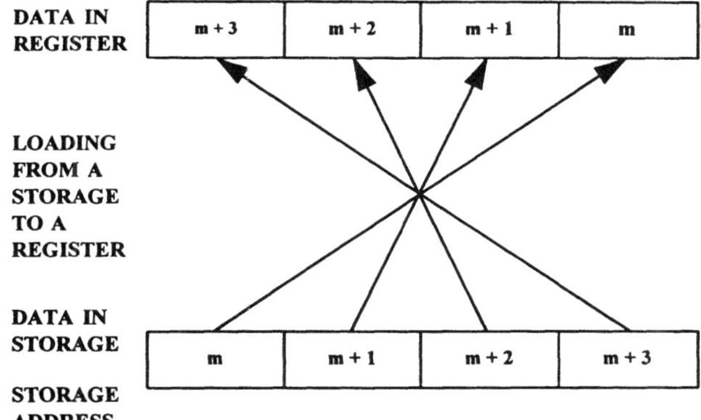

Figure 12.17 Byte-by-byte mapping for Little Endian and Big Endian modes.

12.3.5 Operational principles

Discussions pertaining to the Micro Channel participants often involve the terms *master* and *slave*. It is helpful to acquire an understanding of these terminologies prior to looking at the implementations. Master is the name given to the participants that drive the address bus and the data control signals. A master can be of three possible types: *system master, bus master,* and *DMA controller.* A system controller is the default master that controls the channel when it is idle. A bus master is an adapter implementation which arbitrates for use of the channel when needed. A DMA controller is the third kind of bus master and it monitors the arbitration bus, rather than initiating arbitration for the channel. A participant that sends or receives data under the control of the master is referred to as a slave. Slaves can be of three different types, based on what component they are interacting with. These are an *I/O slave,* a *memory slave,* and a *DMA slave.* An I/O slave is selected by its address within the I/O address space. A memory slave gets selected by its address within the memory address space. A DMA slave is selected by arbitration, or optionally by its address within the memory address space. The participants' individual master-slave relationships are shown in Fig. 12.18, with the Micro Channel bus as the common medium. Out of the six implementations described here and pictured in Fig. 12.19, the bus master and the three slaves are adapter implementations. This means that any Micro Channel card can be classified within the four variations of adapters categorized here.

The arbitration process on the Micro Channel bus, which is the mechanism of allocating control of the bus to one of the adapters cur-

Signals index:
ARBS - Arbitration bus signal
ADDR - Address bus signal
DATA - Data bus signal
IRQ - Interrupt request signal
OMCS - Other Micro Channel signals

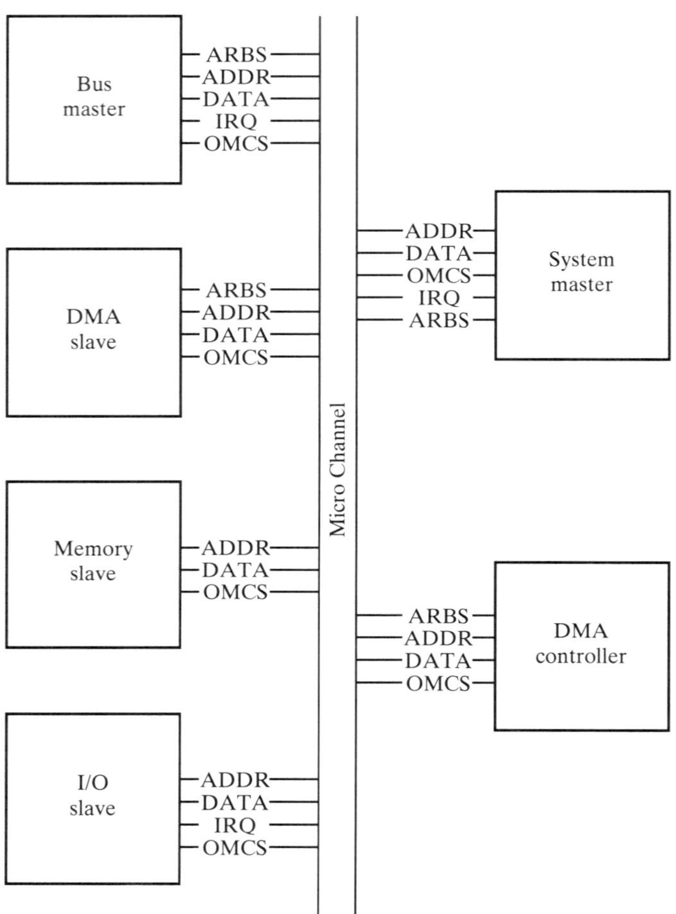

Figure 12.18 Micro Channel structure on the System/6000.

rently requesting service, makes use of either a fairness protocol or a priority sequence to ensure balanced availability of the bus to all devices attached to it.

A single segment of the operation involves the following ordered steps: (1) an arbitration request is made, (2) the central arbitrator issues an arbitrate signal when the Micro Channel bus becomes avail-

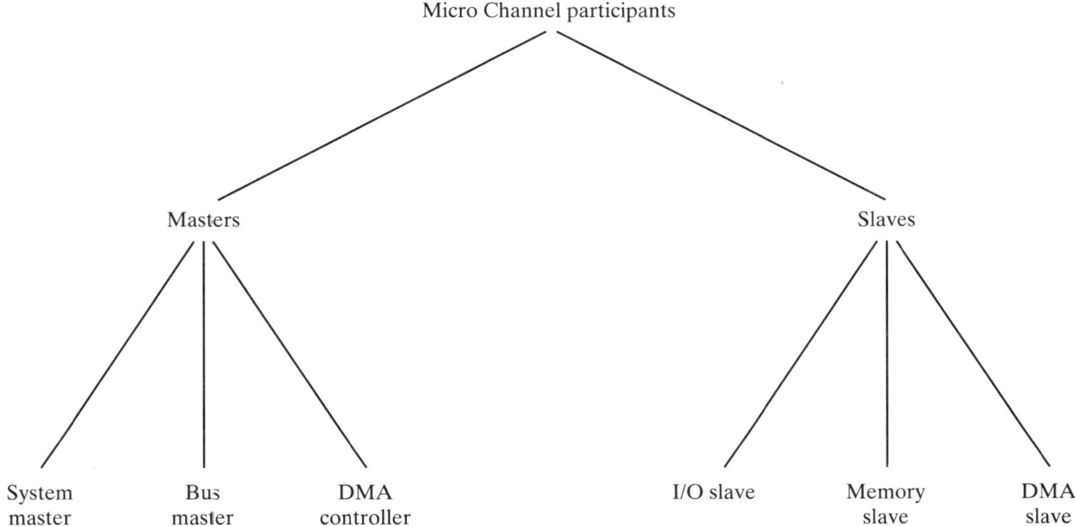

Figure 12.19 Classification of different Micro Channel adapter implementations.

able, (3) the requesting device places its arbitration level on the arbitration bus and continues to monitor the bus for comparison of the arbitration levels, (4) the arbitration level is selected, and (5) the arbitrate signal is changed to a grant signal, thereby giving the master device controlling this arbitration level the permission to use the bus.

12.3.6 Streaming data support

Streaming data procedure is a newly implemented feature of the Micro Channel bus that has been made available with the System/6000 product line. This feature provides the ability to transfer multiple data cycles within a single bus envelope. In other words, it allows for multiple data read or write cycles to be executed with the cost of a single device selection. The amortization of the device selection overhead across the total packet doubles the data transfer capability of the bus.

In order to best understand the streaming data feature, it should be compared with the basic transfer capability in lieu of pointing out the differences. Figure 12.20 illustrates both the transfer cycles. In the basic transfer mode, the following key events occur as a result of signals being issued by the bus master:

ADDR: An (I/O or memory) address is placed on the address bus.

$S(0,1)$: The write-status signal is activated. The status signal for a read operation is $S(1,0)$. The $S(0,0)$ and $S(1,1)$ combinations are not used.

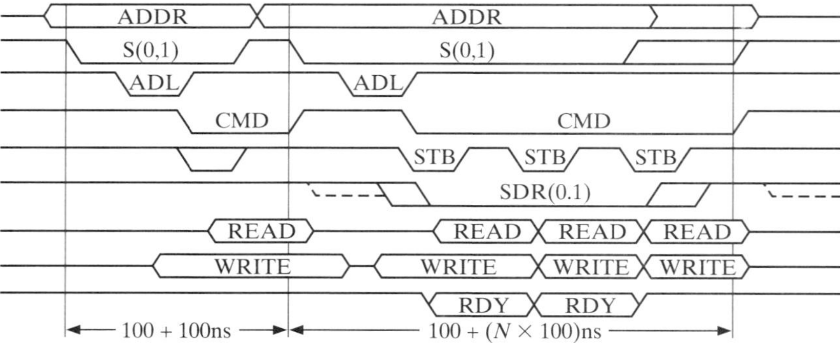

Figure 12.20 Basic transfer and streaming data cycles. (*Copied with permission from IBM.*)

ADL: An address decode latch is issued to allow an adapter to latch
            the already decoded address.

_____ :   Device selection occurs.

CMD: The command signal is activated for approximately 100 ns to
            control the data transfer. Its trailing edge indicates the end of
            the bus cycle.

WRITE: Data is transferred.

The cost for device selection is 100 ns. The actual transfer takes 100 ns.
Thus, the cost of a basic transfer cycle is 200 ns every time a transfer
is made.

The streaming data feature is similar, except for the fact that there
is a set of additional signals involved in the process, and a block of data
gets transferred with a single device selection. The following key signals are issued:

ADDR: The bus master places an address on the address bus.

S(0,1):   The bus master activates the write-status signal.

ADL: An address decode latch is issued to allow an adapter to latch
            the already decoded address.

_____ :   Device selection occurs.

SDR(0,1):   The bus slave issues this signal to indicate that it supports the
            streaming data feature and also provides for speed-matching
            between bus master and bus slave. If the slave does not drive
            these signals, then the cycle is completed as a basic transfer.

CMD: The command signal is activated for approximately 100 ns to
            control the data transfer.

STB: The bus master issues this control signal for data transfer.

WRITE: Data is transferred.

The cost for device selection remains 100 ns. Each transfer takes 100 ns. As there are three write cycles in Fig. 12.20, the streaming data transfer time is $100 + (100 \times 3) = 400$ ns. Thus, the generic formula for estimating streaming data transfer time costs is $100 + (100 \times n)$ ns, where n indicates the number of read or write cycles.

In addition to the 32-bit streaming data mode discussed above, an alternate mode of transferring 64 bits simultaneously is defined in the Micro Channel architecture. In this mode, data is moved over a 32-bit address bus, using line-multiplexing techniques. This effectively expands the 32-bit data bus into a 64-bit data bus with 32 data lines plus 32 address lines. The 64-bit cycle begins as a 32-bit basic transfer cycle. The selected slave indicates through its response that it supports 64-bit streaming operations. During a transfer to the slave, the master starts the streaming data strobe signal and gates the data onto the data and address buses. During a transfer to the master, the master tristates the address bus after driving the command signal active, and later the slave gates the data onto the data and address buses. The 64-bit streaming transfer then proceeds like a 32-bit streaming transfer. As a result, a remarkable level of performance improvement is achieved. Some of the high-end configurations of the System/6000 support this feature.

It is useful to know that the Micro Channel architecture allows for increasing the already impressive data transfer rate to an amazing 160 MB/s when implemented with a data cycle time of 50 ns on a 64-bit data path. This implementation of the bus will be available when hardware technology can take advantage of it.

Data may be paced during the 40-MB/s streaming data procedure only. This process of *data pacing* allows slaves to introduce momentary pauses in the data transfer. The need for this feature arises when a slave can support streaming data, but not at a fast enough pace. A special signal related to the channel-ready status enables the data-pacing function. The bus master inspects the state of the signal. If it is inactive during read, it indicates that the slave did not have valid data in this clock period. If it is inactive during write, it indicates that the slave did not accept the data; hence the transfer needs to be repeated.

12.3.7 Data parity handling

Very often errors are caused by card-seating problems and electromagnetic interferences in the machine. The data parity feature provides an improved error detection mechanism with data handling on the Micro Channel bus. Its functionality is independent in the sense that parity and nonparity devices can be mixed. Support for data parity is controlled by a special signal, called the data parity enable signal. The presence or lack of this signal indicates to a master whether data parity is supported on the particular card. For write operations, the data parity function, if supported, is triggered when the bus master activates the data parity enable signal. The slave checks this parity. If found incorrect, the slave issues its channel check signal. For read operations, the data parity function is triggered by the slave (instead of the bus master) activating the data parity enable signal. The bus master checks this parity. If found incorrect, the bus master interrupts the system.

12.3.8   Address parity handling

This feature provides for the verification of correct addressing on the Micro Channel bus. The address parity, in combination with the data parity function, ensures the integrity of the information flow to the appropriate destinations, with minimal impact on performance. The support for address parity is controlled by a signal driven by the bus master. The signal is called the address parity enable signal. All slaves supporting address parity check this signal. If address parity is correct, the selected slave notifies the bus master that it was selected by activating a signal called the card-selected feedback signal. If the address parity is incorrect, the slaves supporting address parity signal an exception by issuing their channel check signal.

Both data and address parity are optional features. The parity checkings can only occur between devices that have the capability. The difference between the nature of the two protocols is that data parity is provided by the provider of the data, whereas address parity is always driven by the master.

12.3.9   Synchronous exception handling

Synchronous channel check provides for the signaling of errors synchronously with a transfer in progress. Unlike the PS/2 product line, where exception-handling was asynchronous, the System/6000 has provided a more reliable and superior error-detection capability. As seen above, exceptions are signaled on the Micro Channel bus with the channel check signal. In the case of a DMA operation, the slave issues the channel check signal. This is followed by the bus master suspending processing and subsequently generating an interrupt. The hardware interrupt issued, in turn, invokes a utility program to handle the exception condition. In the case of a PIO operation, the adapter activates the channel check signal. As a result, the transfer is halted in the same bus cycle that caused the exception, and an error recovery utility program is invoked to handle the exception condition.

Described in this section are the key Micro Channel interface definition features whose implementations were announced with this System/6000 product line. The functions, features, and benefits of the three key functionalities—namely, streaming data protocol, data and address parity handling, and synchronous exception handling—form the basis for many future design strategies.

12.4 STORAGE SUBSYSTEM

The transcending design goals in the storage device subsystem are performance, cost, device interface, upgradeability, and device availability. Keeping these requirements in perspective, the SCSI bus interface was found to be best suited for the System/6000's storage subsystem. SCSI (small computer system interface) has long lost its literal meaning. Today, most people know SCSI (pronounced "scuzzy") as a versatile computer bus interface and command set specification, with its official description specified in the ANSI standard X3.131-1986 specifications. An interesting observation comes to mind with respect to the positioning of the SCSI bus on the system; it is the only bus that can be placed external to the housing of the machine (i.e., when connected to external devices). Figure 12.21 exhibits the positioning of the SCSI bus with respect to the machine's mechanical packaging.

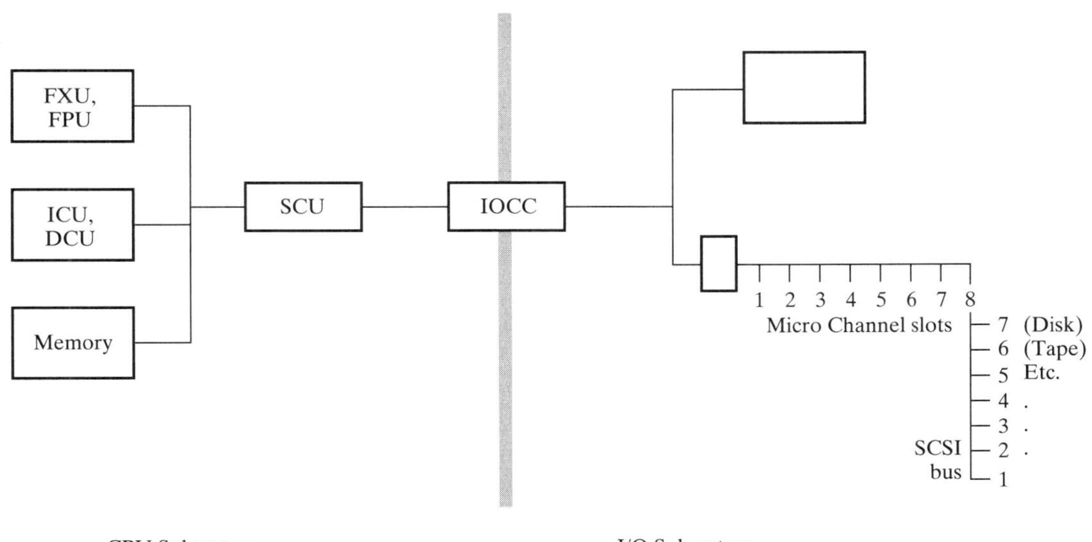

Figure 12.21 Positioning of the SCSI bus.

12.4.1   SCSI basics

Perhaps the biggest strength of the SCSI bus is that it provides device-independent connections. Being a bus-level implementation rather than a device-level implementation like the IDE (integrated drive electronics), ESDI (enhanced small device interface), and ST-506 (Seagate's standard) device interface standards, the SCSI enjoys a definitive luxury for versatility. It is able to attach intelligent peripheral devices such as hard disks, diskette drives, CD-ROMs, printers, plotters, and scanners, without having to discriminate among them. SCSI's attachment feature is unimportant, as it can be in the form of an adapter on the Micro Channel bus, or as an integrated unit on the planar board. What is important is that SCSI allows assorted types of peripherals to be connected in a daisy-chained fashion.

The physical specifications of SCSI allow for a maximum of eight devices to be attached to a single SCSI bus on a computer. Devices attached to the bus are numbered and are referred to as SCSI devices. Each unit has a unique identification (ID) number of its own. This SCSI device ID is really a bit-significant representation of the SCSI address, which is derived from one of the bus signal lines. Of the devices numbered from 0 through 7, the one with the largest number has the highest priority.

The logical specification permits a SCSI attachment feature to allow each SCSI device to have up to eight logical units. These logical units are not attached directly to the SCSI bus. Instead, they are divisions within a SCSI device. Conceptually, a device controller can be thought of as the SCSI device and the device itself as the logical unit. Both a SCSI device number as well as a *logical unit number* (LUN) are required in order to access any logical unit. Note that of all the devices, only two devices actually communicate at any given time, since SCSI is a shared bus. When two devices are communicating, one acts as an *initiator* and the other as a *target*.

Multifarious configurations of SCSI are possible, as the bus not only permits the host computer System/6000 to communicate with its peripherals and other hosts, but also allows one of its peripherals to communicate with another peripheral. The participants involved are illustrated in Fig. 12.22.

12.4.2   SCSI bus signals

A close look at this device interface standard reveals that SCSI is an 8-bit parallel I/O bus. It consists of a total of 18 signals, with 9 signals used for control and the remaining 9 for data (8 data lines and 1 parity line). The control signals, in accordance with the bus phases, decree

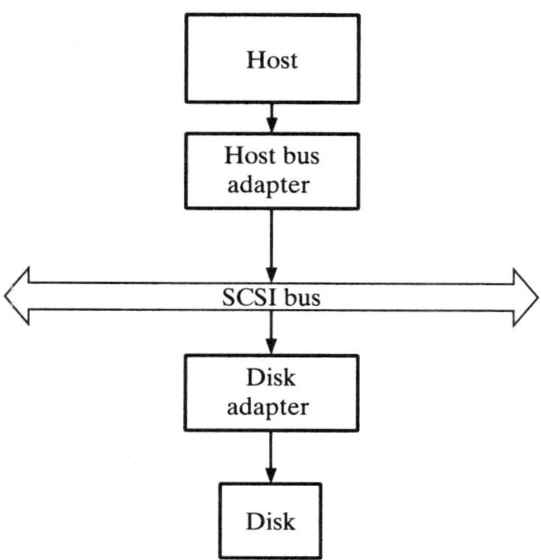

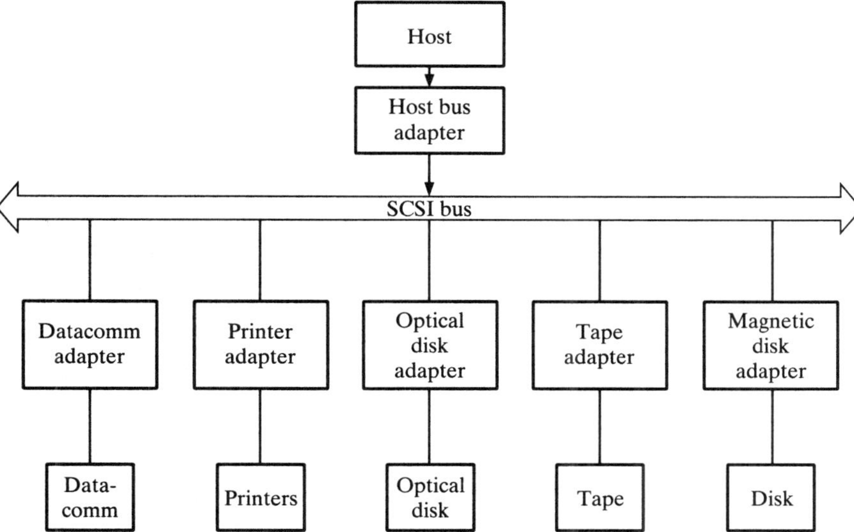

Figure 12.22 Possible participants in a SCSI transfer.

the direction in which the data is to be transferred. The bidirectional data lines act under the direction of these control signals to transfer information in the guided direction.

Two different electrical specifications are supported by the SCSI bus:

- single-ended
- differential

The single-ended driver and receiver configuration uses TTL (transistor-transistor logic) levels. It uses a voltage line between 0 and 5 volts. With such a small range of voltage change, this implementation of SCSI bus can be used reliably with a maximum cable length of up to 6 m. Typically, the single-ended SCSI is only used for attachments within a cabinet. The differential driver and receiver configuration, on the other hand, uses two signal lines for each voltage, and the signal value depends on the voltage difference between the two lines. The differential SCSI supports a cable length up to 25 m. Both types of electrical specifications are supported by the System/6000.

12.4.3 SCSI protocol

The SCSI protocol consists of a prescribed set of rules like any other protocols. Often, an example helps to relate a concept better, if reviewed before delving into the theory. Consider the following scenario between two devices (an initiator and a target) for a read operation. The initiator arbitrates for the bus, gets the bus, and subsequently sends its command to the target device. The bus is freed at this point. The target decodes the command sent by the initiator, and it becomes ready to send/receive data. The target now arbitrates for the bus, makes a connection with the initiator, and subsequently transfers data to it. With the data transfer done, a status byte is transferred and the bus is freed.

The design of the SCSI protocol calls for a scheme for bus arbitration. Bus arbitration is required so that device(s) can bid for the bus in order to transfer data across devices. The arbitration protocol works as follows:

```
device waits for a free bus
device wanting to use the bus puts its SCSI ID on the bus
if there is no higher SCSI ID bidding for the bus, then
      device gains control of the bus
else
      other device (with higher SCSI ID) gets the bus
```

The communication over the SCSI bus is controlled by a sequence of states called *bus phases*. There are seven distinct phases—the bus-free phase, arbitration phase, selection/reselection phase, command phase, data in/out phase, status phase, and message in/out phase. Each phase is described here in light of the key events that are associated with the target and the initiator.

Phase 1: Bus-free

This phase indicates that no device is using the bus and that it is available for use at this time.

Phase 2: Arbitration

One device is permitted to gain control of the bus so that it is able to become an initiator or a target. The method of gaining control is as follows:

1. The device waits for a bus-free stage to occur.
2. Following a minimal bus-free delay, the device arbitrates for the bus, using its busy signal and one of its eight data signals that corresponds with its SCSI ID number. While the busy signal tells other devices on the bus that the bus is in use, the data signal's role is to bid for the bus.
3. The arbitration protocol (previously explained) is used to grant the bus to one of the bidding devices. As there is a one-to-one correspondence between the eight data signals and the eight supported devices, the data signal that got sent out by a bidding device remains unique for an iteration.
4. Following a brief delay (called the arbitration delay) during which the arbitration protocol chooses the nominee, the device with the highest SCSI ID number is granted the bus. A select signal is asserted by the chosen device to mark the end of this arbitration phase.

Phase 3: Selection/reselection

The chosen device places its own SCSI ID and the target's SCSI ID on the bus, in order to inform the target device about its proposed involvement. The target in turn acknowledges the selection request and allows the initiator to enter the next phase. It should be mentioned here that normally the initiator selects the target to perform a read or write operation. However, a reselection may also occur when a preempted target needs to reconnect to an initiator to continue an already scheduled operation that was started by the initiator until it got suspended by the target.

Phase 4: Command

A command is transferred from the initiator to the target. It starts off with the target requesting information. The initiator then places the requested values on the bus, and subsequently the target reads the data off the bus. In this way, the target continues to read the rest of the data until all the bytes are read. This data received is the SCSI command descriptor block (CDB). CDBs may be either 6 bytes or 10 bytes in size, depending on the SCSI command codes.

Phase 5: Data in/out

The actual transfer of data occurs in this phase. The process is referred to as data-in when data is sent from the target to the initiator. Conversely, the process is called data-out when data is sent from the initiator to the target.

Phase 6: Status

The target sends a status byte to the initiator, indicating the completion of the command.

Phase 7: Message in/out

In this phase, the target and the initiator may pass messages to each other to convey information about the bus. The message-in phase allows message(s) to be sent from the target to the initiator, while the message-out phase permits them to be sent from the initiator to the target. A typical example of this message in/out phase might be an advise to abort the current command owing to some abnormal condition, or to establish a data transfer speed for data transfers.

The order in which these phases occur on the SCSI bus follows a prescribed sequence. A finite-state automaton given in Fig. 12.23 explains all the transition states. Note that a reset condition in this protocol can always abort at any phase in its state of progress. If a reset does happen, then the subsequent phase will always be the bus-free phase.

12.4.4   Buffering

The SCSI adapter interface connects the Micro Channel bus to the SCSI bus. It provides an interface for connecting assorted devices to the computer system. In this machine, quite a few functions have been implemented in hardware to improve performance of the interface. The

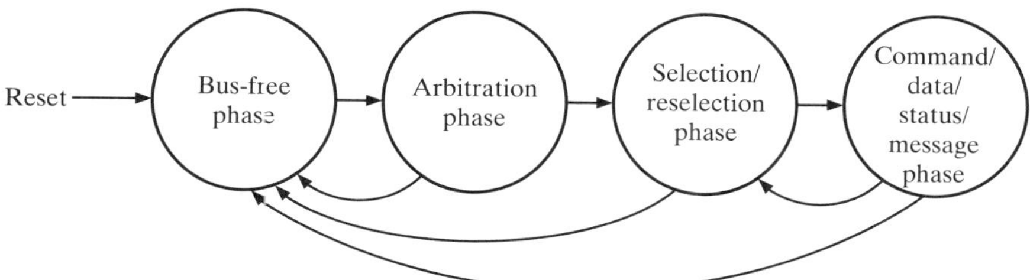

Figure 12.23 A finite-state automaton showing the possible transition states for the SCSI protocol.

SCSI adapter acts as an initiator as well as a target, depending on the component it is dealing with. Figure 12.24 illustrates the dual role of the SCSI adapter when it interacts with its storage device and then with the Micro Channel bus. In other words, the SCSI adapter behaves as an initiator when transferring data from or to the storage device. And it assumes the role of a bus master when transferring buffered data from or to the Micro Channel bus.

The controller uses the DMA transfer mode to move all system data. This transfer is done in bursts of 4 to 128 bytes, with the default being 64 bytes. Although disk cache controllers are considered a desirable investment for boosting the performance of data transfer here, the architecture of System/6000 eliminates the need to have one implemented separately. The AIX operating system makes use of a huge virtual address space and its single-level store feature to treat the main storage as the disk cache controller. By doing so, not only is the need for a disk cache controller fulfilled, but the probability of finding a cache hit also increases by an order of magnitude over the typical controller cache approach. Also, access to a file contained in the system

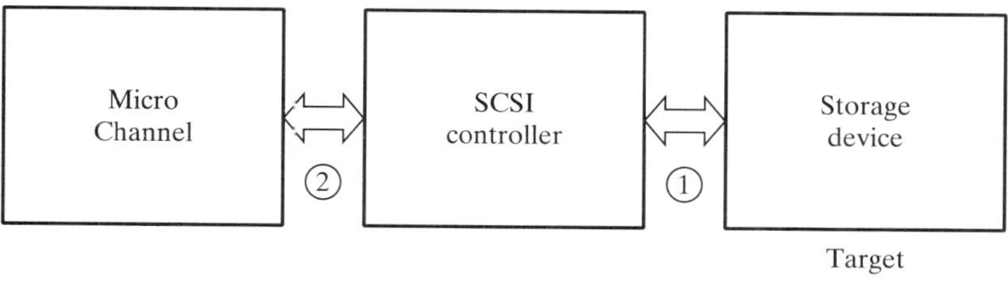

① Initiator

② Bus master

Figure 12.24 Dual-personality of a SCSI controller as (1) an initiator and (2) a target, when transferring data between Micro Channel and a storage device.

memory includes only the memory access cost and not an I/O bus transaction (which is far more expensive). Such cache hits, therefore, not only eliminate physical device latency but also eliminate the I/O transaction associated with a disk cache controller. In this way, the System/6000 is able to achieve a notable performance edge over regular disk cache designs, and it implements its adapters without a cache. A small 0.5-KB data buffer on the SCSI controller card is still necessary, however, to perform a speed-matching function. Data needs to be buffered when being transferred from/to the Micro Channel bus. There is a good reason for doing this. Since the data transfer rate of the SCSI bus is in the order of magnitude of ten times less than that of the Micro Channel, it makes sense to buffer the data in order to provide speed-matching between the 40-MB/s Micro Channel bus (with streaming data support) and the 4-MB/s SCSI bus.

During a SCSI read operation, data gets sent to the Micro Channel bus from the SCSI device in bursts whenever the buffer is flushed. Meanwhile data continues to flow from the SCSI device into this buffer in preparation for the next burst. When this buffer becomes empty, the Micro Channel bus is released. A SCSI write is identical to the read operation, except for the direction of the transfer.

12.4.5 SCSI mailbox

A processor's read or write request is propagated over to the I/O subsystem using a memory I/O operation. This processor cannot afford to stay idle by waiting around for this I/O to occur. So, a mailbox-like scheme is implemented in the controller which can be instrumental in relieving the host by off-loading the requests in a safe place until they can be made to execute. Once the processor relinquishes control of the I/O request, the commands get treated like a queued task for the SCSI bus that is autonomous of the processor's involvement. These commands are stored in RAM memory until the SCSI bus becomes ready to service them. There are 32 mailboxes in total. Thirty are used to store commands to SCSI devices, with the remaining two being used for controller hardware purposes and to pass unexpected condition status.

From an operational perspective, the elements of a mailbox function are quite simple. The process consists of two steps. In the first step, the host loads mailbox bytes 0 to 23 with command parameters. In the second step, the host clears mailbox bytes 24 to 31, which are used by the I/O controller to signal its completion status. After loading a mailbox, no host involvement is necessary. Using the steps explained above, commands to a single SCSI device can be queued by chaining several mailboxes.

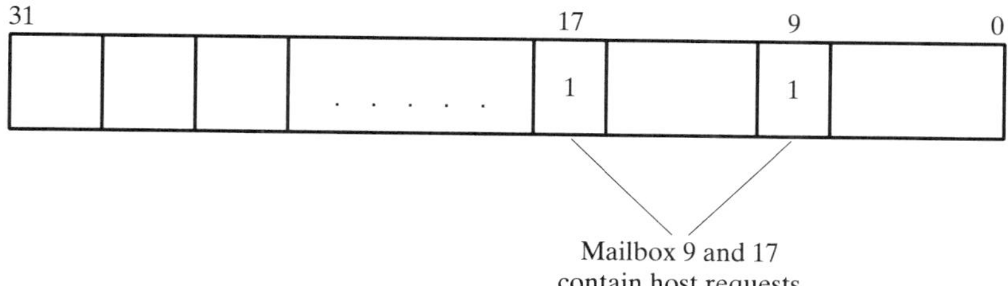

Figure 12.25 Interrupt status register (ISR) holding pending mail requests in its cells (9 and 17 in the figure).

How and when do these queued commands get serviced? Upon completion of the currently executing SCSI task, the host is interrupted by the I/O controller. When this interrupt occurs, the host reads a 32-bit register called the interrupt status register (ISR). Each bit in ISR corresponds to one mailbox. An "on" bit with a 1 in it indicates that the corresponding mailbox is holding pending request(s) in it, as illustrated in Fig. 12.25. All mailboxes with outstanding requests are enqueued to the SCSI bus. Theoretically, all of the 30 mailboxes' commands could get serviced simultaneously if there were so many of them remaining outstanding. The scheme not only lessens the burden on the interrupt handlers but also minimizes the host processing time.

12.4.6   SCSI I/O controller logic

The SCSI I/O controller consists of two principal logic chips—one handles the SCSI protocol, and the other manages the Micro Channel transfers and related control functions. The SCSI control logic is implemented using a Western Digital chip. By handling the protocol at a hardware level, the benefits achieved are twofold. First, the burden is lessened on the main controller microprocessor, and second, low SCSI connection times are achieved. The second chip that handles the management functions is implemented using Intel's 80C186 microprocessor. Its functions are to regulate the Micro Channel transfers, oversee the mailboxes, supervise the SCSI chip, test the integrity of the SCSI bus, and control the 0.5-KB FIFO buffer (first-in first-out describes its buffering scheme). Positioning of these two chips can be viewed in Fig. 12.26. Other relevant components on the I/O controller are the ROM and the RAM modules which serve as the microprocessor memory for instructions and data. A custom CMOS gate array on the controller card houses the FIFO buffer, the mailbox area, and affiliated internal interface logic.

All the devices supported on this machine comply with the SCSI standards defined by ANSI document X3.131-1986. Beyond this func-

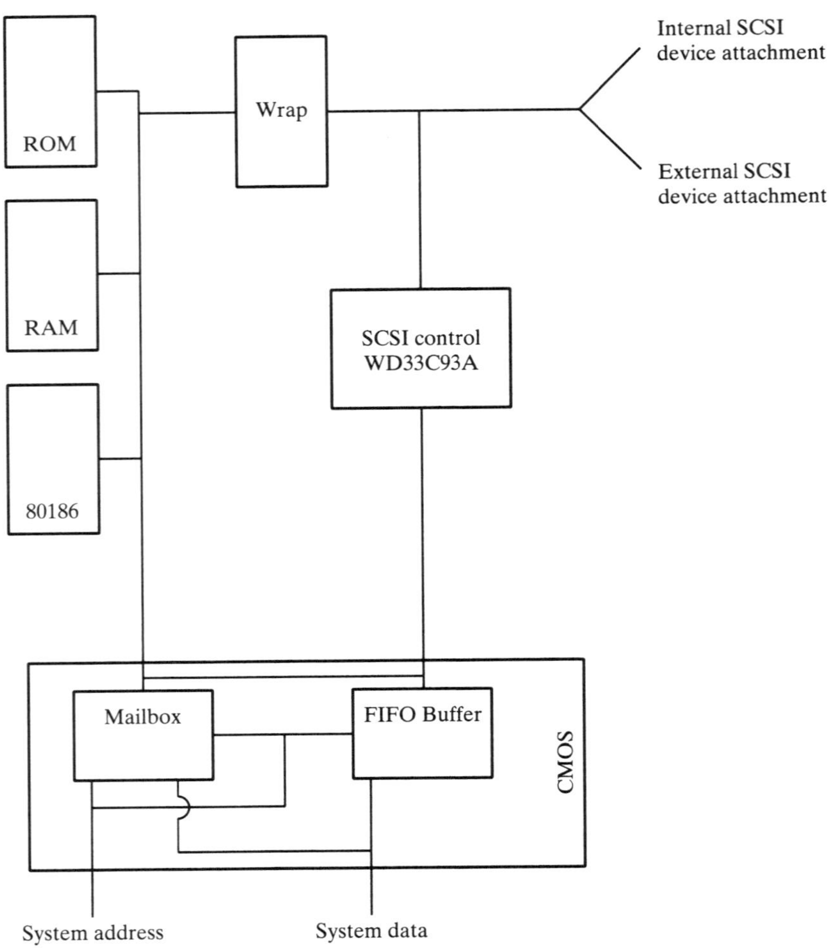

Figure 12.26 Block diagram for SCSI I/O controller.

tionality, devices may also adhere to additional features of SCSI such as the SCSI-2.

12.4.7 Beyond SCSI

SCSI-2 is an extension of the original SCSI interface which is defined by the X3T9.2 subcommittee. Enhancements to SCSI evolved into this new standard in order to support changing technology, new applications, and greater performance requirements. This SCSI-2 standard is supported by the System/6000. Several of its new features and functions have helped the user community to standardize specifications. Some of the noteworthy enhancements are:

- *Common command set (CCS):*   Eighteen SCSI commands are now defined in the CCS, so that vendor-specific command implementations can be avoided.

- *Wide SCSI:*   This option adds a second cable of 68 conductors (rather than the normally used 50 conductors), in order to provide a 16-bit data path. Using this feature increases the transfer rate.

- *Fast SCSI:*   This option doubles the synchronous data transfer speed when used with high-quality cables and differential drivers and receivers.

- *Command queuing:*   Multiple commands from an initiator to the same logical unit can be queued using this feature.

- *Command set enhancements:*   Enhanced command sets now support new device types like scanners, CD-ROMs, and optical memory devices.

Support for SCSI-2 is growing rapidly. All of the controller cards that are currently in use in the System/6000 can be made to support the SCSI-2 standard, if used with the right microcode.

SCSI-3 is an evolving standard that will expand the horizons of the SCSI-2 and SCSI interfaces. Like SCSI-2, it is being defined by the X3T9.2 subcommittee. The features that the SCSI-3 specifications have attempted to address will pave a path in a future direction to where evolving needs and faster data transfer speeds will bring the technology to new thresholds. Some of the key issues that SCSI-3 specifications will try to address are:

- *Fiber-optic option:*   Using a fiber medium will greatly increase the data transfer bandwidth.

- *Devices per bus:*   The upper limit for the maximum permissible number of devices will be increased beyond the current capacity.

- *Auto-configuration:*   This option will allow automatic initialization of the newly added devices on the bus.

12.5 BUS BANDWIDTH AND PERFORMANCE

This chapter discusses the three different buses in its three separate sections. The first bus that was described was the SIO bus. It interfaces the SCU to the ICU and DCU. This bus has an extremely high bandwidth, as it runs at the processor's speed. Based on the speed of the processor, the memory bandwidth of the SIO bus may vary from 160 MB/s (on the 20-MHz machines which were available when the product line was first announced) to an amazing 1000 MB/s. The memory bandwidth is derived from (1) the number of lines that interface to the processor's memory, and (2) the processor speed. For example, a 50-MHz processor equipped with a full-size cache containing a 128-bit memory bus interface will have a memory bandwidth of 800 MB/s. But the same 50-MHz processor, if configured with a half-size cache, has a 64-bit memory bus interface and a reduced memory bandwidth of 400 MB/s.

The second bus described here is the Micro Channel bus, which currently operates with a data transfer rate of 40 or 80 MB/s, depending on the machine model and implementation. By observing the bandwidth difference of the Micro Channel bus as compared to that of the SIO bus, one can get a good idea of the speed at which things happen in the processor subcomplex, as compared to the I/O subcomplex.

Lying external to the Micro Channel bus is the SCSI bus, which has a maximum data transfer rate of 4 MB/s. If SCSI-2 is implemented, then the data transfer rate can go up to 10 MB/s.

As one exits from the core to the peripherals of the machine, two trends are quite prominent. First, bandwidth of the buses decreases dramatically, and second, buffering between buses increases significantly. An analogy can be made between the high-bandwidth path from the core of the processor to its low-bandwidth I/O subsystem and an eight-lane highway system feeding into a two-lane street, which in turn opens into a single-lane path. In the case of road systems, the speeds of the vehicles are adjusted (i.e., lowered) in order to compensate for the reduced capacity to handle traffic. But in the case of buses in computer systems, speed cannot be compromised. So, multiple levels of buffering schemes are provided to queue up data and transfer them in bursts.

Presented here is a table summarizing the performance levels of the buses found on the System/6000, in terms of their data transfer rates.

Bus type	Peak data transfer rate
SIO (62.5-MHz clock)	1000 MB/s
SIO (20-MHz clock)	160 MB/s
Micro Channel (64-bit)	80 MB/s
Micro Channel (32-bit)	40 MB/s
SCSI-2	10 MB/s
SCSI	5 MB/s

12.6 SUMMARY

Reliability and availability are the most noteworthy features in System/6000's I/O subsystem. The error-correction mechanisms, along with the interruptable and restartable memory-scrubbing feature with retest capability, enhance the machine's hardware integrity to an impressive extent.

The SCU is the key component which is responsible for arbitrating all the communications between the processor subcomplex (ICU, FXU, and DCU), main memory, and I/O. It generates the memory control signals upon receipt of I-cache reload, D-cache reload, and D-cache storeback requests. Furthermore, it acts as the bus master for the memory bus and the SIO bus. In addition, the SCU is also responsible for providing a data path for I/O load/store operations between the CPU and the respective I/O device.

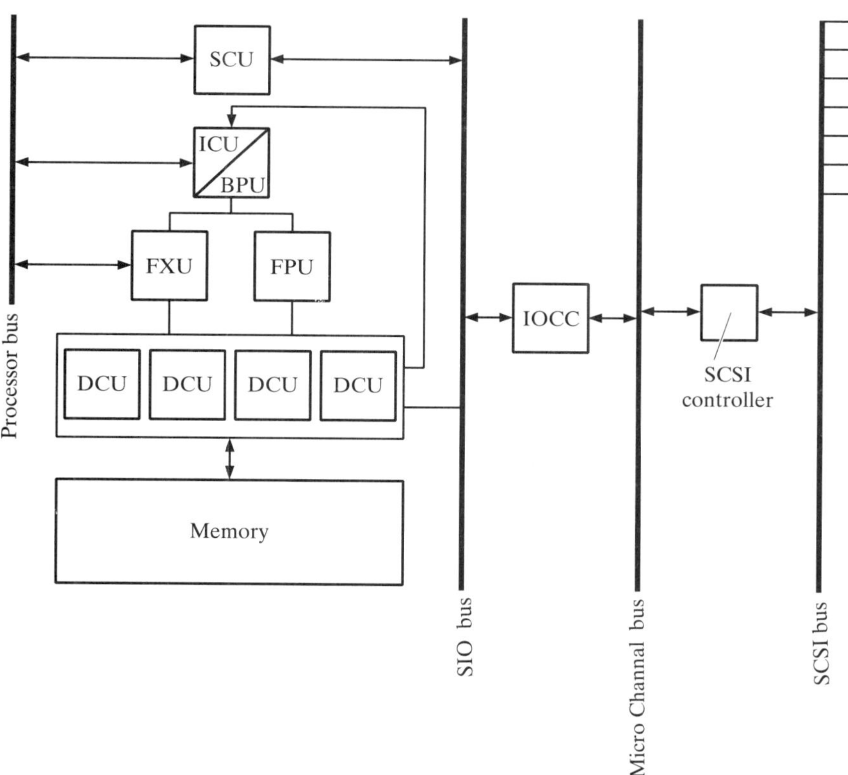

Figure 12.27 Positioning of the various buses—memory, SIO, and SCSI.

The SIO bus interfaces with the IOCC. The IOCC in turn interfaces with the Micro Channel bus at its other end. The principal function of the IOCC is to move data between the memory subsystem and the device(s) attached to the adapters on the Micro Channel bus. A view from the global perspective of the hardware architectural layout reveals this IOCC to be a conceptual barrier between two domains, namely, (1) the processor and memory complex, and (2) the I/O device and storage complex. Figure 12.27 further illustrates the concept.

The Micro Channel bus extends to the multifarious adapters, providing a medium for the transfer of data. All adapter cards attached to the Micro Channel slots adhere to the standard Micro Channel characteristics.

The SCSI bus further extends the reachability of the Micro Channel bus to an assortment of storage devices. The ability to support more than one kind of device off a single adapter is what makes SCSI a popular choice—it is not only the number of devices per se, but also the kind of the device(s) that can be supported by a single adapter. Figure 12.27 illustrates an end-to-end layout of the different buses in the System/6000, to facilitate understanding of the dataflow through the different buses of the memory and I/O subsystem.

Together with the memory, I/O, and storage subsystems, this machine contributes a high level of performance, in addition to providing an impressive degree of reliability, upgradeability, and configuration flexibility. Much of this performance level was achieved without having to exploit the optimal capabilities of components like the Micro Channel bus, which on its own accord is capable of delivering even higher data transfer rates than what are presently implemented. The closely knit design of the performance-crafted components has been the key to achieving this new frontier in computer performance engineering. The overall performance of the machine is no surprise, as its sophisticated processor complex is complemented by an equally impressive memory and I/O subsystem.

System/6000 Software Subsystem—Systems Perspective

Architecture of AIX

This chapter introduces a system perspective for the software subsystem of the System/6000. It introduces the AIX kernel in light of its characteristic components, infrastructure, and communication mechanisms. Although some basic terms and concepts are reviewed, familiarity with UNIX is assumed.

13.1 OPERATIONAL COMPONENTS OF THE KERNEL

There have been references made about the fact that the AIX system supports the illusion that the processes have "life" and files have "places." These two entities, processes and files, are the central concepts in the AIX system model. A *file* (defined as a collection of bytes logically grouped together) and a *process* (defined as a program in its state of execution) together form an operational entity, where file is the piece of data and process is the rule that acts upon the file. If the idea is extended further, it becomes evident that working with files involves devices and management of devices, while working with processes involves the management of processes. A logical block diagram of an AIX kernel, displayed in Fig. 13.1, shows the two main subsystems for process and device management side by side. This well-known layout is similar to a traditional UNIX system. The vertical separation between the device management subsystem and the process manage-

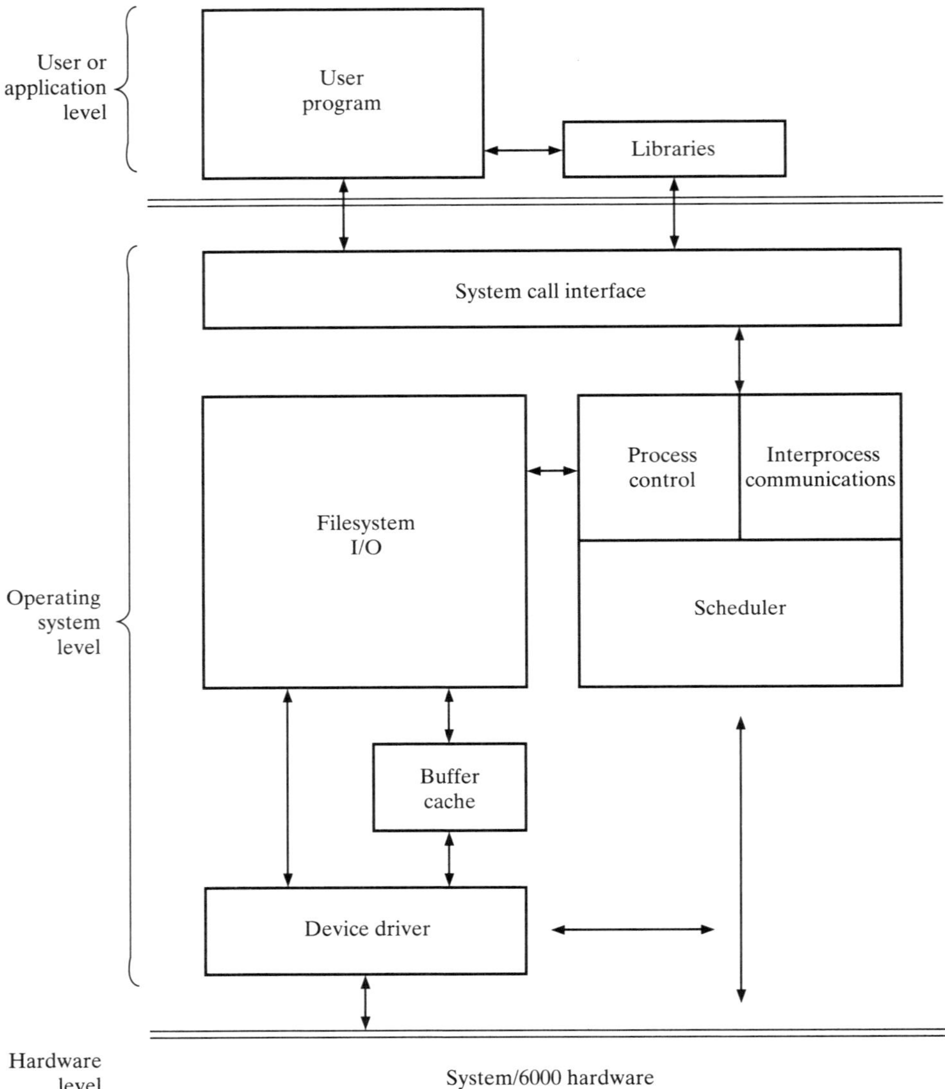

Figure 13.1 Logical block diagram of an AIX kernel.

ment subsystem reflects their functional roles. The two horizontal separations emphasize the positioning of the functional components of AIX between the application level and the hardware level.

The role of each component is significant in its own way as each affects the overall working of the operating system. User programs make use of libraries (using subroutine calls) to communicate with the kernel via *system calls*. Libraries are repositories for common routines that programs use to perform a task. They are linked with the programs at compile, load, or run-time and become a part of the program. System calls are similar to ordinary functions in high-level languages like C and are covered in detail in Chap. 15. For the purpose of discussion here, they can be thought of as primitives that allow a program to use the operating system services. When a program enters the operating system it accesses the file subsystem and/or the process subsystem. The *file I/O subsystem* handles dataflow and the I/O aspect of program execution. It uses a buffered as well as a nonbuffered mode to interface with the I/O device drivers and coordinate file I/O. The *process subsystem,* on the other hand, handles the orchestration of processes. This orchestration is a top-level abstraction of all the tasks, including interprocess communication as well as process scheduling management. The process management concepts are described further in Chap. 14. Details about the file system, memory management, and device drivers are covered in Chap. 16.

13.2   STRUCTURE OF THE AIX KERNEL

A *kernel* in generic operating system terminology denotes a nucleus of software that plays the role of system orchestrator and provides facilities necessary for implementing system services. These services can be functions to access filesystems, provide support for network protocols, or similar facilities. The kernel is a single binary image that supervises all process management, scheduling, and I/O using system calls to interface to the application world. The majority of the kernels' source code is written in C, with a small amount in assembly language.

The kernel's responsibilities can be split up into three functional domains:

1. Process management

2. System call subsystem

3. Memory, I/O, and file management

Each of the domains is discussed in detail in Chaps. 14, 15, and 16.

13.3   FEATURES OF THE AIX KERNEL

The AIX kernel distinguishes itself from traditional UNIX systems by virtue of its unique characteristics. Although its infrastructure is based on a System V Version 3 kernel, a myriad of characteristic features sets it apart from traditional UNIX systems.

The kernel structure in AIX has been extended to support preemption and real-time processing capabilities. The second distinguishing feature of the AIX operating system is that its kernel is pageable. The next noteworthy feature is its virtual memory management scheme which provides support for an exceedingly large address space (2^{52} or 4 petabytes) and performs several vital functions. Additionally, support for a dynamic load facility in AIX was adopted to allow parts of programs and kernel extensions to be dynamically loaded without intervention. Also, a true system management architecture is implemented to provide definition and management of the complex relationships of the objects in the system. In addition to the kernel structure modifications, some of the key components such as the filesystem have been enhanced to provide greater reliability. The storage subsystem generalizes the storage space concept by implementing logical volumes. The I/O subsystem in AIX has been augmented to support functions like mapped files, prepaging, data pacing, and asynchronous I/O handling, which are discussed in detail in Chap. 16. It can be observed from the high-level discussion here that a lot of the AIX kernel is essentially the same as in traditional UNIX systems, while much of it has been augmented to provide a superior environment above and beyond what UNIX developers have attempted before.

13.4 EXTENDING THE AIX KERNEL

The AIX kernel can be expanded by adding *kernel extensions*. This is a unique characteristic of AIX where kernel extensions can be added to an operational environment without preempting any ongoing activity. Attributes like new device drivers, system calls, kernel services, and private kernel routines can be added to the existing kernel to extend its functions. The direct benefit of being able to customize the kernel allows implementation of new timer services, customized interrupt handlers, pinned shared memory segments, and other useful facilities. Figure 13.2 demonstrates the different types of kernel extensions that can be implemented.

Extending the kernel essentially means the same thing as altering the kernel. As useful as this feature is, if exercised without caution, it can be as disadvantageous as it is advantageous when correctly implemented. Any process executing in the user mode can extend (or alter) the kernel, provided it has root privilege. The operation is done by invoking a privileged subroutine called *sysconfig*. The other way of altering the kernel configuration is by changing the tunable parameters. Values of the tunable parameters can be modified using the *smit* utility (discussed in Chap. 8), which in turn updates the information in the ODM database (also described in Chap. 8).

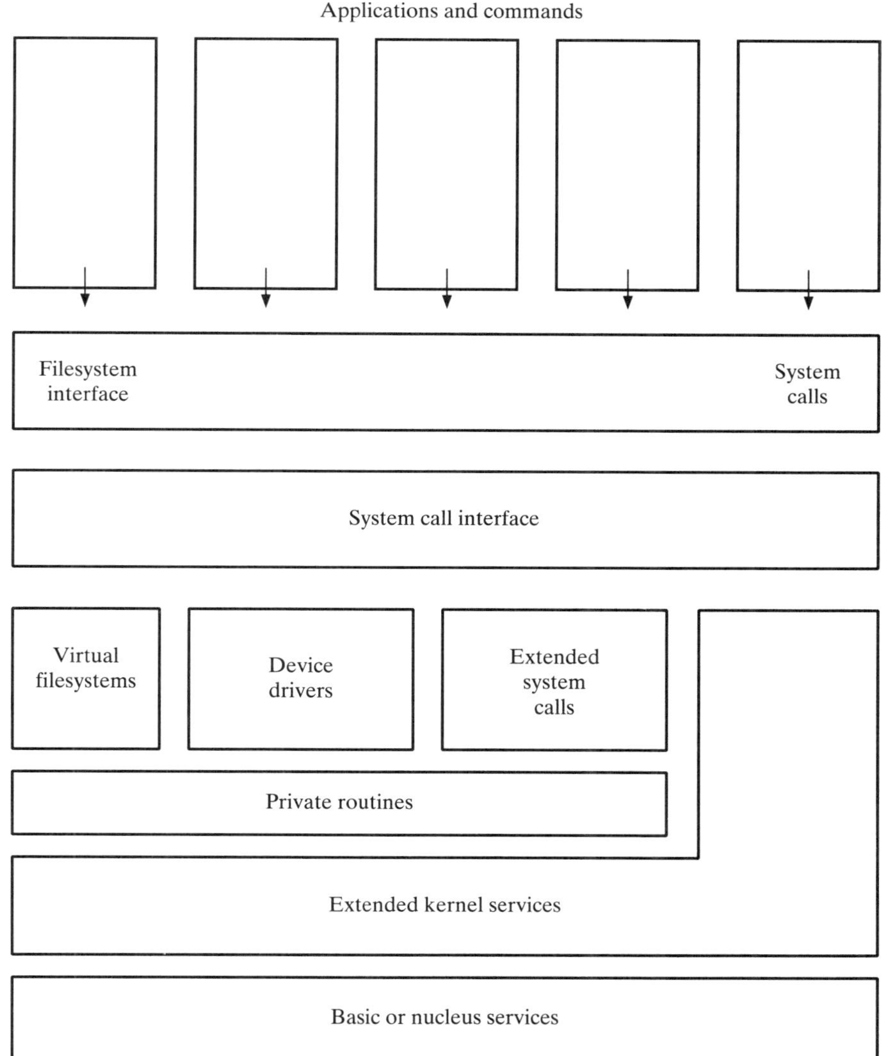

Figure 13.2 Types of kernel extensions.

13.5 AIX PROGRAMS, PROCESSES, AND PROCESS GROUPS

A program is an executable piece of code, and process is the name given to the program in its state of execution. When a program executes, it essentially submits a pattern of bytes to the CPU. This byte stream is interpreted as *instructions* (called *text*), *data,* and *stack.* The bytes that are instructions traverse through the maze of the CPU subcomplex;

they trace a pipelined flow through the branch processing unit, the fixed point unit, and/or the floating point unit. Chapter 9 of this book describes and traces the fate of each instruction down its respective path. The bytes that are data are made available when needed (either through the cache, TLB, or memory) by the instructions. The bytes that are stack-related facilitate a collated sequence of subroutine calls during the program's execution.

Like traditional UNIX systems, AIX handles the execution of several programs concurrently by scheduling them in a time-shared manner. Just as several programs may be executed as multiple processes, multiple processes can also execute a copy of a single program. Since the sequence of instructions in an individual process are self-contained, one process does not cross over or violate the private space of another process. When and if processes do need to communicate with each other, they do so via system calls.

An executable program is created by compiling a high-level language or assembly language source code. The process entity is created using system calls. The *fork* system call is the primary vehicle for creating processes under UNIX and AIX systems. Every time a *fork* system call creates a new process, the original process is referred to as the *parent* process and the newly created process is called its *child* process. A parent may have more than one child. However, the converse is not true; a child cannot have more than one parent. The operating system tracks each process by a unique tag called the *process identification number,* or *pid,* which is assigned to a newly created process as soon as it is created. As in the case of human reproduction in which a child inherits its parent's traits, the genealogy of inheritance in the case of process creation follows the same principle. A child process duplicates all of its parent's characteristics, except for the process identification number, or pid.

An executable user program is loaded into memory for execution using the *exec* system call. Once loaded, the program becomes a process and begins executing. As in all UNIX systems, during its execution, the process changes states constantly, depending on whether it is active or waiting with regard to the other processes on the system. It is often easier to think about processes being in a state of dynamic equilibrium. Every time a process changes its state, it follows a well-defined set of rules, as illustrated by a directed graph (digraph) in Fig. 13.3. The nodes in the digraph represent the various states that the process can assume. The edges in the digraph represent the events in the state change of a process. How does one determine what state transitions are permitted? A state transition between two states is legal as long as there is an edge from the first state to the second state.

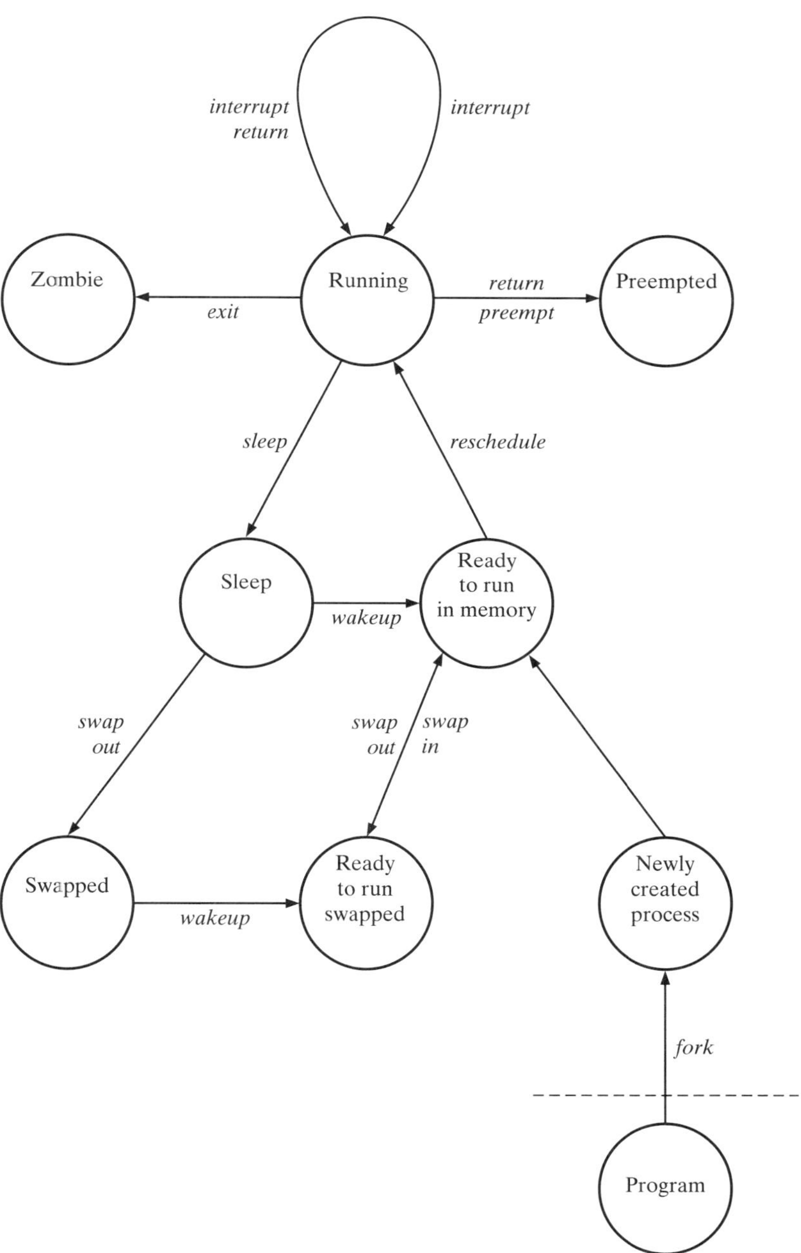

Figure 13.3 Digraph showing state transitions from a high-level perspective.

A process is terminated using the *exit* system call. Usually the parent is notified upon the termination of a process. If a process needs to suspend execution until one of its child processes has terminated, it may do so using the *wait* system call. Sometimes a variation of *wait* is used, called *wait3,* which allows the parent process to acquire information about the cause of child process termination and resource utilization during its life span.

The mechanisms described here for process creation, suspension, and termination form the basics of how processes operate under AIX. Figure 13.4 conceptualizes the effect that *fork, exec, wait,* and *exit* have on the fate of a process. In fact, to execute any program on AIX one has to make use of the *exec* system call (in one of its six variations). In a simple example of a user executing the *ls* command, the command language interpreter, i.e., the shell, first *forks* off a child process, which subsequently *execs* to overlay its image with that of the new program, *ls. ls* completes execution and exits thereafter; consequently, the parent process (the shell), whose execution was halted until now, comes out of the *wait* state.

Processes under AIX are organized into *process groups.* It is a term applied to a group of processes that are related. Typically, a set of processes under a process group have the same parent and very often are associated with the same terminal. Process groups provide a means of communicating with a collection of related processes. The system never changes the process group of a process that has one. However, a new process group can be assigned to any process when there is a need to deliberately dissociate a process from its default process group. This is done with the help of a system call named *setpgrp.* Disassociating a process from its process group is a common practice in the writing of daemons or programs that need to remain detached from terminal(s).

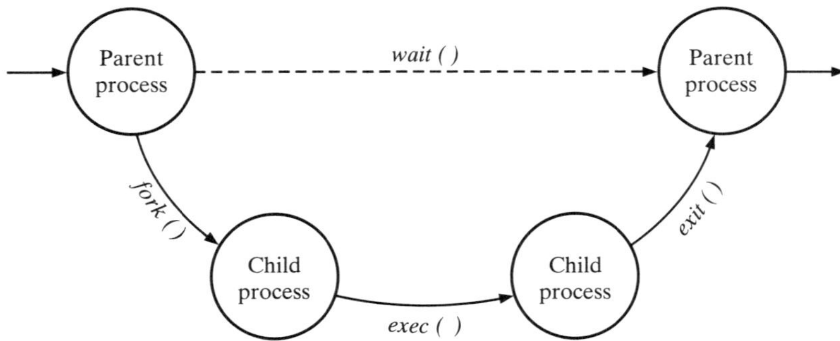

Figure 13.4 Process management system calls.

13.6   AIX NOTIFIERS

AIX provides a number of ways to inform itself and the rest of the system about the occurrence of miscellaneous events. There are three primary vehicles for notification:

- signals
- interrupts
- traps

Signals are notification events used to notify a process or group of processes. Each signal has an associated action that defines how a signal is to be handled when it is delivered to a process. Since signals are asynchronous, a process never knows when/if it is going to receive a signal. So, upon receiving a signal, a process succumbs to the signal's default action (unless an explicit signal handler has been coded into the application). Signals can be sent

- by the kernel to a process (or processes)
- by one process to another process (or to itself)

Every signal is associated with a type of event or condition and has a unique number representing it. For purposes of making a signal more readable, every signal has been assigned a name tag which is defined in a header file on the system called *signal.h*. The primary method of posting a signal for process(es) and process groups is through the usage of system calls, *kill* and *killpg*. The method used to handle a signal on the recipient's side is specific to the signal's action. But in general, signals are either ignored, blocked, or caught (with the exception of two signals, SIGKILL and SIGSTOP). The signals found in *signal.h* are described here.

SIGHUP	1—hangup, generated when terminal disconnects
SIGINT	2—interrupt, generated from terminal special char
SIGQUIT	3—quit, generated from terminal special char
SIGILL	4—illegal instruction (not reset when caught)
SIGTRAP	5—trace trap (not reset when caught)
SIGABRT	6—abort process
SIGEMT	7—EMT instruction
SIGFPE	8—floating-point exception
SIGKILL	9—kill (cannot be caught or ignored)
SIGBUS	10—bus error (specification exception)
SIGSEGV	11—segmentation violation

SIGSYS	12—bad argument to system call
SIGPIPE	13—write on a *pipe* with no one to read it
SIGALRM	14—alarm clock timeout
SIGTERM	15—software termination signal
SIGURG	16—urgent contention on I/O channel
SIGSTOP	17—stop (cannot be caught or ignored)
SIGTSTP	18—interactive stop
SIGCONT	19—continue (cannot be caught or ignored)
SIGCHLD	20—sent to parent on child stop or exit
SIGTTIN	21—background read attempted from control terminal
SIGTTOU	22—background write attempted to control terminal
SIGIO	23—I/O possible, or completed
SIGXCPU	24—CPU time limit exceeded
SIGXFSZ	25—file size limit exceeded
SIGMSG	27—input data is in the HFT ring buffer
SIGWINCH	28—window size changed
SIGPWR	29—power-fail restart
SIGUSR1	30—user defined signal 1
SIGUSR2	31—user defined signal 2
SIGPROF	32—profiling time alarm
SIGDANGER	33—system crash imminent; free up some page space
SIGVTALRM	34—virtual time alarm
SIGMIGRATE	35—migrate process*
SIGPRE	36—programming exception
SIGVIRT	37—AIX virtual time alarm
SIGGRANT	60—HFT monitor mode granted
SIGRETRACT	61—HFT monitor mode should be relinquished
SIGSOUND	62—HFT sound control has completed
SIGSAK	63—secure attention key

Interrupts are asynchronous events that are generated by the kernel or a device. The name is given to them as they indeed "interrupt" the execution of the current process. When a process is preempted, the con-

---

* This signal is specific to the transparent computing facility (TCF) which is supported by AIX running on PS/2 and S/370. TCF gives a view of a single system image and enables migration of processes between processors at run-time. Although kernel hooks for this signal may persist, TCF is not available on AIX running on the System/6000.

trol is transferred to a special set of routines in the kernel called interrupt handlers. An interrupt handler routine services the interrupt and, after completion, transfers control back to the current process to continue execution.

Traps are synchronous events that are normally caused by the system hardware. As in the case of interrupts, a process may not decide how to react to the trap. Control is passed on to trap handlers in the kernel and the trap handler code takes control. In the case of a trap, a process may or may not resume execution, depending on the nature of the trap. There is another type of notifier, *exceptions,* which are also synchronous events like the traps. They directly relate to the currently executing instruction. A common example is a divide-by-zero error. The only notable difference between exceptions and traps is in the resulting handler code modules.

13.7   INTERNAL REPRESENTATION OF AIX FILES

AIX features a variety of files. The word "file" is so generic that one cannot be sure if a file is a piece of data on disk or the disk itself. Since the early days of UNIX, one of its hallmarks has been to treat files, disks, terminals, etc., the same way. This is still true today. As much as this abstraction facilitates the portability of a UNIX system and application software, it can also confuse users. This section describes the different file types and explains how the kernel handles access to files.

13.7.1   File types

A regular file in AIX is not different from traditional UNIX systems. It is just a sequence of bytes with one or more names. A file can be created using either the *open* or *creat* system calls, and can be written to or read from using the basic *read* or *write* system calls. Directories that organize files hierarchically are no different from regular files, except they have a structure imposed on them by the system.

AIX also supports two other file types. They are

- pipes
- device special files

Pipes are like regular files and data is stored in them in the same manner as in regular files. But they differ from regular files in that their data is ephemeral. The contents, being transient in nature, can only be read in a first-in first-out (FIFO) manner. Also, once the data is read from the pipe, the data disappears and cannot be read again. Pipes are useful in a variety of applications where a transient data stream

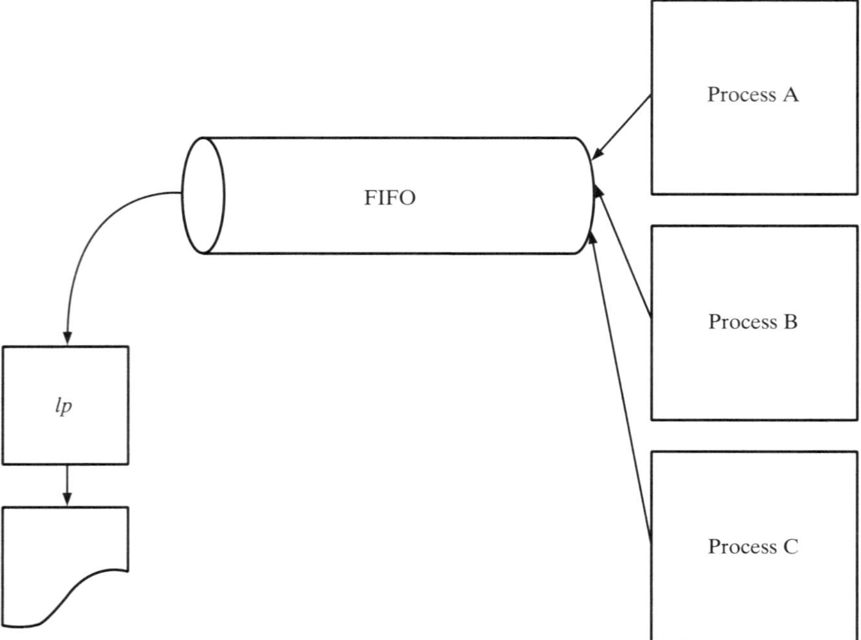

Figure 13.5 Process communicating through a pipe.

makes more sense than a regular file, or in a situation where arbitrary processes need to be communicated with even though one does not know the process(es) at the other end of the pipe (refer to Fig. 13.5).

Hardware devices on AIX and other UNIX systems have filenames and can be accessed by the same system calls that are used for regular files. The jargon used to refer to these devices is *device special files*. All device special files specify devices and therefore their file inodes do not reference any data. Instead, the inode indicates the device type and its logical unit number. Direct references to these device special files are primarily made by the kernel. Users and applications never have to worry about these dependencies. Even the kernel does not worry much about the device-specific dependencies. Most dependencies are segregated in the device drivers. Details about device drivers are covered in Chap. 16. For the discussion here, it will be sufficient to state that the kernel insulates the device dependencies completely from application programs.

13.7.2 Kernel file data structures

The internal representation of a file on a UNIX system is specified in an index block (sometimes called an index node) which contains the description of the disk layout of the file data and allied information such as permissions and ownerships. The term index node has been abbreviated to *inode* over the years and today most of the UNIX community knows it by this shortened name. This inode is the most precious structure as far as files are concerned. It contains all the pertinent information about the file, except for the file name. Initially inodes exist in a static form on disk. Thereafter, they are read into an in-core inode table and remain resident in memory (see Fig. 13.6). Whenever a new file is created, an unused inode is assigned to it. Note that, although a file may have multiple names, all of the *hard links** map back into the same inode (Fig. 13.7). As far as accessing data is concerned, each inode contains eight pointers which point directly to data blocks. Each data block is 4 KB in size. For larger files, the inode contains a pointer which points to a block of indirect pointers; this block contains 1024 pointers which in turn point to data blocks. For even larger files, the inode contains a pointer which points to a block of pointers (1024), each of which points to a further block of pointers (512), each of which points to a data block. Figure 13.8 conceptualizes the structural layout of how data block addresses are stored and accessed in the inode, depending on the size of the file. In principle, these single, double, and triple indirect access methods can be extended to handle quadruple and quintuple indirect blocks, but the current structure has sufficed in practice and no immediate extension is deemed necessary, keeping in mind the current requirements of file sizes required by the industry. The size of data blocks is usually consistent within a filesystem but may vary between two dissimilar filesystems. For example, the size of each data block on the native AIX filesystem is 4 KB, whereas each data block of the CD-ROM filesystem is 512 bytes. Besides data blocks, a filesystem also contains what is called a *superblock* to describe the state of the filesystem. It contains information about the size of the filesystem, number of inodes, the list of free inodes and other housekeeping data.

From the perspective of the kernel, there are three primary data structures associated with every opened file on the system:

- the file table
- the in-core inode table
- the user file descriptor table

---

* Hard links are one of the two types of links normally found under UNIX systems. The other kind of link is a *symbolic link,* which uses a new inode for the file or directory being linked.

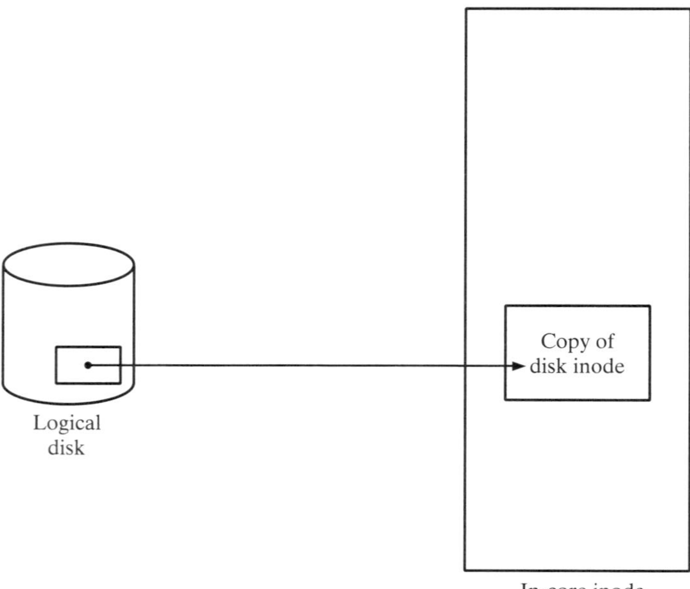

Figure 13.6 Two different representations of the same inode.

The first two tables are global structures, while the third one is local to a user process. The user file descriptor table is organized using the file descriptors associated with opened files of that process as indices to each cell. Three file descriptors are assigned for every process by default, in order to support the standard input (*stdin*), standard output (*stdout*), and standard error (*stderr*) streams. Whenever a file is opened by a process for reading or writing, a new entry is entered into this table. Each entry of this user file descriptor table indexes into the file table, which maintains the byte offset in the file where the subsequent read/write will start. This file table in turn, points to the in-core inode table. Each entry of the in-core inode table is a generic inode, rightfully referred to as a *gnode*. It is this *gnode* that locates the whereabouts of the data in the file. The three-step linkage of the tables for a traditional UNIX system is shown in Fig. 13.9. In the case of AIX, the file table to the in-core inode table mapping is further abstracted by indexing into a virtual filesystem structure called *vnode,* seen in Fig. 13.10. This abstraction of virtual inodes or vnodes allows the system to deal with remotely mounted non-AIX and non-UNIX filesystems. Since the discussion here is pertinent to the internal representation of files only (and not filesystems), discussion has been restricted to the file-related kernel data structures. Additional details are discussed in Chap. 16.

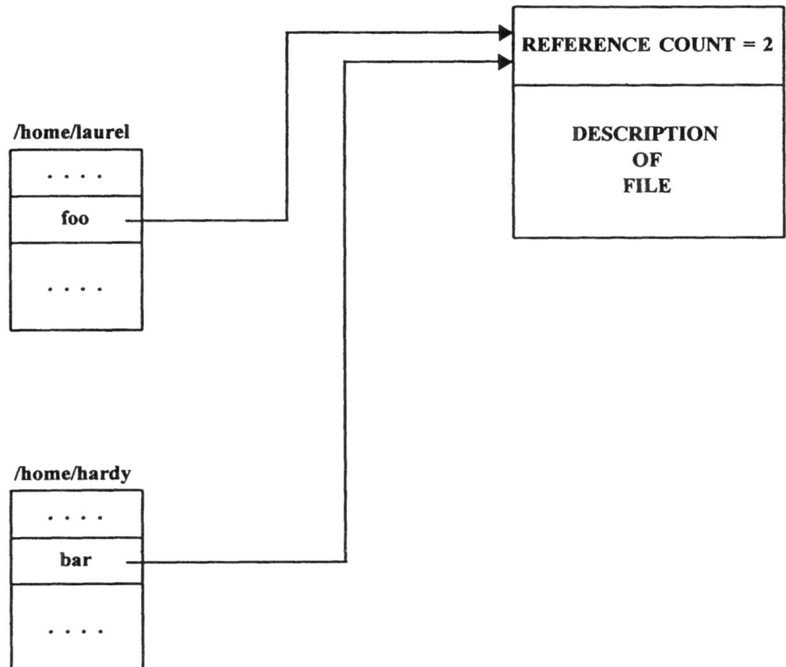

Invoking "ls -li" in hardy's directory shows:

Figure 13.7 A file with multiple names showing a link count of 2.

13.8 BUFFER CACHE

The design of the UNIX filesystems implies a lot of disk I/O. If the UNIX kernel were really to perform every implied disk transfer, the CPU would be idling constantly, waiting for I/O. To address this issue, the kernel allocates a pool of buffers, called the *buffer cache*.* Its intent is twofold. The first is to minimize frequency of disk access by buffering read/write requests, and the second is to act as a cache of recently

---

* The buffer cache is only a data structure and should not be confused with the hardware caches discussed in Chap. 10.

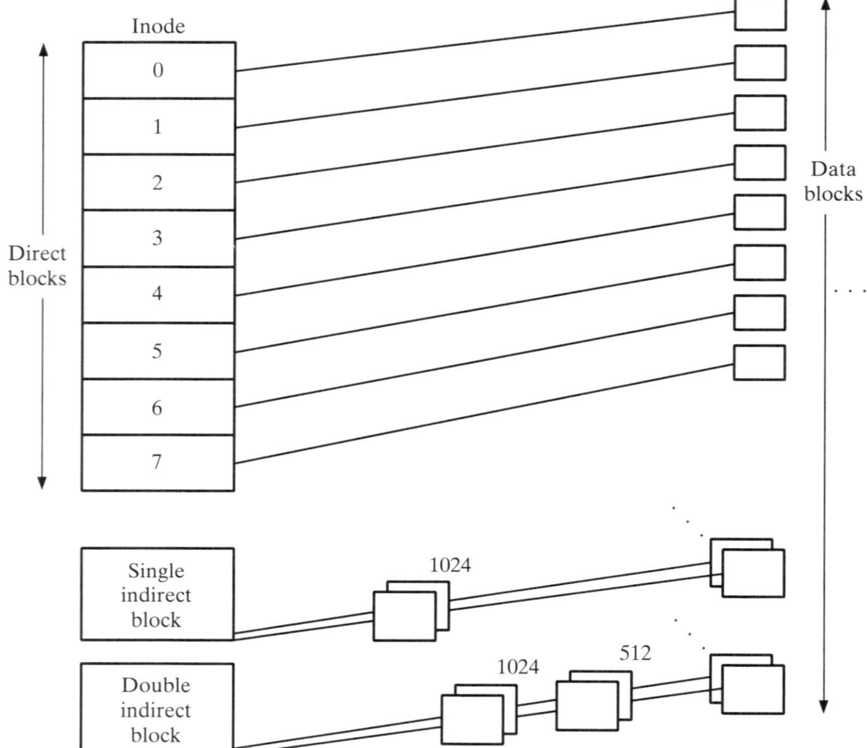

Figure 13.8 Three schemes for storing data block addresses, depending on the size of the file.

used disk blocks. A buffer cache is composed of two parts, (1) a *data buffer* that contains the disk I/O data and (2) a *buffer header* that points to the data array buffer. The buffer header also contains a (logical) device number field and a block number field that uniquely identifies the buffer, along with a status field summarizing the current status of the buffer, as seen in Fig. 13.11. Individual buffer headers are linked together in a buffer pool and remain connected through a doubly linked list.

The overall significance of the buffer cache has diminished in AIX, since AIX uses *mapped files** in its augmented filesystem. This concept of mapped files not only greatly minimizes disk access (when reading from or writing to a file) but also provides a better performance over a

---

* This is a concept of mapping a file into the memory upon *opening* it. The feature is discussed in greater depth in Chap. 16.

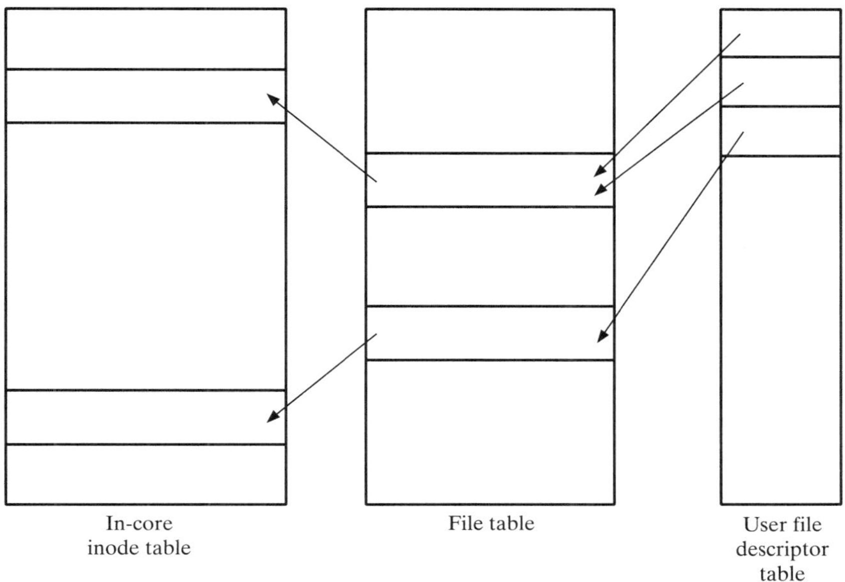

Figure 13.9 Three-step linkage and relationship of in-core inode table, file table, and user file descriptor table in UNIX.

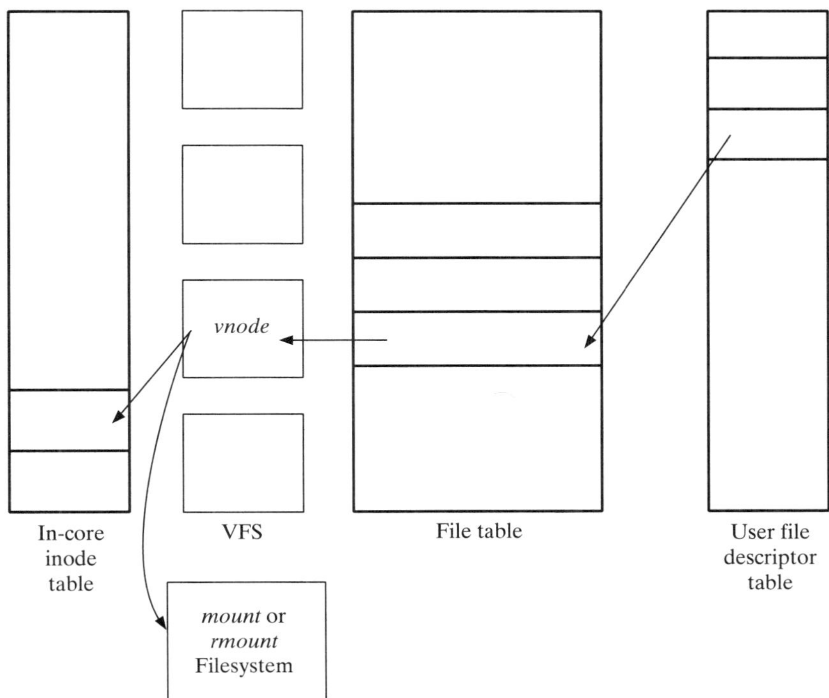

Figure 13.10 Four-step linkage and relationship of in-core inode table, file table, and user file descriptor table in AIX.

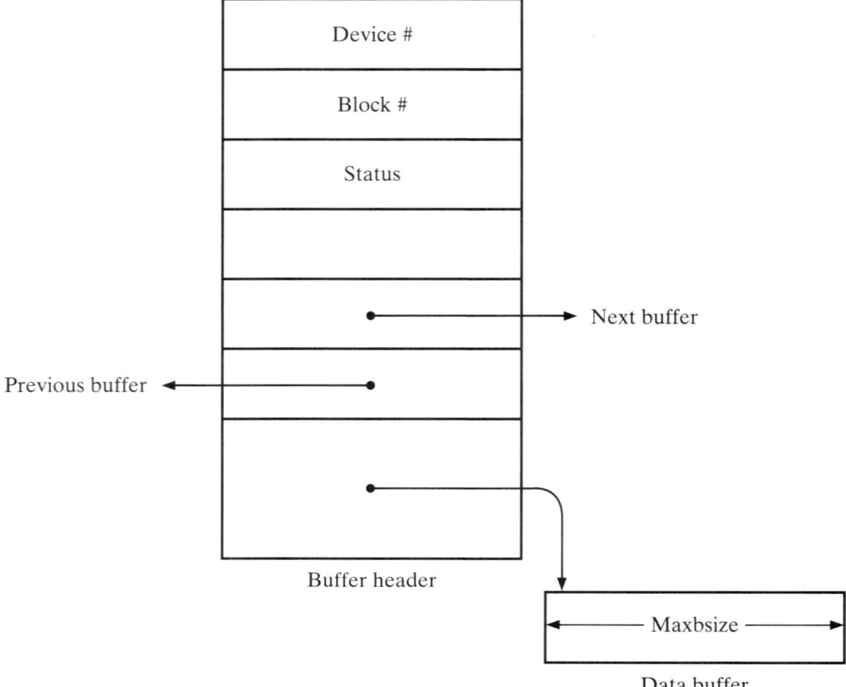

Figure 13.11 Structure of a buffer cache.

traditional buffer cache. The buffer cache continues to have responsibilities for the page device table lists and handling of the superblock during a filesystem mount operation. The buffer header part of the buffer cache is used to handle I/O requests to block devices.

13.9 SUMMARY

The architectural layout and the discussion of the functional characteristics of AIX point to the fact that a lot of the AIX kernel is essentially the same as traditional UNIX systems, while many of its I/O subsystem components, such as the virtual memory manager and the filesystem, have been enhanced to provide a superior environment above and beyond what UNIX vendors had attempted before.

In the chapters to follow, AIX-specific topics will be elaborated upon, while continuing to present a systems perspective of the software subsystem of the RISC System/6000.

Process Management

This chapter describes the process management subsystem for AIX. As such, the low-level process management tasks for AIX are not too different from traditional UNIX systems, but it is the availability of real-time processing capabilities with the AIX kernel running on the System/6000 that makes process control worth revisiting.

A high-level perspective of the generic UNIX processes was formulated in Chap. 13, and the life of processes was reviewed. This chapter describes the basic evolution of process management concepts and extends these into the real-time computing arena.

14.1 PROCESS STRUCTURE

In Chap. 13, a process was defined to be a program in its state of execution. An executable program on disk consists of three areas: (1) a text area which is the code, (2) an initialized area consisting of the data, and (3) a noninitialized area known as the *bss** or heap. As illustrated in Fig. 14.1, when an executable is loaded into memory and undergoes transition to a process, the text area is mapped to one of the 16 segments of virtual memory accessible per process, known as the *text*

---

* This name comes from an assembly language pseudo-operator on the IBM 7090 machine, which was an acronym for "block started by symbol."

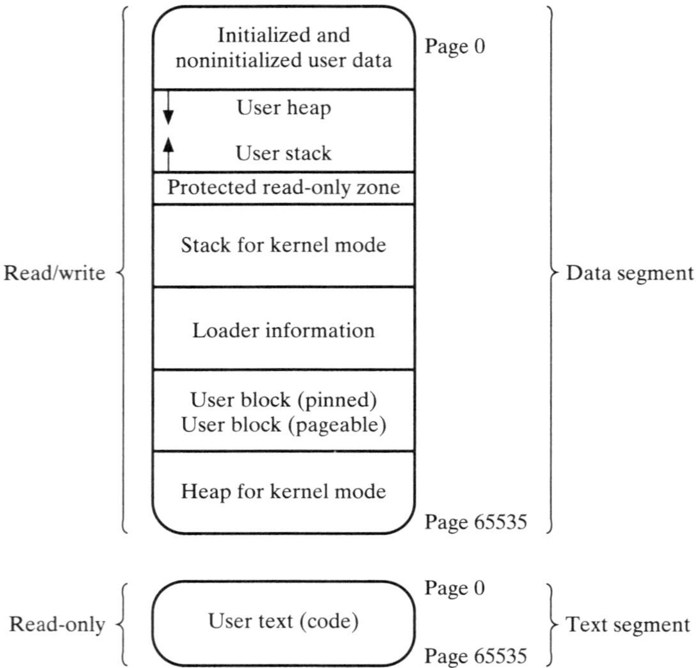

Figure 14.1 Structure of an executable. (*Note*: Each page is 4 KB in AIX.)

segment. This segment is read-only and can be shared by other processes running the same code. The data and *bss* areas are mapped to another virtual memory segment referred to as the *data segment*. This segment is both readable and writable, and private to that process. This data segment can be further broken down into two areas: a *user area* (meant for use when a process is executing in user-mode) and a *kernel area* (meant for use when the process has undergone a mode change and is executing in kernel mode). The kernel area, located at the end of the segment, contains machine-state information for that process, its file descriptor table, and environmental information such as the user ID, current working directory, etc. The user area is at the start of the data segment; here space is allocated for initialized data used for variable declarations, noninitialized data used for function declarations, and dynamically allocated memory. Note that the stacks for the user area and the kernel area are separate (shown in Fig. 14.1).

The data segment is of the type referred to as "working storage." Unlike the text segment, it contains data which is created dynamically as the process runs. It should be noted that this data has no persistent storage on the file system; so, if memory is overcommitted, its contents will get written out to the preallocated area on the paging space. See Chap. 16 for a fuller explanation of how the memory subsystem is managed.

14.2 PROCESS-AFFILIATED KERNEL STRUCTURES

A process, when executing, has no knowledge of other processes on the system. It is the scheduler that manages how and when each process gets the CPU to execute its instructions. This should shed some light on the fact that each process is a distinct, schedulable entity.

Affiliated with each process is a set of data structures. The pertinent ones are *proc* and *u_block* (also referred to as user block or user area).

The *proc* structure contains information related to the scheduler and the dispatcher, such as

state of the process

nice value of the process

process statistics

process priority

user and process identifiers

process link pointers pointing to child and sibling processes

The *u_block* structure, which points to the *proc* structure includes information such as

user credentials

signal management

per-process timer management

user mode address space mapping

audit data

login terminal associated with the process (if any)

user's file descriptor table*

This means that there is a *proc* structure for every process, including kernel processes, running in the system. Each structure is represented by a slot in the process table. There is also a *u_block* structure for every running process and it is stored in the process' private data segment. The difference in their contents is that the *proc* structure contains

---

* This part of the *u_block* is pageable.

information that is needed in memory when a process is swapped out, while the *u_block* structure contains information that need not be in memory when the process is swapped out. Regardless, the in-use *proc* blocks and parts of *u-block* remain pinned in order to avoid page faults in critical sections.

14.3 PROCESS STATES

A typical process moves through multiple states during its life cycle. Unlike the human life cycle, a process can revisit a state during its life. There are six possible states that are stored in the process table entry for every process and can be used to describe a process' state at any given time. The states are described below and their transition states are depicted in Fig. 14.2.

State	Token value	Description
SNONE	0	process slot available
SSLEEP	1	awaiting an event
SRUN	3	runnable
SIDL	4	being created
SZOMB	5	being terminated
SSTOP	6	stopped

The SNONE state signifies that a process slot is available in the process table which the *fork* system call checks during initializing. The SIDL state indicates a process is being created by allocating space in memory to commence execution in the later part of the *fork* system call. The SRUN state can represent a new or a preempted process that is ready to run and is waiting for the CPU. If the process is not a new one, it can be a sleeping process being returned to be scheduled again, or a waiting process resuming execution after having waited on a signal or event, or simply an exiting process from the run state reverting for its next time quantum (recall that exactly one process can run at any given time). The sleep state SSLEEP is encountered for processes that are waiting for I/O, an event to complete, or a resource to become available. The stop state SSTOP represents processes which are waiting for a signal to transition them into the SRUN state. Note that a signal issued by the kernel can result in a sleeping process to transition into a stopped state or a stopped process (that was previously in a sleep state) to transition to a sleep state. Last but not least, there is a terminating state called the zombie state SZOMB, which indicates that a process is exiting, but still occupies its process table slot. As much as

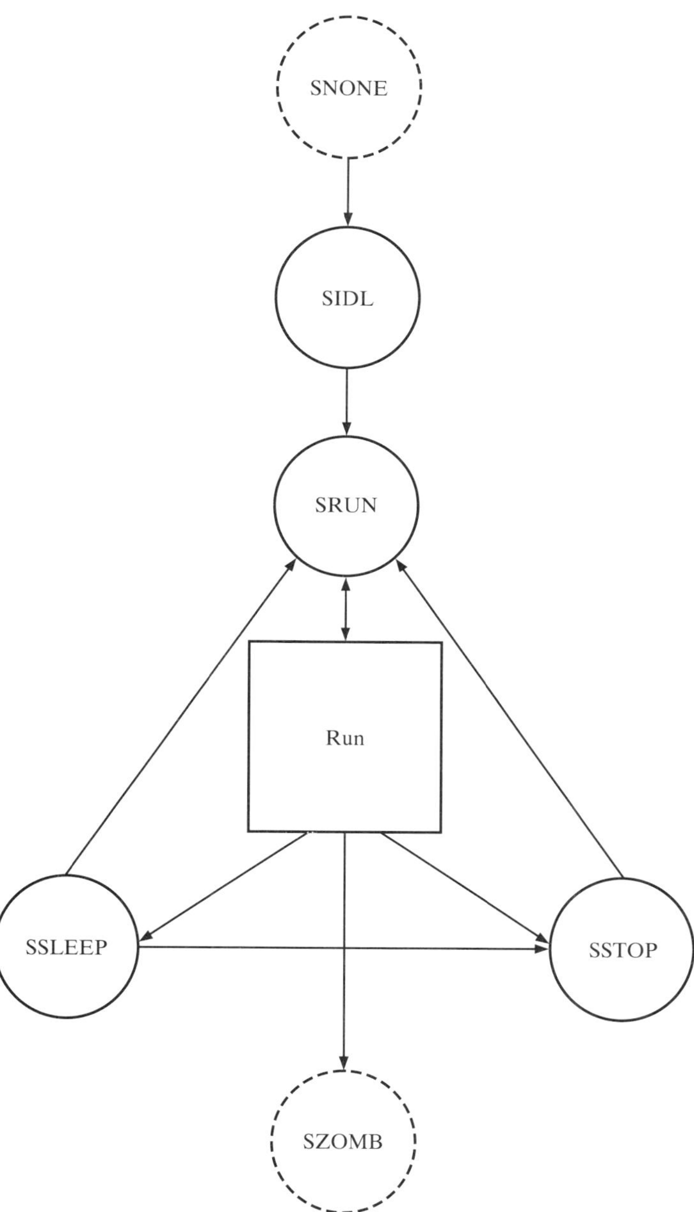

Figure 14.2 AIX process state transition diagram.

this SZOMB state ought to be short-lived, some processes hang around longer than desired, usually because of a parent process' failure to check on the death of its child. Zombie processes can be identified by displaying the process table entries with the help of the *ps* command and finding the processes that appear as "<defunct>" in the command column of the displayed output.

14.4 PROCESS MONITORING

Having been introduced to the process-related data structures on the system and the overall life cycle of the processes, it makes understanding AIX even more meaningful if one is to monitor these ongoing entities at run-time. Many such tools to monitor processes are available.

The *ps* utility is one such tool that allows the user to display processes on the system. Typical information available from the output of *ps* includes: the process identification number of the process (PID), the process identification number of the parent of the process (PPID), the controlling terminal port (TTY), the owner of the process (UID), the name of the owner of the process (USER), the CPU utilization (CPU), the memory utilization (MEM), the process state (STAT or ST), the nice value of the process (NICE), the priority value of the process (PRI), the resident set size (RSS), the text resident set size (TRS), and the paging space used (SIZE). A sample output shown below gives the essence of what kinds of information can be reported using *ps*.*

```
PID   TTY STAT    TIME  PGIN  SIZE  RSS    LIM  TSIZ  TRS  %CPU  %MEM  COMMAND
   0     - S    1:08     6     8    8     xx     0    0   0.0   0.0  swapper
   1     - S    1:50    27   148  216     xx    21   32   0.1   1.0  init
 514     - R 3274:17     0    12   12     xx     0    0   0.0   0.0  kproc
 771     - S    2:33     0    16   16     xx     0    0   0.0   0.0  kproc
1028     - S    0:00     0    16   16     xx     0    0   0.0   0.0  kproc
1599     - S    0:00     0   108   40  32768     2    8   0.0   0.0  biod
2391     - S    0:23    24   144  232     xx    24   36   0.0   1.0  cron
2808     - S    0:13     9    48   72     xx     1    4   0.0   0.0  syncd
2834     - S    0:00     0    24   24     xx     0    0   0.0   0.0  kproc
3096     - S    0:00    13   176  256     xx    21   28   0.0   1.0  srcmstr
3578     - S    0:00    16   240  324     xx    39   56   0.0   1.0  errdemon
```

---

* The output for *ps* may vary somewhat based on the options used with the command. The command used for this specific output was "*ps cvg.*"

PID	TTY	STAT	TIME	PGIN	SIZE	RSS	LIM	TSIZ	TRS	%CPU	%MEM	COMMAND
3618	-	S	0:01	13	124	184	32768	16	24	0.0	1.0	syslogd
3968	-	S	0:00	0	16	16	xx	0	0	0.0	0.0	kproc
4133	-	S	0:00	52	232	456	32768	180	188	0.0	2.0	sendmail
4414	-	S	0:00	3	180	48	32768	2	8	0.0	0.0	biod
4795	-	S	0:01	0	16	16	xx	0	0	0.0	0.0	kproc
4949	hft/0	S	0:02	31	104	380	32768	303	276	0.0	1.0	ksh
5420	-	S	0:00	2	104	136	32768	6	12	0.0	1.0	portmap
5679	-	S	0:00	14	172	248	32768	26	40	0.0	1.0	inetd
5940	-	S	0:19	68	412	784	32768	243	340	0.0	3.0	snmpd
10589	-	S	0:00	3	84	120	32768	11	12	0.0	0.0	writesrv
10854	-	S	0:00	8	76	112	32768	47	28	0.0	0.0	hcondmn
11079	-	S	0:00	9	120	180	32768	26	36	0.0	1.0	bootpd
11388	hft/0	R	0:00	0	128	208	32768	34	48	0.0	1.0	ps
11619	-	S	0:00	11	84	140	32768	47	28	0.0	1.0	infod

More detailed information on processes may be obtained with the use of *crash,* which is a useful dump analyzer cum operating-system monitoring tool. A crash output is displayed below to give a taste of the kind of detailed information that can be tracked. The process chosen in this example is called *init,* and it happens to occupy slot (SLT) #1 in the process table. Some of the hard-to-find information includes process-subsystem-related details regarding sibling and child processes, state of signals, dispatcher- and scheduler-related information for the process, and memory subsystem details like address space. The ones that are extremely useful for debugging are described in detail in the next paragraph.

In the output displayed below, the link fields are chain pointers. There is a *child* pointer that points to a child, and a *sibling* pointer that links child processes together. The dispatch fields are used by the dispatcher, where the *prior* pointer links to a chain of processes with the same priority, the *next* pointer points to the succeeding process on the run list, *pevent* and *wevent* point to the pending events and awaiting events, respectively. Additional fields like *suspend* indicate the signal-nesting level and the *process-waiting-for* field shows exactly what the process is waiting for (events, in this case). The scheduler fields are used by the scheduler. The *pri* field marks the dispatch priority, *nice* gives the nice value, *lpri* gives the lock priority, and *wpri* gives the wait priority. The field containing miscellaneous information displays the handle of the process private segment. The signal field that follows gives details about the pending, masked, caught, and ignored signals in double word formats, where each bit represents a signal number. The statistics field displays information about the process image size.

```
> proc - 1

SLT ST     PID    PPID    PGRP    UID  EUID  PRI  CPU    EVENT   NAME

   1 s       1      0       0       0     0   60    0              init
          FLAGS: swapped_in no_swap wake/sig locks
Links:    *child:0xe3003600 *siblings:0x00000000 *uidl:0xe3000100
    *wchanl(real):0x00000000 *lcklst:0x00000000
    selchn:0x00000000
Dispatch Fields: *prior:0xe3000100 *next:0xe3000100
    pevent:0x00000020 wevent:0x00000004
    polevel:0x000000ad *lockwait:0x00000000
    *eventlst:0x00000000 *wchan(hashed):0x00000000 suspend:0x0001
    process waiting for: event(s)
Scheduler Fields: pri: 60 nice: 20 lpri:127 wpri:127 flags:0x 0
  repage:0x00000000 scount:0x00000000 *snext:0x00000000 *sback:0x00000000
Misc: adspace:0x00001004 *ttyl:0x00000000
        *p_ipc:0x00000000 *p_dblist:0x00000000 *p_dbnext:0x00000000
Signal Information: cursig:0x00 sigstate:0x00
    pending:hi 0x00000000,lo 0x00000000 sigmask:hi 0x00000000,lo 0x00000000
    sigcatch:hi 0x00000001,lo 0x18783eff sigignore:hi 0x7ffffffe,lo
0xe786c000
Statistics: size:0x0000008a(pages) audit:0x00000000
```

crash is a tool capable of displaying any kernel data structure or memory locations. Although crash is one of the most (if not the most) powerful tools to monitor processes in the kernel, it requires a detailed knowledge of AIX's internal data structures. As most of the main kernel data structures have been covered in this book, it is expected that the reader will be able to use crash effectively when needed.

14.5 PROCESS PRIORITY

The dispatcher and the scheduler are the two main components of the kernel that drive a process.

The *dispatcher* is a function which facilitates having the most-favored priority process run at any given time. The dispatcher is invoked at the occurrence of an interrupt or when the currently running process relinquishes control of the CPU in order to perform I/O or to time-slice with other processes. Note that the dispatcher does not recompute process priorities, but instead chooses the best-suited process to run based on its existing priority.

The AIX *scheduler* consists of two parts. One of them is the real-time clock interrupt handler that executes every system timer tick (which is 10 ms). The second part recomputes the process priority every hundred clock ticks (which is 1 second). A nonfixed priority process is charged for every timer tick of CPU it uses by incrementing a field called *p_cpu* in the particular process table entry. Then every hundredth timer tick (which is 1 second), the priority of all processes is recalculated. Subsequently the dispatcher is called to ensure that a process, which may now have a more favored priority, gets dispatched. Note that the recomputation task is performed by halving the CPU value (p_cpu) for all processes, whether they are in a runnable, sleep, or stopped state, and then converting the value into a new priority for each process. This explanation is better understood from the algorithm below.

$$\text{priority} = \text{nice value} + \text{PUSER} + \left(\frac{\text{p} - \text{cpu}}{2}\right)$$

The value of PUSER is a constant, with a default value of 40. It is not a tunable parameter.

The scheduler is often referred to as the *swapper;* in fact, this is how the scheduler process can be identified in a *ps* listing (included in Sec. 14.4). The duality of terms can lead to confusion. As stated before the swapper is the process which handles context-switching, i.e., it swaps processes in and out of the CPU and does so based on a priority scheme. A context switch does not, however, involve a swapping out of the process from main memory to disk. AIX implements two policies for managing memory:

- swapping
- demand paging

When the system is running normally, that is, it is not thrashing, the policy used is demand paging. This mechanism will, when memory is overcommitted, free up memory by "stealing" pages of memory belonging to a process. (Note that this may or may not involve I/O.) When the system thrashes, the policy implemented is swapping. Here the most memory-intensive processes are suspended for a period of time until the system has recovered. When a process is suspended, all memory belonging to that process is freed up. So, the process is said to be swapped out of memory. In summary, the process named swapper, performs dispatching, scheduling, and swapping. It only performs swapping when the system is deemed to be thrashing.

What has been described thus far pertains to normal processes only. For real-time processes, the priority has to remain unaffected, or in other words, the value of p_cpu should not be subjected to recomputation. It becomes necessary that the real-time processes be run at a higher priority than the swapper. On RISC System/6000-running AIX, the swapper process runs with an execution priority of 16. To avoid preemption by the swapper the time-constrained real-time processes run at a fixed priority more favored than 16.

In the priority hierarchy ladder there are three categories of process priorities, namely, (1) *interrupt handler priority,* (2) *real-time priority,* and (3) *user process priority.* An interrupt handler enjoys the most-favored priority on the system in order for it to be able to preempt a running process to respond on time to an external event. The real-time processes have the next level of precedence in the priority hierarchy (Fig. 14.3). Any process that has been assigned a fixed value between 0 and 40 behaves as a real-time process. Such processes run until they voluntarily relinquish the CPU by entering a sleep state or an interrupt causes them to get bumped by causing the dispatcher to run a process with a more favored priority. Recollect that this trait of the dispatcher was mentioned earlier in this chapter where a timer interrupt occurring every 10 ms was inevitable. Thus, it can be stated that the dispatcher's running of the most-favored process, at least as frequently as 10 ms, is tied to the inherent design of AIX on the System/6000. The user process priority is a volatile entity and is constantly redefined throughout its life span. At its birth, a process inherits its parent's priority and over the period of time its value changes based upon its CPU consumption. A process priority has a large degree of variance and can assume up to 86 possible values. There are several catalysts that govern a user process priority, the prime one being the CPU usage.

Permissible priority values for real-time processes = 0 to 40

Permissible priority values for user processes = 41 to 127

14.6 CONTEXT SWITCHING

Context switching is not specific to AIX or UNIX; instead, it is a generic phenomenon found in operating systems with round robin schedulers, where at the end of each time quantum an interrupt is generated from the timer. Processing the timer to switch the CPU to another process requires saving all the registers for the current process and loading the registers for the new process. This task is known as a *context switch.* Context switch time is pure overhead. The time to perform a context switch depends on the cause of the context switch. The cost of a context switch owing to an external interrupt is different from that of one caused by expiration of a process' time-slice, which in turn is different from a context switch occurring due to the voluntary sleep of a process. These varying costs of context switches directly affect performance of the system.

AIX supports a set of unique features that enables it to achieve an exceedingly fast context switch time. Traditional UNIX systems do not allow a context switch while executing in the kernel mode. But AIX has

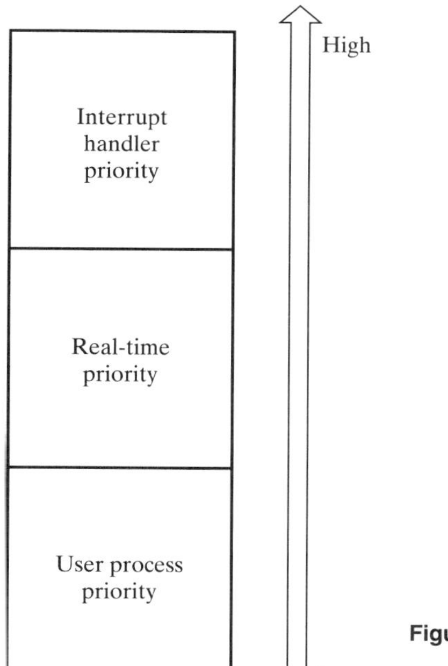

Figure 14.3 Priority hierarchy.

a fully preemptable kernel which does permit such a context switch to happen. Not only is a context switch possible under AIX, but the mechanism is speeded up dramatically because of the presence of a unique data structure for the dispatcher.

There are 128 process-scheduling run queues under AIX that correspond directly to the 128 priorities supported by the dispatcher. Each run queue is a circularly linked list of runnable processes having the same priority. An array of pointers, called the *run queue pointer array* (RQPA), serves as the repository for head pointers to each of the circular doubly linked lists. The system maintains another array, called the *bit array,* with 1-bit flags to indicate which of the run queues are nonempty. This complex data structure is presented in Fig. 14.4. As long as there is one process in the run queue of that priority level, the bit flag in the bit array remains enabled. So, when choosing which process should be run next, the dispatcher only has to look at the bit array to determine the most-favored priority run queue that is occupied. The algorithm is as follows:

```
compute the most favored priority level
index into the array of run queues
access the head pointer pointing to the run queue
select the process at the head of the run queue
dispatch the process
```

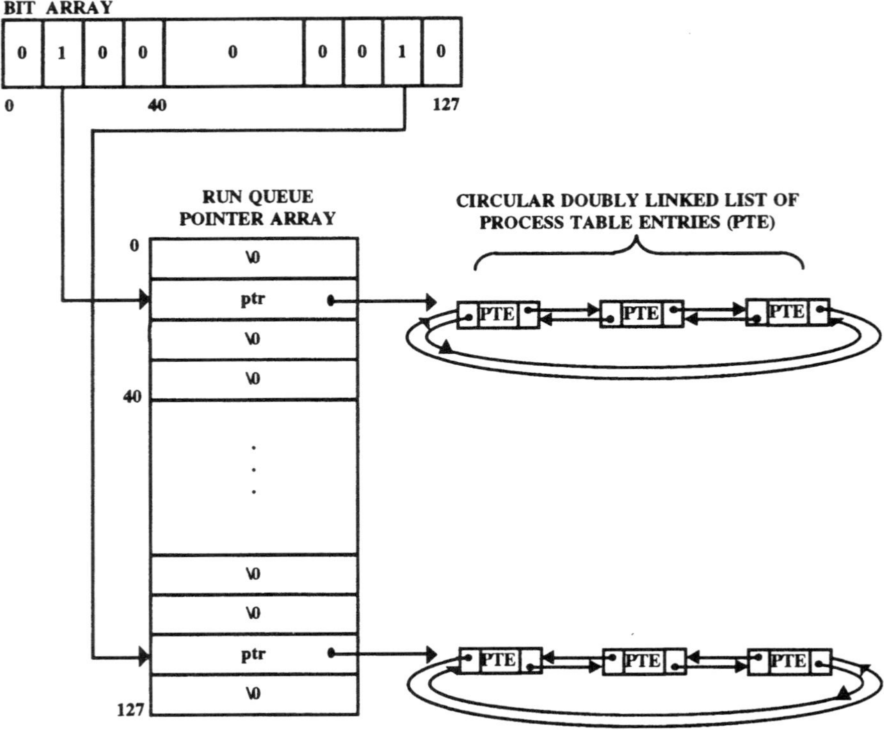

Figure 14.4 Data structure layout for the AIX process dispatcher. Indices 0 to 40 of the RQPA point to real-time processes and indices 41 to 127 point to user processes.

Following the expiration of the scheduler's time quantum, if the process is still runnable, it is placed at the end of the run queue, and the new head of the linked list is dispatched. In this way, the dispatcher is able to implement a round robin scheme within processes of equal priority. The main gain of this implementation in AIX over traditional UNIX is an exceedingly fast context switch, since the dispatcher does not have to traverse long queues, even if there were several runnable processes outstanding.

14.7 PROCESS SCHEDULING

The process-scheduling mechanism in AIX is no different from traditional UNIX systems. The scheduler belongs to a general class of operating schedulers known as *round robin with multilevel feedback*. UNIX process management unifies the temporal diversification in the activities by merging all the computations as processes, thereby making a process the only schedulable entity. Processes are given a time quantum when the scheduler selects one for the CPU from its multilevel priority queue. The highest run-queue level at which incoming user processes can enter the process-scheduling subsystem is 40. (Recall that all processes inherit a PUSER value of 40 plus a nice value varying between 0 and 39 which can be changed via the *nice* or *renice* system calls.) New processes start life with a CPU value (p_cpu) of 0, as shown in Fig. 14.5. In all of the 128 circularly linked process scheduling run queues that correspond to the 128 permissible priorities supported by the dispatcher, the time quantum for time-slicing increases

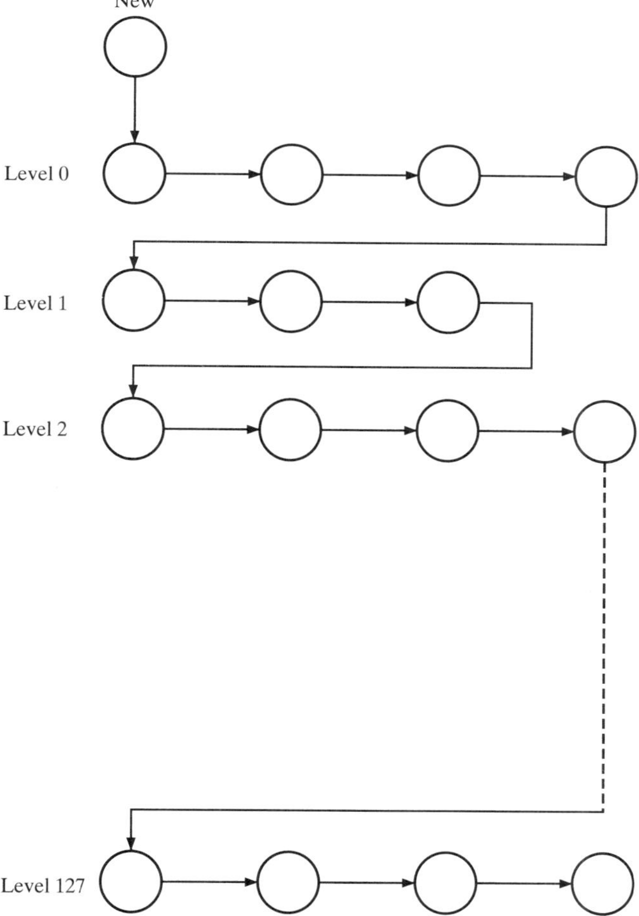

Figure 14.5 Process scheduling.

with the lower level. In other words, CPU-bound processes tend to stay at lower levels and I/O-bound processes hover around higher levels. A process is time-sliced every quantum, and the CPU time used in this interim is charged to that process.

When a context switch occurs to make another process runnable, the overhead encountered in the operation may or may not be charged to the right process. Although the enhanced context switch mechanism in AIX lessens the context switch overhead time, it does not eliminate it.

The process time measurement activity is tied to the clock handler and is carried out by sampling the usage of the CPU at the clock-tick instants. The system keeps time with a hardware clock that interrupts the CPU at a fixed, hardware-dependent rate. The frequency of this interrupt is 100 times a second for the System/6000. This means that the best granularity of time that the AIX kernel can provide is 10 ms. If a process is to wake up after one clock tick, and then go away before the next tick, no CPU utilization would be attributed to its p_cpu field. Due to the coarse clock granularity and the snapshot-oriented mechanism of process timing in UNIX and AIX, errors occur easily, as depicted in the time line in Fig. 14.6. The occurrence of an interrupt (such as the clock interrupt) affects the CPU utilization of the running process. But there is no feature to account for the time spent by the CPU in handling interrupts caused by other processes. The small magnitude of errors, when added up and compared against cumulative system statistics, results in a rather significant quantity—not small enough to be ignored, especially on loaded systems. Those familiar with the mainframe world may recall the problems of low resolution and large variability in time measurements.

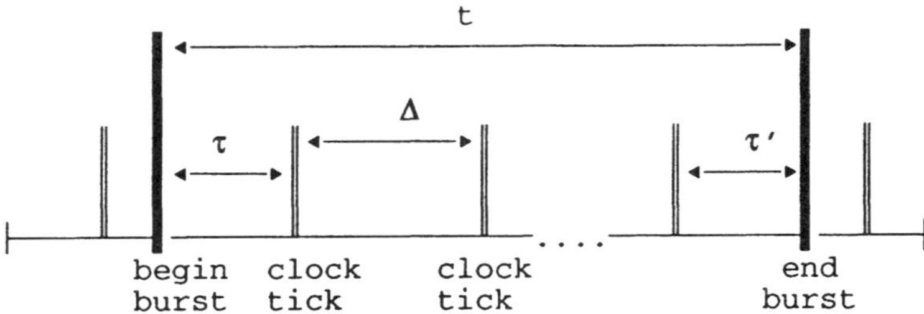

Figure 14.6 Process time measurement. Δ is the clock-tick interval (10 ms); t is the time quantum (CPU burst); τ and τ' are the positive and negative errors created in measuring the interval.

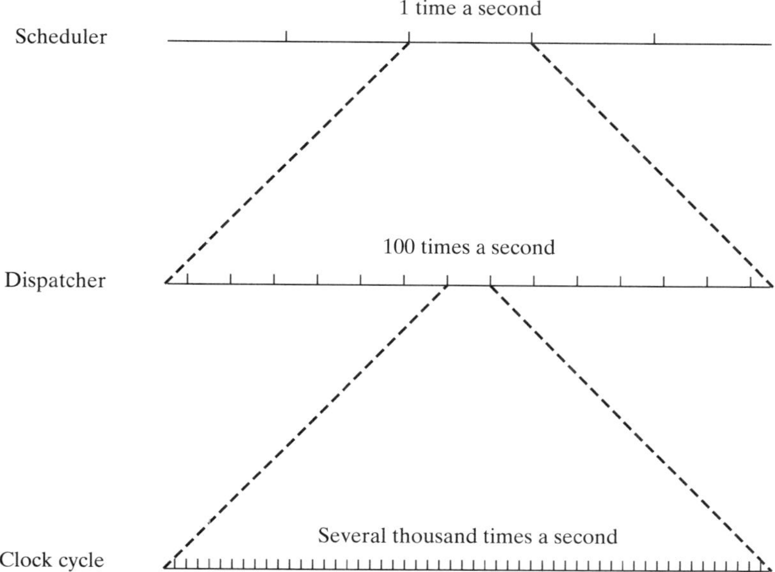

Figure 14.7 A conceptual layout for timing done at three nested levels—
the scheduler, dispatcher, and the clock.

Timing is done at three nested levels (presented in Fig. 14.7), i.e. the
scheduler, the dispatcher, and the clock cycle level. While the scheduler
recomputes the priority of all processes every second, and the dispatcher increments the utilization of the current process by one for
every hundredth of a second, the system has several thousand oppor-
tunities in the interim to raise interrupt(s). In order to address finer
time measurements, a hardware-based timer facility is available on
the System/6000 which enables programs to measure time intervals
with high resolution.

14.8 TIMER SERVICES

Timer services to conduct high-resolution measurements are available
to programmers via two methods:

- kernel services*
- user subroutines

---

* Refer to Chap. 15 for a detailed reference on kernel services.

14.8.1 Hardware timer

There are two facilities available for making hardware timings. The first one is the hardware clock, which is a 64-bit real-time clock that is based on two 32-bit registers. It is used to maintain the time of the day. The upper part of the clock is incremented every second. The lower part is logically incremented every nanosecond, but actually updated once every ten machine cycles.*

The second facility is a 32-bit decrementer that can be used as an interval timer. It has the same resolution and constraints as the lower part of the hardware clock.

14.8.2 Timer services

There are three kinds of services that can be used:

- Kernel timer services
- POSIX timers
- UNIX timers

The kernel services offer four timer services and one time-of-day timer service (refer to Chap. 15) that provide kernel extensions with the ability to be notified when a period of time has passed. The services provided are

- Time-of-day kernel service:

  curtime
- Timer kernel services:

  talloc

  tstart

  tstop

  tfree

The user subroutines, based on POSIX compliance specifications (refer to Chap. 7), are to be used for developing code that is portable across heterogeneous platforms. The POSIX subroutines offered are:

---

* The speed of the oscillator crystal determines the increment interval of this lower part of the real-time hardware clock. For example, a processor running at 50 MHz (equivalent to a cycle time of 20 ns) increments this register once every 200 ns, as compared to a 25-MHz processor which will be able to update this register no more frequently than every 400 ns.

gettimerid

incinterval

absinterval

getinterval

The UNIX subroutines that provide for compatibility with System V systems, BSD systems, and other AIX systems (such as AIX PS/2, AIX RT, and AIX/370) are the following:

alarm

ualarm

getitimer

setitimer

14.9   INTERRUPT AND EXCEPTION HANDLING

The hardware uses the same mechanism to report both interrupts and exceptions. When either event occurs, the machine saves its current state and takes an unconditional branch to a special location where the handler code is located. Depending on the cause for the preemption, the handler code determines whether the event is an exception or an interrupt, and consequently performs different processes accordingly.

Interrupts are triggered asynchronously and seldom have anything to do with the currently executing instruction. Exceptions are synchronous events and are directly related to the currently executing instruction. Timer ticks are interrupts and the divide-by-zero operation is an example of exception. Page faults are also treated like interrupts, except that the interrupted program is made nondispatchable until the page fault is resolved.

Interrupts are asynchronous events that are generated by the operating system or a device. The occurrence of an interrupt indeed interrupts the execution of the current process. The process is preempted and the control is transferred to what are called *interrupt handlers*. The appropriate interrupt-handler-routine services the interrupt and, after its completion, it transfers control back to the current process to continue execution. Since an interrupt itself can be interrupted by a higher priority interrupt, AIX saves an abbreviated context for the interrupt and links a representation of each one together using a region called *current machine state area* or *csa** as seen in Fig. 14.8.

---

* This is possible because an interrupt handler does not require an entire state definition like a process.

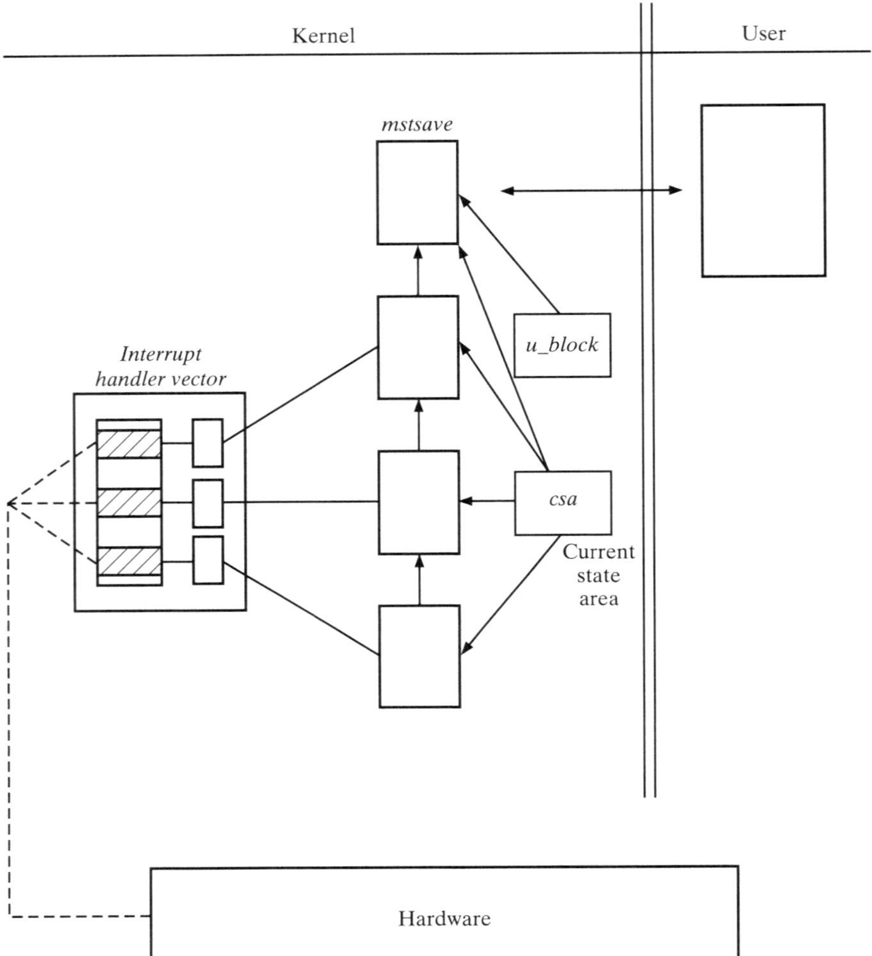

Figure 14.8 Handling of interrupts.

The system tracks these regions by the user's *u_block* structure and a pointer to the *csa* area. Although there are numerous types of interrupts with different interrupt priorities on the system, there are essentially two types of interrupt levels (see Fig. 14.9) associated with them. The first is called a *system interrupt*. These are generated by base hardware components, such as the real-time clock. The second kind of interrupt is referred to as a *device interrupt*. These are caused by the system's interaction with assorted devices. Interrupt priorities associated with the individual interrupts are essentially a hierarchy by which pending interrupts are serviced. A device's interrupt is selected

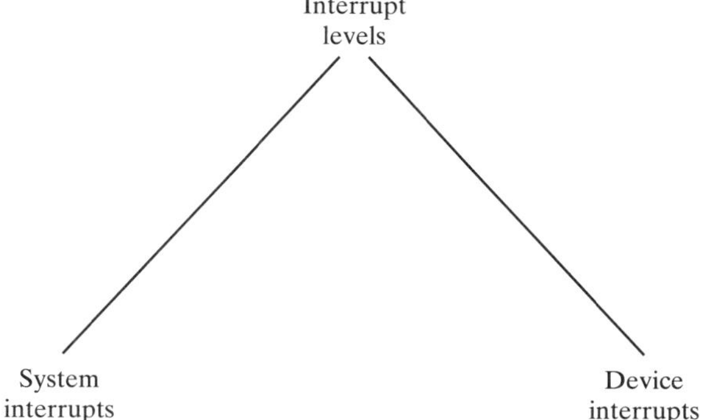

Figure 14.9 Interrupt levels.

based on its maximum interrupt latency requirements and the corresponding device driver's interrupt execution time. As far as interrupt processing within the system is concerned, this operation is provided by the branch processing unit hardware* and its three registers, namely, the MSR (machine status register), the SRR0 (save and restore register), and the SRR1.

The exception handling mechanism enables the executing instruction to specify the type of action to take. Exceptions are handled differently depending on whether they occur while executing in user mode or kernel mode. The default consequence of an exception in user mode causes a signal to be sent to the process indicating the type of exception. If an exception handler is defined, cleanup action is taken to free up the process' storage and affiliated resources. Exception handling in the kernel mode extends the capability of the traditional UNIX mechanism by allowing these exception handlers to be stacked on a per-process or per-interrupt handler basis.

14.10 INTERPROCESS COMMUNICATION

The choice of interprocess communication (IPC) is generally governed by the quantity of data to be communicated between processes and the frequency of exchange between processes. No matter which IPC mechanism is used, each has a minimum overhead cost associated with it and an upper limit on the bandwidth that it can handle gracefully. In the context of IPCs, *overhead* refers to the time required to transfer the

---

* Covered in detail in Chap. 11.

smallest message, and *bandwidth* refers to the maximum permissible rate at which transfer can occur.

There are several IPC mechanisms available under AIX. The list includes

- Pipes
- Message queues
- Shared memory
- Semaphores
- Sockets
- Streams

14.10.1 Pipes

Pipes are the most basic of the IPC mechanisms. They are like regular files and data is stored in them in the same manner. Where they differ from regular files is that their data is ephemeral. Their contents are transient in nature and can only be read in a first-in first-out manner. Once the data is read from pipes, the data disappears and cannot be read again.

Pipes are used in applications where a simple transient data stream makes more sense than a regular file, or in situations where arbitrary processes need to communicate even though the processes at the other end of the pipe are unknown (refer to Fig. 14.10). When multiple processes write to a pipe, the write operations remain atomic and data from one write operation never gets interleaved with data from other processes. However, it should be noted that the pipes do not preserve message boundaries. So, if one process is to write two 32-byte messages

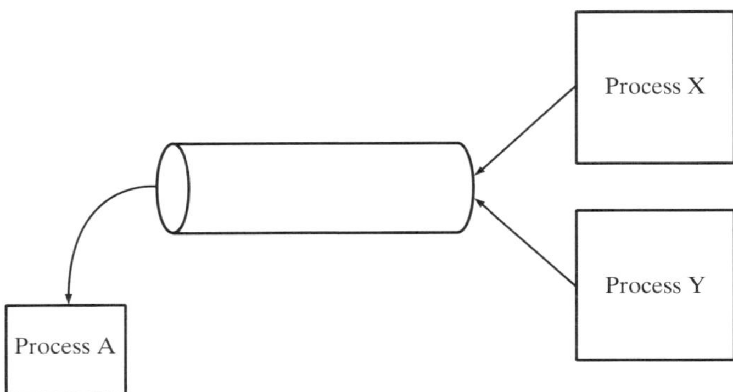

Figure 14.10 Pipes.

into the pipe, the reader process at the other end of the pipe has no way of interpreting whether the contents represent two 32-byte messages or four 16-byte messages. Here the application needs to do its own housekeeping for maintaining message boundaries.

There are two kinds of pipes, *unnamed* pipes and *named* pipes. When using unnamed pipes there is no way for processes without a common ancestor to communicate. So, a process has to create a pipe and then fork off a child process, in order to be able to have both processes (i.e., the parent and the child) share the same set of file descriptors to read and write from the pipe. Named pipes (also called FIFOs) overcome this shortcoming. Since they are identified by a file name, the file descriptor information can be passed to another process which may be unrelated.

Unnamed pipes are opened using the *pipe* system call, and named pipes are created using the *mknod* system call.

14.10.2   Message queues

Message queues provide a more flexible means of communications than pipes or sockets. Unlike pipes or sockets, message queues do not require a process to be waiting for a message.

All messages have an associated message queue identifier, using which, processes can read or write messages to arbitrary queues. This identifier is like a file descriptor in the case of an open system call and is used to reference the queue header. In comparison to pipes, there is no requirement that a process be waiting for a message on a particular queue before another process can write a message to that queue. This means that a process is able to write a message to a queue and exit, and have the message read by another process at some later time. Unlike pipes, messages provide a specific header format so that applications do not have to worry about interpreting message boundaries. Every message on a queue has three attributes: a message *type, length* of the data portion of the message, and the *data* itself. With a variable length data field available, it is easier to structure and manage the data using message queues.

A message queue is a linked list of messages which has been grouped and named as a set. Fig. 14.11 exhibits messages on a queue, showing queue headers, a linked list of message headers, and pointers from the message headers to a data area.

The most frequent operations performed with this IPC facility are (1) creating or accessing of a message queue, (2) removing or controlling the parameters associated with a message descriptor, and (3) transmission (sending or receiving) of a message. There are four system calls to handle these operations. The *msgget* system call opens or creates a

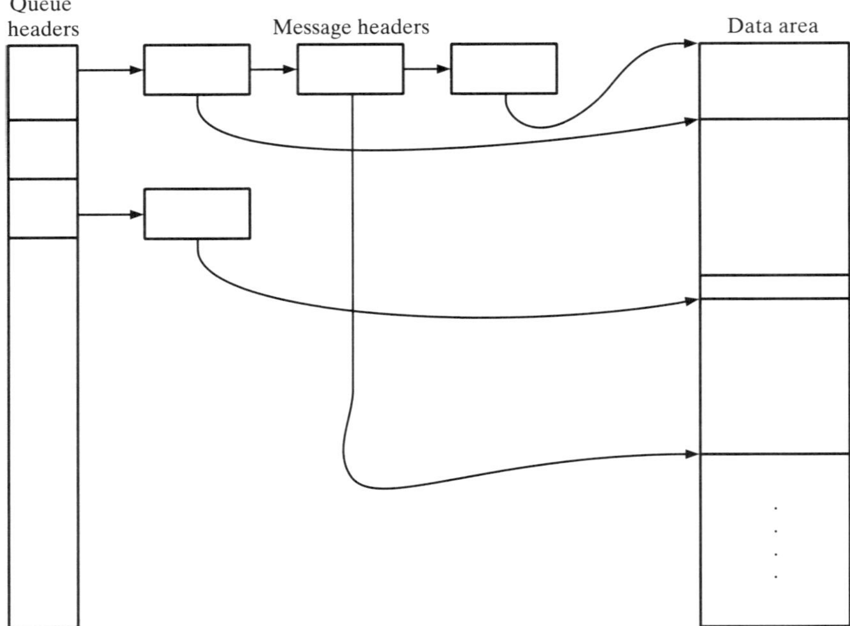

Figure 14.11 Messages on a queue showing queue headers, a linked list of message headers, and pointers from the message area to a data area.

message queue by traversing the message queue array to locate a possible match and allocating a new queue structure if no match is found. The *msgctl* system call is used to query the status of the message queue, set selected status fields, or to remove the queue, when needed. The remaining two system calls, *msgsnd* and *msgrcv,* are similar; one sends and the other receives a message.

14.10.3 Shared memory

Shared memory provides IPC capability to processes. It is unique in that it is the only IPC method that does not require the data to be communicated between processes to be copied. For large chunks of data this is ideal, as it eliminates severe performance problems that can arise from large data movements inside the system. Although AIX protects one process from accessing the memory space of another process, a common memory space can be made available among multiple processes using a set of special system calls. Even though a shared memory capability allows data-sharing under AIX, it remains the responsibility of the processes sharing the memory to devise a synchronization scheme to serialize access to it. This IPC facility on its own does not provide locks or access control among the processes. Although reading from shared memory may be safe, writing to it can result in severe contention problems leading to deadlocks if proper care is not taken.

The system calls for manipulating shared memory are similar to the system calls for messages queues. The *shmget* system call creates a new region of shared memory or returns an existing one, the *shmat* system call logically attaches a region to the virtual address space of a process, the *shmdt* system call detaches a region from the virtual address space of a process, and the *shmctl* manipulates various parameters associated with the shared memory. Note that the low-level instructions to read/write to shared memory are no different from how processes read from and write to standard memory.

Access to a shared memory region is gained by invoking the *shmget* system call that searches the shared memory table for a matching key and subsequently returns a numeric ID. A per-process segment table entry provides access to the descriptor associated with the ID. The ID references entries in the kernel's segment information table, which in turn describes a segment of memory. Under the current implementation of AIX, a process may attach to a maximum of 10 shared memory segments at any given time. Chapter 16 elaborates on the memory segments and explains how a memory of a process is divided into 16 segments, of which 8 (segments 3 to 10) are always available for shared memory and 2 more (segments 11 and 12) can be made available if needed. This is illustrated in Fig. 14.12.

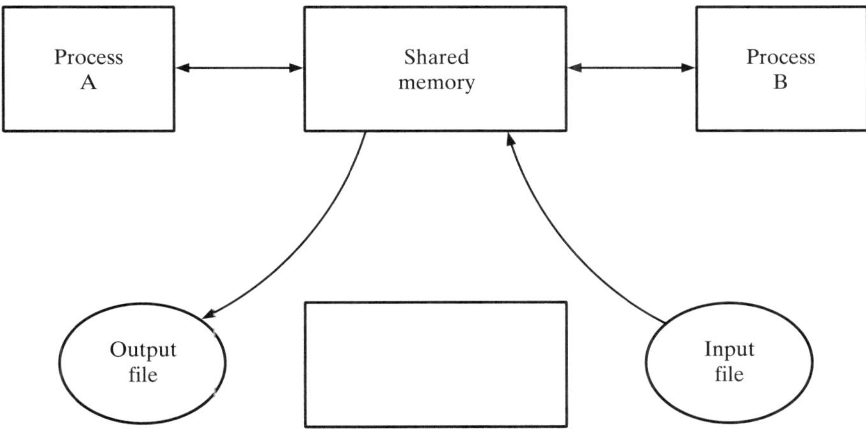

Figure 14.12 Data movement between two cooperating processes using shared memory.

14.10.4 Semaphores

Semaphores are a synchronization primitive. Although semaphores are not exactly IPC mechanisms, they can be regarded as IPC catalysts since they provide a means to synchronize access to shared resources (most commonly, shared memory segments). Semaphores can be used by a variable number of unrelated processes. The semaphore facilities found in AIX have their earliest root going back to Dijkstra's Dekker algorithm, published in 1968, which described an implementation of two atomic operations which incremented and decremented an integer counter, depending on the value. Being atomic in their operation, only one of them could succeed at any given time. The semaphores in AIX and UNIX are a generalization of Dijkstra's atomic operations where they are used as flags to prevent cooperating processes from using the same resource at the same time.

The most common use of semaphores is in synchronizing access to shared memory segments. A semaphore's value can be 1 when memory is available, and its value can toggle to 0 when the memory becomes unavailable. A process accessing this shared memory is required to check the availability of the resource (i.e., when value is 1) prior to accessing it. Assuming the resource is available, the first thing the process does is to decrement the value (to ensure that it can retain exclusive access to the resource). After the process has finished modifying the shared memory, the last thing it does is to increment the value (to allow another process to access the resource). When a semaphore's value toggles between 0 and 1, as seen in the previous example, the type of semaphore is referred to as a *binary* semaphore. On the other hand, when a semaphore takes up general values (0 or positive) to deal with situations with more than two participants, it is called a *counting* semaphore.

The semaphore-related system calls are similar to the system calls for messages queues and shared memory. Allocation of and access to semaphores is based on possession of a *key,* so that processes without a common ancestry can coordinate use of the same sets of semaphores. The *semget* system call creates and gains access to a semaphore set associated with the key; the system returns an integer that serves as the semaphore identifier (called *semid*) for the semaphore set created. Each *semid* points to a set of semaphores and a data structure that contain information about the semaphores. There is a *semop* system call which performs an atomic set of operations on the semaphores associated with the *semid*. It reads the list of semaphore operations (supplied to *semop* as a parameter), verifies that the semaphore numbers are legal and ensures that there is permission to perform the operations. In case of a violation, the *semop* request fails. The third system-call-related semaphore is *semctl,* and it controls miscellaneous operations on the set such as initialization or removal of a set. The basic data structures for semaphores are illustrated in Fig. 14.13.

Of the IPC mechanisms discussed so far, the message queues, shared memory, and semaphores are exceedingly similar in their implementation. All of them feature an equivalent set of system calls, as shown in Fig. 14.14.

14.10.5 Sockets

Sockets are communication channels that enable unrelated processes to exchange data locally or over networks. They are invoked using the *socket* system call. Although they can be used for IPC on the local machine, their primary use has been for remote communications across hosts.

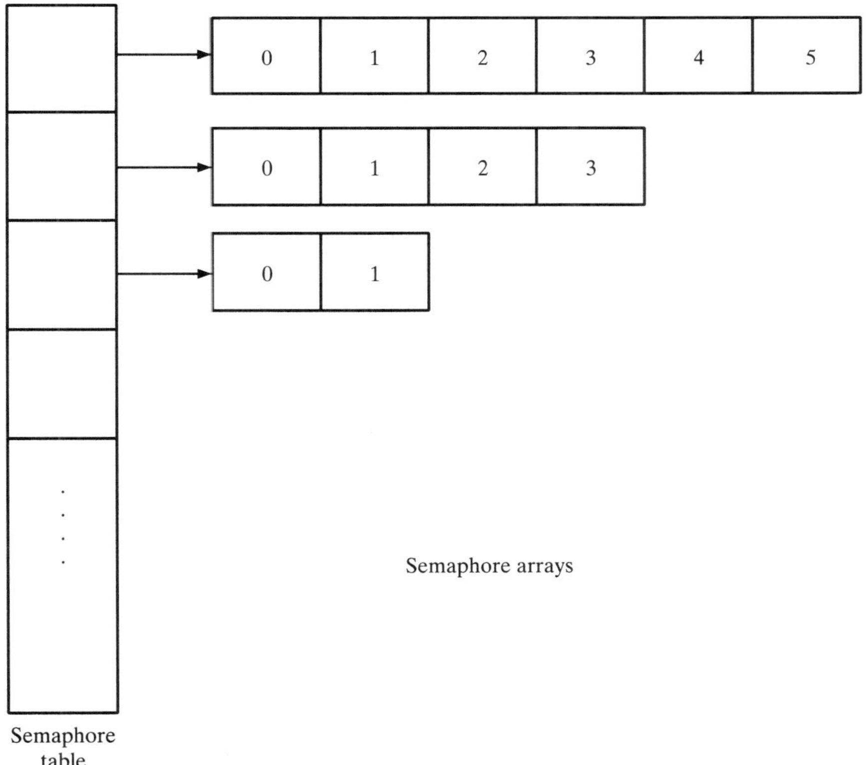

Figure 14.13 Semaphore data structures.

Operations	MESSAGE QUEUE	SEMAPHORE	SHARED MEMORY
system call to create or open	`msgget`	`semget`	`shmget`
system call for control operations	`msgctl`	`semctl`	`shmctl`
system calls for IPC operations	`msgsnd` `msgrcv`	`semop`	`shmat` `shmdt`

Figure 14.14 System calls used for message queue, semaphore, and shared memory.

Sockets move associated data in accordance with a referenced protocol. They make use of underlying drivers to transport information from a process on one system to a participating process on the other, as seen in Fig. 14.15.

The kernel structure for a socket consists of a layered implementation. It has three layers: a *socket layer* which provides the interface with the system calls, a *protocol layer* containing the protocol modules for communication, and a *device layer* holding the drivers that control the network devices. Using sockets, processes can communicate in a client-server mode: a server process listens to a socket from one end of a bidirectional communications path, and client processes communicate with the server via another socket on the other end of a communications path (which may be on a different machine). The internal connections and routing of data from client to the server are maintained by the kernel itself.

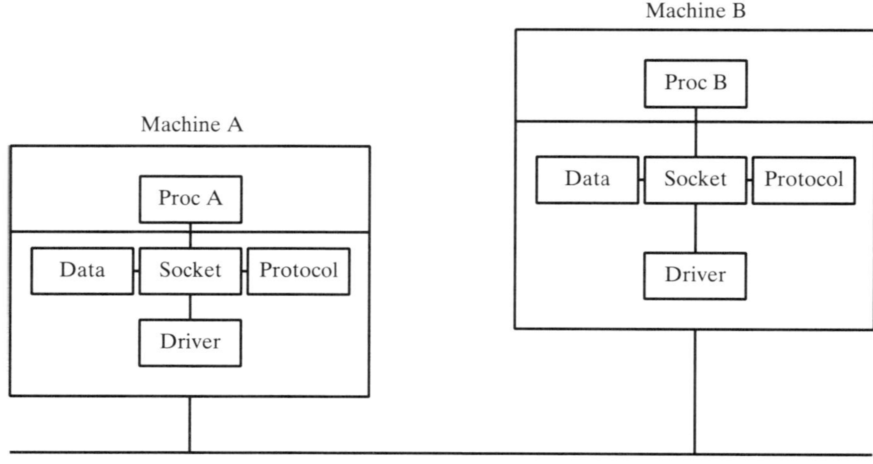

Figure 14.15 Socket.

14.10.6   Streams

Streams is an adaptable suite of tools and facilities for development of AIX and traditional UNIX system communication services. It supports implementation of services ranging from networking protocol suites to device drivers. Streams allows one to define standard interfaces for I/O within the kernel and between the kernel and the rest of the AIX system. The key benefit is that the association mechanism is simple and open-ended. A plethora of applications ranging from networking protocol suites to device driver specifications is supported by this versatile set.

To describe how a stream works, it can be thought of as a full-duplex processing and data transferring path between a driver in kernel space and a process in user space. It provides a conduit by linking three components together: a *stream head,* a *driver,* and one or more *modules* in between. Figure 14.16 shows the layout of the components. The system calls made by the user-level process on a stream are processed by the stream head. The stream head in turn communicates with the module(s). Modules modify the data representation, and pass the information downstream to the driver, which in turn communicates with the external interface.

Streams uses queues as basic data structures that include status information and pointers for message-processing routines and stream administration. Queues are allocated in pairs, one with a lower address for read-side (upstream) and the other for write-side (downstream). Each driver, module, and the stream head are assigned a pair of queues, as a module is added to the stream. Data is passed between the driver, stream head, and modules in sets of data structures called *messages.* A streams message consists of one or more message blocks, each comprising a triplet of a header, a data block, and a data buffer. Within a stream, messages are distinguished by a *type* indicator. Some message types sent upstream may induce specific action by the stream head such as sending a signal to the user process, while others carry information only within the stream.

The basic operation of a streams driver is similar to that of a traditional character I/O driver. It consists of multiple associated nodes accessed by using an *open* system call. Typically, each filesystem node corresponds to a separate minor device for that driver. If one minor device is opened multiple times, subsequent *open* calls return a file descriptor referencing the stream. Processes sharing the same minor device share the same stream to the device driver. A user process sends data to the device using a *write* system call, and receives data from the device using a *read* system call once the device is open. These calls are compatible with the traditional character I/O mechanism. A *close* system call closes the driver and dismantles the associated streams once the last open reference to the stream is completed. The rate of message

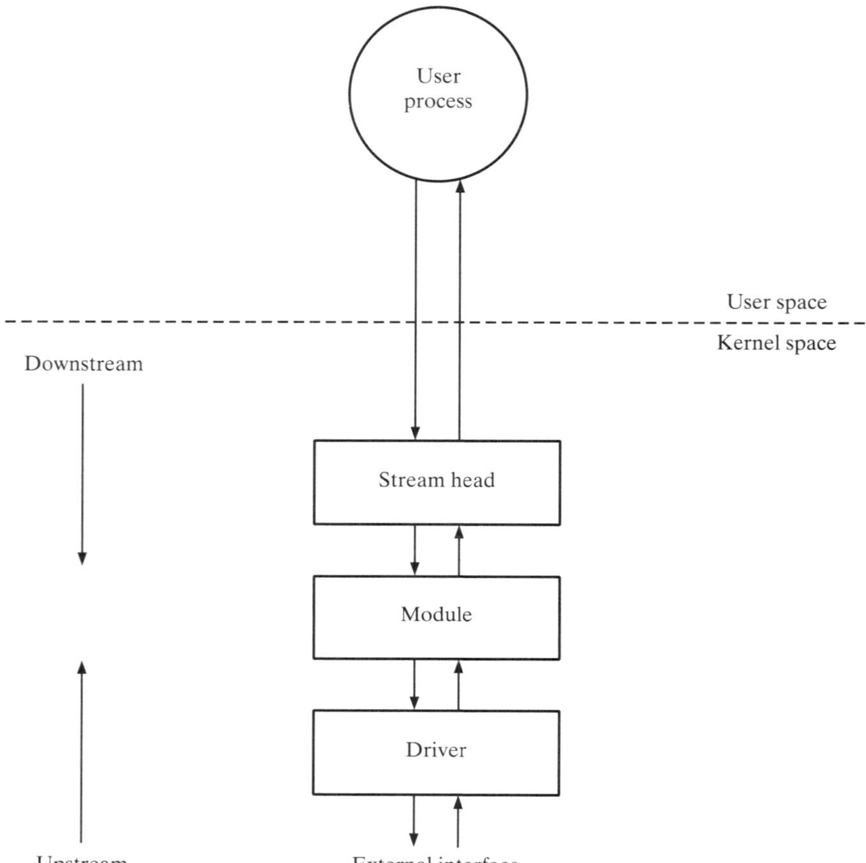

Figure 14.16 Structure of a simple stream.

transfer between modules, drivers, stream head, and the processes is controlled by a mechanism called *flow control*. It is a local and voluntary process to each stream that limits the number of characters that can be queued for processing. This, in turn, limits buffer and related processing at any queue. If the stream exercises flow control on the user, the *write* call blocks until flow control is relinquished and does not return until count bytes are sent to the device. Then, *exit* is called to finish the user process, close open files, and dismantle the stream, if appropriate.

Benefits of streams are that it provides a flexible, reusable, and portable set of tools for development. It standardizes service interfaces that are governed by a set of protocols. It creates data communication service modules and provides capability to manipulate modules from the user level. This allows interchange of modules with common service interfaces and changes the service interface to a streams-user process. Thus, user-level programs, network architectures, and higher-level protocols can be independent of underlying protocols and physical communication media. Further, higher-level services can be created by selecting and connecting lower-level services and protocols. The same protocol module can be used with different drivers on different machines by implementing compatible service interfaces. From a user's perspective, modules can be dynamically selected and interconnected without the hassle of kernel programming, assembly, or linking.

14.11 SUMMARY

An understanding of the concept of a program or process is only complete when one is able to understand not only the structure of a process but also the allied data structures in the user's and the kernel's world. The process life cycle under AIX is no different than under traditional UNIX systems, but it is the presence of advanced context-switching mechanisms, priority queue handling, and a preemptable kernel that makes the AIX process different. In terms of time measurement and timer services, the high-resolution timestamping, made available through kernel extensions, gives AIX an edge over traditional UNIX systems.

The basics of UNIX process management concepts have been kept concise here, as that material can be found in any of the numerous textbooks on the UNIX operating system. Concepts that highlight the capabilities of the RISC System/6000 in areas like support for real-time computing have been emphasized in the discussion.

System Calls and Kernel Services

This chapter describes the services rendered by the AIX kernel to user processes and the extensions offered by the kernel. User processes access most services through what are called *system calls*. Other services like process scheduling are implemented as kernel processes or as routines that execute periodically within the kernel. The AIX kernel on this machine also offers dynamic extendibility and customized kernel extensions.

The purpose of this chapter is not to introduce or explain how individual UNIX system calls work, but to extend the discussion of system calls to kernel services that are available under AIX on the System/6000. Thereafter, the dynamic extendibility feature of the AIX kernel is explained along with the kernel extension facilities.

15.1 SYSTEM CALLS

Execution of a user process is divided into two levels: user and kernel. Whenever a user process requires an operating system service, it executes a system call. This system call performs a momentary *mode switch* from the *user mode* to the *kernel mode* in order to respond to the process' request (refer to Fig. 15.1). A mode switch is obligatory in order to make use of the privileged services that the kernel has access to, such as manipulation of the process status register. Although the kernel distinguishes one process from another by referencing its inter-

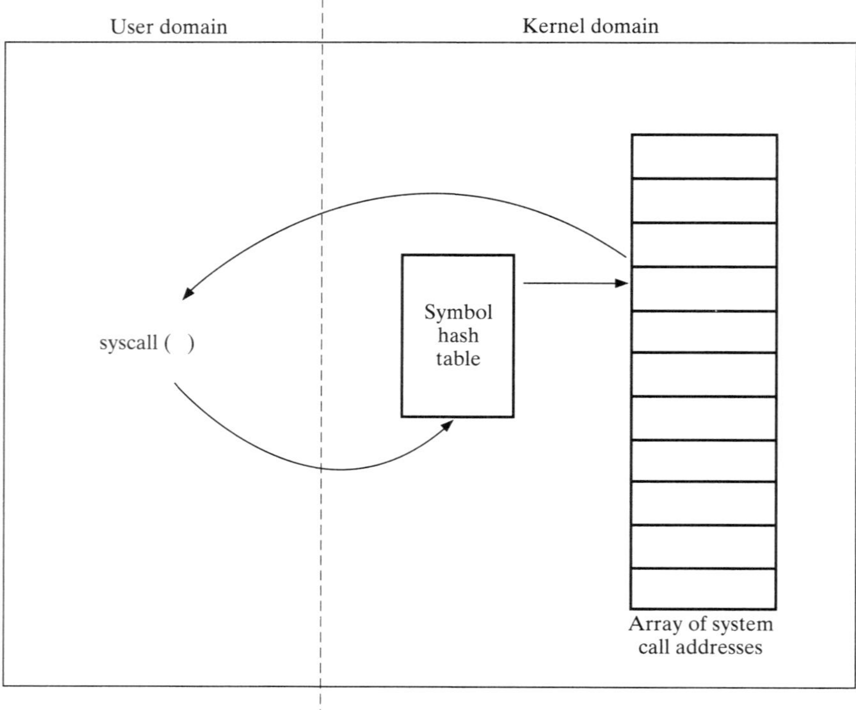

Figure 15.1 Mode switch on AIX.

nal data structures, the underlying hardware of the System/6000 has no clue about processes. The hardware merely views the system in terms of kernel mode and user mode. As illustrated in Fig. 15.2, a kernel is able to differentiate between processes P_1, P_2, P_3, and P_4 along the horizontal axis, and the hardware distinguishes the mode of execution on the vertical axis. It should be understood that execution of a user process in two modes does not mean that there are two processes at any instant; it merely means that the kernel runs on behalf of the user process to handle allocation of resources, etc. For executing any simple program or command, mode switching happens more often than one would expect. Consider catenating a file called */tmp/foo* and redirecting its contents to the terminal device */dev/tty01*. The mode switches (system calls) that take place are highlighted in boldfaced fonts within the algorithm that describes the example from the system perspective of AIX.

Command issued: `cat /tmp/foo > /dev/tty01`

Processes

<table>
<tr><td></td><td>P_1</td><td>P_2</td><td>P_3</td><td>P_4</td></tr>
<tr><td>User
mode</td><td>U</td><td></td><td>U</td><td>U</td></tr>
<tr><td>Kernel
mode</td><td></td><td>K</td><td></td><td></td></tr>
</table>

Figure 15.2 Processes and modes of execution.

Participating Process	Participant's Action
shell	**read** the command line
	parse the command line arguments
	fork a child process and **wait** for it to finish
child	**close** stdout and **open** /dev/tty05
	exit if open fails else **dup** /dev/tty05
child	**exec** /bin/cat
cat	**open** /tmp/foo
cat	**read** /tmp/foo
	write stdout (/dev/tty05)
cat	**exit** and **signal** the parent (the shell)
shell	**write** out a prompt for next command

This scenario of redirecting the contents of a file to a terminal device manifests several sets of underlying system calls. The process-related calls are *fork()*, *exec()*, *wait()*, *exit()*, and *signal()*. File-related system calls used are *open()*, *dup()*, and *close()*. The I/O-related system calls are *read()* and *write()*. All of the system calls shown in this example are standard on traditional UNIX systems as well as on AIX and, hence, are not discussed in any further depth. When invoked from user programs, these system calls perform a mode switch, make use of the kernel services, and continue executing the user application.

Each mode switch from user mode to kernel mode can be categorized on the basis of the action that initiates it. There are two primary kinds of hardware and software actions that gain an entry into the kernel.

1. Hardware interrupts and traps

2. Software interrupts and traps

System calls are referred to as being a special case of software interrupts. The CPU is allowed to be interrupted asynchronously. The occurrence of an interrupt normally causes the kernel to save its current context, service the interrupt, and then resume processing its current context.

Although system calls are invoked just like subroutines, there are some fundamental differences between them. It is necessary to reiterate that they run in the kernel mode when invoked. By doing so, they use certain kernel processes to perform miscellaneous asynchronous tasks. In addition to these basic traits, system calls on AIX are unique in the sense that they are pageable (with some restrictions). They are also preemptable by higher-priority processes to facilitate real-time processing support. Also, new system calls may be added dynamically. Recognize that adding a new system call essentially means extending the kernel by adding to its base set of kernel services.

15.2 KERNEL SERVICES

AIX supplies a set of routines that provides the run-time kernel environment to programs executing in kernel mode. This basic set of routines is referred to as *kernel services*. The programs that run in kernel mode are not conspicuously visible to the user, but they can be displayed using the *pstat* or *ps* commands, if required. Kernel services offered by AIX span a very wide range of functional areas. These services are primarily used by kernel extensions. The main categories of kernel services are shown in Fig. 15.3, and each is discussed in terms of its features, functions, and commonly used routines.

Process and exception management (P&EM) kernel services are provided by the base AIX kernel and are responsible for new kernel process creation, serialization of processes, and signal handling. In addition, certain traditional UNIX kernel services are also incorporated in here, in order to support ported code from other variants of UNIX and previous versions of AIX. Commonly used P&EM kernel services are:

creatp	Creates a new kernel process
initp	Initializes a kernel process after its creation
e_post	Notifies a process of the occurrence of event(s)
e_wait	Forces a process to wait for the occurrence of an event
wakeup	Activates processes sleeping on the specified channel
lockl	Imposes a lock to serialize access to a resource
unlockl	Releases a conventional process lock
setjmpx	Allows saving the current execution state or context

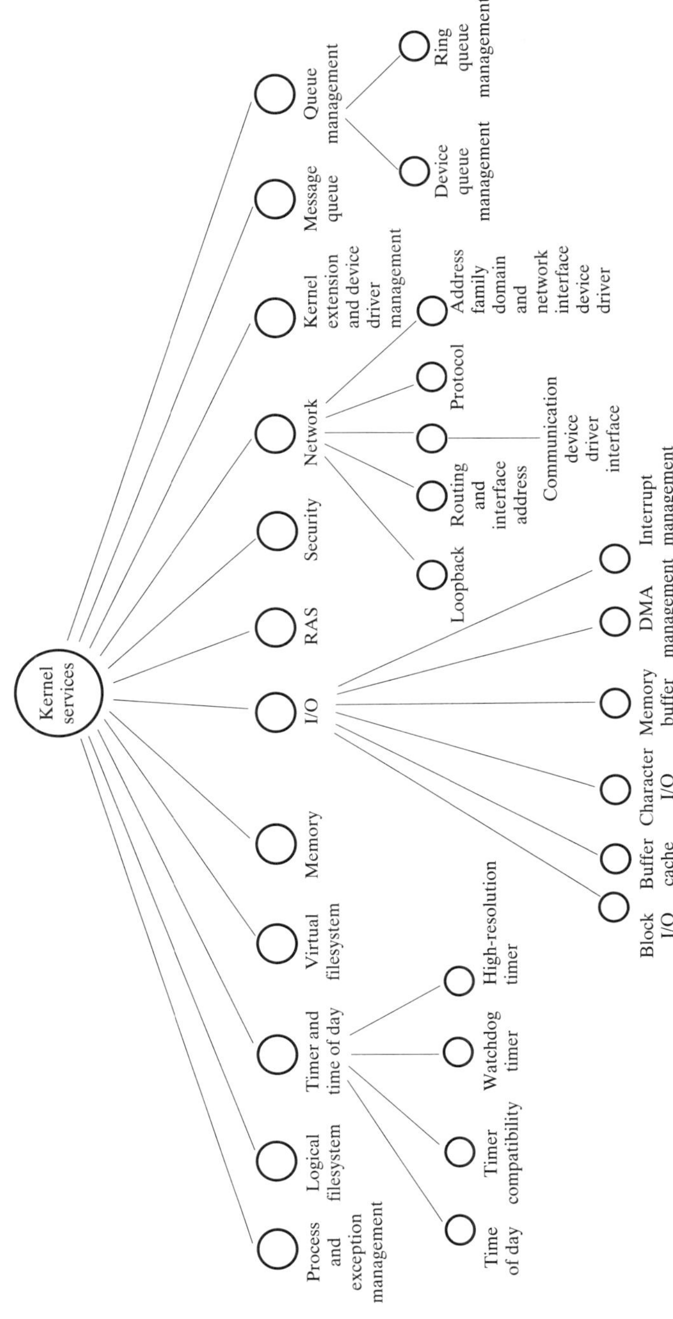

Figure 15.3 Taxonomy of kernel services.

Logical File System (LFS) services allow processes running in kernel mode to open and manipulate files in the same way that user-mode processes do. Since system calls can have data access limitations, a set of filesystem calls are provided with a kernel-only interface. Commonly used LFS kernel services are:

fp_open	Opens a regular file
fp_opendev	Opens a device special file
fp_close	Closes a file
fp_read	Performs a read operation on an open file
fp_write	Performs a write operation on an open file
fp_access	Checks for access permission to an open file
fp_fstat	Acquires the attributes of an open file
fp_ioctl	Issues a control command to an open file

Virtual File System (VFS) kernel services provide a standard interface and act as the basic building blocks for writing a virtual filesystem. They can be used to create and/or free vnodes across various filesystem types without having to worry about physical filesystem dependencies. VFS services that can be used across the various filesystem types to enable the logical filesystem to operate independently of the filesystem type are:

gfsadd	Adds a filesystem type to the *gfs* table
gfsdel	Deletes a filesystem type from the *gfs* table
vn_get	Adds a vnode to the existing list of vnodes for the designated filesystem
vn_free	Frees a previously allocated vnode
vfsrele	Points to a virtual filesystem structure
lookuppv	Retrieves the vnode that corresponds to the named path

Memory kernel services give the ability to dynamically allocate and free memory, pin and unpin processes, manipulate virtual memory objects, and move data between user and kernel memory. Data can also be moved between the kernel and an address space other than the current process address space, using a cross-memory service feature. Commonly used memory kernel services are:

xmalloc	Allocates memory (similar to *malloc* in the user mode)
xmfree	Frees allocated memory
init_heap	Initializes a new heap
pin	Pins the address range in the system address space
unpin	Unpins the address range

Message queue kernel services render the equivalent of normal message queuing functions for programs executing in user mode to the kernel extensions. The most frequent use for these message queue kernel services is as IPC channels to allied kernel processes or user-mode processes. Available message queue kernel services are:

kmsgctl   Queries the status of the message queue, sets selected status fields, or removes the queue, when needed

kmsgget   Opens or creates a message queue by traversing the message queue array to locate a possible match and allocating a new queue structure if no match is found

kmsgsnd   Sends a message using a previously defined message queue

kmsgrcv   Receives a message from a message queue

Reliability-availability-serviceability services are collectively referred to as the RAS kernel services. They address the reliability, availability, and serviceability aspects of the software and hardware. Occurrences of errors and failures are recorded so that they may be examined at a later time. In the event of a fatal error, a kernel service called *panic* gets invoked, which triggers a system dump and captures the data areas that are cataloged in the master dump table. Some of the RAS kernel services are:

panic   Crashes the system (note: It gets invoked in the event of a catastrophic failure to perform a system dump)

errsave   Writes an entry in the system error log when a hardware or software failure is detected

Timing kernel services furnish an array of utilities that address various timing-related aspects of the global system. In order to structure their roles, the services are further grouped into four functional categories referred to as (1) time-of-day (TOD) kernel services, (2) timer compatibility kernel services, (3) watchdog timer kernel services, and (4) high-resolution timer (HRT) kernel services. Each type of service contributes to the time- and timer-related issues of the kernel. The TOD service maintains the systemwide time-of-day timer values and can be used to access or set the time on the system. The timer compatibility service provides backward compatibility with earlier versions of AIX by handling application timeouts and the callout table entries. The watchdog timer service furnishes a low-overhead, moderate-resolution timer which can be used to timestamp events without causing any serious overhead. The HRT services provide fine-grain timing functions that can be used to conduct critical measurements with as fine as 10 ms granularity. Following are the commonly used kernel services:

curtime	Reads the current time
ksettimer	Sets the systemwide TOD timer
tstart	Submits a timer request
tstop	Cancels a pending timer request
delay	Suspends the calling process for the specified number of timer ticks
talloc	Allocates a timer request block (structure is called *trb*)
tfree	Deallocates a timer request block

Security kernel services determine the privilege state of a process and, as a result, facilitate controlling the auditing system and access rights. There is only one security kernel service in the current implementation of AIX.

suser	Determines the privilege state of a process by checking to see if the process has any effective privilege

Network kernel services is a cluster of four types of network-related functions. The first is the address family domain and network interface device driver (AFD/NIDD) services, and it facilitates addition/removal of protocols and network interface drivers from network switching tables. The second set of functions is the routing and interface address kernel services, which supports the network route addition/deletion functionalities for remote hosts and gateways. The third set of functions is referred to as the loopback kernel services; it allows debugging in a simulated environment for development of new network protocols without introducing network variables. The fourth function is the protocol kernel service which enables a raw protocol handler to pass packets up through sockets so a protocol can be implemented in the user space. Finally, there is a set of functions called the communications device handler interface (CDHI) kernel service that provides a standardized interface between network interface drivers and AIX communications device drivers.

Commonly used network kernel services are:

if_attach	Adds a network interface to the network interface list
if_detach	Removes a network interface from the network interface list
rtalloc	Allocates a route consisting of a destination address and a reference to a routing entry
rtfree	Frees the routing table entry by freeing the *mbuf* structure that is associated with the route
rtrequest	Carries out a request to alter the contents of the routing table
rtredirect	Forces a routing table entry to be redirected through a given gateway

net_attach   Opens a communications I/O device handler

net_detach   Closes a communications I/O device handler

I/O kernel services are better described as six separate categories: (1) block I/O services which enable asynchronous I/O transfers to take place in fixed size blocks, (2) buffer cache services which manage user access to device drivers through block special files for filesystem compatibility services and mounts, (3) character I/O services that manage the read/write operations to character devices like keyboards, terminals, etc., (4) DMA management services that coordinate the DMA operations between adapters and memory, (5) interrupt management services that enable/disable interrupt levels in the system, and finally (6) memory buffer services which provide facilities to acquire, release and manipulate memory buffers.

Commonly used I/O kernel services are:

bread   Reads the specified block's data into a buffer.

bwrite   Writes the specified buffer's data.

getblk   Assigns a buffer to the specified block.

purblk   Purges the specified block from the buffer cache.

getc   Retrieves a character from a character list.

putc   Places a character at the end of a character list.

waitcfree   Checks the availability of a free character buffer.

m_get   Allocates a memory buffer from the memory buffer pool.

m_pullup   Shuffles an *mbuf* chain so that a given number of bytes is in contiguous memory in the data area of the head *mbuf* structure.

m_free   Frees an *mbuf* structure.

d_init   Initializes a DMA channel.

d_clear   Frees a DMA channel.

d_mask   Disables a DMA channel.

d_move   Provides a means of accessing the data while a DMA transfer is being performed on it. Since this service accesses the data through the same system hardware as that used to perform the DMA transfer, it can guarantee the data to be consistent. It can also access data that is hidden from normal processor accesses.*

Device and ring queue kernel services are methods of queuing requests from one kernel process to another. They are based on a client-server model. For AIX on the System/6000, the services have

---

* Refer to the discussion on page hiding in Chap. 16.

been streamlined and the functions have been reduced. With virtual interrupts no longer supported by AIX, the device and ring queue services are primarily left serving as compatibility structures for software ports from previous versions of the AIX operating system. Commonly used services are:

creatq	Creates a device queue
dstryq	Deletes the specified device queue
attchq	Creates a path to a device queue
detchq	Removes a path to a device queue
enque	Places a queue element into a specified device queue
deque	Removes an element from the device queue
waitq	Waits for a queue element to be placed on a device queue
queryi	Provides information about device queues
rqc	Creates a ring queue in the kernel heap
rqd	Deletes a ring queue from the kernel queue
rqputw	Puts a queue element on the specified ring queue
rqgetw	Returns the next element from the specified ring queue

Device driver management/kernel extension services include general purpose kernel loading and binding services and device driver binding services. Commonly used services are:

devswadd	Adds a device entry to the device switch table
devswdel	Removes a device driver entry from the device switch table
iostadd	Registers an I/O statistics structure used for updating I/O statistics reported by the *iostat* facility (covered in Chap. 8)
pio_assist	Provides a programmed I/O exception handling mechanism for routines performing programmed I/O
uexadd	Adds a systemwide exception handler for catching user-mode process exceptions
uexdel	Deletes a previously added systemwide exception handler

A kernel service in general can either be called in both the process and the interrupt environments, or exclusively in the process environment. Table 15.1 provides the names of the available kernel services under AIX, along with the environment from which they can be called. For the syntax and options of each one of these services, one should refer to the product documentation.*

---

* Technical reference: *Kernel and Subsystems,* volume 4 (SC23-2385-00).

TABLE 15.1   Kernel Services

Command	Process environment	Interrupt environment
ackque	✓	
add_arp_iftype	✓	✓
add_domain_af	✓	✓
add_input_type	✓	✓
add_netisr	✓	✓
add_netopt	✓	✓
as_att	✓	
as_det	✓	
attchq	✓	
audit_svcbcopy	✓	
audit_svcfinis	✓	
audit_svcstart	✓	
bawrite	✓	
bdwrite	✓	✓
bflush	✓	
binval	✓	
blkflush	✓	
bread	✓	
breada	✓	
brelse	✓	✓
bwrite	✓	
canclq	✓	
cfgnadd	✓	
cfgndel	✓	
clrbuf	✓	✓
clrjmpx	✓	✓
copyin	✓	
copyinstr	✓	
copyout	✓	
creatd	✓	
creatp	✓	
creatq	✓	
curtime	✓	✓
d_align	✓	✓
d_cflush	✓	✓
d_clear	✓	✓
d_complete	✓	✓
d_init	✓	✓
d_mask	✓	✓
d_master	✓	✓
d_move	✓	✓
d_roundup	✓	✓
d_slave	✓	✓
d_unmask	✓	✓
del_arp_iftype	✓	✓
del_domain_af	✓	✓
del_input_type	✓	✓
del_netisr	✓	✓
del_netopt	✓	✓
delay	✓	
deque	✓	
detchq	✓	

(Continued)

TABLE 15.1   Kernel Services (*Continued*)

Command	Process environment	Interrupt environment
devdump	✓	✓
devstrat	✓	✓
devswadd	✓	
devswdel	✓	
devswqry	✓	✓
dmp_add	✓	
dmp_del	✓	
dmp_prinit	✓	
dstryd	✓	
DTOM *macro*	✓	✓
epost	✓	✓
e_sleep	✓	
e_sleepl	✓	
e_wait	✓	
e_wakeup	✓	✓
enque	✓	
errsave	✓	✓
find_arp_iftype	✓	✓
find_input_af	✓	✓
find_input_type	✓	✓
fp_access	✓	
fp_close	✓	
fp_fstat	✓	
fp_getdevno	✓	
fp_getf	✓	
fp_hold	✓	
fp_ioctl	✓	
fp_lseek	✓	
fp_open	✓	
fp_opendev	✓	
fp_poll	✓	
fp_read	✓	
fp_readv	✓	
fp_rwuio	✓	
fp_select	✓	
fp_write	✓	
fp_writev	✓	
fubyte	✓	
fubyte	✓	
fuword	✓	
getadsp	✓	
getblk	✓	
getc	✓	✓
getcb	✓	✓
getcbp	✓	✓
getcf	✓	✓
getcx	✓	✓
geteblk	✓	
geterror	✓	✓
getexcept	✓	✓
getpid	✓	✓
getppidx	✓	

TABLE 15.1   Kernel Services (*Continued*)

Command	Process environment	Interrupt environment
getuerror	✓	
gfsadd	✓	
gfsdel	✓	
i_clear	✓	
i_disable	✓	✓
i_enable	✓	✓
i_init	✓	
i_mask	✓	✓
i_reset	✓	✓
i_sched	✓	✓
i_unmask	✓	✓
if_attach	✓	✓
if_detach	✓	✓
if_down	✓	✓
if_nostat	✓	✓
ifa_ifwithaddr	✓	✓
ifa_ifdstwithaddr	✓	✓
ifa_ifwithnet	✓	✓
ifunit	✓	✓
init_heap	✓	
initp	✓	
io_att	✓	✓
io_det	✓	✓
iodone	✓	✓
iostadd	✓	
iostdel	✓	
iowait	✓	
kgethostname	✓	✓
kgettickd	✓	✓
kmod_entrypt	✓	
kmod_load	✓	
kmod_unload	✓	
kmsgctl	✓	
kmsgget	✓	
kmsgsnd	✓	
ksettickd	✓	
ksettimer	✓	
lockl	✓	
loifp	✓	✓
longjmpx	✓	✓
lookupvp	✓	
looutput	✓	✓
m_adj	✓	✓
m_cat	✓	✓
m_clattach	✓	✓
m_clget *macro*	✓	✓
im_clgetm	✓	✓
m_clgetx	✓	✓
m_collapse	✓	✓
m_copy *macro*	✓	✓
m_copydata	✓	✓
m_copym	✓	✓

(*Continued*)

TABLE 15.1   Kernel Services (*Continued*)

Command	Process environment	Interrupt environment
m_dereg	✓	
m_free	✓	✓
m_freem	✓	✓
m_get	✓	✓
m_getclr	✓	✓
m_getclust *macro*	✓	✓
m_getclustm	✓	✓
m_gethdr	✓	✓
M_HASCL *macro*	✓	✓
m_pullup	✓	✓
m_reg	✓	
MTOCL *macro*	✓	✓
MTOD *macro*	✓	✓
M_XMEMD *macro*	✓	✓
net_attach	✓	
net_detach	✓	
net_error	✓	✓
net_sleep	✓	
net_start	✓	
net_start_done	✓	✓
net_wakeup	✓	✓
net_xmit	✓	✓
net_xmit_trace	✓	✓
NLuprintf	✓	
panic	✓	✓
peekq	✓	✓
pfctlinput	✓	✓
pffindproto	✓	✓
pidsig	✓	✓
pgsignal	✓	✓
pin	✓	
pincf	✓	
pincode	✓	
pinu	✓	
pio_assist	✓	✓
prochadd	✓	
prochdel	✓	
purblk	✓	
putc	✓	✓
putcb	✓	✓
putcbp	✓	✓
putcf	✓	✓
putcfl	✓	✓
putcx	✓	✓
qryds	✓	
queryd	✓	
queryi	✓	✓
queryp	✓	
raw_input	✓	✓
raw_usrreq	✓	✓
readq	✓	
rqc	✓	

TABLE 15.1   Kernel Services (*Continued*)

Command	Process environment	Interrupt environmen
trqd	✓	
rqgetw	✓	
rqputw	✓	
rtalloc	✓	✓
rtfree	✓	✓
rtinit	✓	✓
rtedirect	✓	✓
rtrequest	✓	✓
schednetisr	✓	✓
selnotify	✓	✓
setjmpx	✓	✓
setpinit	✓	✓
setuerror	✓	
sig_chk	✓	
sleep	✓	
subyte	✓	
suser	✓	
suword	✓	
talloc	✓	
tfree	✓	✓
timeout	✓	✓
timeoutcf	✓	
trcgenk	✓	✓
trcgenkt	✓	✓
tstart	✓	✓
tstop	✓	✓
uexadd	✓	
uexblock	✓	✓
uexclear	✓	✓
uexdel	✓	
uiomove	✓	
unlockl	✓	
unpin	✓	✓
unpincode	✓	
unpinu	✓	✓
uprintf	✓	
untimeout	✓	✓
uphysio	✓	
ureadc	✓	
uwritec	✓	
vec_clear	✓	
vec_init	✓	
vfsrele	✓	
vm_att	✓	✓
vm_cflush	✓	
vm_det	✓	✓
vm_handle	✓	
vm_makep	✓	
vm_mount	✓	
vm_move	✓	
vm_protectp	✓	
vm_qmodify	✓	

(Continued)

TABLE 15.1   Kernel Services (*Continued*)

Command	Process environment	Interrupt environment
vm_release	✓	
vm_releasep	✓	
vm_unmount	✓	
vm_write	✓	
vm_writep	✓	
vms_create	✓	
vms_delete	✓	
vms_iowait	✓	
vn_free	✓	
vn_get	✓	
w_clear	✓	✓
w_init	✓	✓
w_start	✓	✓
w_stop	✓	✓
waitcfree	✓	
waitq	✓	
wakeup	✓	✓
xmalloc	✓	
xmattach	✓	
xmdetach	✓	✓
xmemdma	✓	✓
xmemin	✓	✓
xmemout	✓	✓
xmfree	✓	

15.3   KERNEL EXTENSIONS

The set of base kernel services available under AIX can be used by the kernel extensions. A kernel extension knows about these services by importing the symbols that are to be added to the kernel namespace during the binding phase. The symbols are specified through a file called *kernex.exp*. This file also works as an export file for kernel extensions that are to be added to the kernel namespace.

There are two ways to load a new kernel extension into the kernel namespace.

1. The *sysconfig* routine can be used to load the kernel extension. Symbols defined in the kernel extension's exports file during the linking time are added to the kernel namespace.

2. The loader can load additional object files into the kernel to resolve symbols referenced by the new kernel extension. In this case, there are no symbols added to the kernel namespace since the exported symbols are only used to resolve references needed during the load of a new kernel extension.

The kernel namespace can only be expanded by explicitly loading a kernel object file. The symbols added to the kernel namespace are made available to any subsequently loaded kernel object file in the form of imported symbols.

A complete list of all the system calls available under AIX can be found in the product manual.* A set of privileged system calls that can be used for writing one's own kernel extensions is provided here. The list given in Table 15.2 shows which system calls are available to the kernel extensions, and which ones are restricted to kernel processes.

---

* Calls and subroutine reference: *Base Operating System,* volume 1 (SC23-2198-00).

TABLE 15.2   System Calls

System calls	Kernel extensions	Kernel processes
disclaim		✓
getdomainname		✓
getgidx	✓	✓
getgroups		✓
gethostid	✓	✓
gethostname		✓
getpeername		✓
getpgrp	✓	✓
getppid	✓	✓
getpri	✓	✓
getpriority	✓	✓
getrlimit		✓
getrusage		✓
getsockname		✓
getsockopt		✓
gettimer		✓
getuidx	✓	✓
resabs		✓
resinc		✓
restimer		✓
semctl		✓
semget	✓	✓
semop		✓
setdomainname		✓
seteuid	✓	✓
setgid	✓	✓
setgidx	✓	✓
setgroups		✓
sethostid	✓	✓
sethostname		✓
setpgid	✓	✓
setpgrp	✓	✓
setpri	✓	✓
setpriority	✓	✓
setreuid	✓	✓
setrlimit		✓
setsid	✓	✓
settimer		✓

(Continued)

TABLE 15.2   System Calls (*Continued*)

System calls	Kernel extensions	Kernel processes
setuid	✓	✓
setuidx	✓	✓
shmat		✓
shmctl		✓
shmdt		✓
shmget		✓
sigaction		✓
sigprocmask		✓
sigstack		✓
sigsuspend		✓
sysconfig		✓
times		✓
ulimit	✓	✓
umask	✓	✓
uname		✓
unamex		✓
usrinfo		✓
utimes		✓

15.4 DYNAMIC BINDING

The binding steps involve relocating symbols and resolving external references while combining object modules and libraries to form an object file. Traditional UNIX systems use a static binding process where all symbols and references are resolved at compile time (see Fig. 15.4), which means that the resulting object file must contain all the code that will be needed during the execution of the file. AIX uses a dynamic binding technique that permits symbols to be resolved and relocated at run-time. There are two types of dynamic bindings.

1. *load*-time binding

2. *exec*-time binding

In *load*-time binding, the symbols are resolved upon explicit loading of a program. The *load* system call permits the program to load ancillary modules at its discretion, thereby facilitating the reduction of the size of an executable file. In *exec*-time binding, the symbols are resolved when the *exec* system call grants control to the program to initiate execution.

15.5 SUMMARY

Processes use system calls to utilize the resources on the system. Since the kernel owns all the resources on the system it becomes necessary for the user processes to go through a mode switch before being able to use the kernel's services. System calls on AIX are preemptable by

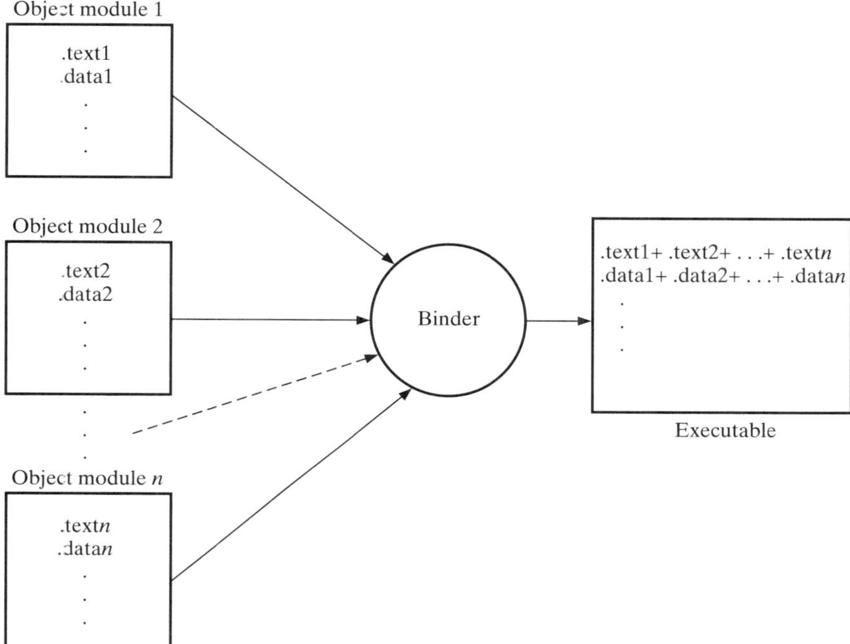

Figure 15.4 The symbol resolution process.

higher-priority processes to facilitate real-time processing support. Also, the kernel can be dynamically extended beyond its base set of services. Extensions to the kernel are possible in any of the subsystems including device drivers, system calls, kernel services, and even private kernel routines. While some kernel services can be called in both the process and the interrupt environments, others are restricted to the process environment. The set of base kernel services available under AIX are used by kernel extensions.

In addition to user processes on the system there are privileged processes that run in the kernel address space, i.e., */unix*. These processes running in the kernel mode have access to additional system calls for carrying out privileged tasks. Even in the kernel address space, there is a distinction made between two types of uses of system calls. There is a set of system calls that can be used by kernel extensions, and another set that is available to kernel processes only. User mode processes in kernel mode can only use system calls that have their parameters passed by value, and the kernel routines executing under user mode processes cannot directly use a system call having reference parameters. The latter restriction is imposed because when system calls with reference parameters access a caller's data, they are accessing storage across a protected domain.

Chapter

16

File, I/O, and Memory Management

This chapter provides a tour of the I/O subsystem of AIX. Internal data structures related to file, I/O, and memory are explained in light of their functions, features, and benefits. The discussion begins with a design overview of the filesystem and is followed by a detailed description of the logical filesystem, physical filesystem, mapped files, and the journaled filesystem. The virtual memory subsystem is discussed next, in terms of its page replacement, memory load control, and code pinning policies. Finally, a description of the I/O management and its key features is presented from a systems point of view.

16.1 AIX FILESYSTEM

The AIX filesystem has a logical view of the file layout, as well as a physical view of the file organization. The logical perspective is referred to as the *logical filesystem* and the physical view of the file layout is called AIX's *physical filesystem*. The logical filesystem includes the traditional inverted tree structure as seen on all UNIX systems. Directories, links, etc., are all considered a part of the logical filesystem. Three different filesystem types are supported by AIX:

journaled filesystem

network filesystem

CD-ROM filesystem

The journaled filesystem specifies the native AIX filesystem. The network filesystem specifies the filesystem type that permits files residing on remote machines to be accessed as though they resided on a local machine. The CD-ROM filesystem allows the contents of a CD-ROM to be accessed through the normal filesystem interface (like open, read, and close).

16.1.1 Physical filesystem

The physical filesystem maintains the system's perspective of the devices. To interface the logical filesystem with the physical filesystem, an intermediate layer of abstraction is introduced, the *virtual filesystem*. Because of this abstraction, AIX is able to support foreign file and filesystem types. Figure 16.1 illustrates the interfacing role of the virtual filesystem. The virtual filesystem permits user processes to access files using a universal system call interface, regardless of the location or the type of the file. Figure 16.2 demonstrates how the presence of a virtual filesystem changes the "standard UNIX" access to a file.

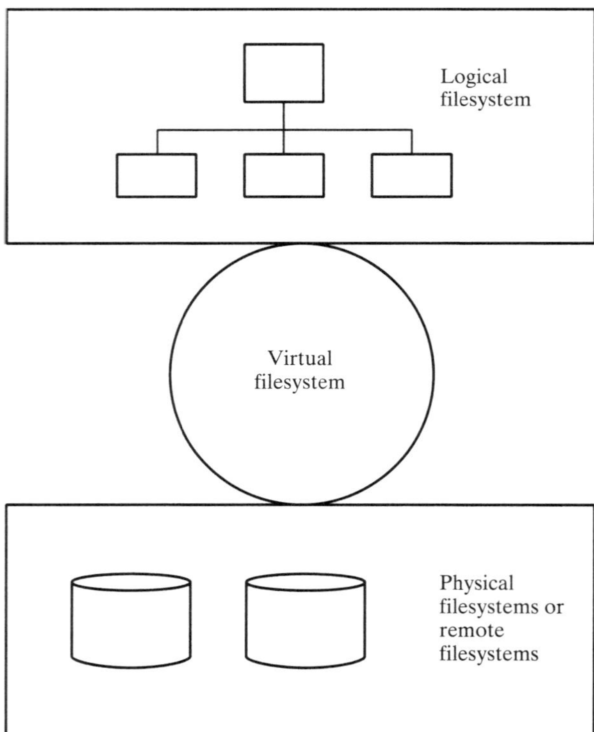

Figure 16.1 Virtual filesystem.

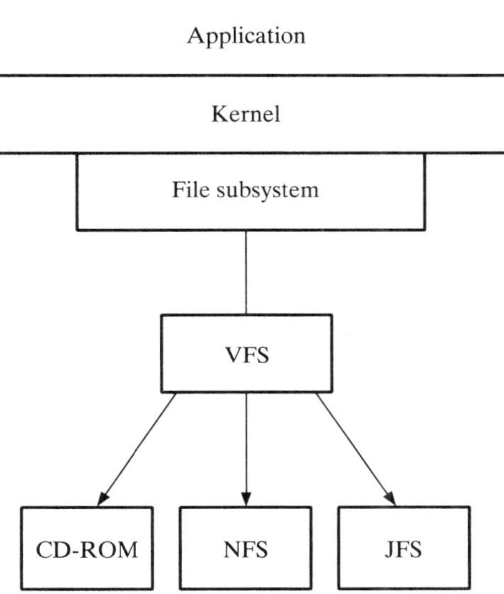

Figure 16.2 Virtual filesystem permitting generalization for file access.

An access to a file begins with one of the user file descriptors pointing to the file table, and the file table in turn pointing to the *vnodes*. The *vnode* references an affiliated *gnode* in the in-core inode table and also points to a structure called *vfs* that describes the mount (for example */home* or */usr*) that supports the file in question. This *vfs* structure has a reference pointing to a data structure called *gfs* which describes the type of the filesystem, and another reference pointing back to the directory *vnode* upon which it is mounted. The *gfs* structure states whether the filesystem in question is a journaled filesystem, network filesystem, or a CD-ROM filesystem. Depending on which filesystem type is being pointed to, the *gfs* structure indexes into two structures: a structure called *vfsops* that determines the set of operations apropos to this filesystem (such as *mount, unmount, sync,* etc.) and a structure named *vnodeops* that describes a set of functions (such as *link, mkdir, mknod*) that can be performed on *vnodes* from this filesystem. Figure 16.3 delineates the course through the tables and structures to complete the picture.

16.1.2 Memory mapped files

When a user opens a normal file under AIX to read from, write to, or append to, the file is automatically mapped to memory to provide what are called *mapped files*. That is, normal file access under AIX bypasses the buffer cache subsystem that traditional UNIX systems use. By having files mapped to the system memory, the cost for a read or write to a

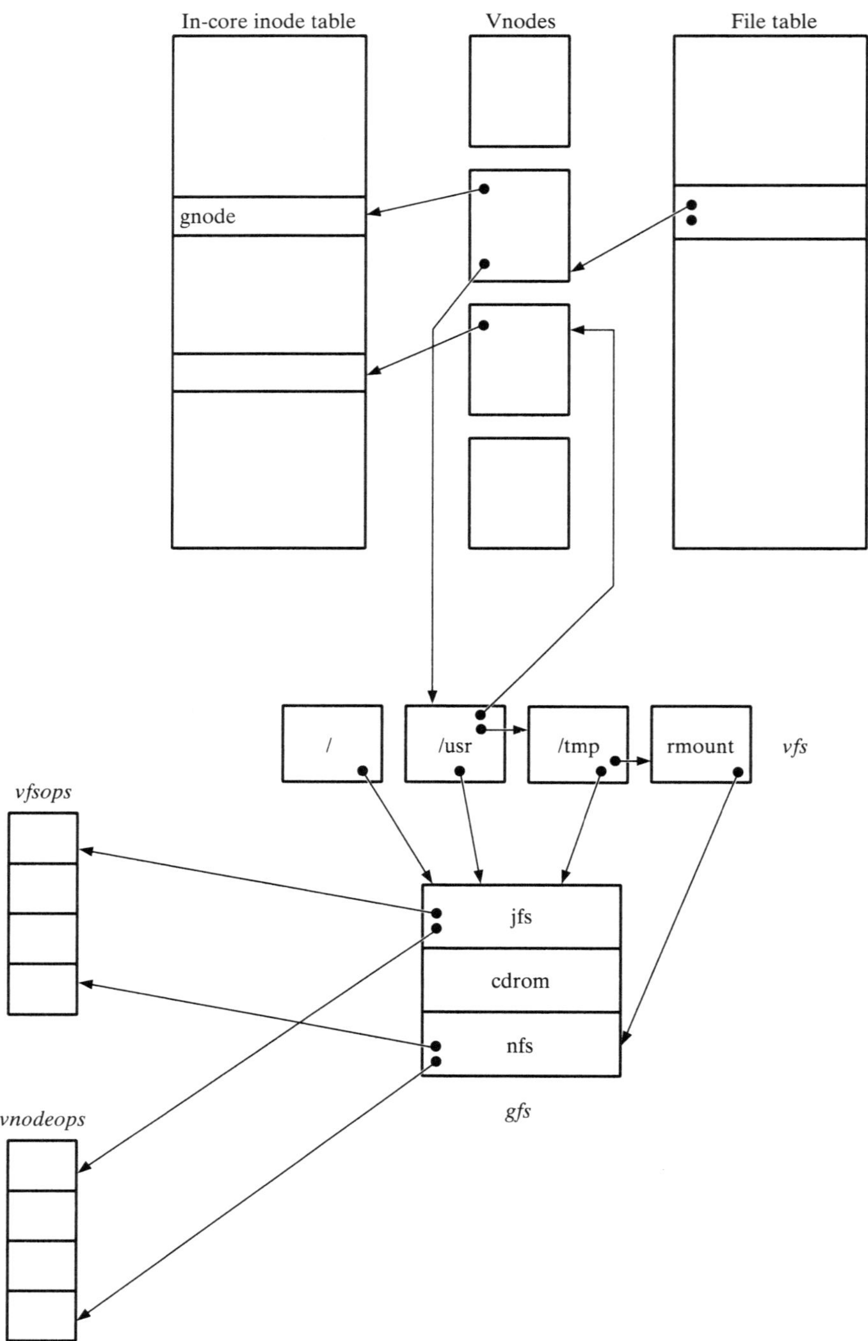

Figure 16.3 VFS data structures.

file is diminished to merely the cost for a memory write. This greatly enhances I/O performance. Although upon being opened, files get mapped implicitly by default, explicit mapping can also be requested using a set of special-purpose system calls.

There are two system calls, *mmap* and *shmat,* that provide capability for multiple processes to map the same region of an object such that they share addressability to that object. As far as choosing one over the other, the *shmat* call is used when there are a few files to be mapped simultaneously to their entirety and memory regions need to be shared among unrelated processes. The *mmap* call, on the other hand, is used when many files are to be mapped simultaneously, portability of the application is vital across other UNIX platforms, and there is a need to map a portion of the file.

If mapped explicitly, the file is accessed by address rather than by *read* and/or *write* system calls. There could be a performance tradeoff here; while explicitly mapped files save on the overhead cost of the *read/write* system calls, they lose the benefit of the system write-behind feature.

16.1.3   I/O pacing

Interactive processes on the system occasionally suffer from long response times when used in environments with heavy I/O on a moderately loaded system. Although this is quite normal in multiuser time-sliced environments, the interactive applications in particular are noticed by the user community. The reason for this symptom should be evident: it has to do with pending I/O requests being the bottleneck. *I/O pacing* is a feature of the memory manager that can put an upper limit on the number of I/O requests that can be outstanding against a file at any given time. When this limit is exceeded the process with pending I/O requests is suspended (by putting it to sleep) long enough so that the outstanding requests can be processed and a lower threshold level is reached. In traditional UNIX systems, including previous releases of AIX, users occasionally encountered a multiple-second delay when another application was performing a large number of writes to a disk. As most writes are asynchronous, long queues can build up which cause several seconds' worth of delay. The disk I/O pacing feature eliminates this problem. However, there may be instances with real-time computing requirements where this feature can hurt processes performing intensive I/O. Keeping in mind the diverse requirements for response time, this feature has been made a selectable option rather than hard-coded.

By default, pacing remains disabled. One may enable pacing in AIX using *smit* and specifying the number of pages for upper and lower limits to suitable values if large I/O-intensive jobs on the system inhibit interactive response time.

16.2 JOURNALED FILESYSTEM

Traditional UNIX systems could not guarantee recovery from a crash without loss of files. The method of recovery depended excessively on utilities and the savvy of the system administrator. AIX does away with the UNIX-like way of storing and recovering information by implementing a persistent storage management scheme. The mechanisms implemented by AIX in this area are radically different from traditional UNIX systems. AIX implements a level of abstraction on top of the physical media called *logical volume*. This logical volume not only enhances the reliability of the files in the filesystems but also eradicates the limitations of static filesystem size.

16.2.1 Logical volume manager

The logical volume manager (referred to as LVM from here on) is a paradigm that addresses the concept of virtual disks (called logical volumes) to address the evolving need of the storage subsystem. The LVM on the System/6000 provides a layer of abstraction between the logical partition perceived by the users and the actual physical partition viewed by the operating system (refer to Fig. 16.4). LVM consists of two major subsystems.

1. LVM subroutines

2. Logical volume device driver (LVDD)

The LVM subroutines can be accessed through the logical volume data structures and the logical volume device driver configuration routines, as seen in Fig. 16.5. The logical volume device driver interface is at a higher level than that of a physical device and allows an abstraction of device-specific dependencies (refer to Fig. 16.6 to view the interface layout).

The principal benefit of implementing the LVM paradigm is that it allows the extension of files, filesystems, and raw partitions to multiple physical media, without modification to existing system or application software. Since the logical volume is an abstraction, it can be made larger than the underlying physical volumes. Logical volumes can also be mirrored on multiple physical volumes to improve performance for data access and provide a greater reliability for sensitive data sets. The LVM supports transparent software bad-sector remapping which means that it has the ability to detect and relocate bad sectors autonomously.

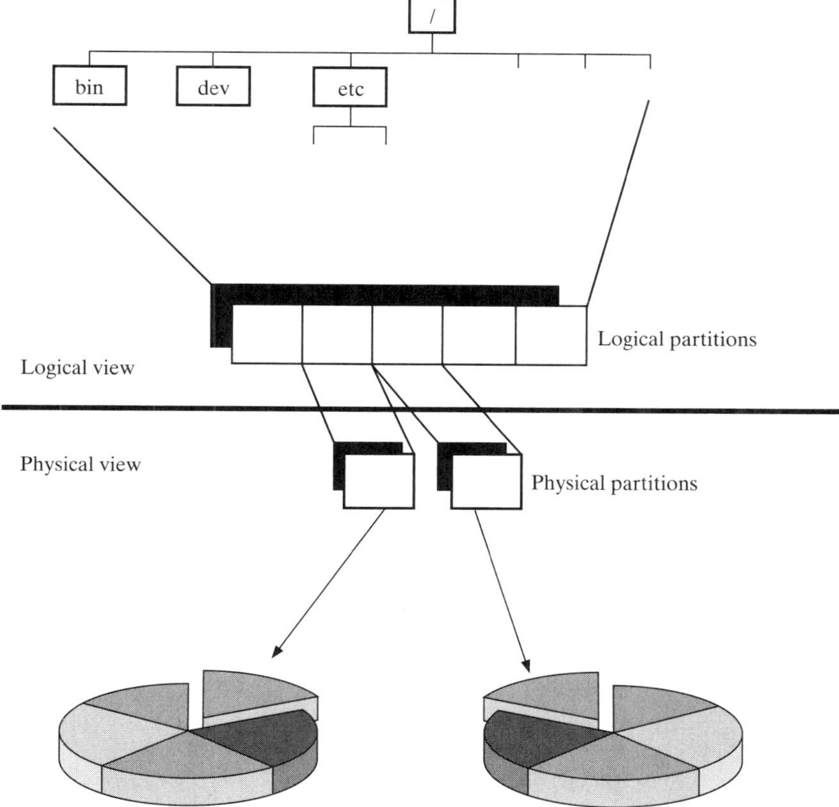

Figure 16.4 Abstraction of logical and physical partitions using the LVM.

The size of a logical volume can be increased dynamically on a running system without impacting logged-on users. The only thing a user notices is that before increasing the logical volume size, the filesystem is fuller than it is after the resizing operation. The access to logical volumes is transparent with no alteration to the interface through which users and system administrators communicate with the AIX filesystem on the System/6000.

Before delving into the details of the LVM, there are some terms that need explaining.

Physical volume.   Physical volume (PV) refers to a physical disk.

Logical volume.   The term logical volume (LV) refers to a logically grouped area. This area appears as if it were a device to the applica-

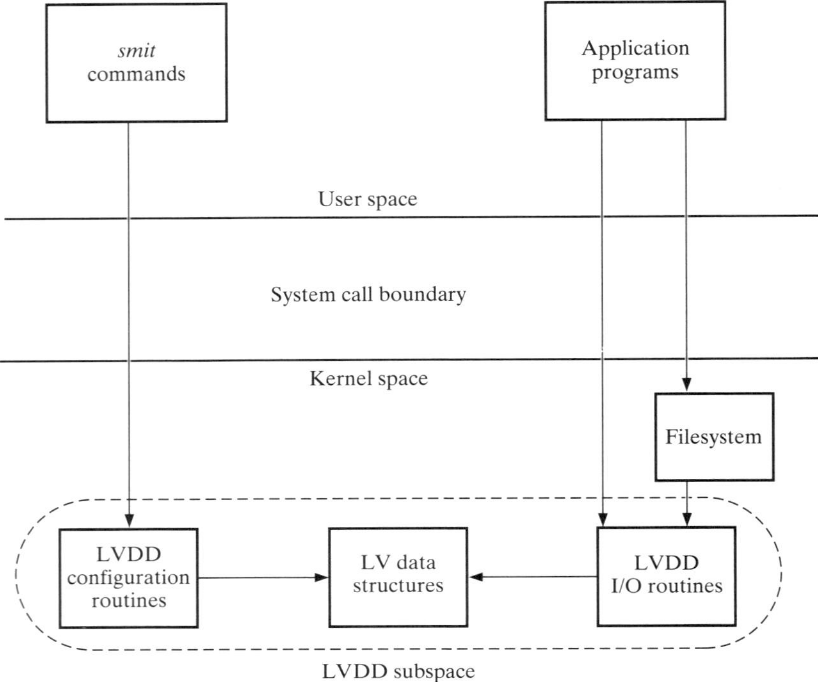

Figure 16.5 LVM execution model.

tions and as a disk to the users. A logical volume, in actuality, is simply a mapping to areas of physical volume(s). Since a logical volume can map to multiple physical volumes, its size can be larger than any one physical volume. The most common use of a logical volume is for a filesystem.

Volume group.   As the name suggests, a volume group (VG) is a collection of physical volumes. A volume group may contain different disk types.

Physical partition.   For the LVM, a physical partition (PP) is the smallest unit of disk space allocation.

Logical partition.   A single logical partition (LP) points to one or more physical partitions.

Figure 16.7 maps the newly introduced terms to an illustration to further explain the positioning of each of these components. As shown, the physical volume is the primary system storage device. The information pertinent to the physical volume and the volume group to which it belongs is organized within selected data areas within the physical volume. The areas are referred to as the *physical volume reserved area*

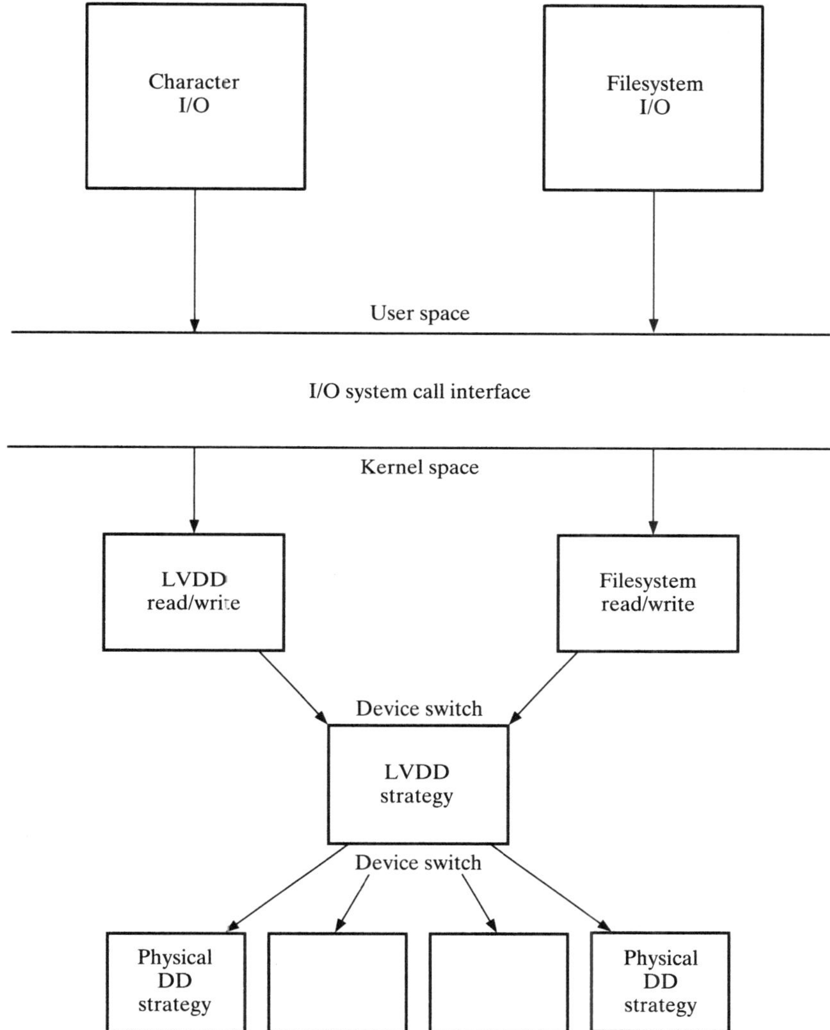

Figure 16.6 Logical volume device driver interface.

and the *volume group reserved area*. LVM uses the information stored in these reserved areas to orchestrate its tasks. Note that the size of these areas needed to describe a physical volume may vary from system to system, since its description depends upon the number of physical volumes and logical volumes constituting the storage space. Following the contents of these two essential reserved areas, a small fraction of the space is used to store the *bad sector relocation pool*. The remainder of the space on the physical volume stores the user data. Figure 16.8 shows the organization of the data area, bad sector reloca-

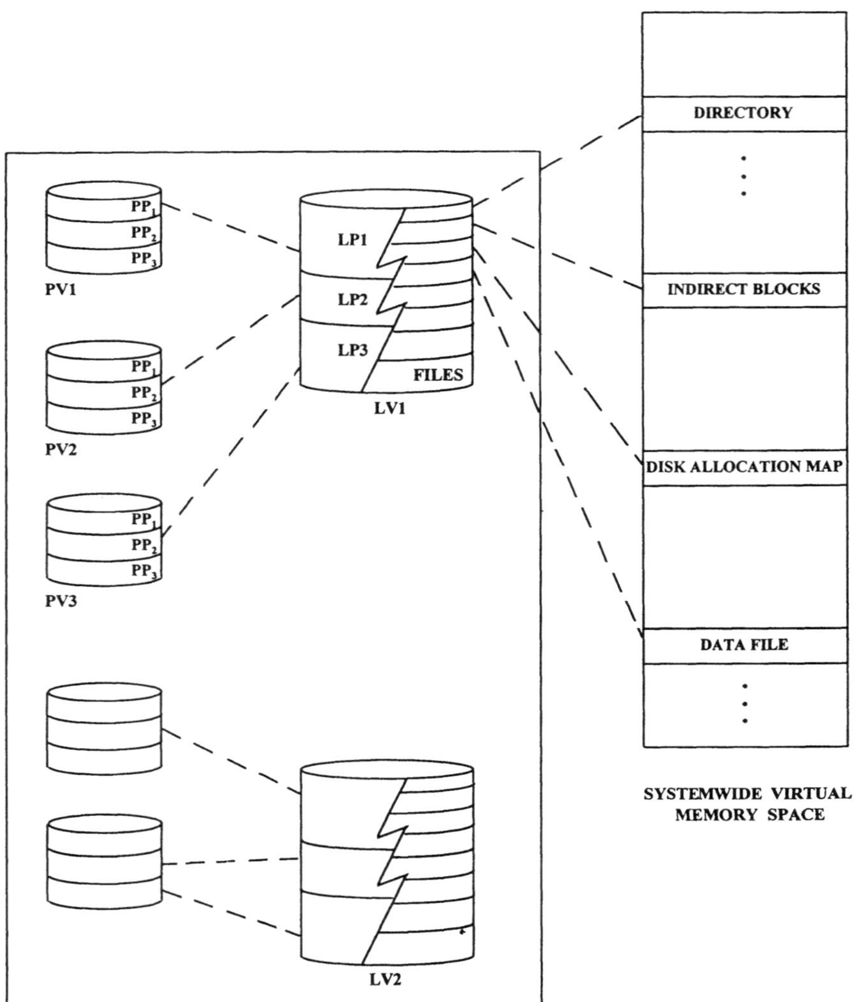

Figure 16.7 Mapping of physical and logical volumes.

tion pool, volume group reserved area, and physical volume reserved area on a physical volume.

The LVM acts as a device driver. It receives requests such as *open, read, write, ioctl,* and *close,* and performs the tasks necessary to complete the operations. For example, a *read* call to a logical volume is converted to the appropriate operation on physical volumes, and subsequently is passed to the physical device driver. The LVM synchronizes the I/O and, in turn, responds to the initial logical request for that *read* operation.

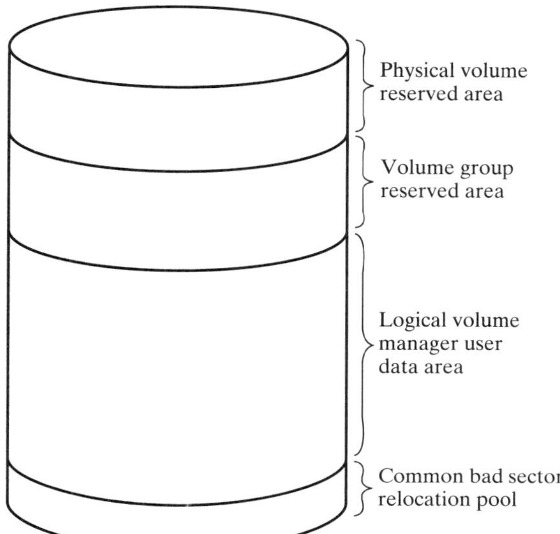

Figure 16.8 Physical volume organization.

In general, applications use the logical volume device nodes as a "normal device" and access it using standard *read, write,* and *ioctl* system calls. The flow of block as well as character (raw) I/O are handled by the LVDD's *strategy* routine. The driver *strategy* entry point then translates the logical address to a physical address (handling bad sector relocation and mirroring) and calls the appropriate physical disk device drivers. Once the I/O has been completed, the physical device driver calls a routine named *biodone,* which in turn invokes the LV I/O completion handling routine. Once this has been completed, *biodone* is called upon again to notify the requester that the I/O is now completed.

Like any regular device driver, the LVM driver is split into two parts: the top half and the bottom half. The top half contains the *open, close, read, write,* and *ioctl* entry points. The bottom half contains the *strategy* entry point-block read and write code.

The code in the top half of the LVM device driver runs in the context of a user process address space. When commands like *ioctl* are used to manipulate a volume group and its associated logical and physical volumes, the *ioctl* call passes through an entry point called *lv_ioctl* (an abstraction for the logical volume layer). Like this one, a complete set of I/O entry point routines is provided. The entry points are:

lv_open   Called by the filesystem when a device is opened or a logical
              volume is mounted.

lv_close   Called by the filesystem when a logical volume is unmounted or when the last *close* has occurred on the open file corresponding to the device.

lv_read   Called by the *read* system call to translate character I/O to block I/O requests.

lv_write   Called by the *write* system call to translate character I/O to block I/O requests.

lv_ioctl   Serves as an entry point for the *ioctl* call and also implements most of the driver programming interface. The commands for this entry point and details about how to write drivers for the LVM, can be referenced from the product documentation.*

The bottom half of the LVM device driver features several layers, including the device *strategy* entry point. This *strategy* routine is a code that is called to process all logical block requests. This part of the LVM, i.e., the bottom half, validates I/O requests, translates logical addresses to physical addresses, handles mirroring and bad sector relocation, and actually starts the I/O. Unlike the top half of the LVM device driver, this part runs in the interrupt context and is not permitted to block.

The different layers of the bottom half of the LVM device driver are:

Strategy.   Performs logical request validation, initialization, termination, and serialization of logical requests (when block ranges overlap).

Mirror consistency manager.   Ensures integrity of the mirrored data (i.e., if mirroring is enabled on the system).

Scheduler.   Schedules physical requests for logical operations.

Status area manager.   Tracks availability of physical volumes and the state of physical extents.

16.2.2   Disk mirroring

Mirroring refers to the replication of data stored in a logical block. The LVM controls mirroring through the use of the *ioctl* system call, as seen in Fig. 16.9. AIX can be *singly mirrored,* i.e., configured to maintain two copies of data. If there are three copies, then data is said to be *doubly mirrored.* As implied from its definition, mirroring, if enabled, requires double the disk space (at a minimum) for the mirrored data. This feature remains disabled by default. If required, mirroring may be enabled using the *smit* tool. Data may be mirrored for high availability or for higher performance.

---

* *Writing a Device Driver for AIX Version 3.2* (GG24-3629-01).

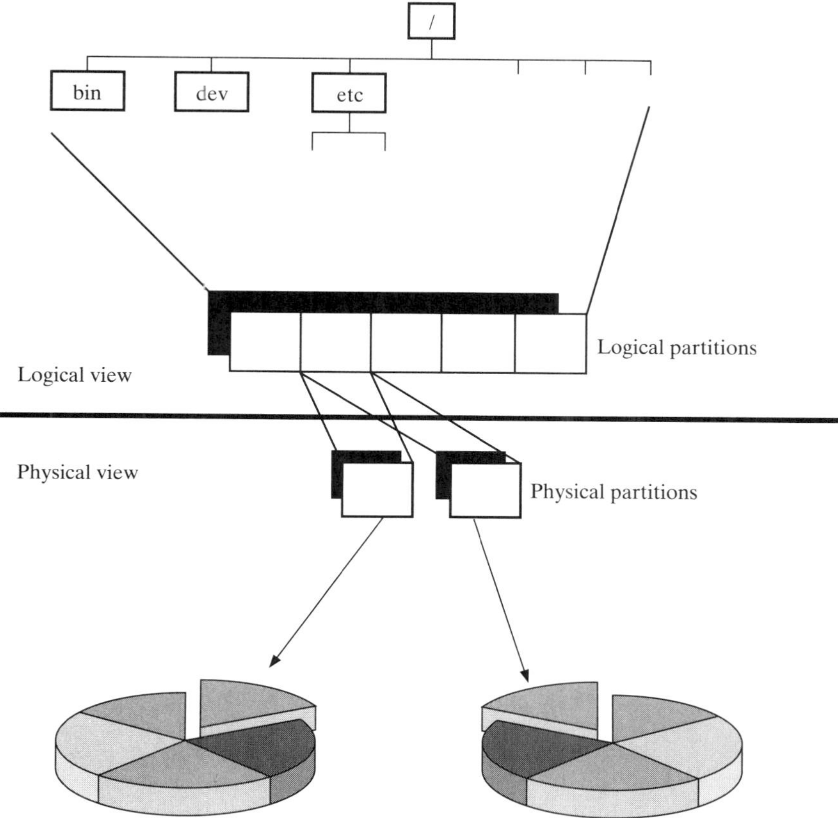

Figure 16.9 Disk mirroring (singly mirrored).

Mirroring for high availability is done to deal with situations when/if data becomes unavailable owing to media defects, a catastrophic drive failure, controller malfunction, etc. By mirroring data, the LVM is able to transparently recover from the loss of one copy of the data. When access to one copy of data is denied, the LVM redirects I/O intended for the missing data to the secondary or tertiary copy. As useful as this feature is for handling critical data, careful planning is a prerequisite when setting up the volume group for mirroring. Consider an example where a configuration of two physical volumes is being used with a filesystem that has been singly mirrored for a total of two separate copies of the filesystem. If the two copies of the filesystem are housed on separate disks, then one disk's failure would still retain access to an alternate copy of the data. But had only one disk maintained both physical volumes, a disk failure would have resulted in a complete loss of data, thereby defeating the purpose of mirroring for high availability.

Mirroring for higher performance is performed if there are data blocks that are subjected to intensive I/O, primarily owing to excessively frequent *read* operations. Having multiple copies of a data block which can be accessed in parallel by concurrent *read* requests renders quicker data access than one without disk mirroring. If implemented, the mirrored copies should be distributed across multiple physical disks for optimal performance. On systems equipped with sufficient hard drives and disk space to spread the mirrored blocks, performance for *read* access is achieved by the system by scheduling to access the copy of the mirrored block that costs the least to retrieve. For *write* operations, copies of a mirrored block get scheduled to be written whenever feasible, meaning that the block is not considered written until the last copy of its associated mirrored block has been updated. Usually the total time required to write the copies of a mirrored block approximates the time it takes to write the slowest copy of a mirrored block. Note that lack of careful configuration planning to ensure proper distribution of mirror copies across disjoint physical disks can result in performance degradation instead of performance enhancement. In conclusion, mirroring is not always the best way to achieve high performance. Its gain is significant when data is mirrored for the purposes of frequent *read* access, rather than frequent *write* access.

16.2.3 Bad block relocation

This is another configurable feature that can be enabled or disabled based on the need. There are two kinds of errors that may be encountered by the LVM:

1. soft errors

2. hard errors

Based on the type of error encountered, the LVM takes the appropriate actions.

When the LVM detects a soft (correctable) read error, it attempts to rewrite the data, with *write* verification to the physical drive potentially correcting the error. Either of two things can happen. If there is no support for *write* verification on the disk drive and the LVM rewrite fails, the soft error gets treated as a hard error. On the other hand, if the disk drive supports *write* verification, the *read* succeeds; this is followed by the LVM performing a *write* operation to the relocated area and relocating the sector.

When the LVM detects a hard (uncorrectable) error, it relocates the sector. The operation is performed using a pool of data sectors that is maintained for this purpose. All subsequent I/O is then directed to the new sector. If the data is mirrored, then LVM redirects the failed *read* to another copy of the data and subsequently relocates and rewrites the relocated bad sector. When no mirroring of the data is available, the LVM returns an error. Later, when the sector is updated, it gets relocated and again capable of storing data.

16.3 MEMORY SUBSYSTEM

The memory subsystem internals of AIX differ fundamentally from those of traditional UNIX operating systems. IBM rearchitected the memory management scheme to make the best use of this machine's hardware architectural features. The virtual memory concepts have evolved from a predecessor machine, the IBM RT, and have been improved upon in the System/6000. The concepts have been extended in this computer system to provide an address space that is a thousand times larger than what it was in the RT. It is the hardware architectural components that facilitate this awesome storage space. In regard to the storage space, there are three fundamental objects that form the infrastructure of the memory subsystem; they are (1) real memory, (2) virtual memory, and (3) disk space. The real memory frames and the virtual memory pages of the System/6000 are divided up into basic units, each of which is 4 KB in size. The disk space on this machine is also partitioned into basic units called blocks, each of which is 4 KB.

real memory	$\rightarrow$	frames (each 4 KB in size)
virtual memory	$\rightarrow$	pages (each 4 KB in size)
page space	$\rightarrow$	blocks (each 4 KB in size)

From the system's perspective, virtual memory encompasses both real memory and disk (the filesystem and the paging space). A virtual memory address may point to a page on disk or to a page in real memory, depending on whether the reference is being made to an active or an inactive portion of the program. A roadmap of the general page mapping concept is illustrated in Fig. 16.10, where a virtual page number from the virtual address space indexes into a table called the external page table (XPT) to resolve whether to go to the paging area or to go to the real memory. If the address is meant for the paging space then it directly points to the location on the paging space. But if the address is to point to the real memory, it must derive its real page number prior to accessing the real memory. This real page number is generated from a structure called the page frame table (PFT).

As far as addressability goes, the AIX kernel, in conjunction with the System/6000 hardware components, provides a per-process address space of 4 gigabytes (2^{32}) and a total system address space of 4 petabytes (2^{52}). The upper limit on real memory supported by the 32-bit

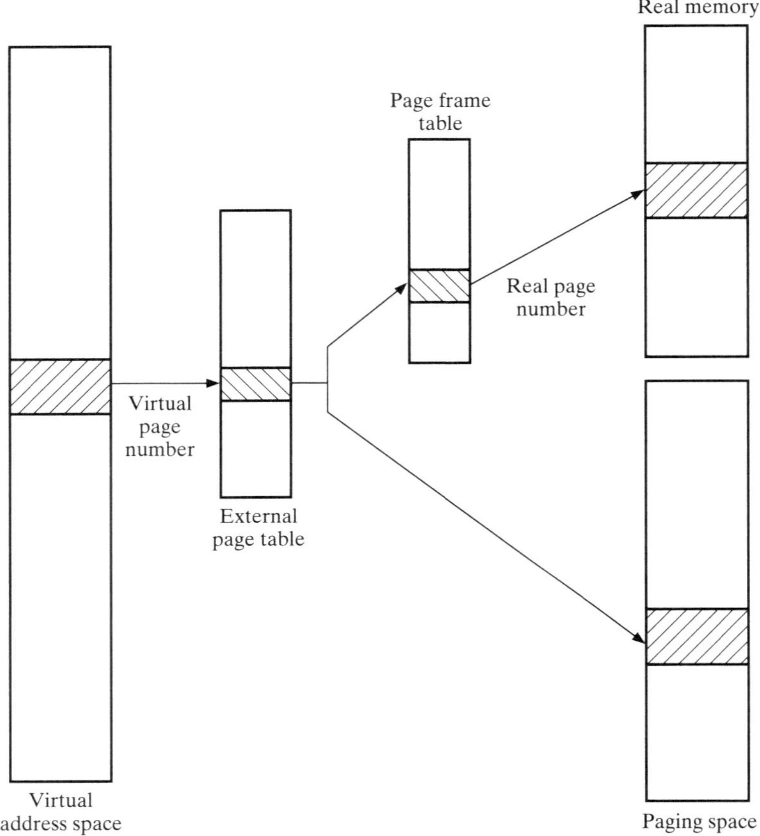

Figure 16.10 Roadmap of the general page mapping mechanism.

implementation of the power architecture is 4 gigabytes and a vast virtual memory address space is achieved using a segmented memory addressing model. Think about the total systemwide virtual address space of the System/6000 consisting of 2^{52} bytes that is divided into approximately 16 million (2^{24}) 256-MB (2^{28}) segments. Each segment in turn can contain up to 64,000 (2^{16}) pages.

Associated with each process is an array that holds the addresses of 16 segments, which happen to be the range of virtual memory addressable by that process. Since there are 16 segments, each of which is 256 MB in size, the total process address space can be expressed by the following calculation:

$$(\text{number of segments}) \times (\text{size per segment}) => \text{process address space}$$
$$16 \times 256 \text{ MB} => 4 \text{ GB}$$

For a running process, its array containing the addresses of the 16 segments addressable by the process itself are held in the 16 segment registers (implemented in the hardware and located in the fixed point unit on the CPU planar).

16.3.1 Segmented memory

A segmented memory model is employed by the System/6000. Access to segments is regulated by the mode (i.e., kernel mode versus user mode) in which the process is serving at that instant. For kernel processes, this is not a problem, as they always run in kernel mode. But processes executing in user mode have access to a limited number of segments; they have *read/write* access to segment 2 and any shared data segments that the process may have attached, and *read* access to segments 1 and 13. The remaining segments cannot be accessed by user-mode processes directly.* This description of the process address space is better understood with the help of a diagram; the layout of the segments is illustrated in Fig. 16.11.

From the kernel's perspective, text and data in segments 0 and 11 through 15 serve all processes, while the other segments are process-specific. Segment 0 houses the text and data for the base kernel along with kernel extensions (if any). Segments 1 and 2 are private for each process and remain protected from being accessed by other processes. Segments 3 through 10 are shared data segments and can be used to hold explicitly mapped files, or as shared memory for processes that have requested access via a shared memory system call (refer to Sec. 16.1.2). Continuing with the role of each segment, segments 11 and 12 are used to manage the kernel structures used by the virtual memory manager (VMM). Segment 13 is the shared text segment and holds text loaded from shared objects, such as *libc.a*. Segment 14 serves as the kernel data segment, which holds kernel structures, data, and, most important of all, the *proc* table.[†] Finally, segment 15 is reserved for I/O addresses. Figure 16.12 gives a graphical depiction of where each of the 16 segments points to.

Segments that point to additional data structures need some more explanation. Segment 0, which contains the kernel text and data, includes the heap and its allied control structures. Segment 1 contains

---

* In order to access an area other than what is referenced by segments 1, 2, 13, and shared data segments (if attached), a user process either has to be in kernel mode or access an address in the virtual memory address space indirectly by opening a pseudo-device called *kmem,* located in the */dev* directory.

[†] This is a large data structure, implemented as an array of structures, with each structure holding information pertaining to each of the processes on the system, such as process priority, process link pointers to child and sibling processes, etc. To give an idea about the size of the *proc* structure, AIX reserves 16 MB for it. Chapter 14 describes the *proc* structure in greater detail.

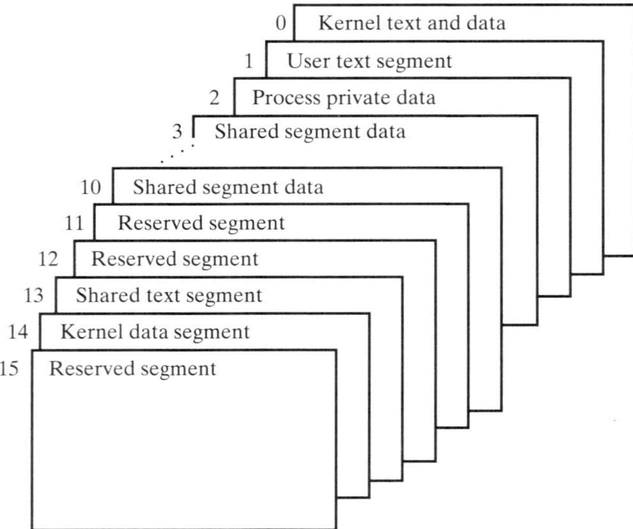

Figure 16.11   Segmented memory.

the user process text, i.e., the code. Segment 2 is the process private segment and it includes the initialized data, uninitialized data, user heap, user stack, system call error code variable *errno,** kernel mode stack (used by auto variables in kernel extensions), and user block. Segment 11 is allocated for use by the VMM to refer to kernel structures such as the page frame table, hash anchor table, page device table, and segment control block. The *page frame table* (PFT) is a structure that is allocated at boot time with one entry for each frame of physical memory. This PFT is referenced whenever the cache and the TLB[†] have failed to provide a real address. The PFT is actually two parallel nonpageable tables with a *hash anchor table* to hold the hashed list of pages and to refer to a *segment information table*. This segment information table contains entries (each of which is called a *segment control block*) to describe each segment in the system. The different kinds of segments recognized by the VMM are discussed later in this section.

Continuing with the description of subsequent segments, segment 12 is allocated for use by the VMM to reference the page table area con-

---

* It is a global variable that holds an error code to indicate why a system call failed.

† The term *cache* has been kept generic, without making any distinctions between the data and instruction cache so that the description here can hold good for all POWER chips with separate as well as combined caches. TLB is an acronym for translation lookaside buffer, a hardware structure which is responsible for translating virtual page numbers to real page numbers.

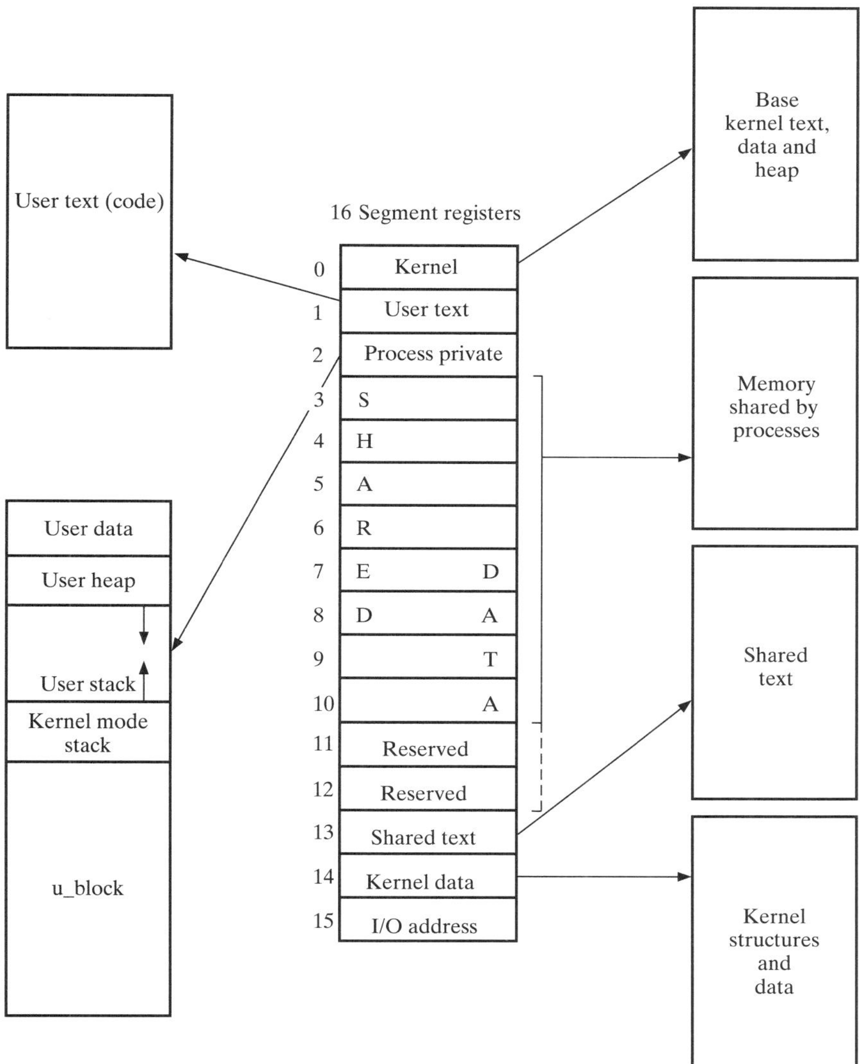

Figure 16.12 Segmented memory of the AIX kernel.

taining the external page table and area page map. The *external page table* (XPT) is a collection of structures that are used to construct an external page table for every working segment by having each of its entries describe the location of that page, primarily pointing out whether the page in question is in real memory or on the page space. References made about the remaining segments are straightforward and have been discussed in the previous paragraph.

16.3.2 Virtual memory management

As described earlier, virtual memory segments are partitioned into fixed-size units called *pages*. Each page's size is 4 KB. A page can be in real memory or on disk until needed. Similarly, real memory is divided into fixed-sized units called *page frames*. The role of the virtual memory manager (VMM) is to manage the allocation of real memory page frames and to resolve process references to virtual memory pages that are not currently in real memory. Figure 16.13 shows how a 4-bit index into the segment registers is used, and how a page offset into the virtual segment table is derived from an effective address to access an element.

There are several subcomponents within the VMM. They are

Segment manager

Virtual page manager

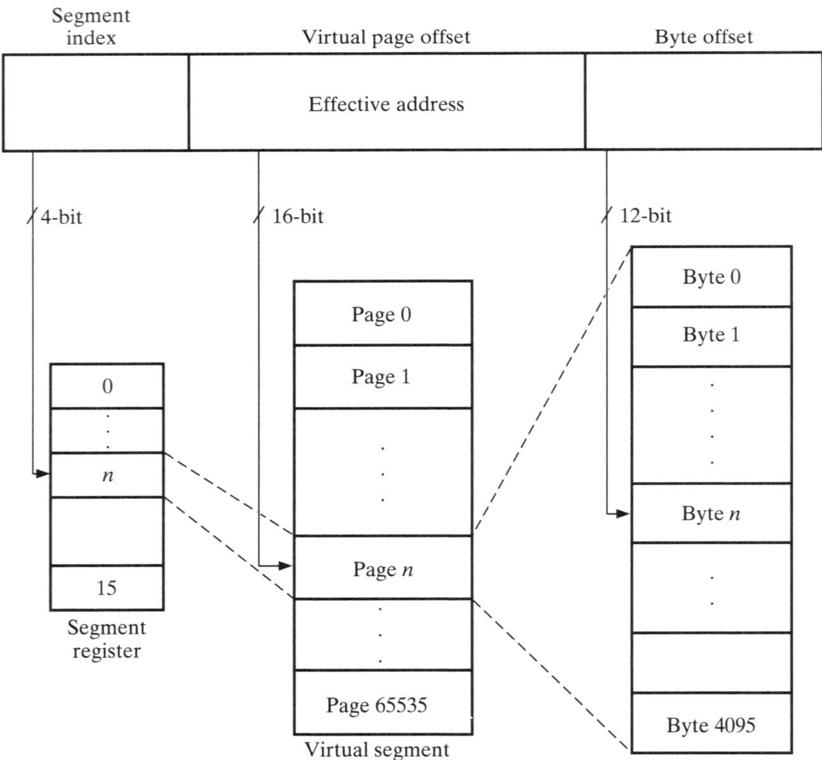

Figure 16.13 Accessing an element in virtual memory using the 16 segment registers, virtual segment, and byte offset.

Page frame manager

Page fault handler

Persistent storage manager

The segment manager provides functions to create, modify, copy, and destroy virtual memory segments. The virtual page manager manages the mapping of virtual memory pages to disk slots on external storage. The page frame manager orchestrates the allocation and deallocation of physical memory page frames to virtual pages and the lists of free pages frames, mapped page frames, and page frames in use, for I/O operations. The page fault handler is responsible for handling the page faults which occur when a referenced virtual address is not mapped within the PFT. The persistent storage manager provides database memory, transaction processing, locking, and logging services for the physical filesystem.

The VMM distinguishes between types of segments based upon the function performed by them and the way they are backed to external storage when paging occurs. There are three kinds of segments that are recognized by the VMM:

- *Working storage segments.* These include dynamically allocated structures and variables, and copy-on-write mapped pages* that do not have a permanent backing storage.

- *Persistent storage segments.* AIX on System/6000 accesses all files as mapped files. This means that program and/or file access begins with a few initial pages getting copied into virtual storage segments. Subsequent pages are "page-faulted in" on demand.

- *Client segments.* This type of segment includes pages that are brought in via NFS or any other type of remote filesystem.

Figure 16.14 shows the different segment types supported by AIX on the System/6000.

16.3.3 Page replacement

The VMM maintains a list of free page frames that it uses to accommodate pages that must be brought into memory. Unless a virtual memory page is pinned, it may become paged out when extra memory frames are needed. In a memory-constrained environment, the VMM

---

* Mapped files may be read-only, read-write, and copy-on-write. The phrase *copy-on-write* refers to the fact that any changes made to the data are stored in the paging area and not written back to the original file. Only an *fsync* system call will cause the pages to be written back to disk.

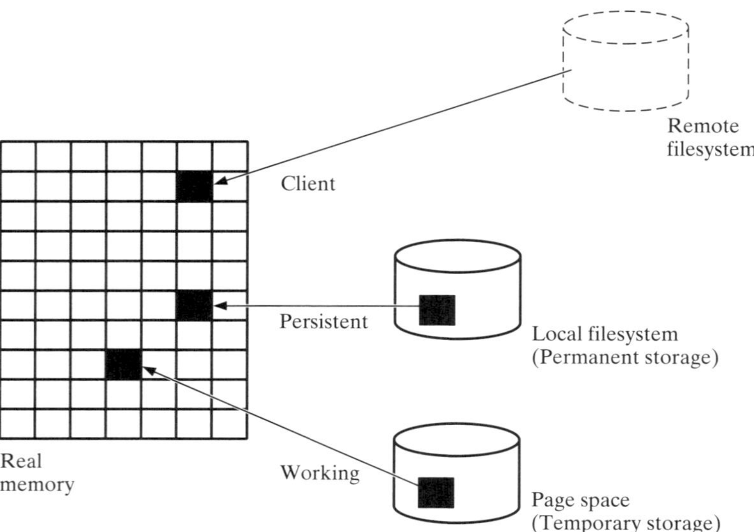

Figure 16.14 Different segment types supported by AIX.

occasionally replenishes the free list (number of empty page frames in memory) by removing some of the current data from real memory, effectively "stealing" the real memory frames. The virtual memory pages whose page frames are to be stolen are selected using an algorithm called the page-replacement algorithm.

The page replacement algorithm is governed by two key artifacts. The first one is the use of repaging statistics. A *repage fault* differs from a new *page fault* in the sense that the page in question, which is known to have been referenced recently, is referenced again and is not found in memory because the page has been replaced since it was last accessed. A perfect page replacement scheme would eliminate repage faults entirely (excluding memory size constraints) by always stealing frames from pages that are not going to be referenced again. This is not feasible to implement, as it requires knowledge of future page references. However, it is possible to reduce the effect of the repaging phenomenon by using statistics of its past behavior. The second criterion used is the distinction between computational memory and file memory among the memory-resident pages. A *computational memory* differs from a *file memory* in the sense that the former consists of the pages belonging to working storage segments or program text segments and the latter consists of the remaining pages.

The technique used to select pages to be replaced is based on one of the generic page replacement algorithms known as the *clock hand algorithm*. It makes use of a referenced bit for each page to determine what pages have been used, i.e., referenced recently. When the page replacement routine is invoked, it cycles through the page frame table, examining each page's referenced bit. If a page is found unreferenced and is replaceable, it is placed on the free list. If a selected page is found modified since it was last written to the disk (filesystem space or the page space), the page is written out prior to being placed on the free list. If a page was referenced, it is not selected for page out; instead, its reference bit is reset. Additional intelligence, added to the page replacement policy under AIX, ensures that the computational pages get fair treatment. What this means is that if a huge data file is to be read into memory sequentially, it should not page out text pages which are likely to be reused soon. The VMM attempts to keep the size of the free list around a fixed range. If page faults or system demands cause the free list size to fall below the low threshold, the page replacement algorithm frees up enough pages to make the free list larger than the high threshold, so as to maintain a consistent size of the free list.

16.3.4 Memory load control

When a process references virtual memory pages that are on disk, the referenced page must be paged in. This creates I/O traffic and delay. If the main memory is fully occupied and there aren't any free pages left, *thrashing* may happen. Thrashing is the result of incessant I/O to the paging disk, wherein processes encounter page faults almost as soon as they are dispatched. To eradicate this phenomenon, a load control algorithm is implemented that detects when the system is beginning to thrash, and consequently suspends active processes (by putting them to sleep and freeing up all the memory they are using) until the system has recovered from thrashing.

This load control feature is settable as well as tunable. This means that one can disable the memory load control feature of the operating system if no suspension of active processes owing to detection of thrashing is desired, or if compatibility with earlier versions of AIX, which lacked this load control feature, is needed. As far as tuning goes, the memory load control feature can be fine-tuned to best meet the requirements of an individual system and its workload.

The memory load control mechanism works by attempting to determine if there is a scarcity of memory frames for the set of active processes on the system. This inference is made by the scheduler once every second. Based on an analysis of the previous second's snapshot, the scheduler determines if processes are to be suspended or activated. If it is to suspend processes, the nominated processes are marked up and are consequently suspended at the earliest opportunity that the system gets to put the processes in user mode.

16.3.5   Code pinning

When code and data associated with a device driver is pinned in real memory (that is, exempt from being paged out to disk), response time for that device improves dramatically as there is no time lost to page faults. If not used properly, pinning can result in serious performance problems on the system throughput.

16.4   I/O MANAGEMENT

I/O management under AIX has two characteristic traits, namely an asynchronous I/O facility and a page hiding property. Other functionalities are no different than those of traditional UNIX systems.

16.4.1   Asynchronous I/O

The term *synchronous I/O* alludes to the notion that I/O occurs while one waits for it to complete. In contrast, asynchronous I/O does not cause applications to wait. This, in general, improves performance since the I/O operations and the applications can both progress at the same time. Transaction processing applications, such as databases, are able to take a big advantage of this feature for performing overlapped compute tasks and I/O.

This facility is an implementation of the POSIX Asynchronous Input and Output Interface 1003.4 document. The functions provided by the asynchronous I/O facilities are (1) nonblocking I/O, (2) cancellation of I/O requests, and (3) notification of I/O event completions. The nonblocking I/O facility allows the applications to proceed with their execution without being blocked; it does so by queuing the requests and allowing the application to continue execution. Cancellation of I/O requests works only if the request is still in the queue and its I/O operations have not yet started. Notification of I/O event completions are handled by either having the application poll for the status of that I/O operation periodically or by sending an asynchronous notification status to the application using the SIGIO signal.

Multiple asynchronous I/O requests may be issued on the same device by one or more applications. But remember that, since the operations are performed asynchronously, the order in which the I/O calls are handled may not be the order in which they were issued.

16.4.2   Page hiding

In System/6000, data can be located in the cache, system memory, or in a DMA (direct memory access) buffer. DMA services move the data between these three locations. For every DMA transfer, the DMA device drivers flush the data from the cache to memory. They then hide the page, preventing the data from being put back into the processor cache. There is a counter that counts the number of times a page is hidden for DMA. A page need not be hidden except when the counter goes down from 0 to 1 and it need not be revealed except in the situation when the count goes from 1 to 0. This count is most relevant in operations like logical volume mirrored writes, where a failure to make sure that the same number of calls has been made to the routine initializing a block mode DMA transfer as well as to the routine completing the transfer can result in incorrectly hidden pages and data loss.

16.5 SUMMARY

The three key concepts used in the evolution of the augmented I/O storage facility of the System/6000 are derivatives of some of the well-known early computer systems. The large virtual memory of this machine and the integration of file subsystems with logical volumes and virtual memory were evolved from computer systems like the IBM System/38 and the earlier operating system, MULTICS, which is regarded as the ancestor of the present-day UNIX. The third component, which is the innovation of database memory, was derived from IBM 801, an experimental machine developed at the Thomas J. Watson Research Center. All of the three traits were combined and first implemented in an integrated manner on the IBM RT. Later, the concepts were improved upon and incorporated in the RISC System/6000. This made it possible to deliver AIX as the only implementation of the UNIX operating system with unique I/O and storage features that stand out above and beyond the traditional UNIX-based systems.

Bibliography

Agarwal, A., Hennessy, J., and Horowitz, M., "Cache Performance of Operating Systems and Multiprogramming Workloads," *ACM Transactions on Computer Systems,* 6(4), November 1988, pp. 393–431.

Agrawala, A.K., Sanghi, D., and Noh, S.H., "Process Timing in UNIX," Technical report, Dept. of Computer Science, Univ. of Md., 1989.

AIX Version 3.1 RISC System/6000 As A Real Time System (GG24-3633-00), IBM Corporation, 1991.

AIX Version 3.2 for RISC System/6000, Kernel Extensions and Device Support Programming Concepts (SC23-2207-01), IBM Corporation, 1992.

AIX Version 3.2 for RISC System/6000, Performance Monitoring and Tuning Guide (SC23-2365-01), IBM Corporation, 1992.

AIX Version 3.2 for RISC System/6000, Technical Reference: Base Operating System and Extensions, Volume 1 (SC23-2382-00), IBM Corporation, 1992.

AIX Version 3.2 for RISC System/6000, Technical Reference: Base Operating System and Extensions, Volume 2 (SC23-2383-00), IBM Corporation, 1992.

AIX Version 3.2 for RISC System/6000, Technical Reference: Kernel and Subsystems, Volume 4 (SC23-2385-00), IBM Corporation, 1992.

Alpert, D., "Memory Hierarchies for Directly Executed Language Microprocessors," Ph.D. thesis, Stanford Univ., 1984.

Auslander, M.A., "Managing Programs and Libraries in AIX Version 3 for RISC System/6000 Processors," *IBM Journal of Research and Development,* vol. 34, January 1990.

Bach, M.J., *The Design of the UNIX Operating System,* Prentice Hall, Englewood Cliffs, NJ, 1986.

Bakoglu, H.B., Grohoski, G.F., and Montoye, R.K., "The IBM RISC System/6000 Processor: Hardware Overview," *IBM Journal of Research and Development,* vol. 34, January 1990.

Bakoglu, H.B. and Whiteside, T., "RISC System 6000 Hardware Overview," *IBM RISC System/6000 Technology,* IBM Corporation, Austin, Texas, 1990.

Bowlds, P.A., *Micro Channel Architecture: Revolution in Personal Computing,* VNR Computer Library, 1991.

Chakravarty, D., "Automation in Clinical Biochemistry & Laboratory: Computer Applications in Medicine." K.L. Mukherjee (ed.), *Medical Laboratory Technology: Procedure Manual for Routine Diagnostic Tests,* Tata-McGraw-Hill, vol. 3, chap. 32, pp. 960–984, 1988.

Chakravarty, D., "Benchmarking under AIX," *Focus Tech J.,* vol. 1, no. 4, pp. 20–21.

Chakravarty, D. and Chakravarty, A., "Architectural Dependencies Related to Performance Measurements under UNIX," Computer Measurements Group Transactions, Summer 1992. Republished in *International CMG Conference Proceedings,* December 1992.

Cocke, J. and Markstein, V., "The Evolution of RISC Technology at IBM," *IBM Journal of Research and Development,* vol. 34, January 1990.

Comer, D.E., *Operating System Design—Volume II: Internetworking with Xinu,* Prentice Hall, Englewood Cliffs, N.J., 1987.

Cook, J.A. and Wolfsthal, Y., "Dynamic Binding in AIX Version 3," *AIXpert,* pp. 30–40, Fall 1991.

Ferrari, D., Sezzari, G., and Zeigner, A., *Management and Tuning of Computer Systems,* Prentice Hall, Englewood Cliffs, N.J., 1983.

Forrer, T.R., Frazier, G.R., Mathis, J.R., and Tsao, G.W., "Storage Subsystem," *IBM RISC System/6000 Technology,* IBM Corporation, Austin, Texas, 1990.

Gibbs, G.B., "Demystifying the Object Data Manager," *AIXtra,* p. 49–62, April 1992.

Guide to OSF/1: A Technical Synopsis, O'Reilly & Associates, Inc., Calif., 1991.

Grohowski, G.F., Kahle, J.A., Thatcher, L.E., and Moore, C.R., "Branch and Fixed-Point Instruction Execution Units," *IBM RISC System/6000 Technology,* IBM Corporation, Austin, Texas, 1990.

Grove, R.D. and Oehler, R., "RISC System 6000 Processor Architecture," *IBM RISC System/6000 Technology,* IBM Corporation, Austin, Texas, 1990.

Hall, B.C. and O'Brian, K., "Performance Characteristics of Architectural Features of the IBM RISC System/6000," *4th International Conference on Architectural Support for Programming Languages and Operating Systems,* 1991, pp. 303–309.

Hardell, W.R., Jr., Hicks, D.A., Howell, L.C., Jr., Maule, W.E., Montoye, R., and Tuttle, D.P., "Data Cache and Storage Control Units," *IBM RISC System/6000 Technology,* IBM Corporation, Austin, Texas, 1990.

Henry, G., "IBM RT Architecture and Design Decisions," *RT Personal Computer Technology,* Form No. SA23-1057, IBM Corporation, 1986.

Hester, P.D., "RISC System 6000 Hardware Background and Philosophies," *IBM RISC System/6000 Technology,* IBM Corporation, Austin, Texas, 1990.

Hester, P.D., Hollaway, J.T., and May, F.T., "Hardware Description," *RT Personal Computer Technology,* Form No. SA23-1057, IBM Corporation, 1986.

Hill, M.D., "Aspects of Cache Memory and Instruction Buffer Performance," Ph.D. thesis, Univ. of California at Berkeley, Calif., 1989.

Hill, M.D. and Smith, A.J., "Evaluating Associativity in CPU Caches," *IEEE Transactions on Computers,* 38(12), pp. 1612–1630, December 1989.

Hokenek, E., and Montoye, R.K., "Leading Zero Anticipator (LZA) in the IBM RISC System/6000 Floating Point Execution Unit," *IBM Journal of Research and Development,* vol. 34, January 1990.

Hoskins, J., *IBM RISC System/6000, A Business Perspective,* John Wiley & Sons, Englewood Cliffs, N.J., 1991.

Hwang, K. and Briggs, F., *Computer Architecture and Parallel Processing,* McGraw-Hill Series in Organization and Architecture, McGraw-Hill, N.Y., 1984.

IEEE, "Portable Operating System Interface for Computer Environments (POSIX)," 1003.1-1988, *IEEE,* 1988.

Keller, T.W., "AIX 3.2 Memory Load Control," *AIXpert,* pp. 17–25, February 1992.

Kernighan, B.W., and Pike, R., *The UNIX Programming Environment,* Prentice Hall, Englewood Cliffs, N.J., 1984.

Jain, R., *The Art of Computer Systems Performance Analysis,* John Wiley & Sons, N.Y., 1991.

Lewis, E., "Performance Tuning: Theory and Practice," *AIXtra,* pp. 48–56, March/April 1993.

Loukides, M., *System Performance Tuning,* O'Reilly & Associates, Inc., Calif., 1991.

Mano, M.M., *Computer System Architecture,* 2d ed., Prentice Hall, Englewood Cliffs, N.J., 1982.

McKusick, M.K. and Karels, M., "Performance Improvements and Functional Enhancements in 4.3BSD," Computer System Research Group, Dept. of Computer Science and Electrical Engineering, Univ. of California at Berkeley, Calif.

Montoye, R.K., Hokenek, E., and Runyon, S.L., "Design of the IBM RISC System/6000 Floating Point Execution Unit," *IBM Journal of Research and Development,* vol. 34, January 1990.

Nicholson, J.O., "Micro Channel Features," *IBM RISC System/6000 Technology,* IBM Corporation, Austin, Texas, 1990.

Nicholson, J., Neal, D., Dhawan, S., Arimilli, R., and Siegel, D., "RISC System/6000 I/O Structure," *IBM RISC System/6000 Technology,* IBM Corporation, Austin, Texas, 1990.

Olsson, B., Montoye, R., Markstein, P., and NguyenPhu, M., "RISC System/6000 Floating-Point Unit," *IBM RISC System/6000 Technology,* IBM Corporation, Austin, Texas, 1990.

Pasha, S.Z. and Welbon, E.H., "Performance-Directed Design Guidance Using Simulation," *IBM RISC System/6000 Technology,* IBM Corporation, Austin, Texas, 1990.

Patterson, D.A. and Sequin, C.N., "A VLSI RISC," *Computer,* 15, no. 9, pp. 8–21, September 1982.

Pescatore, J.C., Jr., "The Micro Channel Architecture: An Adapter Designer's Perspective," Master's thesis, Duke University, 1989.

POWERstation and POWERserver, Hardware Technical Information General Architectures, (SA23-2643-02), IBM Corporation, 1992.

POWERstation and POWERserver, Hardware Technical Information Options and Devices, (SA23-2646-00), IBM Corporation, 1992.

POWERstation and POWERserver, Hardware Technical Reference Micro Channel Architecture, (SA23-2647-00), IBM Corporation, 1992.

Przybylski, S.A., *Cache and Memory Hierarchy Design: A Performance-Directed Approach,* Morgan Kaufmann Publishers, Inc., 1990.

Przybylski, S.A., "Performance-Directed Memory Hierarchy Design," Ph.D. thesis, Stanford Univ., 1988.

Puzak, T.R., "Cache Memory Design," Ph.D. dissertation, Univ. of Mass., 1985.

Ratiu, I.M. and Bakoglu, H.B., "Pseudorandom Built-in Self-Test Methodology and Implementation for the IBM RISC System/6000 processor," *IBM Journal of Research and Development,* vol. 34, January 1990.

Ritchie, D.M. and Thompson, K., "UNIX Timesharing," *CACM,* vol. 57, no. 6, part 2, pp. 1931–1946, July/August 1978.

SCSI—Architecture and Implementation, (GG24-3507-00), IBM Corporation, 1990.

SCSI—Understanding the Small Computer System Interface, NCR Corporation, Prentice-Hall, Englewood Cliffs, N.J., 1990.

Special Issue on Software Performance Engineering of CMG Transactions, no. 60, Spring 1988.

Stone, H.S., *High-Performance Computer Architecture,* Addison-Wesley Series in Electrical and Computer Engineering, 1987.

UNIX Programmer's Reference Manual (PRM), 4.3 Berkeley Software Distribution, Computer Systems Research Group, Computer Science Division, Univ. of California, Berkeley, 1986.

Warren, H.S., Jr., "Instruction Scheduling for the IBM RISC System/6000 Processor," *IBM Journal of Research and Development,* vol. 34, January 1990.

Writing a Device Driver for AIX Version 3, (GG24-3629-00), IBM Corporation, 1991.

Index

ABOUT THE AUTHOR

Dipto Chakravarty has been involved in developing and teaching AIX and POWER architecture to the technical staff of IBM Advanced Workstation Division and worldwide. Mr. Chakravarty's prior experience includes expert consulting with Bell Atlantic, DEC, Apple, the U.S. Army, and several other organizations. He is a recognized expert in performance tuning of UNIX on RISC architectures.

Mr. Chakravarty's research interests include performance monitors and remote node emulators for distributed systems, and VLSI.